MANAGEMENT of Finance

a guide for the non-specialist

David Cox
Michael Fardon

consultant
Roger Petheram

Published by Osborne Books Limited
Unit 1B Everoak Estate
Bromyard Road
Worcester
WR2 5HN
Tel 01905 748071
e-mail books@osbornebooks.co.uk
www.osbornebooks.co.uk

Printed by the Bath Press, Bath.

British Library Cataloguing in Publication Data
A catalogue record for this book is available from the British Library

ISBN 1 872962 23 8

CONTENTS

ACKNOWLEDGEMENTS

The authors wish to thank the following for their help with the production and editing of the book: Frank Adcock, Jean Cox, Michael Gilbert, Jon Moore and Anita Sherwood.

Particular thanks go to Roger Petheram of Worcester College of Technology for reading the text, commenting upon it, checking answers, and always being prepared to discuss any aspect of the book.

Thanks are also due to The Body Shop International PLC for permission to reproduce extracts from their Report and Accounts and to the Royal Mint for permission to use images of coins.

THE AUTHORS

David Cox has more than twenty years' experience teaching management and accountancy students over a wide range of levels. Formerly with the Management and Professional Studies Department at Worcester College of Technology, he now lectures on a freelance basis and carries out educational consultancy work in accountancy studies. He is author and joint author of a number of textbooks in the areas of accounting, finance and banking.

Michael Fardon has extensive teaching experience of a wide range of business and accountancy students at Worcester College of Technology. He is now a writer and educational consultant in the area of business and finance.

INTRODUCTION

Management of Finance provides a practical guide to business finance for the non-specialist. It is suitable for practising managers, and for students on first level degrees and courses such as Higher National, National Examining Board for Supervision and Management (NEBSM), Certificate in Management Studies (CMS), Diploma in Management Studies (DMS), and Master of Business Administration (MBA).

The book, which assumes no prior knowledge of finance, starts by looking at the part played by business in the economy and the role of the finance function in organisations. It then moves on to the area of financial accounting by studying the financial statements of profit and loss, balance sheet, and cash flow – including the way in which financial performance can be monitored through accounting ratios and other techniques. The management accounting section covers costing systems and methods – showing how they can help with financial decision making, planning and control. The final section of the book looks at business planning and explains how business information can be analysed and presented. It concludes by showing how a formal business plan is prepared.

In writing the book we have sought to avoid the use of accounting jargon and technical knowledge. Instead, we have focused on practical applications so that the non-financial manager can see the benefits of the various accounting techniques. In particular, the book contains numerous examples and Case Studies within the text. At the end of all except the last chapter there are various activities – some take the form of discussion topics, others are numerical and invariably require a conclusion to be drawn. Comprehensive answers to all the activities are provided in Appendix B.

Throughout the book, we have borne in mind the wide range of readers so that it will be appropriate to managers and students of all disciplines. Thus it is applicable to organisations in both the private and public sectors and also to voluntary organisations – many of the examples, Case Studies and activities are relevant to all sectors.

The objectives of *Management of Finance* are to give you:

- a good knowledge of the terminology used in financial accounting and management accounting
- an understanding of accounting statements

- the ability to ask detailed questions of those who prepare accounting statements
- the knowledge to use financial information to help with decision making, planning and control of the organisation
- an appreciation that accounting statements have their limitations

We wish you well with your studies.

David Cox

Michael Fardon

Summer 1997

Section 1

finance in context

This first section looks at the part played by business in the economy and the role of finance in organisations

customers

suppliers

£

PRODUCTS & SERVICES

£

PRODUCTS & SERVICES

sole traders — partnerships — limited companies

national economy

accountants

1 THE ROLE OF BUSINESS IN THE ECONOMY

this chapter covers ...

- *the types of business organisation in the economy*
- *the objectives of business*
- *the main forms of business organisation*
- *the range of sources of finance for business*
- *the concept of added value and the effect on the economy*

INTRODUCTION

In this first chapter we take an overview of business and the effect it has on the economy – both in the local economy where the business is situated and in the national economy – and on the contribution made to central government through the payment of taxes.

We begin by looking at the different types of business organisations, their place in the economy, and their objectives (which will not be solely the profit motive). We turn our attention then to the forms in which a business might be organised – as a sole trader, a partnership, or a limited company.

Finance is invariably a key issue for most businesses – financial resources enable it to function: we look at the main sources of finance available.

We conclude with the process of buying goods and services and then 'adding value' before they are sold at a profit. The added value concept shows how money flows into the economy – both local and national – as the business pays its costs. Central government benefits through the payment of taxes.

TYPES OF BUSINESS ORGANISATION

A walk around any medium-sized town will reveal evidence of a wide variety of business organisations: bus services, telephones, the Post Office, banks, shops, restaurants, pubs, etc, together with superstores and manufacturing/service businesses often located at 'out-of-town' retail and business parks. All of these businesses use financial resources to generate money from sales which contributes to the local and national economies through, for example:

- the payment of wages to employees
- the payment of rates to the local authority
- the purchase of goods and services, both locally and nationally
- the collection of Value Added Tax on sales
- the payment of tax on profits

We can classify the different types of business organisations (see fig 1.1) by distinguishing between:

- public sector and private sector organisations
- type of industry (note that the term 'industry' includes the service sector)

public sector and private sector organisations

Public sector organisations are owned directly or indirectly by central or local government. They are not all businesses as such, although the trends for business goals such as profit and efficiency are becoming more dominant. Examples of public sector organisations include the National Health Service and the Post Office.

Private sector organisations are owned by private individuals in the form of companies, partnerships and sole trader businesses. Examples include well known names such as Marks and Spencer, W H Smith and ICI.

types of industry

Primary industry produces the raw materials used by other businesses; examples include oil, gas, mining, agriculture and fishing.

Manufacturing industry (the *secondary sector*) processes the raw materials into finished products; examples include the aircraft industries, electronics and pharmaceuticals.

Service industry (the *tertiary sector*) does not produce manufactured items but provides services such as transport, financial services (banking and insurance) and tourism.

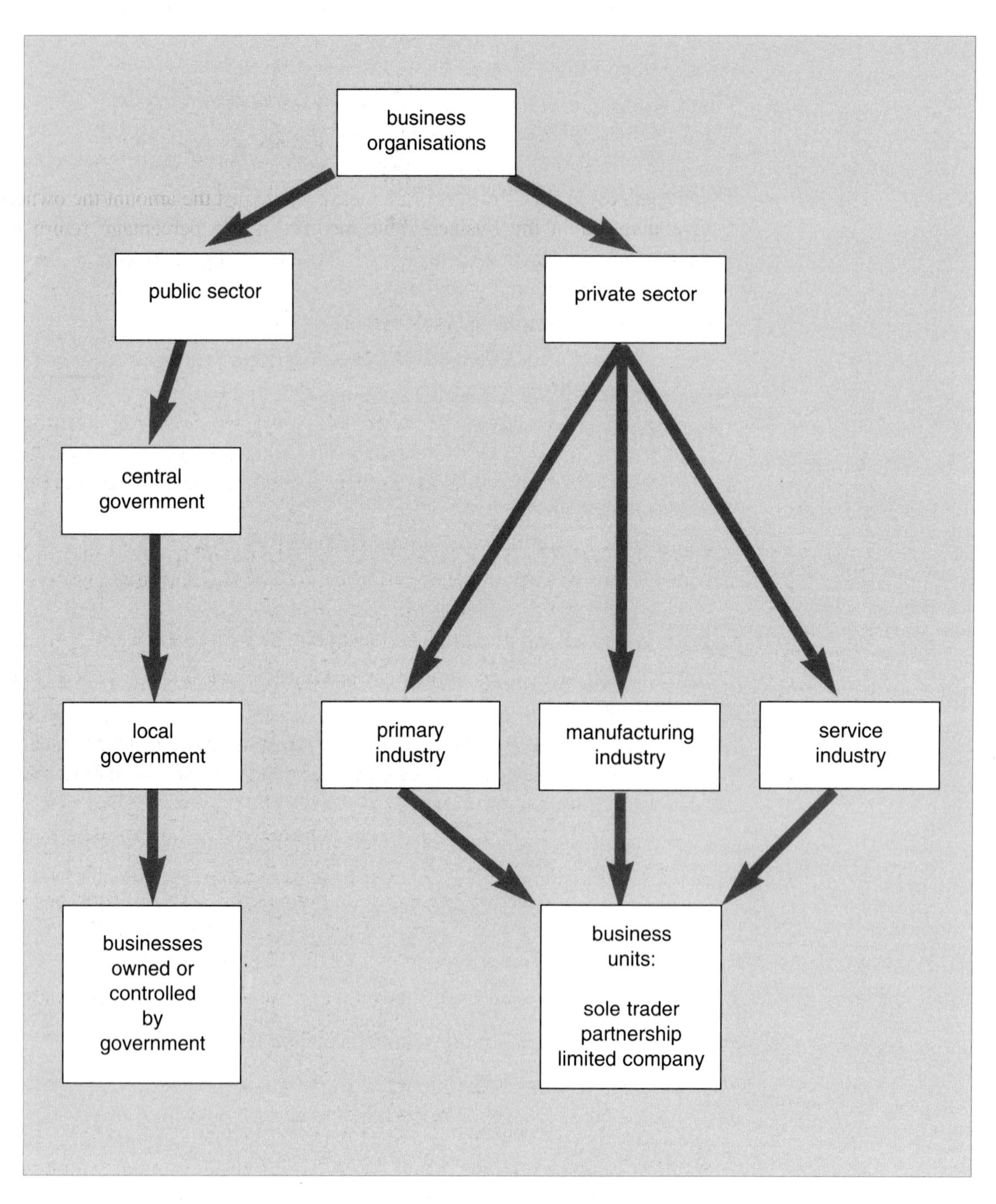

Fig 1.1 Types of industry and business organisation

OBJECTIVES OF BUSINESS ORGANISATIONS

profit

For most businesses the *profit motive* remains the most important objective. A business needs to generate sufficient profit to enable the owners to be able to draw a reasonable amount from the business each year, or for shareholders to be paid dividends. Profit is often measured against the amount the owners have invested in the business: this measure is the percentage return on capital, which can then be compared with last year's figure, or with the return of similar businesses. In this way, we can establish a 'yardstick' against which to compare the current performance of the business.

other objectives

Once the profit motive has been satisfied, and particularly as a business increases in size, a range of other objectives is developed. Some of these relate closely to the business and its output, others to wider issues. Examples include:

- *quality* – to improve the quality of the product, through better design and engineering, adding value to the output by providing better facilities, better training for the workforce
- *research and development* – providing money and facilities to enable research to take place, which may or may not lead to the development of new products
- *increase in market share* – developing the business and its products to make it more attractive to customers, so taking market share from rivals and ensuring long-term profits in the future; a growth in size will also enable the business to take advantage of economies of scale – doing more business but at a lower cost
- *social policy* – such as benefiting society by sponsorship of sport and the arts; raising levels of wages and standards of education in developing countries; donating money to political parties and other causes
- *environmental issues* – taking initiatives to improve the environment, such as becoming more energy efficient, and reducing waste

the three 'E's

The objectives of a business organisation should incorporate the three 'E's:

- *effectiveness* – that the actual output achieved, in terms of products or services, is the same as the planned output for the period
- *efficiency* – that output is achieved with the lowest level of resources, ie there is no waste or slack capacity

- *economy* – that the purchases made by the business or organisation are bought at the lowest possible cost consistent with quality and quantity

FORMS OF BUSINESS ORGANISATION

Most businesses in the private sector are organised in the form of a sole trader, partnership or limited company. The one that is chosen will depend on a number of factors, which include:

- *capital available* – the amount of money that the owner or owners put into the business
- *nature of the business* – for example, a supermarket chain will have a different form of business organisation to a corner shop
- *degree of expertise* – as well as technical expertise in the products of the business, other skills may be needed 'in-house', eg marketing, finance, computers
- *barriers to entry* – several industries preclude the entry of small business, eg it would be impossible to establish a bank run by one person
- *other factors* – size of the market, level of competition, degree of specialisation, whether trade is within the UK, European Union or internationally

A comparison of sole traders, partnerships and limited companies is given in fig 1.2.

sole trader

A sole trader is an individual in business

Sole traders run shops, small factories, farms, garages, etc, either in their own name, or under a suitable trading name. The businesses are generally small because the owner usually has limited resources – or capital – with which to start and profits are often low. Any profits remaining after the sole trader has taken out drawings for personal expenses are usually retained into the business.

There are a number of advantages of being a sole trader:

- *independence* – the business can be run as the owner thinks fit, without the need to consult anyone else
- *personal service* – a small business supervised by the owner invariably gives a better service than a large, impersonal organisation
- *simplicity* – the business is easy to establish and there are none of the legal costs of drawing up partnership agreements or limited company documentation

	SOLE TRADER	PARTNERSHIP	LIMITED COMPANY
legal status	the sole trader *is* the business	the partners *are* the business	a separate legal entity from the shareholders
members	one – the sole trader	from two partners to a normal maximum of twenty partners	minimum of two shareholders; no maximum
liability	liable for entire debt of business	partners are each liable for entire partnership debt	shareholders can lose only their investment (either the amount already paid, or promised to be paid)
legislation	none specific	Partnership Act 1890	Companies Act 1985 (as amended by the Companies Act 1989)
regulation	none specific	written or oral partnership agreement	Memorandum and Articles of Association
management	sole trader runs the business	all partners normally take an active part	run by directors and other authorised officials
share of profits	all to owner	shared equally (Partnership Act), or in proportions set out in partnership agreement	dividends paid to shareholders
taxation	income tax on profits	each partner liable for income tax on their share of profits	corporation tax on profits
financial accounts	private; not available to public	private; not available to public	made available to the public at Companies House
main sources of finance	own savings, bank overdrafts, loans, grants	savings of partners, bank overdrafts, loans, grants	shareholders, bank overdrafts, loans, grants

Fig 1.2 Comparison of forms of business organisation

There are also disadvantages of being a sole trader:

- *responsibility* – there is no one to share the risks and responsibilities of running the business
- *time* – long hours are often worked
- *lack of expertise* – the sole trader may have limited skills in areas such as finance and marketing

For a sole trader, there are also a number of financial considerations:

- *capital* – does the owner have sufficient money to start the business?
- *tax* – as a self-employed person, the sole trader will have to pay Income Tax and National Insurance Contributions
- *liability for debt* – the owner has unlimited liability for the debts of the business: this means that if the business should fail, the owner's personal assets may be used to pay off debts
- *providing security to a lender* – a lender will invariably require security to cover borrowings: often such security will be the home of the sole trader

partnership

A partnership is a group of individuals working together in business with a view to making a profit.

A partnership is simple to establish and involves two or more people running a business together. The partners are the business. Examples of partnerships include groups of doctors, dentists, accountants, and solicitors.

A partnership – often known as a 'firm' – can either trade in the name of the partners, or under a suitable trading name. For example if M Smith & G Jones set up a glazing business, they could call themselves 'Smith and Jones & Co' or adopt a more catchy name such as 'Classy Glass Merchants'. Note that the '& Co' does *not* mean that the partnership is a limited company.

A partnership does not have to be registered anywhere but it is often advisable for partners to have a partnership agreement drawn up by a solicitor. This will state what capital is being invested by each partner, how profits are split, and what will happen if there is a dispute. In a partnership each individual partner is personally liable for the debts of the business.

limited company

A limited company is a separate legal entity, owned by shareholders and run by directors.

A limited company is quite different from a sole trader in that it has a legal identity separate from its owners. The owners – the shareholders – are not personally liable for the company's debts, but can be made so if they are asked by a lender to provide security (eg their homes).

A company is managed by directors appointed by the shareholders (also known as members). In the case of many small companies the shareholders *are* the directors. A limited company must be registered at Companies House. An annual return and financial statements must be sent each year to Companies House by the company. The rules for running the company must be set out in the *Memorandum and Articles of Association*, a copy of which must also be sent to Companies House. There is much paperwork involved in establishing and running a limited company.

A limited company can be referred to as either

- a *private limited company* (abbreviated to *Ltd*), or
- a *public limited company* (abbreviated to *plc*)

Most small or medium-sized businesses which decide to incorporate (form a company) become private limited companies. If, however, they are larger, with an issued share capital of over £50,000, they can register as a public limited company. A plc *can* be quoted on the Stock Exchange (or related markets), but not all take this step.

FINANCE FOR BUSINESS

The financial needs of a business will often determine the form of the business organisation. For example, running a corner shop has fewer financial needs than a supermarket chain: thus the former is more likely to be a sole trader, while the latter is usually a public limited company.

Sole traders generally rely on their own financial resources, together with bank borrowing. Partnerships and limited companies on the other hand have more sources of finance that they can call upon. They need these further financial resources because their businesses are generally on a larger scale.

The common sources of finance for each form of business organisation and the purposes for which the money will be required are set out below.

sole trader

sources A sole trader has to rely heavily on his or her own resources to finance the business. Sources of finance include:

- savings
- sale of possessions, eg selling a house and buying a smaller one
- possible redundancy payments

- loans from family and friends
- loans from external sources – banks, government agencies
- grants from central/local government, the European Union, and other organisations
- hire purchase and leasing
- profits from the business

needs

A sole trader will use the money for two main purposes when starting or expanding a business:

- *long-term* purchases such as premises, vehicles and equipment
- *short-term* requirements such as buying stock, paying bills, paying wages

partnership

sources

Partnerships can normally raise more money than sole trader businesses because there are more individuals who can contribute money to the enterprise. Further sources of finance for partnerships include:

- contributions from partners active in the business
- contributions from partners who are not active in the business; these partners are normally referred to as 'sleeping partners' – they provide the money, share in the profits, and let the other partners get on with running the business

needs

The financial needs of a partnership are largely the same as those of a sole trader business, but are usually on a larger scale:

- *long-term* purchases such as premises, vehicles and equipment
- *short-term* requirements such as buying stock, paying bills, paying wages

limited company

sources

Limited companies are the largest form of business enterprise. Finance is provided by individuals and financial institutions – such as pension funds and unit trust managers – buying shares in the company. The way the investment is made will depend on the size of the company:

- *small private limited company* – the shareholders may well be the directors who run the company

- *medium-sized private limited company* – the shares may be sold to other companies or investors looking for a good return on their money
- *large public limited companies* – the shares may be sold to the public through a public issue (and then traded on the Stock Exchange)

Limited companies will also rely on other forms of external financing such as bank loans, hire purchase, leasing, and debt factoring (selling debts to a finance company).

needs

Limited companies, like sole traders and partnerships need finance for long-term and short-term purposes. They may also need finance for the acquisition of other companies and businesses.

CASE STUDY

OUTPUT SERVICES – PARTNERSHIP OR LIMITED COMPANY?

This Case Study looks at a small business wishing to expand. It highlights the advantages and disadvantages of partnerships and limited companies, and looks at the sources of, and needs for, finance.

situation

James Curry has been running a computer bureau as a sole trader for two years. His business, Output Systems, has involved managing the accounts and payroll of a number of local firms on his computer. He has worked from home and made a substantial profit in the first two years. He realises, however, that he must diversify to develop the business and he has suggested to Joe Harvey, a friend of his, that they join forces. Joe Harvey's interest is also in computers and he has been specialising in producing promotional literature for local firms and organising mailshots for them under the name 'Intermail Services'. Joe has agreed that they could pool their resources and offer a useful package of computer services, trading under the name of 'Output Services'. They seek professional advice from a solicitor and an accountant as to whether they should form a partnership or a limited company. They also ask about the financial aspects of their proposals.

solution

the solicitor's advice

liability

If they form a *partnership,* they are both individually and collectively responsible for all the debts of the partnership. If they form a *limited company* it is a separate legal entity, responsible for its own debts. They will become directors, ie employees of the company, and not strictly speaking liable for its debts, but . . .

security

If a partnership borrows from the bank, the partners will invariably have to offer a mortgage of their homes as security. If they become directors of a company and the company borrows, the directors may be asked to guarantee the borrowing and support the guarantee with a mortgage over their homes – ie the position of personal liability with respect to security is little changed whether they are partners or directors.

documentation

A partnership is often (not always) formalised in a written Partnership Agreement which the solicitor can draw up for them. The formation and registration of a limited company require much more documentation (including the Memorandum and Articles of Association) and are therefore more expensive in terms of legal fees. Running a limited company also involves more paperwork such as maintaining the minutes of meetings, filing accounts and annual returns.

The solicitor suggests that, on the face of it, a partnership would be the cheaper and simpler alternative, subject to their being able to get on with each other (the Partnership Agreement could cover cases of disputes).

the accountant's advice

taxation

Each partner is liable for personal Income Tax on his share of the profits and also for National Insurance Contributions. A limited company is subject to Corporation Tax on its profits and the directors are additionally liable on their salaries for Income Tax and National Insurance Contributions (which are also payable by the company).

audit and accounts

Neither a partnership nor a small company is required to have its accounts audited (larger companies must have their accounts audited). Companies must send a set of their accounts each year to Companies House where they are available for public inspection, although smaller companies can submit abbreviated accounts. The accountant's fees for a limited company will generally be higher than for a partnership.

raising of finance

It is often easier for a limited company to raise funds as there are generally individuals and companies ready to take shares in a small company as a form of investment. The accountant points out that this form of investment is more readily available to larger companies. This form of finance is not available to partnerships which rely more heavily on the introduction of capital by the partners.

conclusion

James and Joe decide that, as they work well together, they will choose the simpler and cheaper option of forming a partnership. They will ask the solicitor to draw up a Partnership Agreement for them and the accountant to advise on finance and taxation. They bear in mind that, if the business expands further, they may, in the future, form a limited company, but only if their personal tax bills justify the action (ie if they are paying tax at higher rates), and if they need to raise further finance from outside investors who want to buy shares in the proposed company.

BUSINESS ORGANISATIONS AND ADDED VALUE

the concept of added value

As a business spends money on its running costs – materials, components, expertise, overheads, and so on – it is *adding value* to its product. It is putting money and resources into a product or service which it can then sell at a profit. To take a simple example, a farmer can sell the apples that the farm grows. But the farmer can also *add value* to the apples by processing them – into apple juice, cider and apple pies. These processes will cost the farmer in terms of materials and overheads, but they will also enable the farmer to charge more in the long run because *value has been added* to the product.

The diagram below shows how selling a product or service involves:

- *costs* which add value to the product/service
- *money received from sales* which is then used to pay costs and also to provide a profit for the owner(s) of the business

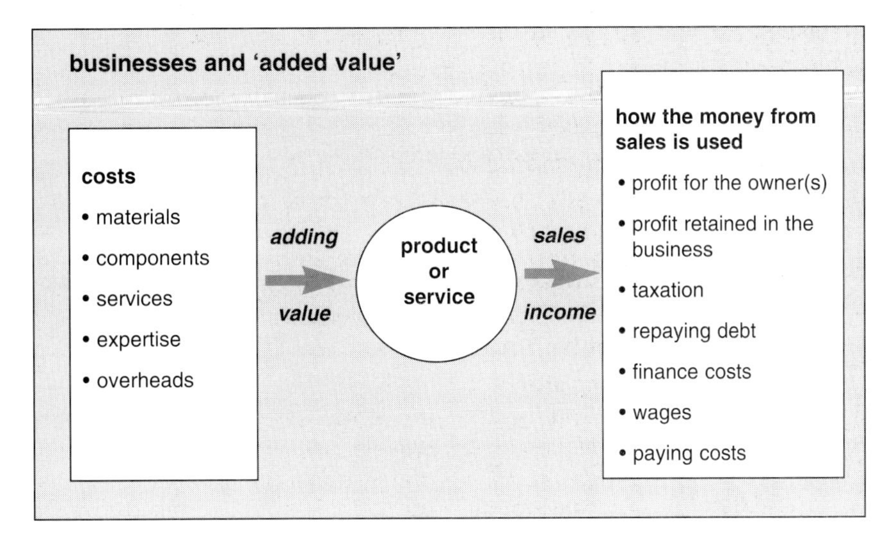

the distribution of added value

When a business has sold its 'added value' product or service it will receive its money in due course: this will then be *distributed.* The diagram above shows how the money is used.

profit for the owner(s)

Whether the business is a sole trader or a limited company, the owner(s) of the business will want to see a return on the capital invested. For the sole trader and partnership, profit can be taken in the form of *drawings* – money taken out of the business. Shareholders' profits are distributed in the form of *dividends* on the company's shares.

profit retained in the business

It is normal and sensible practice to retain some of the profit in the business so that it can be invested in new products/services and equipment. The business should be looking ahead to develop its range in order to make increasing profits in the future.

taxation

Business profits are taxable. Sole traders and partners pay *income tax* on their business profits; limited companies pay *corporation tax* on their profits. Businesses and their owners therefore have to set aside a proportion of their profits for paying tax to the Inland Revenue. Also if VAT is charged by a business on its product, the VAT will have to be paid to HM Customs & Excise (set off against VAT paid on the purchases a business makes).

repaying loans

Many businesses finance part of their operations through loans from banks and other providers of finance. Part of the cash generated by the business will therefore have to be allocated for repayment of capital (the actual amount borrowed) and interest (the cost of that finance).

finance costs

Finance costs include *interest* and *fees* paid on loans, and bank charges made for operating the business bank account.

wages

The *wages* and *salaries* bill can be high if the business is labour-intensive.

paying costs

The costs listed in the left-hand box of the diagram will need paying for – the money in effect goes full circle. These costs include materials, services used, the business running expenses (overheads).

added value and the economy

The concept of added value illustrates how businesses interact with all aspects of the local and national economy. The process of added value creates a trading cycle which is continually:

- buying in goods and services
- adding value
- selling the product/service
- distributing the money received

In this way, money is generated and contributed to the local economy (through payment of wages, local goods and services), the national economy (goods and services, finance costs, exports) and central government (taxation, Value Added Tax, National Insurance Contributions). Thus individual businesses contribute to the wealth of the economy through the process of added value.

CASE STUDY

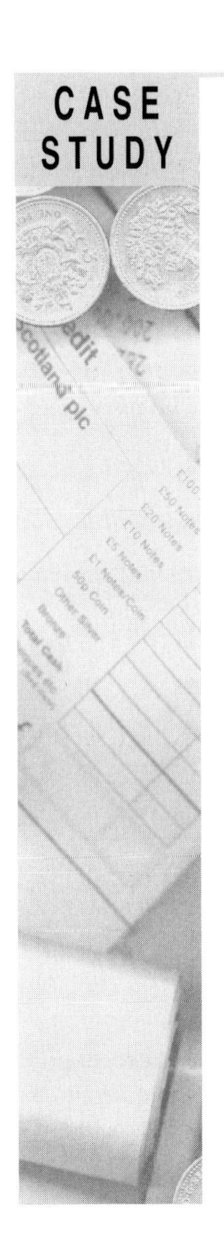

TOYISSON MOTORS – NEW FACTORY

situation

Toyisson Motors is a Far-Eastern manufacturer of family cars. In order to establish a stronger presence in the European market the company has decided to locate a new factory on a 'green-field' site in the north-east of England. The UK government has put together a package of grants to encourage the company to establish itself in this part of the country.

How will the arrival of this new enterprise benefit

- the local economy of the north-east?
- the UK national economy?
- central government?

solution

The decision to build a new factory will create employment – not only for those working at the factory, but also at suppliers of goods and services. In fact, it has been estimated that, for every one person employed by a new factory such as this, at least one other job is created.

local economy

Construction workers will build the factory and make improvements to local roads. Payment of their wages, and the purchase of building materials will flow into the local economy.

Once the factory is operational, the wages of employees, together with payments to local suppliers of components and services will benefit the local economy. Toyisson Motors will pay business rates on its factory to the local authority – which will be able to provide better services in its area.

UK national economy

There will be benefits from payments by Toyisson Motors to suppliers. The

national economy will also benefit from the export of some of the cars made at the new factory and the need for the UK to import fewer cars: this will boost the country's balance of trade (the difference between earnings from the export of goods and the import of goods from abroad).

central government

Toyisson Motors will make payments to various government departments, eg

- Value Added Tax collected on sales made, less VAT on goods purchased – paid to HM Customs & Excise
- Corporation Tax paid to the Inland Revenue on profits made by the company in the UK
- Income Tax collected by the company as statutory deductions from employees' wages – paid to the Inland Revenue
- National Insurance Contributions – another statutory payment which comprises deductions from employees' wages and a contribution by the company – paid to the Inland Revenue

With all these benefits flowing down to the local and national economies and to central government, there is no doubt that the new factory, if successful, will bring added value to the UK. By offering an initial package of grant aid to establish the new factory, the government hopes that the UK economy will receive much greater benefits in the longer term.

- Organisations can be classified into public sector or private sector.
- The types of industry are
  - primary, producing raw materials
  - manufacturing, processing raw materials into finished products
  - service, providing services such as transport, financial services, tourism
- Whilst the profit motive is a primary objective of most businesses, there are other objectives, such as:
  - quality
  - research and development
  - increase in market share
  - social policy
  - environmental issues
- A business can be formed as a sole trader, or a partnership, or a limited company.
- Sole trader and partnership businesses are simpler and less expensive to establish than limited companies, but the directors of a limited company have limited liability, unlike sole traders and partners who are fully liable for business debts.

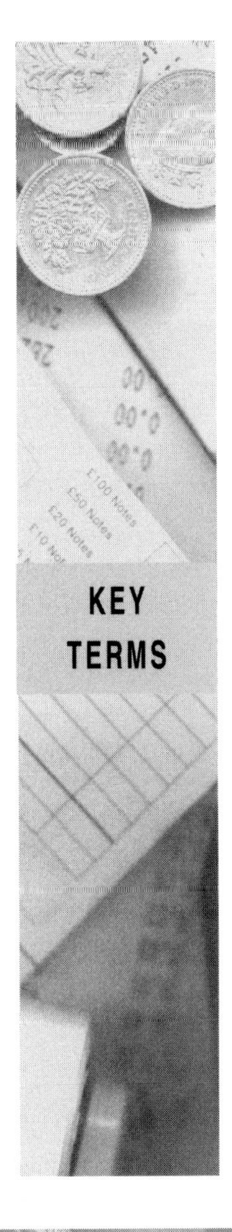

- Partnerships and limited companies provide more scope for raising external finance than a sole trader business; all types of businesses invariably rely on bank borrowing as a form of finance.
- A business adds value to goods and services and then sells them at a profit. The payment by the business of its costs helps money to flow into the local and national economies, and to central government through the payment of taxes.

Having taken an overview of business in this chapter, in the next we turn to a detailed examination of the role of accounting in business, and of the personnel involved in the accounting function.

sole trader – an individual in business with a view to making a profit

partnership – a group of individuals working together in business with a view to making a profit

limited company – a separate legal entity, owned by shareholders and run by directors

public limited company – a company, registered as a plc, with an issued share capital of more than £50,000; may be quoted on the Stock Exchange (or related markets)

private limited company – any limited company which is not a public limited company

added value – spending money on a product or service so that it gains value and can be sold at a profit

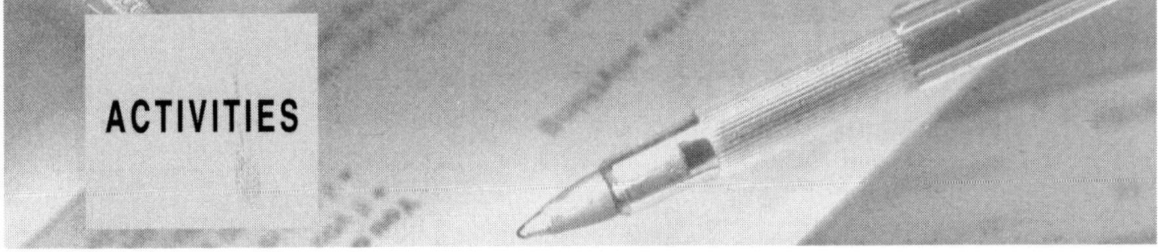

1.1 Identify an organisation with which you are familiar and consider the following:

- Is the organisation in the public or private sector? What does it do?
- In what type of industry is the organisation – primary, manufacturing or service?
- What do you see as the main objective of the organisation? Does it set any objectives itself? What secondary objectives does it have?
- Give examples of how the organisation incorporates the three 'E's of effectiveness, efficiency and economy

1.2 Prepare for a group discussion on forms of business organisations by identifying four existing businesses: one a sole trader, one a partnership, one a private limited company, and one a public limited company.

For each business, report on:

- its name and location of premises
- its products or services
- its size (which might be measured in terms of turnover/sales, number of employees, number of locations, profits, share of market)
- the reasons for its current form of business organisation (is this likely to change in the near future?)
- its sources of finance

Information should be obtained from personal contacts, the financial pages of newspapers, company reports, Companies House. (Note: it may not be possible to research fully all aspects of each business organisation.)

Discuss your findings with the members of your group.

1.3 Compsoft Limited is a recently established business which provides computer service and repairs to local businesses. The management has the following figures of costs and income for the first year in business:

Costs		£
Spare parts for repairs		25,000
Software and computer supplies bought for resale		72,000
Wages and salaries		42,000
Rent and rates of premises		11,000
Finance costs:	interest paid on bank loan	3,000
	leasing of office equipment	12,000
Income		
Receipts from repairs		100,000
Sales of software and computer supplies		108,000

- How much added value has been achieved by the company during the year?
- How has the money received as income been used by the business? How would you advise the directors of Compsoft to utilise any surplus money?
- Calculate the percentage of
  - the cost of spare parts
  - the cost of software and computer supplies

  against the respective income figures. Discuss the reasons for any differences in the percentages.

1.4 Discussion topics:

- What will be the impact on the local economy of the closure of:
  - a department store?
  - a farm?
  - a factory (production is to be transferred to the Far East)?
  - a college?
  - a bank?
- How might there be a conflict between different business objectives, eg maximising profits, increasing market share, spending money on research and development, environmental issues?
- What will be the financial effect on local retail businesses of
  - a new 'out-of-town' shopping centre?
  - the opening of a branch of a major burger company?
  - the setting up of a telephone banking operation on a nearby 'green-field' site?

2 THE ACCOUNTING FUNCTION

this chapter covers ...

- *the need for accounting records*
- *the people who are interested in aspects of the accounts*
- *an overview of the accounting system*
- *the need for different accounting periods*
- *the main accounting personnel and their roles*
- *the differences between financial accounting and management accounting*

INTRODUCTION

Why does a business have to keep 'books'?
Who is interested in the accounts?
What is the difference between an auditor and an accountant?
When do we use management accounting?

These are questions often asked about 'accounts'. Many people see the accounting function of a business as an administrative task that doesn't add value to the products or services of the business, or generate profits. In this chapter (and throughout the rest of the book) we will attempt to dispel some of these myths! We will look at why there is a need for accounting records, and the people who will be interested in them. We will take an overview of the accounting system, distinguish between the key accounting personnel, and conclude with a look at the differences between financial accounting and management accounting.

THE NEED FOR ACCOUNTING RECORDS

All businesses, and most other organisations, are required by law to keep accounting records – the 'books' – of their financial transactions. There are several parties who will be interested in various aspects of the accounts, as shown in fig 2.1 on the opposite page.

WHO IS INTERESTED IN THE ACCOUNTS?	*WHAT ARE THEY INTERESTED IN?*	*WHY ARE THEY INTERESTED?*
Owner/shareholders	• Has the business made a profit? • Can the business pay its way? • What was the sales (turnover) figure?	• To see how much money can be paid by the business as drawings or dividends • To assess if the business will continue in the foreseeable future • To see if the business is growing
Inland Revenue	• Has the business made a profit?	• To calculate the tax due on profits
H M Customs and Excise	• What was the sales (turnover) figure? • What were the figures for purchases and expenses?	• To ensure that, if appropriate, the business is registered for VAT (Value Added Tax) • To ensure that VAT returns are completed on time and that any payment due is made within the timescales
Bank manager	• Has the business made a profit? • What is the bank balance or overdraft? • What is the value of the business' assets?	• To check if the business can afford to make loan repayments • To assess how far the bank is financing the business • To assess the value of security available to cover lending
Employees and trade unions	• Has the business made a profit? • Can the business pay its way?	• To see if the business can afford pay rises • To assess if the business will continue to trade in the foreseeable future
Debtors (who owe the business money)	• What is the value of the business' assets? • Can the business pay its way?	• To see if the business has the financial strength to carry out work contracted to it • To assess the ability of the business to meet liabilities which might fall due, eg guarantees and warranties
Creditors (to whom the business owes money)	• Can the business pay its way? • What is the value of the business' assets?	• To assess if the business is able to pay its debts as they fall due • If the business should fail, how much are the creditors likely to receive?
Competitors	• What was the sales (turnover) figure? • What is the value of the business' assets?	• To see if the business is expanding or declining • To calculate whether the business can be taken over

Fig 2.1 Interested parties to the accounts of a business

THE ACCOUNTING SYSTEM

It is essential that the financial transactions of the business are recorded in a way that is both precise and standardised, as they will be of interest to a number of parties, not least the owner or shareholders.

The accounting system operates at two levels:

- *book-keeping* – the day-to-day recording of financial transactions
- *accounting* – the use of book-keeping records to prepare analytical statements (eg profit and loss account) which are used to monitor the business and provide a basis for making financial decisions

The accounting system is the process of recording financial information from documents (such as invoices and receipts) into the accounting records, checking that the information has been recorded correctly, and then presenting the information in a way which enables the owners and managers of the business to review progress. It can be summarised as follows:

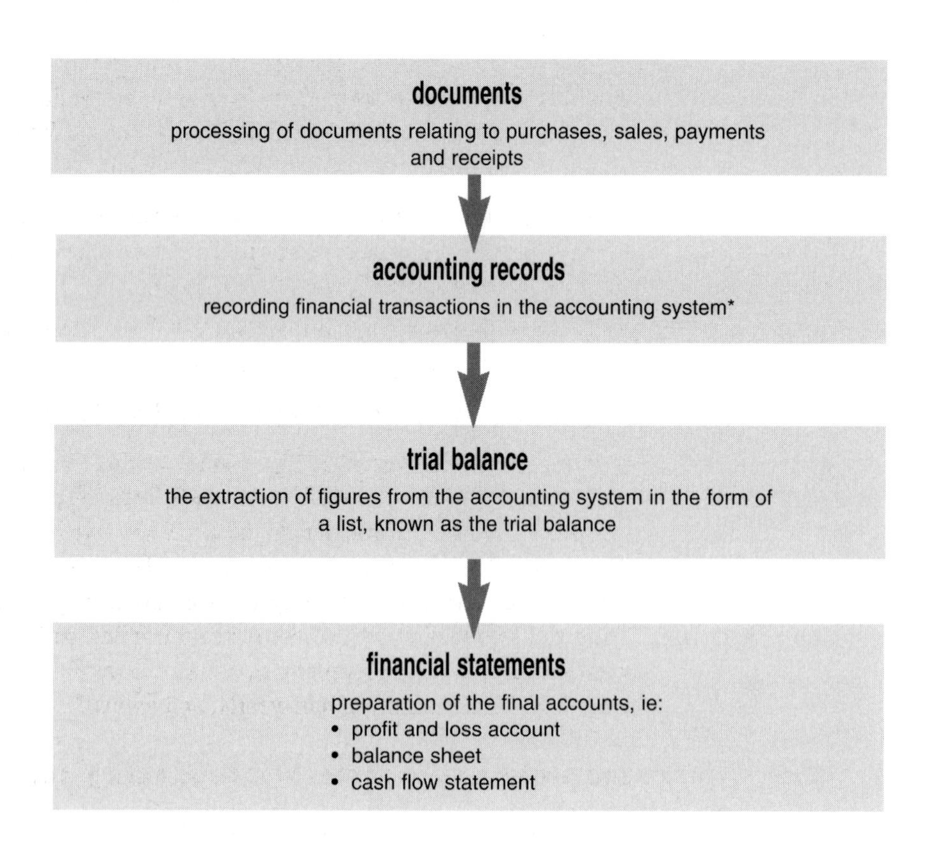

* Most businesses use an accounting system based on the double-entry book-keeping system, whereby each financial transaction is recorded in the accounts twice.

As noted above, the final accounts of a business comprise:

- *profit and loss account* – which shows the amount of profit or loss made during the accounting period
- *balance sheet* – which shows the assets, liabilities and capital at the end of the accounting period
- *cash flow statement* – which shows the movements of money (in the form of cash itself and the bank account) into and out of the business during the accounting period (note that this statement is more common for larger businesses)

We will be studying the final accounts in more depth in the next few chapters. An understanding of the final accounts will enable us to assess how well the business is performing year-on-year, and also against its competitors and the industry average.

ACCOUNTING PERIODS

As we have seen, the accounting system records day-to-day financial transactions, and then uses the information, at regular intervals, to prepare the financial statements of profit and loss account, balance sheet and cash flow statement.

The statements are linked – a profit and loss account and cash flow statement cover a time period, while a balance sheet shows the state of the business on the last day of the time period, for example:

- profit and loss account **for the year ended** 31 December 1997
- balance sheet **as at** 31 December 1997
- cash flow statement **for the year ended** 31 December 1997

The time period covered by the profit and loss account is known as the *accounting period.* Generally, for each individual business, accounting periods cover the same length of time, for example the year-ended 31 December 1997, year-ended 31 December 1998, and so on. As you will see with this example, the last day of one accounting period is immediately followed by the first day of the next accounting period. While accounting periods can cover any length of time, the most common are monthly, quarterly (three monthly), half-yearly, and annually.

monthly and quarterly accounting periods

Many businesses monitor their progress on a monthly and/or quarterly basis. Thus, at the end of each month, or quarter, they will produce financial statements. These are then used within the business to assess the level of activity and profitability in the accounting period, and the state of the company – in terms of assets and liabilities – at the end of the period. Such monthly and quarterly financial statements are often used in conjunction with a budgeting system, where targets are set for key activities of the business – eg sales, purchases, expenses – often up to twelve months ahead. The budget figures are then compared with what actually happened and, if necessary, corrective action can be taken for the next accounting period. Note that the monthly or quarterly accounts will be included in total figures for the business' financial year: see annual accounting periods, below.

With computer accounting programs, it is a simple task to print out the profit and loss account and balance sheet at the end of each month or quarter.

half-yearly accounting periods

Public limited companies (whose shares are quoted on the Stock Exchange) send information to their shareholders and financial analysts in the form of half-yearly results. These give some information on the company's progress during the first half of the financial year; however, the amount of detail supplied is less than that contained in the formal 'annual report and accounts' – also, the information has not been verified by the auditors (outside accountants who check the figures on behalf of the shareholders).

annual accounting periods

Virtually every organisation – from sole trader through to the largest multinational corporation, and central and local government – produces annual accounts. There is, historically, no particular reason for choosing to report results once a year, except that it represents a reasonable time period over which to monitor progress.

There is no requirement for final accounts to end on a particular day in each year, although 31 December is a popular financial year-end for limited companies. Many sole traders and partnerships choose the year-end date of 31 March because the tax year ends on 5 April. The financial year-end, however, does not have to fit in with the end of a month.

The annual financial statements of limited companies are sent to the shareholders and a copy is filed with Companies House (where they are available for inspection).

Some public limited companies also issue an annual summary financial statement to shareholders; these give less information than the full annual accounts.

ACCOUNTING PERSONNEL

book-keeper

Anyone can keep the 'books' of a business; the important point is that they must be kept – by the owner, or by a full or part-time book-keeper (or book-keepers) employed for the purpose. Book-keepers do not have to be qualified (although many are). The role will vary from someone coming in for half-a-day a week to write up the books of a small business, to hundreds of people being employed by larger companies and using powerful computer systems.

The 'books' will vary from handwritten records (stationery shops sell accounting books designed especially for the smaller business) to computer accounting systems. Nowadays computers have come down in price so much that they can be afforded by virtually all businesses. There are a wide range of computer accounting programs available – from 'off-the-shelf' software which is more than adequate for smaller companies' needs, through to specialist programs which can be adapted to meet the needs of much larger companies and central and local government.

accountant

The role of the accountant – who will, invariably, be professionally qualified – is to check, summarise, present, analyse and interpret the accounts for the benefit of the owner/owners and other interested parties. There are two types of specialist accountant:

- *financial accountant*, mainly concerned with external reporting
- *management accountant*, mainly concerned with internal reporting

However, in smaller businesses, the two roles are often combined and the work undertaken by one accountant.

The function of the ***financial accountant*** is very much concerned with financial transactions, and with using the information produced by the book-keeper. The financial accountant extracts information from the accounting records in order to provide a method of control, for instance over debtors, creditors, cash and bank balances. The role also requires the preparation of year-end financial statements, and may also include negotiation with the Inland Revenue on tax matters for the business. Limited companies, in particular, must comply with the accounting requirements of the Companies Act (see Chapter 6), and with the relevant accounting standards (see pages 49–50). The Companies Act requires the directors of a company to report annually to shareholders, with certain minimum financial accounting information being disclosed.

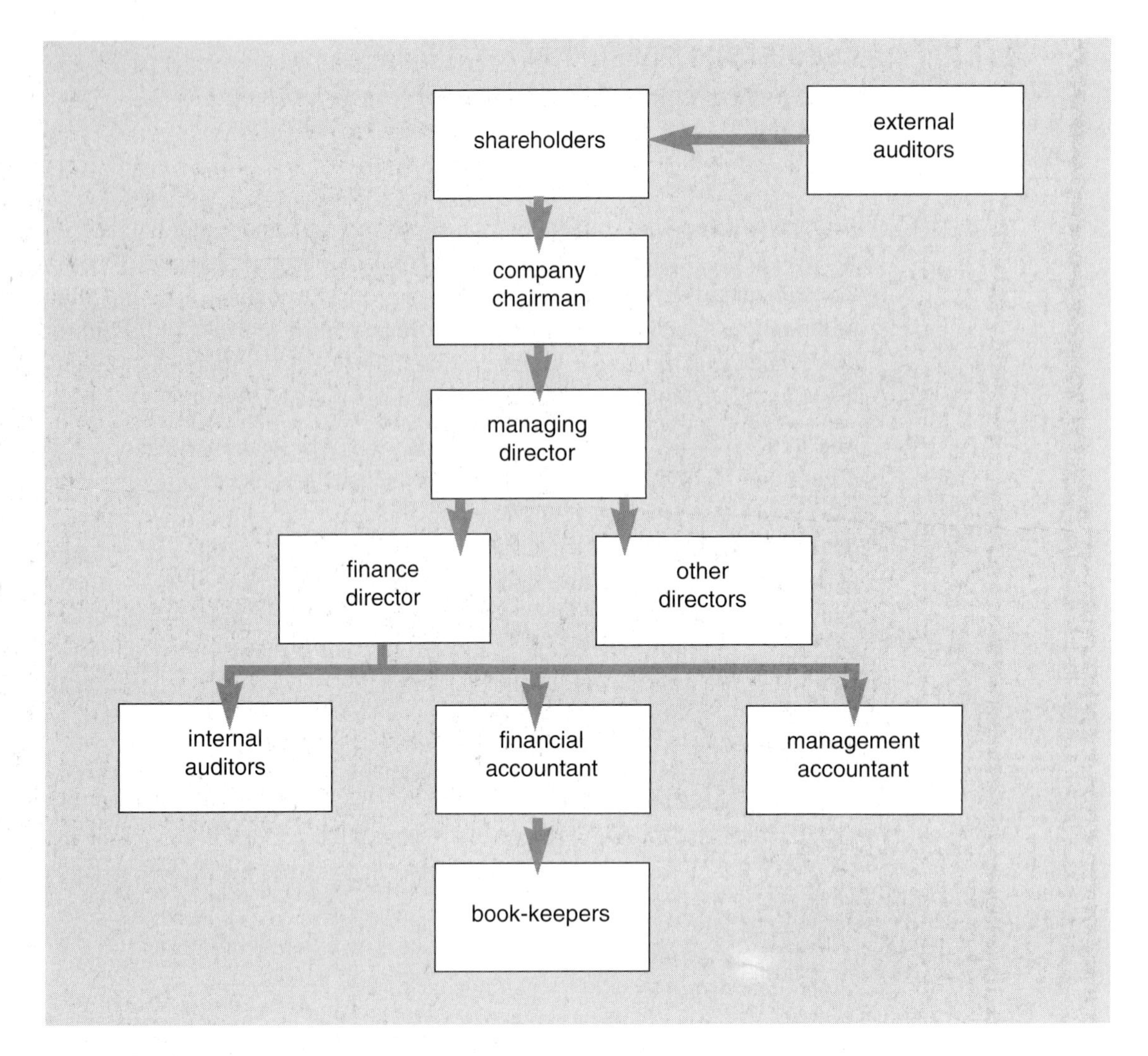

Fig 2.2 Organisation chart of accounting personnel

The ***management accountant*** obtains information about costs – eg the cost of labour, materials, overheads – and interprets it and prepares reports for the owners or managers of the business. In particular, the management accountant is concerned with financial decision making, planning and control of the business.

auditors

Auditors are accountants whose role is to check that accounting procedures have been followed correctly. There are two types of auditors:

- external auditors
- internal auditors

External auditors are independent of the firm whose accounts are being audited, but work within a framework of Auditing Standards (issued by the Auditing Practices Board). The most common type of audit conducted by external auditors is the statutory audit of a limited company. In this, the auditors are reporting to the shareholders of a company, stating that the legal requirements laid down in the Companies Act have been complied with, and that the accounts represent a 'true and fair view' of the state of the business. External auditors are usually appointed by the shareholders at the Annual General Meeting of the company.

Not all companies need to have their accounts audited. Companies with an annual turnover below a certain figure (currently £350,000) are exempt from audit requirements.

Internal auditors are employees of the business which they audit. Their duties are concerned with the internal check and control procedures of the business, for example setting down the procedures for the control of cash, authorisation of purchases, and disposal of property. The nature of their work requires that they should have a degree of independence within the company; they often report directly to the financial director.

organisation of accounting personnel

Fig 2.2 on the previous page shows the inter-relationship of the accounting personnel described; the business in this instance is a medium-sized limited company.

FINANCIAL ACCOUNTING AND MANAGEMENT ACCOUNTING

Much of the material that we will cover in this book is concerned with financial accounting and management accounting. *Financial accounting* is involved with financial transactions that have happened already and with the preparation and interpretation of financial statements: profit and loss account, balance sheet, and cash flow statement. *Management accounting* deals with all aspects of costing information, and reporting to management the effect on the business in the future, eg the result of:

- reducing/increasing selling prices
- developing new products or services
- switching resources from one product or service to another
- closing one department or division of the business

The table below shows the differences between financial accounting and management accounting. However, as mentioned earlier, in smaller companies and organisations, the differences between these two types of accounting may become blurred and both might be undertaken by the same accountant.

financial accounting	management accounting
historical Records past financial transactions; covers previous year's trading; looks backwards.	***recent past and future*** Performance reports containing financial information on recent past, and projections for future.
for outsiders Financial statements prepared for shareholders, creditors, bank, Inland Revenue, Registrar of Companies.	***for insiders*** Available only to managers, directors, and owners (but not to shareholders generally); may be made available to bank.
outsiders make the rules The Companies Act specifies the accounting information that must be prepared; also the Inland Revenue has requirements; the accountancy professional bodies set standard accounting practice.	***insiders make the rules*** The content of reports and the principles used can be suited to the activities of the business and the requirements of its managers.
a 'true and fair' view Financial accounting is required to present a 'true and fair' view of the financial affairs of the business.	***a useful report*** The main requirement of management accounting is to produce information that will enable the business to conduct its activities more effectively.
timing Generally there is little urgency to produce financial accounts; financial statements are normally produced once a year.	***timing*** Management accounting information is prepared as frequently as circumstances demand; speed is often vital as information may go out-of-date very quickly.

Fig 2.3 Differences between financial accounting and management accounting

CHAPTER SUMMARY

- We have seen the legal requirement for businesses and most other organisations to keep accounting records, and the various parties who will have an interest in some aspect of the accounts.

- The accounting system commences with the processing of documents relating to purchases, sales, payments and receipts, and concludes with the production of the financial statements of profit and loss account, balance sheet, and cash flow statement.

- Accounting periods are used as time periods over which the progress of the business can be monitored.

- The two main areas of accounting are *financial accounting* and *management accounting.* The former is most concerned with the recording of financial transactions that have already happened and with the preparation and interpretation of financial statements; the latter deals with all aspects of costing information – both in the recent past and in estimates for the future – and in the preparation of reports for the owners and managers of the business.

In the next section of the book we look in more detail at the financial statements of profit and loss account, balance sheet, and cash flow statement.

KEY TERMS

accounting records	the 'books' of the business or organisation in which financial transactions are recorded
double-entry book-keeping	the method by which most accounting records are kept – it involves making two entries in the accounts for each financial transaction
financial statements	the final accounts: profit and loss account, balance sheet and cash flow statement
profit and loss account	shows the amount of profit or loss made during the accounting period
balance sheet	shows the assets, liabilities and capital at the end of the accounting period
cash flow statement	shows the movements of money into and out of the business during the accounting period
accounting period	time period covered by the final accounts: monthly, quarterly, half-yearly or annually
financial accountant	concerned with all aspects of financial transactions and, in particular, preparation and interpretation of financial statements

management accountant	involved with internal reporting to management, and with financial decision making, planning and control of the business
auditors	accountants whose role is to check that accounting procedures have been followed correctly

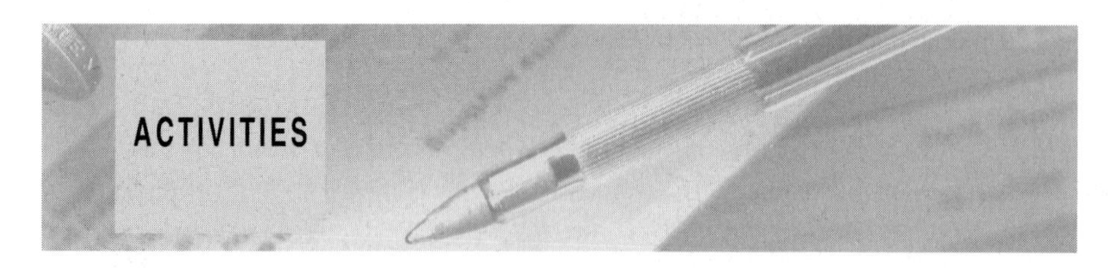

ACTIVITIES

2.1 Investigate the financial structure of an organisation with which you are familiar. In particular:

(a) Identify the type of financial statements produced and their frequency. Who are the interested parties to these statements? Why is this?

(b) What is the purpose of the main financial statements used by the organisation?

(c) Produce an organisation chart of the finance function.

(d) Identify the roles of financial accountant and management accountant (even if the organisation uses different job titles). What work is each responsible for?

(e) What other job titles are used within the finance function? What work is each responsible for?

(f) Who are the external auditors of the organisation? When were they appointed, and how much do they earn for the audit? Obtain a copy of the most recent audit report – does the wording assure you that all is well with the organisation's finances?

2.2 For an organisation with which you are familiar, write job descriptions for

- the financial accountant
- the management accountant

What particular skills are required for these jobs?

2.3 Discussion topics:

- How does an accountant add value to an organisation?
- Which is more important, to produce goods and services, or to account for them?

Section 2

financial statements

This section of the book takes a detailed look at financial accounting and, in particular, at the form of the financial statements:

- ***profit and loss account***
- ***balance sheet***
- ***cash flow statement***

profit and loss account

sole traders

—

partnerships

—

limited companies

cash flow statement

balance sheet

3 BASICS OF FINANCIAL STATEMENTS

this chapter covers ...

- *the definition of a profit and loss account*
- *the structure and layout of a profit and loss account*
- *the definition of a balance sheet*
- *the structure and layout of a balance sheet*
- *the concept of depreciation and its application to the financial statements*
- *an introduction to the cash flow statement*
- *the links between the financial statements*
- *the purposes of financial statements, including their part in enabling owners and managers to monitor performance, and their role in raising finance for the business*
- *the scope of the 'rules' of accounting*

INTRODUCTION

In this chapter we look at the three financial statements:

- profit and loss account – which shows the profitability of the business
- balance sheet – which shows the assets, liabilities and capital of the business
- cash flow statement – which shows the movements of money into and out of the business

In particular we look at the 'how and why' of the profit and loss account and balance sheet using, as examples, a relatively small sole-trader business. In the chapters which follow, we shall be studying in detail cash flow statements (Chapter 5), and the more complex financial statements of limited companies (Chapters 4 and 6).

Towards the end of this chapter we shall consider the purposes for which the financial statements are used, and the 'rules' of accounting under which they are prepared.

PROFIT AND LOSS ACCOUNT

A profit and loss account is a financial statement which summarises the revenue and expenses of a business for an accounting period and shows the overall profit or loss.

The profit and loss account summarises information from the accounting records:

- the sales (or turnover) of the business
- the cost of sales made by the business
- the overheads of running the business, such as administration, wages, rent paid, telephone, interest paid, travel expenses

The amount of sales is the *revenue* of the business, while the cost of sales and overheads are the *expenses* of the business.

layout of a profit and loss account

In broad terms, the profit and loss account consists of a calculation

REVENUE *minus* EXPENSES *equals* PROFIT OR LOSS

If revenue is greater than expenses, then the business has made a profit; if expenses are greater than revenue, then a loss has been made.

Fig 3.1 on page 35 shows an example profit and loss account for a sole trader, ie one person in business. For other business units, such as partnerships and limited companies, the profit and loss account shows how the net profit is shared amongst the owners of the business – an agreed share of profits to each partner, dividends to shareholders in a limited company. (We will look in more detail at the financial statements of limited companies in Chapters 4 and 6.)

The profit and loss account is presented in a *vertical* format, ie it runs down the page. Two columns are used for money amounts; the right-hand money column contains sub-totals and totals, while the left-hand money column is used for listing individual amounts, eg of overheads, which are then totalled and carried to the right-hand column.

The layout of the profit and loss account shown on page 35 – with the two levels of profit – gross profit and net profit – is suitable for a *trading business* which buys and sells goods. The layout, can, however, be adapted to suit the needs of different types of business. A *service sector business* such as an accountancy firm, for example, may show 'fee' income in place of sales. A *manufacturing business*, on the other hand, uses a separate manufacturing account to calculate production cost which is then transferred into profit and loss account in place of (or addition to) purchases (see Chapter 9).

The amounts for **sales** and **purchases** include only items in which the business trades – eg a clothes shop buying clothes from the manufacturer includes the amount incurred in its purchases figure; when the clothes are sold the amount is recorded as sales. By contrast, items bought for use in the business, such as a new till for the shop, are not included with purchases but are shown as assets on the balance sheet.

Cost of sales represents the cost to the business of the goods which have been sold in this financial year. Cost of sales is:

	opening stock	(stock bought previously)
plus	purchases	(purchased during the year)
minus	closing stock	(stock left unsold at the end of the year)
equals	cost of sales	(cost of what has actually been sold)

Gross profit is calculated as:

sales – cost of sales = gross profit

If cost of sales is greater than sales, the business has made a gross loss.

Overheads are the running costs of the business – known as *revenue expenditure.* The categories of overheads used vary according to the needs of each business.

Net profit is calculated as:

gross profit – overheads = net profit

If overheads are more than gross profit, the business has made a net loss.

The net profit is the amount the business earned for the owner during the year, and is subject to taxation. The owner can draw some or all of the net profit for personal use – the accounting term for this is *drawings.* Part of the profit might well be left in the business in order to help build up the business for the future. Profit does not necessarily equal cash in the bank available for spending; it may already have been invested back in the business.

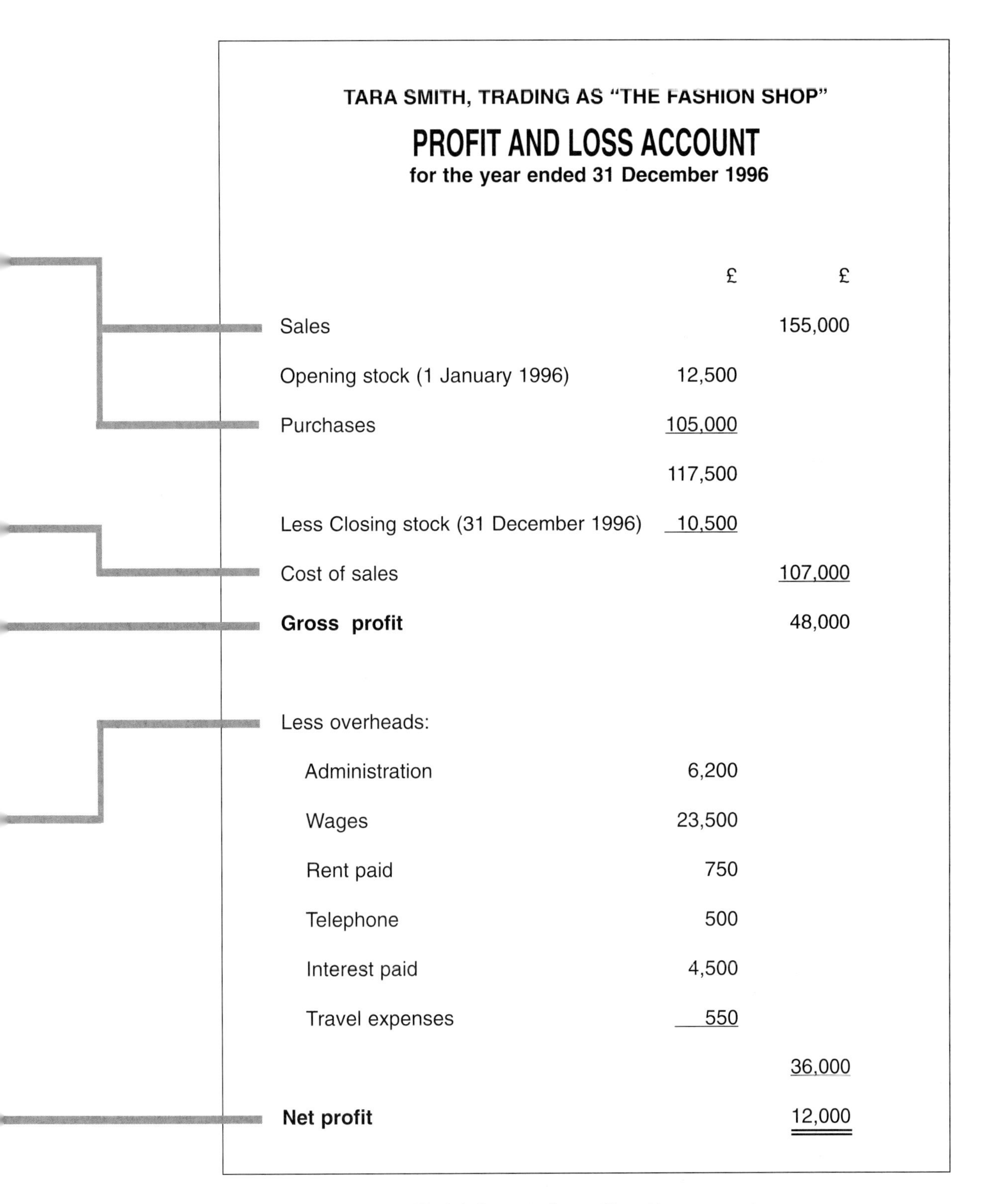

TARA SMITH, TRADING AS "THE FASHION SHOP"

PROFIT AND LOSS ACCOUNT

for the year ended 31 December 1996

	£	£
Sales		155,000
Opening stock (1 January 1996)	12,500	
Purchases	105,000	
	117,500	
Less Closing stock (31 December 1996)	10,500	
Cost of sales		107,000
Gross profit		48,000
Less overheads:		
Administration	6,200	
Wages	23,500	
Rent paid	750	
Telephone	500	
Interest paid	4,500	
Travel expenses	550	
		36,000
Net profit		12,000

Fig 3.1 Layout of a profit and loss account

BALANCE SHEET

A balance sheet is a financial statement which shows the assets, liabilities and capital of a business at a particular date.

Balance sheets are different from profit and loss accounts (which show profits for an accounting period); by contrast balance sheets show the state of the business at one moment in time – things could be somewhat different tomorrow; in fact a balance sheet is often described as a 'snapshot' of a business at one moment in time.

The balance sheet lists:

- the *assets* (amounts owned by the business), such as premises, vehicles, stock for resale, debtors (amounts owed by customers to the business), cash, bank (if not an overdraft)
- the *liabilities* (amounts owed by the business), such as creditors (amounts owed by the business to suppliers), bank overdraft and loans
- the *capital,* the amount of the owner's finance put into the business, plus profits made over time

The figures for the amounts of the assets, liabilities, and capital are taken from the accounting records of the business.

layout of the balance sheet

The balance sheet shows the value of the assets used by the business to make profits and how they have been financed. This concept may be expressed as follows:

ASSETS *minus* LIABILITIES *equals* CAPITAL

Thus the balance sheet shows the asset strength of the business, in contrast to the profit and loss account, which shows the profits from trading activities.

Fig 3.2 on page 39 shows an example of a balance sheet for a sole trader. The balance sheet is presented in a vertical format, and assets and liabilities are listed under the headings of fixed assets, current assets, current liabilities, long-term liabilities, and capital.

By accounting tradition, fixed and current assets are listed starting with the most permanent, ie premises, and working through to the most liquid, ie nearest to cash: either cash itself, or the balance at the bank.

Note the distinction between *capital expenditure* and *revenue expenditure*:

- capital expenditure – the purchase of fixed assets (shown in the balance sheet)
- revenue expenditure – the cost of overheads (shown in the profit and loss account)

the concept of capital

The concept of capital as a liability of a business is sometimes difficult to appreciate. It is important to realise that the assets and liabilities of a business are treated separately from the personal assets and liabilities of the owner. For example, if a group of people decided to set up in business they would each agree to put in a certain amount of capital to start the business. As individuals they regard their capital as an investment, ie an asset which may, at some time, be repaid to them. From the point of view of the business, the capital is a liability, because it is owed to the owner or owners. In practice, it is unlikely to be repaid as it is the permanent capital of the business (unless the business ceases trading or is sold on).

capital, drawings and net profit

To the owner's capital is added net profit for the year, while drawings – the amount, withdrawn by the owner during the year – are deducted, ie:

	owner's capital at start of year
plus	net profit for the year
minus	owner's drawings for the year
equals	closing capital at end of year

This calculation leaves a closing capital at the balance sheet date which balances with the net assets figure – the balance sheet *balances.* (Note that drawings are not included amongst the overheads in the profit and loss account because they are a payment to the owner rather than being made to 'third parties'.)

In partnership balance sheets the same details, ie capital, net profit, and drawings, are shown for each partner, together with other items which relate specifically to the way in which the partners have agreed to share profits and losses.

In limited company balance sheets (see Chapters 4 and 6), details of the share capital issued by the company are shown, together with retained profits for the year, ie profit after payment of dividends to the shareholders.

Fixed assets comprise the long-term items owned by a business which are not bought with the intention of selling off in the near future, eg premises, machinery, motor vehicles, office equipment, shop fittings, etc.

Current assets comprise short-term assets which change regularly, eg stock of goods for resale, debtors (amounts owed to the business by customers), bank balances and cash. These items will alter as the business trades, eg stock will be sold, or more will be bought; debtors will make payment to the business, or sales on credit will be made; the cash and bank balances will alter with the flow of money paid into the bank account, or as withdrawals are made.

Current liabilities are due for repayment within twelve months of the date of the balance sheet, eg creditors (amounts owed by the business to suppliers), and bank overdraft (which is technically repayable on demand, unlike a bank loan which is negotiated for a particular time period).

Working capital is the excess of current assets over current liabilities, ie current assets minus current liabilities = working capital. Without adequate working capital, a business will find it difficult to continue to operate. Working capital is also often referred to as net current assets.

Long-term liabilities are where repayment is due in more than one year from the date of the balance sheet; they are often described as 'bank loan,' 'long-term loan,' or 'mortgage.'

Net assets is the total of fixed and current assets, less current and long-term liabilities. The net assets are financed by the owner(s) of the business, in the form of capital. Net assets therefore equals the total of the 'financed by' section – the balance sheet 'balances'.

Capital is the owner's investment, and is a liability of a business, ie it is what the business owes the owner.

TARA SMITH, TRADING AS "THE FASHION SHOP"

BALANCE SHEET

as at 31 December 1996

	£	£
Fixed assets		
Premises		100,000
Shop fittings		20,000
		120,000
Current assets		
Stock	10,500	
Debtors	10,500	
Bank	5,450	
Cash	50	
	26,500	
Less Current liabilities		
Creditors	16,500	
Working capital		10,000
		130,000
Less Long-term liabilities		
Loan from bank		50,000
NET ASSETS		80,000
FINANCED BY		
Capital		
Opening capital		75,000
Add net profit		12,000
		87,000
Less drawings		7,000
Closing capital		80,000

Fig 3.2 Layout of a balance sheet

DEPRECIATION OF FIXED ASSETS

In your studies of financial statements you will come across references to 'depreciation,' among the overheads in the profit and loss account and in the fixed asset section of the balance sheet.

Depreciation is the estimate of the amount of the loss in value of fixed assets over a specified time period.

Fixed assets, for example machinery and vehicles, reduce in value – or depreciate – as time goes by, largely as a result of wear and tear. For example if you buy a new car on Thursday you will not be able to sell it for the same price the following Thursday; it will have dropped in value – depreciated – by a substantial amount in that time.

depreciation in financial statements

To provide a more accurate view of the financial state of a business, depreciation of fixed assets is recorded in the financial statements as follows:

- the amount of depreciation for the year is included as an overhead in profit and loss account; the effect of this is to *reduce* the net profit
- the value of fixed assets shown in the balance sheet is *reduced* to reflect the amount that they have depreciated *since the assets were bought*

The reason for making these adjustments for depreciation is because the business has had the use of the fixed assets during the year: the estimated fall in value of the assets is recorded in profit and loss account, which now shows a more accurate profit figure while, in the balance sheet, fixed assets are reduced in value to indicate their approximate 'true' value.

an example of depreciation in financial statements

Tara Smith tells you that she wishes you to show £2,000 for depreciation of shop fittings in her financial statements for 1996. As a result she will include an overhead for depreciation of £2,000 in her profit and loss account (which will reduce her net profit to £10,000). In the balance sheet the £2,000 will reduce the value of the shop fittings as shown below:

Balance sheet as at 31 December 1996

	£	£	£
Fixed Assets	*Cost*	*Depreciation to date*	*Net*
Premises	100,000	–	100,000
Shop fittings	20,000	2,000	18,000
	120,000	2,000	118,000

depreciation – a non-cash expense

It is very important to understand that depreciation is a non cash expense. Unlike most of the other overheads in profit and loss account, no cheque is written out, or cash paid, for depreciation. In cash terms, depreciation causes no outflow of money. As depreciation is a non-cash expense, it is *not* a method of providing the cash to replace the asset at the end of its life. (In order to do this, it would be necessary to create a separate fund into which cash is transferred at regular intervals; the fund needs to be represented by a separate bank account, eg a deposit account, which can be drawn against when the new fixed asset is purchased.)

depreciation methods

There are several different ways in which we can allow for the loss in value of fixed assets. All of these are *estimates*, and it is only when the asset is sold or scrapped that we will know the accuracy of the estimate.

The most common methods of calculating depreciation are:

- straight-line method
- reducing balance method

With the *straight-line method*, a fixed percentage is written off the original cost of the asset each year. For example, referring back to Tara Smith's shop fittings, straight-line depreciation of ten per cent per annum will give depreciation amounts of:

1996	£2,000	ie £20,000 x 10%
1997	£2,000	ie £20,000 x 10%
		etc

With the *reducing balance method*, a fixed percentage is written off the reduced balance each year. The reduced balance is the cost of the asset, less depreciation to date. For example, with Tara Smith's shop fittings, reducing balance depreciation of twenty per cent per annum will give depreciation amounts of:

1996	£4,000	ie £20,000 x 20%
1997	£3,200	ie (£20,000 – £4,000) x 20%
		etc

Straight-line depreciation is more often used for fixed assets that are likely to be kept for the whole of their expected lives, eg shop fittings, machinery, office equipment. Reducing balance depreciation is particularly appropriate for assets which depreciate more in their early years and which are not kept for the whole of their expected lives, eg vehicles.

OTHER ADJUSTMENTS TO FINANCIAL STATEMENTS

As well as depreciation of fixed assets, a number of other adjustments are made to the profit and loss account and balance sheet in order to provide a more accurate view of the financial state of the business. These adjustments include:

prepayments

These are payments made in the current accounting period which relate to expenses for the next accounting period. In the financial statements, the amount of the prepayment is:

- deducted from expenses in profit and loss account (because it does not relate to the current accounting period)
- shown as a prepayment in the current assets section of the balance sheet

accruals

These are expenses due in the current accounting period but which have not yet been paid. In the financial statements, an accrual is:

- added to expenses in profit and loss account (because it relates to the current accounting period)
- shown as an accrual in the current liabilities section of the balance sheet

bad debts written off

These are debtors to whom goods or services have been sold but who, despite all efforts, will not pay. In the financial statements, bad debts written off are:

- shown as expenses in profit and loss account (ie the seller is having to 'foot' the bill for not vetting customers sufficiently well)
- deducted from debtors in the balance sheet

provision for bad debts

This is where a provision is made for possible future bad debts – often the provision is calculated as a percentage, eg two per cent of debtors. In the financial statements, provision for bad debts is:

- shown as an expense in profit and loss account (the amount is either the new provision – or the increase in an existing provision – for bad debts)
- deducted from debtors in the balance sheet (so that the figure for debtors represents a reasonable approximation of the amount likely to be collected from debtors)

CASH FLOW STATEMENTS

The profit and loss account, as we have seen, shows the profitability of a business; however, profits are not the same as cash, and a profitable business could well have an increasing bank overdraft. The balance sheet shows the assets used by a business and how they have been financed; however, asset strength does not mean that a business has sufficient cash in the bank to pay its way.

A cash flow statement uses information from the accounting records (including profit and loss account) and balance sheet, and shows an overall view of money flowing in and out of a business during an accounting period.

The cash flow statement concentrates on the liquidity of a business by showing the flows of money coming in and going out during the accounting period. We shall study cash flow statements in detail in Chapter 5 where we shall see how profits, together with changes in assets and liabilities on the balance sheet, have an effect on the cash of the business.

LINKS BETWEEN FINANCIAL STATEMENTS

The three financial statements – profit and loss account, balance sheet, and cash flow statement – cannot be considered in isolation. Each focuses on a particular aspect of the financial state of the business:

- profit and loss account – the profitability of the business
- balance sheet – the asset strength of the business
- cash flow statement – the liquidity of the business

The statements are inter-linked, as shown in fig 3.3. For example:

- receipt of sales income in the profit and loss account becomes a cash inflow in the cash flow statement
- the purchase of a new fixed asset adds to the value of assets in the balance sheet and becomes an outflow of cash in the cash flow statement
- the payment of wages and salaries in the profit and loss account is a cash outflow
- an increase in liabilities (eg raising a loan) is a cash inflow
- an increase in capital is a cash inflow

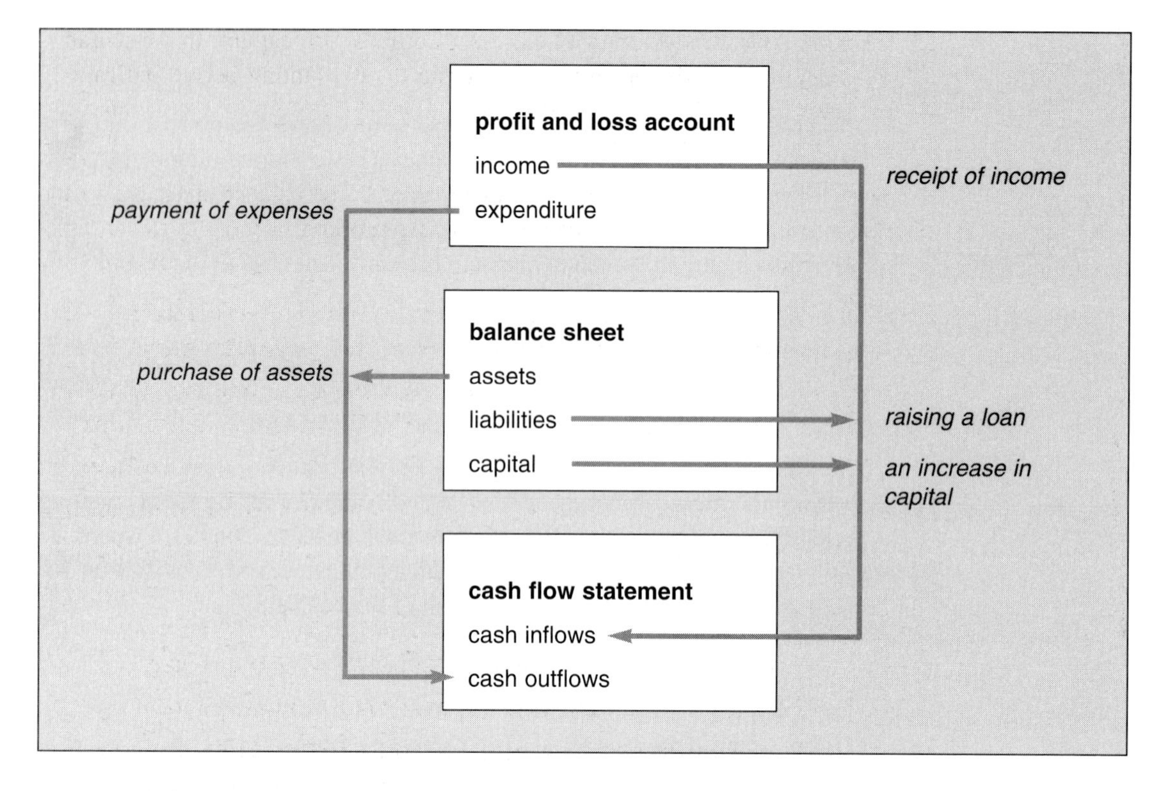

Fig 3.3 Links between financial statements

PURPOSES OF FINANCIAL STATEMENTS

There are, as we have already seen in Chapter 2, various types of users of financial statements. Each user reads the statements for different reasons. The main purposes of financial statements are to:

- inform the owners and managers of the business
- monitor the performance of the business
- secure and maintain finance for the business
- fulfil legal requirements
- assess liability for tax

inform the owners and managers of the business

The profit and loss account informs the owners and managers of the amount of sales, expenses and net profit made during the year, while the balance sheet shows the make-up of the assets, liabilities, and capital. In particular, the amount of profit (or loss) made during the accounting period indicates the level of drawings (sole traders and partnerships), or dividends (limited companies), that can be made.

The relationship between the various amounts shown on the balance sheet will also be considered. For example, owners and managers will look at:

- the value of the business' fixed assets
- the amount of long-term liabilities in relation to capital (generally, the total amount of loans to the business should be less than the capital)
- the figures for current asset and current liability items (is there too much stock? too many debtors? too many creditors? or even too much money in the bank?)

The cash flow statement will inform the owners and managers of the amount of money flowing in and out of the business during the accounting period.

monitor the performance of the business

Here the user of the financial statements will be seeking to compare:

- current performance with that of the previous accounting period
- current performance with budgets and forecasts prepared for the period
- current and past performance with that of similar businesses, so as to make an inter-firm comparison

A first review will be to look at the money amounts of items; a more detailed review will involve the calculation of *accounting ratios* to assess business performance. For example in the profit and loss account, the amounts of sales, expenses and net profit will be of interest. In particular, the net profit to sales, expressed as a percentage, is a key indicator. From the balance sheet, the user will be assessing the strength of the business, in terms of assets, when compared with the previous year's figures. We will look more fully at the analysis of financial statements using *accounting ratios* in Chapter 7.

secure and maintain finance for the business

A lender, such as a bank, will usually want to see the last three years' financial statements (where available) before agreeing to provide finance. Here the lender will be looking to see that profits have been made. Although the past is not always a guide to what will happen in the future, it does give an indication of the abilities of the people who own and run the business. Before agreeing finance, the bank will consider a number of questions about the business – enquiring about profitability, and particularly the value and type of the assets shown by the balance sheet.

is the business profitable?

For a business that has already secured finance, the lender will wish to see each year's profit and loss account, balance sheet and cash flow statement as they become available, and may also ask for information on a monthly or quarterly basis. The lender is looking at, amongst other things, whether the business continues to be profitable and whether the business is generating cash.

what is the value of the assets?

A lender, such as a bank, will also be concerned about the strength of the assets. Most lenders take some form of security from a borrower and, for businesses, this usually means a mortgage (or charge) over assets and, in particular, the buildings. Potential lenders will assess the value of the assets from the balance sheet and decide the best security to take, while existing lenders will look to see if the value of their security has increased.

how much is the business borrowing?

The amount of loans in relation to the capital of the owner(s) – the *'gearing'* – will also be considered. As a general rule, the loans should be less than the capital, otherwise the lender will ask the question 'whose business is it – yours or ours?' The amounts of loans in relation to capital are compared by means of the gearing ratio; a high gearing ratio shows that loans are high in relation to capital.

fulfil legal requirements

One of the legal requirements of a limited company is to produce accounts which are prepared in accordance with the terms of the Companies Acts (see Chapter 6). The shareholders are sent a copy of the accounts, and a copy is filed at Companies House, where it is accessible to members of the public. In this way, users can obtain the information that they need from the accounts. For sole traders and partnerships, there is a legal requirement to keep accounting records and to calculate profit or loss; however, these accounts are not available to the public.

assess liability for income tax and corporation tax

Sole traders and partners are liable for *income tax* as individuals. Thus, when a sole trader business makes a profit, the person running the business must show the profit on his or her tax return, along with any other income; similarly, partners must show their share of the profits from the partnership.

As noted above, sole traders and partnerships are required to prepare accounts in order to assess taxation liabilities. Accordingly, many such businesses use the services of an accountant, who will be able to prepare the accounts and deal with the Inland Revenue on behalf of the owners.

Limited companies are different from sole traders and partnerships in that they are legal bodies in their own right. As such they account directly to the Inland Revenue for the tax due on their profits; this tax is *corporation tax*. It is calculated on the profit before any distribution of profits (in the form of dividends) is made to the shareholders.

THE "RULES" OF ACCOUNTING

The regulatory framework forms the "rules" of accounting. Broadly, there are two sets of rules to consider when preparing financial statements:

- accounting concepts
- accounting standards

If the same rules are followed, broad comparisons can then be made between the financial results of different businesses.

accounting concepts

There are a number of accounting concepts which underlie the preparation of financial statements. These include:

business entity concept

This refers to the fact that final accounts record and report on the activities of one particular business. They do not include the personal assets and liabilities of those who play a part in owning or running the business.

money measurement concept

This means that, in the final accounts, all items are expressed in the common denominator of money. Only by using money can items be added together to give, for example, net profit, or a balance sheet total. The disadvantage of money measurement is that it is unable to record items which cannot be expressed in money terms. For example, a business with an efficient management, and good labour relations, will appear to have the same value as one that is overstaffed and has poor labour relations: only in the longer term, with different levels of profit and balance sheet structure, will the differences between the two become apparent.

A further disadvantage of money measurement is that it cannot take note of inflation. For example, a business achieved sales of £500,000 in 1996 and £525,000 in 1997. Is this an improvement? It depends on the general level of inflation – if inflation was less than five per cent per year, their sales have increased in real terms.

materiality concept

Some items are of such a low value that it is not worthwhile recording them separately in the accounting records, ie they are not 'material'.

Examples:

- Small expense items, such as donations to charities, the purchase of plants for the office, window cleaning, etc, do not justify recording as separate expenses; instead they are grouped together as sundry expenses.
- End-of-year stocks of office stationery, eg paper clips, staples, photocopying paper, etc, are often not valued for the purpose of financial statements, because the amount is not material and does not justify the time and effort involved. This does mean, however, that the cost of all stationery purchased during the year is charged as an expense to profit and loss account – technically wrong, but not material enough to affect the financial statements.
- Low-cost fixed assets are often charged as an expense in profit and loss account, instead of being classed as capital expenditure, eg a stapler, waste-paper basket, etc. Strictly, these should be treated as fixed assets and depreciated each year over their estimated life; in practice, because the amounts involved are not material, they are treated as profit and loss account expenses.

Materiality depends very much on the size of the business. A large company may consider that items of less than £1,000 are not material; a small company may well use a much lower figure. What is material, and what is not becomes a matter of judgement for the accountant.

going concern concept

This presumes that the business to which the final accounts relate will continue to trade in the foreseeable future. The profit and loss account and balance sheet are prepared on the basis that there is no intention to reduce significantly the size of the business or to liquidate the business. If the business was not a going concern, assets would have very different values, and the balance sheet would be affected considerably. For example, a large, purpose-built factory has considerable value to a going concern business but, if the factory had to be sold, it is likely to have a limited use for other industries, and therefore will have a lower market value. The latter case is the opposite of the going concern concept and would be described as a 'gone concern.' Also, in a gone concern situation, extra depreciation would need to be charged as an expense in profit and loss account to allow for the reduced value of fixed assets.

accruals (or matching) concept

This means that expenses and revenues must be matched so that they concern the same goods and the same time period. The profit and loss account should always show the amounts of the expense that should have been incurred, ie the expenditure for the year, whether or not it has been paid – see also accruals and prepayments (page 42.)

consistency concept

This requires that, when a business adopts particular accounting methods, it should continue to use such methods consistently. For example, a business that decides to make a provision for depreciation on machinery at ten per cent per annum, using the straight-line method, should continue to use that percentage and method in the future for this asset. Of course, having once chosen a particular method, a business is entitled to make changes provided there are good reasons for so doing, and a note to the financial statements would explain what has happened. By applying the consistency concept, direct comparison between the financial statements of different years can be made.

prudence concept

This concept, also known as conservatism in accounting, requires that financial statements should always, where there is any doubt, report a conservative figure for profit or the valuation of assets. To this end, profits are not to be anticipated and should only be recognised when it is reasonably certain that they will be realised; at the same time all known liabilities should be provided for: see also depreciation (page 40), and the treatment of bad debts (page 42). 'Anticipate no profit, but anticipate all losses' is a summary of the concept which, in its application, prevents an over-optimistic presentation of a business through the financial statements.

accounting standards

Over the last thirty years, a number of accounting standards have been produced to provide a framework for accounting. The intention has been to reduce the variety of accounting treatments. This framework for accounting is represented by *Statements of Standard Accounting Practice* and *Financial Reporting Standards.*

Statements of Standard Accounting Practice – or SSAPs, as they are usually known – are issued by the Accounting Standards Board. This Board requires accountants to observe the applicable accounting standards, and to disclose and explain significant departures from the standards.

Four of the accounting concepts we have just looked at – *going concern, accruals, consistency* and *prudence* – are detailed in SSAP 2, which is entitled 'Disclosure of accounting policies'. These concepts apply to all final accounts and, in the case of limited companies, are given legal force by the Companies Act. (The other concepts – *business entity, money measurement* and *materiality* – are so fundamental that they are followed in all circumstances.) In order to provide a framework for the preparers of accounts, the Accounting Standards Board has also issued a discussion document entitled 'Statement of Principles' which covers topics such as the objectives and elements of financial statements.

Financial Reporting Standards (FRSs) are issued by the Accounting Standards Board which reviews standards, withdrawing those that are out-of-date and introducing new ones.

Companies Act

The Companies Act 1985 (as amended by the Companies Act 1989) gives details of the accounting requirements to be shown when preparing the financial statements of limited companies (see Chapter 6).

- The three main financial statements are:
  - profit and loss account
  - balance sheet
  - cash flow statement
- The profit and loss account shows the profit or loss for the accounting period. For a trading business, such as a shop, which buys and sells goods, the profit and loss statement shows two levels of profit: gross profit and net profit (or net loss).The profit and loss account can be adapted to suit the needs of other businesses, eg the service sector, or manufacturing.
- The balance sheet shows the assets, liabilities and capital at a particular date; it is a 'snapshot' of the business at the end of the accounting period.
- The cash flow statement shows the money flows in and out of a business during an accounting period.
- Depreciation of fixed assets is included in the financial statements in order to provide a more accurate view of the financial state of the business.

Depreciation is often calculated using:
- *either* the straight-line method
- *or* the reducing balance method

Depreciation is a *non-cash expense.*

- There are close links between the three financial statements, for example:
  - the income in profit and loss account is reflected in the cash inflows in the cash flow statement
  - the purchase of fixed assets is a cash outflow in the cash flow statement
  - a net profit shown in profit and loss account is added to the capital in the balance sheet
- The financial statements are not ends in themselves; instead they are used as a way of informing the owners and managers about the business and to enable business performance to be monitored; they also have a role in raising finance for the business; they are used to assess liability for tax.
- The 'rules' of accounting comprise: accounting concepts, accounting standards and regulations contained within the Companies Acts.

In this chapter we have studied a relatively simple set of financial statements. During the next three chapters, we will look in detail at cash flow statements and the statements prepared by limited companies.

profit and loss account — a summary of the revenue and expenses of a business for an accounting period, which shows the overall profit or loss

gross profit — sales minus cost of sales

cost of sales — opening stock, plus purchases, minus closing stock

net profit — gross profit minus overheads

overheads — the running costs of the business, such as administration, wages, rent paid, telephone, interest paid, travel expenses

balance sheet — the assets, liabilities and capital of a business at a particular date

assets — amounts owned by or owed to the business, either fixed assets or current assets

liabilities — amounts owed by the business, either current liabilities or long-term liabilities

capital — the amount of the owners' finance invested in the business

drawings — the amount withdrawn from a sole trader or partnership business by the owner(s)

depreciation — the estimate of the amount of the loss in value of fixed assets over a specified time period

cash flow statement	statement giving an overall view of money flowing in and out of a business during an accounting period
accounting concepts	part of the regulatory framework of accounting
SSAP	Statement of Standard Accounting Practice; part of the regulatory framework of accounting
FRS	Financial Reporting Standard; part of the regulatory framework of accounting

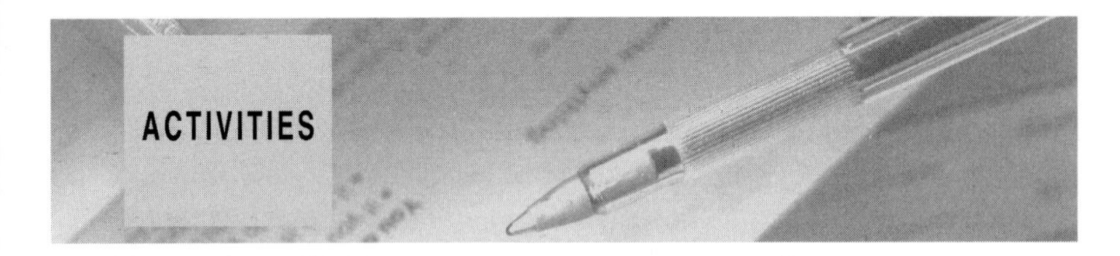

3.1 The following figures are taken from the accounting records of 'Gloria's Garden', a retail florists and garden supplies shop, run by Gloria Golding, at the end of the financial year on 31 March 1997:

	£
Opening stock at 1 April 1996	1,750
Purchases	67,500
Sales	109,950
Closing stock at 31 March 1997	10,400
Wages	16,500
Rent paid	8,450
Telephone	1,430
Interest paid	780
Administration	9,720
Shop fittings at cost	15,000
Depreciation of shop fittings to 31 March 1996	6,000
Debtors	1,450
Creditors	6,250
Cash	150
Bank	1,210
Capital (at 1 April 1996)	16,100
Drawings for year	14,360

Gloria tells you that depreciation of shop fittings for the financial year is to be £3,000.

- You are to set out:
  - the profit and loss account

– the balance sheet

for the financial year ended 31 March 1997

- Cast a critical eye over the financial statements that you have produced and prepare a list of points that you, as financial adviser to the business, would wish to discuss with Gloria.

3.2 The profit and loss accounts and balance sheets for the first two years of trading for Wyvern Stationery are shown below and on the following page. The business, owned by Peter Simpson, sells office and student stationery from a rented shop close to the local college.

Study the accounts and then discuss the following:

- Who are the people interested in reading these financial statements? Explain the purposes for which they will use them.
- What are the particular points that Peter Simpson will note from the profit and loss account? Include a calculation of the net profit percentage for each year, and give a brief comment. Note: the net profit percentage is calculated as follows:

$$\frac{\text{net profit}}{\text{sales}} \times \frac{100}{1} = \text{net profit percentage}$$

- List the main changes that have occurred between the two balance sheet dates. Do you think the business has expanded or declined? What is the evidence for your decision?
- What are the particular points from the statements that Peter Simpson's bank manager will note? Peter's business has an overdraft facility of £3,000, and a bank loan of £2,000.

Peter Simpson, trading as "Wyvern Stationery"
Profit and loss accounts for the year ended 31 December

	last year		*this year*	
	£	£	£	£
Sales		27,500		48,200
Less Cost of Sales		18,300		35,186
Gross profit		9,200		13,014
Less overheads:				
Administration	1,550		1,980	
Wages	520		2,050	
Rent paid	1,000		1,250	
Telephone	330		410	
Interest paid	240		520	
Travel expenses	150		200	
		3,790		6,410
Net profit		5,410		6,604

Peter Simpson, trading as "Wyvern Stationery"
Balance sheets as at 31 December

	last year		this year	
	£	£	£	£
Fixed assets				
Shop fittings		2,000		2,500
Equipment		1,500		2,250
		3,500		4,750
Current assets				
Stock	3,240		7,230	
Debtors	870		1,925	
Bank	1,820		–	
Cash	85		130	
	6,015		9,285	
Less Current liabilities				
Creditors	2,610		4,730	
Bank	–		2,955	
	2,610		7,685	
Working capital		3,405		1,600
		6,905		6,350
Less Long-term liabilities				
Loan from bank		2,000		1,800
NET ASSETS		4,905		4,550
FINANCED BY				
Capital				
Opening capital		6,000		4,905
Add net profit		5,410		6,604
		11,410		11,509
Less drawings		6,505		6,959
Closing capital		4,905		4,550

3.3 Discuss the following and, where appropriate, state the correct accounting treatment:

(a) What is the purpose of

- profit and loss account
- balance sheet

(b) A business depreciated its machinery last year on the reducing balance method; for this year the owner intends to use the straight-line method. By doing this, she says that this will deduct less depreciation from profit and loss account, so her net profit will be higher and her bank manager will be impressed. She says that she might revert back to the reducing balance method next year.

(c) A business has debtors of £30,000. The owner knows that, included in this figure is a bad debt of £2,500. He wants to show £30,000 as debtors in the year-end balance sheet in order to show the asset strength of the business.

(d) Profits for a business were £100,000 last year; this year they are £102,500. Has the business improved?

(e) A district nurse uses her own car for visiting patients; she is reimbursed for petrol and other running expenses so incurred by her employers, a NHS Trust. Should the car be shown on the balance sheet of the NHS Trust?

(f) Most financial statements are prepared on the going concern basis. What other basis can be used, and when is it appropriate to use each method?

4 FINANCIAL STATEMENTS: LIMITED COMPANIES

this chapter covers ...

- *the advantages of forming a limited company*
- *the differences between a private limited company, a public limited company, and a company limited by guarantee*
- *the information contained in a company's Memorandum of Association and its Articles of Association*
- *the differences between ordinary shares and preference shares*
- *the concept of reserves, and the difference between capital reserves and revenue reserves*
- *the appropriation section of a company's profit and loss account*
- *the layout of a company's balance sheet*

INTRODUCTION

In the previous chapter we looked in detail at the profit and loss account and balance sheet of a sole trader business, and also considered how the statements would be different for a partnership. In this chapter we turn our attention to the financial statements of limited companies (cash flow statements are covered in detail in Chapter 5, which follows). Here we will look at the 'internal use' accounts, rather than the detailed accounting requirements of the Companies Act (which will be covered in Chapter 6).

ADVANTAGES OF FORMING A LIMITED COMPANY

A limited company is a separate legal entity, owned by shareholders and run by directors.

The limited company is often chosen as the legal status of a business for a number of reasons:

limited liability

The shareholders (members) of a company can only lose the amount of their investment, being the money paid already, together with any money unpaid on their shares (unpaid instalments on new share issues, for example). Thus, if the company became insolvent (went 'bust'), shareholders would have to pay any unpaid instalments to help repay the creditors. As this is an unlikely occurance, shareholders are in a very safe position: their personal assets, unless pledged as security to a lender, *are not available to the company's creditors.*

separate legal entity

A limited company is a separate legal entity from its owners. Anyone taking legal action proceeds against the company and not the individual shareholders.

ability to raise finance

A limited company can raise substantial funds from outside sources by the issue of shares:

- from the public on the Stock Exchange or the Alternative Investment Market, for the larger public company
- privately from relatives and friends, for the smaller company

Companies can also raise finance by means of debentures (see page 61).

membership

A member of a limited company is a person who owns at least one share in that company. The minimum number of members is two, but there is no upper limit. A member of a company is the same as a shareholder.

other factors

A limited company is usually a much larger business unit than a sole trader or partnership. This gives the company a higher standing and status in the business community, allows it to benefit from economies of scale, and makes it of sufficient size to employ specialists for functions such as production, marketing, finance and personnel.

THE COMPANIES ACT

Limited companies are regulated by the Companies Act 1985, as amended by the Companies Act 1989. Under the terms of the 1985 Act there are two main types of limited company: the larger *public limited company* (abbreviated to 'Plc'), which is defined in the Act, and the smaller company, traditionally known as a *private limited company* (abbreviated to 'Ltd'), which is any other limited company. A further type of company is *limited by guarantee.*

public limited company (Plc)

A company may become a public limited company if it has

- issued share capital of over £50,000
- at least two members (shareholders) and at least two directors

A public limited company may raise capital from the public on the Stock Exchange or the Alternative Investment Market, and the new issues and privatisations of recent years are examples of this. A public limited company does *not have to* issue shares on the stock markets, and not all do so.

private limited company (Ltd)

The private limited company is the most common form of limited company. The term *private* is not set out in the Companies Act 1985, but it is a traditional description, and well describes the smaller company, often in family ownership. A private limited company has:

- no minimum requirement for issued share capital
- at least two members (shareholders) and at least one director

The shares are not traded publicly, but are transferable between individuals, although valuation will be more difficult for shares not quoted on the stock markets.

company limited by guarantee

A company limited by guarantee is not formed with share capital, but relies on the guarantee of its members to pay a stated amount in the event of the company's insolvency. Examples of such companies include charities and artistic and educational organisations.

GOVERNING DOCUMENTS OF COMPANIES

There are a number of documents required by the Companies Act in the setting-up of a company. Two essential governing documents are the *Memorandum of Association* and the *Articles of Association.*

Memorandum of Association, the constitution of the company, which regulates the affairs of the company to the outside world and contains five main clauses:

1. name of the company (together with the words 'public limited company' or 'limited', as appropriate)
2. capital of the company (the amount that can be issued in shares: the authorised share capital)
3. 'objects' of the company, ie what activities the company can engage in; under the Companies Act 1989, the objects can be stated as being those of 'a general commercial company', ie the company can engage in any commercial activity
4. registered office of the company (not the address, but whether it is registered in England and Wales, or in Scotland)
5. a statement that the liability of the members is limited

Articles of Association, regulate the internal administration of the company, including the powers of directors and the holding of company meetings.

ACCOUNTING REQUIREMENTS OF THE COMPANIES ACT

The Companies Act 1985 (as amended by the Companies Act 1989) not only requires the production of accounts, but also states the detailed information that must be disclosed. For larger companies the accounts are audited by external auditors – this is a costly and time-consuming exercise (smaller and medium-sized companies are often exempt from audit – see page 97). The accounts must be submitted within nine months of the financial year-end to Companies House, where they are available for public inspection. A copy of the accounts is available to all shareholders, together with a report on the company's activities during the year.

In this chapter we will study the 'internal use' accounts, rather than being concerned with the detailed accounting requirements of the Companies Act. In Chapter 6 we will look at such 'published accounts', as they are often known.

Before we examine the financial statements in detail we will look first at the principal ways in which a company raises finance: shares. There are different types of shares which appear in a company's balance sheet as the company's share capital.

TYPES OF SHARES ISSUED BY LIMITED COMPANIES

The *authorised share capital* is stated in the Memorandum of Association and is the maximum share capital that the company is allowed to issue. The authorised share capital may not be the same as the *issued share capital*; under company law the issued capital cannot exceed the amount authorised. If a company which has issued the full extent of its authorised share capital wishes to make an increase, it must first pass the appropriate resolution at a general meeting of the shareholders.

The authorised and issued share capital may be divided into a number of classes or types of share; the main types are *ordinary shares* and, less commonly, *preference shares*. These shares usually carry voting rights – thus shareholders have a say at the annual general meeting and at any other shareholders' meetings.

ordinary (equity) shares

These are the most commonly issued class of share which carry the main 'risks and rewards' of the business: the risks are of losing part or all of the value of the shares if the business loses money or becomes insolvent; the rewards are that they take a share of the profits – in the form of *dividends* – after allowance has been made for all expenses of the business, including loan interest, taxation, and after preference dividends (if any). When a company makes large profits, it will have the ability to pay higher dividends to the ordinary shareholders; when losses are made, the ordinary shareholders may receive no dividend.

Companies rarely pay out all of their profits in the form of dividends; most retain some profits as reserves. These can always be used to enable a dividend to be paid in a year when the company makes little or no profit, always assuming that the company has sufficient cash in the bank to make the payment. Ordinary shareholders, in the event of the company becoming insolvent, will be the last to receive any repayment of their investment: other creditors will be paid off first.

preference shares

Preference shares usually carry a fixed percentage rate of dividend – for example, ten per cent of nominal value.Their dividends are paid in preference to those of ordinary shareholders; but they are only paid if the company makes profits. In the event of the company ceasing to trade, the 'preference' will also extend to repayment of capital before the ordinary shareholders.

nominal and market values of shares

Each share has a *nominal* value – or face value – which is entered in the accounts. Shares may be issued with nominal values of 5p, 10p, 25p, 50p or £1, or indeed for any amount. Thus a company with an authorised share capital of £100,000 might state in its Memorandum of Association that this is divided up into:

100,000 ordinary shares of 50p each	£50,000
50,000 ten per cent preference shares of £1 each	£50,000
	£100,000

The nominal value usually bears little relationship to the *market value* . This is the price at which issued – or 'secondhand' – shares are traded. Share prices of a quoted public limited company may be listed in the *Financial Times*.

issue price

This is the price at which shares are issued to shareholders by the company – either when the company is being set up, or at a later date when it needs to raise more funds. The issue price is either at *par* (ie the nominal value), or above nominal value. In the latter case, the amount of the difference between issue price and nominal value is known as a *share premium*: for example – nominal value £1.00; issue price £1.50; therefore share premium is 50p per share.

LOANS AND DEBENTURES

In addition to money provided by shareholders, who are the owners of the company, further funds can be obtained by borrowing in the form of loans or debentures. Both loans and debentures usually carry a fixed rate of interest that must be paid, just like other business expenses, whether a company makes profits or not. As loan and debenture interest is a business expense, this is shown in the profit and loss account along with all other expenses. In the event of the company ceasing to trade, loan and debenture-holders would be repaid before any shareholders.

LIMITED COMPANIES: PROFIT AND LOSS ACCOUNT

A limited company uses the same form of financial statements as a sole trader or partnership. However there are two items commonly found in the profit and loss account of a limited company that are not found in those of other business types:

- **directors' remuneration** – ie amounts paid to directors; as directors are employed by the company, their pay appears amongst the expenses of the company
- **debenture interest** – as already noted, when debentures are issued by companies, the interest is shown as an expense in the profit and loss account

A limited company follows the profit and loss account with an *appropriation section* to show how the net profit has been distributed. Fig 4.1 (see below and opposite) shows an example of a limited company's profit and loss account. (See also Appendix A, page 379, for a specimen format).

The **overheads** of a limited company include directors' remuneration and interest paid on debentures (if debentures have been issued).

The company has recorded a **net profit** of £43,000 in its profit and loss account – this is brought into the appropriation section.

Corporation tax, the tax that a company has to pay, based on its profits, is shown in the appropriation section. We shall not be studying the calculations for corporation tax in this book. It is, however, important to see how the tax is recorded in the financial statements.

The company has already paid **interim dividends** on the two classes of shares it has in issue (ordinary shares and preference shares); these would, most probably, have been paid just over half-way through the company's financial year. The company also proposes to pay a **final dividend** to its shareholders: these will be paid in the early part of the next financial year. Note that a dividend is often expressed as an amount per share, based on the nominal value, eg 5p per £1 nominal value share (which is the same as a five per cent dividend).

Added to **net profit** is a **balance** of £41,000. This represents profits of the company from previous years that have not been distributed as dividends. Note that the appropriation section shows a balance of retained profits at the year-end of £50,000. Such retained profits form a revenue reserve (see page 65) of the company.

ORION LIMITED

PROFIT AND LOSS ACCOUNT

for the year ended 31 December 1997

	£	£
Sales		725,000
Opening stock	45,000	
Purchases	381,000	
	426,000	
Less closing stock	50,000	
Cost of sales		376,000
Gross Profit		349,000
Less overheads:		
Directors' remuneration	75,000	
Debenture interest	6,000	
Other overheads	225,000	
		306,000
Net profit for year before taxation		43,000
Less corporation tax		15,000
Profit for year after taxation		28,000
Less interim dividends paid		
ordinary shares	5,000	
preference shares	2,000	
final dividends proposed		
ordinary shares	10,000	
preference shares	2,000	
		19,000
Retained profit for year		9,000
Add balance of retained profits at beginning of year		41,000
Balance of retained profits at end of year		50,000

Fig 4.1 An example of a limited company profit and loss account

LIMITED COMPANIES: BALANCE SHEET

Balance sheets of limited companies follow the same layout as those we have seen earlier, but the capital section is more complex because of the different classes of shares that may be issued, and the various reserves. Fig 4.2 (on pages 66 and 67) shows the balance sheet of Orion Limited as an example. (A specimen format for a limited company balance sheet is included in Appendix A, page 379).

RESERVES

A limited company rarely distributes all its profits to its shareholders. Instead, it will often keep part of the profits earned each year in the form of reserves. As the balance sheet of Orion Limited shows (see fig 4.2 on page 67), there are two types of reserves:

- capital reserves, which are created as a result of a non-trading profit
- revenue reserves, which are retained profits from profit and loss account

capital reserves

Examples are:

- *Revaluation reserve.* This occurs when a fixed asset, most probably property, is revalued in the balance sheet. The amount of the revaluation is placed in a revaluation reserve where it increases the value of the shareholders' investment in the company. Note, however, that this is purely a 'book' adjustment – no cash has changed hands.

  For example, the following company revalues its property from £500,000 to £750,000.

BALANCE SHEET (extracts)

Before revaluation	£
Fixed asset: property at cost	500,000
Share capital: ordinary shares of £1 each	500,000
After revaluation	
Fixed asset: property at revaluation	750,000
Share capital: ordinary shares of £1 each	500,000
Capital reserve: Revaluation reserve	250,000
	750,000

- *Share premium account.* An established company may well issue additional shares to the public at a higher amount than the nominal value. For example, Orion Limited (fig 4.2) seeks finance for further expansion by issuing additional ordinary shares. Although the shares have a nominal value of £1 each, because Orion is a well-established company, the shares are issued at £1.50 each. Of this amount, £1 is recorded in the issued share capital section, and the extra 50p is the share premium.

A capital reserve cannot be used to fund the payment of dividends.

revenue reserves

Revenue reserves are often the balance of the appropriation section of the profit and loss account: this balance is commonly described as 'profit and loss account balance' or 'balance of retained profits'. Alternatively, they may be transferred from the appropriation section to a named revenue reserve account, such as *general reserve*, or a revenue reserve for a specific purpose, such as *reserve for the replacement of machinery*. Transfers to or from these named revenue reserve accounts are made in the appropriation section of the profit and loss account.

reserves: profits not cash

It should be noted that reserves – both capital and revenue – are *not* a cash fund to be used whenever the company needs money, but are in fact represented by assets shown on the balance sheet. The reserves record the fact that the assets belong to the shareholders via their ownership of the company.

LIMITED COMPANIES: CASH FLOW STATEMENT

Cash flow statements are covered fully in Chapter 5, which follows. Limited company cash flow statements are on pages 80 to 82.

A limited company balance sheet is now illustrated and explained on the next two pages.

Limited company balance sheets usually distinguish between:

intangible fixed assets, which do not have material substance but belong to the company and have value, eg goodwill (the amount paid for the reputation and connections of a business that has been taken over), patents and trademarks; intangible fixed assets are depreciated (or amortised, in the case of goodwill) in the same way as tangible fixed assets.

tangible fixed assets, which have material substance, such as premises, equipment, vehicles.

As well as the usual **current liabilities**, for limited companies, this section also contains the amount of proposed dividends (but not dividends that have been paid in the year) and the amount of corporation tax to be paid within the next twelve months. The amounts for both of these items are also included in the appropriation section of the profit and loss account.

Long-term liabilities are those that are due to be repaid more than twelve months from the date of the balance sheet, eg loans and debentures.

Authorised share capital is included on the balance sheet 'for information', but is not added into the balance sheet total, as it may not be the same amount as the issued share capital.

Issued share capital shows the classes and number of shares that have been issued. In this balance sheet, the shares are described as being fully paid, meaning that the company has received the full amount of the value of each share from the shareholders. Sometimes shares will be partly paid, eg ordinary shares of £1, but 75p paid. This means that the company can make a call on the shareholders to pay the extra 25p to make the shares fully paid.

Capital reserves are created as a result of non-trading profit.

Revenue reserves are retained profits from profit and loss account.

The total for **shareholders' funds** represents the stake of the shareholders in the company. It comprises share capital (ordinary and preference shares), plus reserves (capital and revenue reserves).

ORION LIMITED

Balance sheet as at 31 December 1997

Fixed assets	*Cost*	*Dep'n to date*	*Net*
	£	£	£
Intangible			
Goodwill	50,000	20,000	30,000
Tangible			
Freehold land and buildings	180,000	20,000	160,000
Machinery	230,000	90,000	140,000
Fixtures and fittings	100,000	25,000	75,000
	560,000	155,000	405,000
Current assets			
Stock		50,000	
Debtors		38,000	
Bank		22,000	
Cash		2,000	
		112,000	
Less Current liabilities			
Creditors	30,000		
Proposed dividends	12,000		
Corporation tax	15,000		
		57,000	
Working capital			55,000
			460,000
Less Long-term liabilities			
10% debentures			60,000
NET ASSETS			400,000
FINANCED BY			
Authorised share capital			
100,000 10% preference shares of £1 each			100,000
600,000 ordinary shares of £1 each			600,000
			700,000
Issued share capital			
40,000 10% preference shares of £1 each, fully paid			40,000
300,000 ordinary shares of £1 each, fully paid			300,000
			340,000
Capital reserve			
Share premium account			10,000
Revenue reserve			
Profit and loss account			50,000
SHAREHOLDERS' FUNDS			400,000

Fig 4.2 An example of a limited company balance sheet

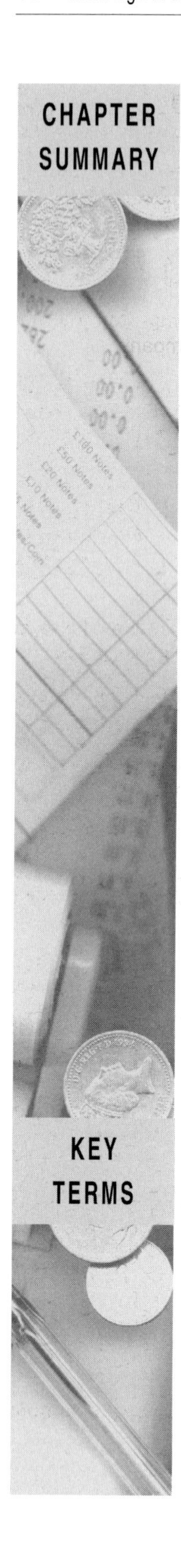

CHAPTER SUMMARY

- A limited company has a separate legal entity from its owners.
- A company is regulated by the Companies Act 1985 (as amended by the Companies Act 1989), and is owned by shareholders and managed by directors.
- A limited company may be either a public limited company or a private limited company.
- The liability of shareholders is limited to any money unpaid on their shares.
- The main types of shares that may be issued by companies are ordinary shares and preference shares.
- Borrowings in the form of loans and debentures are a further source of finance.
- The final accounts of a company include an appropriation section, which follows the profit and loss account.
- The balance sheet of a limited company is similar to that of sole traders and partnerships but the capital and reserves section reflects the ownership of the company by its shareholders:
  - a statement of the authorised and issued share capital
  - details of capital reserves and revenue reserves

This chapter has provided an introduction to the format and the workings of limited company accounts. However, companies vary as much in activity as in size, and you are strongly recommended to investigate sets of company accounts and to make comparisons. As limited companies are obliged by law to make their accounts public, there will be no difficulty in obtaining copies, especially from the larger plcs.

The published accounts of limited companies are covered in Chapter 6. Before reading that chapter you should first study Chapter 5, which examines *cash flow statements* – one of the financial statements found in the accounts of larger companies.

KEY TERMS

limited company	a separate legal entity owned by shareholders and run by directors
limited liability	shareholders of a company are liable for company debts only to the extent of any money unpaid on their shares
shareholder	person who owns at least one share in a limited company; a shareholder is also a member of a company
public limited company	a company, registered as a plc, with an issued share capital of over £50,000 and at least two members and at least two directors; it may raise funds on the stock markets

private limited company – any other company with share capital limited by shares other than a public limited company

Memorandum of Association – the document setting out the constitution of the company, which regulates the affairs of the company to the outside world

Articles of Association – the document regulating the internal administration of the company

ordinary shares – commonly issued type of shares which take a share in the profits of the company but which also carry the main risks

preference shares – shares which carry a fixed rate of dividend paid, subject to sufficient profits, in preference to ordinary shareholders; in event of repayment of capital, rank before the ordinary shareholders

debentures – loans to a company; debenture interest is an expense in profit and loss account

nominal value – the face value of the shares entered in the accounts

issue price – the price at which shares are issued to shareholders by the company

market value – the price at which shares are traded

directors' remuneration – amounts paid to directors as employees of the company; an expense in profit and loss account

dividends – amounts paid to shareholders from the profit of the company; an interim dividend is paid half-way through a financial year; a final dividend is paid at the end of a year

authorised share capital – amount of share capital authorised by the company's Memorandum of Association

issued share capital – the classes and number of shares that have been issued by the company; cannot exceed the authorised share capital

reserves – profits retained by the company; two main types:

- capital reserves, created as a result of a non-trading profit
- revenue reserves, retained profits from profit and loss account

revaluation reserve	capital reserve created by the revaluation of a fixed asset, most usually property; cannot be used for payment of dividends
share premium account	capital reserve created by the issue of shares at a price higher than nominal value, the excess being credited to share premium; cannot be used for payment of dividends

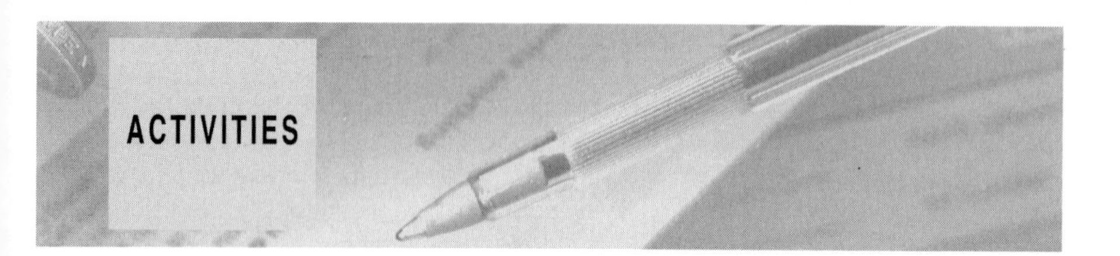

Note: a specimen format for limited company accounts (for internal use) is provided in Appendix A (page 373); this will help when preparing numerical answers.

4.1 The following figures are taken from the accounting records of Jobseekers Limited, a recruitment agency, at the end of the financial year on 31 December 1996:

	£
Issued share capital (£1 ordinary shares)	100,000
Premises at cost	175,000
Depreciation of premises to date	10,500
Office equipment at cost	25,000
Depreciation of office equipment to date	5,000
Goodwill at cost	20,000
Amortisation of goodwill to date	6,000
Stock at 31 December 1996	750
Debtors	42,500
Creditors	7,250
Bank overdraft	13,950
Bank loan	55,000
Net profit for year before taxation	68,200

Corporation tax for the year	14,850
Interim ordinary dividend paid	10,000
Final ordinary dividend proposed	40,000
Retained profit at 1 January 1996	7,350

- Set out
  - the appropriation section of the profit and loss account (starting with net profit)
  - the balance sheet

  for the financial year ended 31 December 1996
- Cast a critical eye over the financial statements that you have produced and prepare a list of points to discuss with the finance director.

4.2 Discuss the following statements (some aspects may need additional research):

(a) "Depreciation of fixed assets is used as a method of saving up the cash to replace the assets when they reach the end of their useful lives."

(b) "There is no need to seek a bank loan to fund the expansion scheme, we can use the cash from the reserves."

(c) "Don't let's write down the goodwill we paid when we bought Bloggs Limited earlier this year; we are improving the service to their former customers so we ought to keep it at the same amount, perhaps even increase the figure."

(d) "I can't see why we say share capital is a liability of the company."

(e) "Although we have made reasonable profits this year we need to plough them back into the company for the future: I suggest we consider not paying dividends to our ordinary and preference shareholders this year. I'm sure that they will see the logic of this ..."

(f) "Let's change our depreciation method this year so that we charge a higher figure in profit and loss account. This will give us lower profits and we'll pay less tax."

(g) "As profits are low this year, let us use share premium account to pay the dividends to shareholders."

5 CASH FLOW STATEMENTS

this chapter covers ...

- *an appreciation of the need for a cash flow statement*
- *the cash flows for each of the main sections of the statement*
- *how the cash flows relate to the main areas of business activity*
- *the interpretation of cash flow statements*

INTRODUCTION

The profit and loss account shows profitability, and the balance sheet shows asset strength. While these two financial statements give us a great deal of information on the progress of a business during an accounting period, profit does not equal cash, and strength in assets does not necessarily mean a large bank balance. The *cash flow statement* links profit with changes in assets and liabilities in the balance sheet, and the effect on the cash of the business.

A cash flow statement uses information from the accounting records (including profit and loss account and balance sheet), and shows an overall view of money flowing in and out of a business during an accounting period.

Such a statement explains to the owner or shareholders why, after a year of good profits for example, there is a reduced balance at the bank or a larger bank overdraft at the year-end than there was at the beginning of the year. The cash flow statement concentrates on the liquidity of the business: it is a lack of cash (a lack of liquidity) that causes most businesses to fail and not poor products or services. The importance of the cash flow statement is such that all but smaller limited companies must include the statement as a part of their accounts. For sole traders and partnerships, the information that the statement contains is of considerable interest to the owner(s) and to a lender, such as a bank.

In this chapter we will look in detail at the cash flows and the layout of the cash flow statement. The format adopted is set out in Financial Reporting Standard No 1 and is used in limited company financial statements. We shall look at two Case Studies – one for a sole trader and one for a limited company. We will also consider how the statements can be interpreted by the user.

FORMAT OF THE CASH FLOW STATEMENT

Cash flow statements are divided into eight sections:

1. Operating activities
2. Returns on investments and servicing of finance
3. Taxation
4. Capital expenditure and financial investment
5. Acquisition and disposals
6. Equity dividends paid
7. Management of liquid resources
8. Financing

The cash flows for the year affecting each of these main areas of business activity are shown in the statement, although not every business will have cash flows under each of the eight sections.

Fig 5.1 on page 75 shows the main cash inflows and outflows under each heading, and indicates the contents of the cash flow statement. On page 76 an example is shown with the figures inserted.

The first section of the cash flow statement – *operating activities* – needs a word of further explanation, particularly as it is the main source of cash flow for most businesses. For this explanation, please see the next page.

operating activities

The net cash inflow from operating activities is calculated by using figures from the profit and loss account and balance sheet as follows:

	operating profit (ie net profit, before deduction of interest)
add	depreciation for the year*
add	decrease in debtors, or *deduct* increase in debtors
add	increase in creditors, or *deduct* decrease in creditors
add	decrease in stock, or *deduct* increase in stock

* Depreciation is added to net profit because depreciation is a non-cash expense, that is, no money is paid out by the business in respect of depreciation charged to profit and loss account.

Note that changes in the main working capital items of stock, debtors and creditors have an effect on cash balances. For example, an increase in stock reduces cash, while a decrease in debtors increases cash.

increase or decrease in cash

The cash flow statement concludes with a figure for the increase or decrease in cash. This is calculated from the subtotals of each of eight sections of the statement.

LAYOUT OF A CASH FLOW STATEMENT

A cash flow statement uses a common layout which can be amended to suit the particular needs of the business for which it is being prepared. A layout – with specimen figures included – can be seen on page 76.

Note: a specimen format is included in Appendix A, page 373.

CASH FLOW STATEMENT

Operating activities

- Operating profit (net profit, before deduction of interest)
- Depreciation charge for the year
- Changes in debtors, creditors and stock

Returns on investments and servicing of finance

- *Inflows:* interest received, dividends received
- *Outflows:* interest paid, dividends paid on preference shares (but not ordinary shares – see below)

Taxation

- *Outflow:* corporation tax paid by limited companies during the year

Capital expenditure and financial investment

- *Inflows:* sale proceeds from fixed assets and investments
- *Outflows:* purchase cost of fixed assets and investments

Acquisitions and disposals

- *Inflows:* sale proceeds from investments and interests in
  - subsidiary companies (where more than 50 per cent of the shares in another company is owned)
  - associated companies (where between 20 per cent and 50 per cent of the shares in another company is owned)
  - joint ventures (where a project is undertaken jointly with another company)
- *Outflows:* purchase cost of investments in subsidiary companies, associated companies, and interests in joint ventures

Equity dividends paid

- *Outflow:* the amount of dividends paid to equity (ordinary) shareholders during the year (where the cash flow statement is for a sole trader or partnership, the *drawings* will be shown)

Management of liquid resources

- *Inflows:* sale proceeds from short-term investments that are almost as good as cash – such as treasury bills (a form of government debt), and term deposits of up to a year with a bank
- *Outflows:* purchase of short-term liquid investments

Financing

- *Inflows:* receipts from increase in capital /share capital, raising/increase of loans
- *Outflows:* repayment of capital/share capital/loans

Fig 5.1 Contents of the cash flow statement

ABC LIMITED
Cash flow statement for the year ended 31 December 1997

	£	£
Operating activities:		
Operating profit (note: before tax and interest)	75,000	
Depreciation for year	10,000	
Decrease in stocks	2,000	
Increase in debtors	(5,000)	
Increase in creditors	7,000	
Net cash inflow from operating activities		89,000
Returns on investments and servicing of finance:		
Interest received	10,000	
Interest paid	(5,000)	
		5,000
Taxation:		
Corporation tax paid (note: amount *paid* during year)		(6,000)
Capital expenditure and financial investment		
Payments to acquire fixed assets	(125,000)	
Receipts from sales of fixed assets	15,000	
		(110,000)
Acquisitions and disposals		
Purchase of subsidiary undertakings	(–)	
Sale of a business	–	–
Equity dividends paid: (note: amount *paid* during year)		(22,000)
Cash outflow before use of liquid resources and financing		(44,000)
Management of liquid resources:		
Purchase of treasury bills	(250,000)	
Sale of treasury bills	200,000	
		(50,000)
Financing:		
Issue of share capital	275,000	
Repayment of capital/share capital	(–)	
Increase in loans	–	
Repayment of loans	(90,000)	
		185,000
Increase in cash		91,000

Notes:

- The separate amounts shown under each main heading can, if preferred, be detailed in a note to the cash flow statement.
- The increase or decrease in cash – shown at the end of the statement – is to be reconciled, in a note, to the change in net debt (short and long-term borrowings, less cash/bank balances) during the accounting period: see page 83.
- Money amounts shown in brackets indicate a deduction or, where the figure is a sub-total, a negative figure.

CASH FLOW STATEMENT OF A SOLE TRADER

This first case study introduces the topic of cash flow statements by looking at a small sole trader business; we then move on to the second case study (page 80) which shows how the statement will be prepared for a limited company.

situation

Samantha Smith runs a children's clothes shop in rented premises in a small market town. Her balance sheets for the last two years are as follows:

BALANCE SHEET AS AT 31 DECEMBER

	1996			1997		
	£	£	£	£	£	£
	Cost	Dep'n	Net	Cost	Dep'n	Net
Fixed assets						
Shop fittings	1,500	500	1,000	2,000	750	1,250
Current assets						
Stock		3,750			4,850	
Debtors		625			1,040	
Bank		220			–	
		4,595			5,890	
Less Current liabilities						
Creditors	2,020			4,360		
Bank	–			725		
		2,020			5,085	
Working capital			2,575			805
			3,575			2,055
Less Long-term liabilities						
Loan from husband			–			1,000
NET ASSETS			3,575			1,055
FINANCED BY						
Capital						
Opening capital			3,300			3,575
Add net profit for year			5,450			4,080
			8,750			7,655
Less drawings			5,175			6,600
Closing capital			3,575			1,055

Note: Interest paid on the loan and bank overdraft in 1997 was £450.

Samantha Smith says to you: "I cannot understand why I am overdrawn at the bank by £725 on 31 December 1997 when I made a profit of £4,080 during the year". She asks for your assistance in seeking an explanation.

CASH FLOW STATEMENT OF A SOLE TRADER

solution

A cash flow statement will give Samantha Smith the answer:

CASH FLOW STATEMENT

for the year ended 31 December 1997

	£	£
Operating activities:		
Operating profit (before interest)	4,530	
Depreciation for year	250	
Increase in stocks	(1,100)	
Increase in debtors	(415)	
Increase in creditors	2,340	
Net cash inflow from operating activities		5,605
Returns on investments and servicing of finance:		
Interest paid		(450)
Taxation:		
Corporation tax paid		not applicable
Capital expenditure and financial investment:		
Payments to acquire fixed assets		(500)
Owner's drawings		(6,600)
Cash outflow before use of liquid resources and financing		(1,945)
Financing:		
Loan from husband		1,000
Decrease in cash		(945)

points to note

- Operating profit for the year (before interest) is calculated as:

net profit for 1997	£4,080
interest for 1997	£ 450
	£4,530

- Depreciation for the year of £250 is the amount of the increase in depreciation to date shown on the balance sheets, that is, £750 minus £500.
- An increase in stock and debtors reduces the cash available to the business (because stock is being bought, debtors are being allowed more time to pay). In contrast, an increase in creditors gives an increase in cash (because creditors are allowing Samantha more time to pay).
- In this example there is no tax paid (because Samantha is a sole trader who will be taxed as an individual, unlike a company which pays tax on its profits); however, the place where tax would appear is indicated on the cash flow statement.
- As this is a sole trader business, drawings are shown on the cash flow statement in place of equity dividends.
- The change in the bank balance is summarised as follows: from a balance of £220 in the bank to an overdraft of £725 is a 'swing' in the bank of minus £945, which is the amount of the decrease in cash shown by the cash flow statement.

explanation to Samantha Smith

In this example, the statement highlights the following points for the owner of the business:

- net cash inflow from operating activities is £5,605, whereas owner's drawings are £6,600; either profits must be increased or drawings must be reduced.
- fixed assets costing £500 have been purchased
- a long-term loan of £1,000 has been raised from her husband
- over the year there has been a decrease in cash of £945, this trend cannot be continued for long
- by the end of 1997 the business has an overdraft of £725, caused mainly by the excessive drawings of the owner
- in conclusion, the liquidity position of this business has deteriorated over the two years, and corrective action will be necessary

CASH FLOW STATEMENT OF A LIMITED COMPANY

situation

The balance sheets of Newtown Trading Company Limited for 1996 and 1997 are as follows:

Balance sheet as at 31 December

	1996			1997		
	£	£	£	£	£	£
	Cost	Dep'n	Net	Cost	Dep'n	Net
Fixed assets	47,200	6,200	41,000	64,000	8,900	55,100
Current assets						
Stock		7,000			11,000	
Debtors		5,000			3,700	
Bank		1,000			500	
		13,000			15,200	
Less Current liabilities						
Creditors	3,500			4,800		
Proposed dividends	2,000			2,500		
Corporation tax	1,000			1,500		
		6,500			8,800	
Working capital			6,500			6,400
			47,500			61,500
Less Long-term liabilities						
Debentures			5,000			3,000
NET ASSETS			42,500			58,500
FINANCED BY						
Ordinary share capital			30,000			40,000
Share premium account			1,500			2,500
Retained profits			11,000			16,000
SHAREHOLDERS' FUNDS			42,500			58,500

Note: Interest paid on the loan in 1997 was £400.

Prepare a cash flow statement for the year ended 31 December 1997 and comment on the main points highlighted by the statement.

solution

Newtown Trading Company Limited
Cash flow statement for the year ended 31 December 1997

	£	£
Operating activities:		
Operating profit (before interest)*	9,400	
Depreciation for year§	2,700	
Increase in stocks	(4,000)	
Decrease in debtors	1,300	
Increase in creditors	1,300	
Net cash inflow from operating activities		10,700
Returns on investments and servicing of finance:		
Interest paid		(400)
Taxation:		
Corporation tax paid		(1,000)
Capital expenditure and financial investment:		
Payments to acquire fixed assets		(16,800)
Equity dividends paid:		(2,000)
Cash outflow before use of liquid resources and financing		(9,500)
Financing:		
Issue of ordinary shares at a premium		
£10,000 + £1,000 =	11,000	
Repayment of debentures	(2,000)	
		9,000
Decrease in cash		(500)

Notes

* Calculation of the operating profit for 1997 before interest, tax and dividends:

	£
increase in retained profits	5,000
interest paid in 1997	400
proposed dividends, 1997	2,500
corporation tax, 1997	1,500
operating profit before interest, tax and dividends	9,400

§ Depreciation charged: £8,900 – £6,200 = £2,700

Both proposed dividends and corporation tax – which are current liabilities at 31 December 1996 – are paid in 1997. Likewise, the current liabilities for dividends and tax at 31 December 1997 will be paid in 1998 (and will appear on that year's cash flow statement).

how useful is the statement?

The following points are highlighted by the statement:

- net cash inflow from operating activities is £10,700
- a purchase of fixed assets of £16,800 has been made, financed partly by operating activities, and partly by an issue of shares at a premium
- the bank balance during the year has fallen by £500, ie from £1,000 to £500
- in conclusion, the picture shown by the cash flow statement is that of a business which is generating cash from its operating activities and using them to build for the future

LINKS TO OTHER FINANCIAL STATEMENTS

As the cash flow statement is one of the three financial statements prepared at the end of an accounting period, it needs to be read in conjunction with the profit and loss account and balance sheet. In order to provide links to the other financial statements, the accounting standard on cash flow statements, FRS1, requires that there should be two reconciliations, between:

- operating profit and the net cash flow from operating activities
- the increase or decrease in cash and the movement in net debt

operating profit with net cash flow from operating activities

We have already seen in the case studies how this reconciliation is prepared: the 'operating activities' section commences with the operating profit and, after adjustments for depreciation and the change in stocks, debtors and creditors, concludes with the net cash flow from operating activities. In practice, the figures making up the reconciliation are invariably shown as a note to the cash flow statement with just the figure for net cash flow being shown on the face of the statement.

change in cash with movement in net debt

This reconciliation requires us to take the final figure on the cash flow statement – the increase or decrease in cash – and reconcile it with changes in net debt. (Note that net debt is the borrowing of the business – eg debentures, loans and overdrafts – less cash/bank balances and other liquid resources). Thus, for ABC Limited (see page 76) the reconciliation could be shown as follows, with specimen figures used:

Reconciliation of net cash flow to movement in net debt

	£
Increase in cash in the period	91,000
Cash to repay loan	90,000
Cash used to increase liquid resources (note: the net purchase of treasury bills)	50,000
Change in net debt	231,000
Net debt at 1 January 1997	(300,000)
Net debt at 31 December 1997	(69,000)

The above indicates that ABC Limited has used a lot of cash this year both to reduce its borrowings by £90,000 and to increase its liquid resources (in the form of treasury bills). As a consequence, the last two lines of the reconciliation show that its net debt has fallen from £300,000 at the start of the year to £69,000 at the end – a reduction of £231,000. (For businesses where borrowings are less than cash/bank balances and other liquid resources, the words 'net funds' are used in place of 'net debt'.)

USING THE CASH FLOW STATEMENT

The cash flow statement is important because it identifies the sources of cash flowing into the business and how they have been used. We need to read the statement in conjunction with the other two financial statements – profit and loss account and balance sheet – and also in the context of the previous year's statements. The following points should also be borne in mind:

- Like the other financial statements, the cash flow statement uses the *money measurement concept* (page 47). This means that only items which can be recorded in money terms can be included; also we must be aware of the effect of inflation when comparing one year with the next.
- We are looking for a reasonable cash flow from operating activities each year – this is the cash from the trading activities of the business.
- Changes in the working items of stock, debtors and creditors need to be put into context. For example, it would be a warning sign if there were large increases in these items in a business with a falling operating profit, and such a trend would put a strain on the liquidity of the business.
- The statement will show the amount of investment made during the year (eg the purchase of fixed assets). In general there should be a link between the cost of the investment and an increase in loans and/or capital – it isn't usual to finance fixed assets from short-term sources, such as a bank overdraft.

- Where there has been an increase in loans and/or capital, look to see how the cash has been used. Was it to buy fixed assets or other investments, or to finance stocks and debtors, or other purposes?
- The statement, as a whole, links profit with changes in cash. Both of these are important: without profits the business cannot generate cash (unless it sells fixed assets), and without cash it cannot pay bills as they fall due.

CHAPTER SUMMARY

- The objective of a cash flow statement is to show an overall view of money flowing in and out of a business during an accounting period.
- A cash flow statement is divided into eight sections:
  1. operating activities
  2. returns on investments and servicing of finance
  3. taxation
  4. capital expenditure and financial investment
  5. acquisitions and disposals
  6. equity dividends paid
  7. management of liquid resources
  8. financing
- Larger limited companies are required to include a cash flow statement as a part of their published accounts. They are also useful statements for sole traders and partnerships.

KEY TERMS

cash flow statement	shows an overall view of money flowing in and out of a business during an accounting period
cash flow from operating activities	operating profit (before interest and tax), plus depreciation for the year, together with changes in the working capital items (stock, debtors and creditors)
returns on investments and servicing of finance	interest received and paid; dividends received
capital expenditure and financial investment	purchase and/or sale of fixed assets and investments
liquid resources	short term investments that are almost equal to cash
financing	issue or repayment of loans or share capital or capital
net debt	borrowings (debentures, loans and overdrafts), less cash/bank balances and other liquid resources

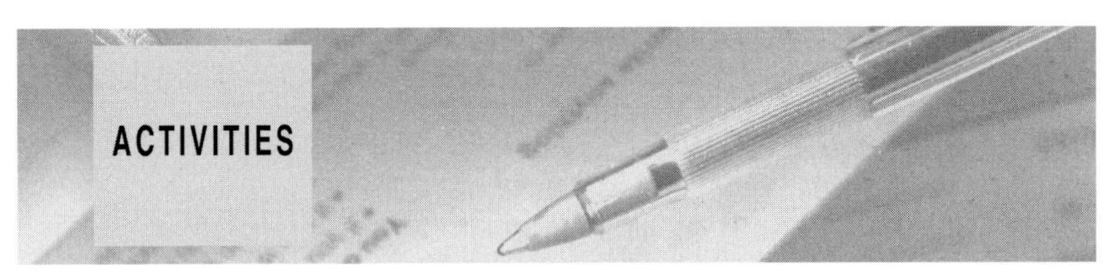

Note: A specimen format for a cash flow statement is provided in Appendix A (page 373); this will help when preparing numerical answers.

5.1 John Smith has run a delicatessen from rented premises for two years. His business has made a profit for each year, but his bank balance has fallen and is now an overdraft. He is puzzled by this and asks you to help him and explain what has happened. His balance sheets are as follows:

Balance sheet as at 31 December

		1996			1997	
	£	£	£	£	£	£
	Cost	Dep'n	Net	Cost	Dep'n	Net
Fixed assets						
Fixtures and fittings	3,000	600	2,400	5,000	1,600	3,400
Current assets						
Stock		5,500			9,000	
Debtors		750			1,550	
Bank		850			–	
		7,100			10,550	
Current liabilities						
Creditors	2,500			2,750		
Bank overdraft	–			2,200		
		2,500			4,950	
Working capital			4,600			5,600
NET ASSETS			7,000			9,000
FINANCED BY						
Capital						
Opening capital			5,000			7,000
Add net profit for year			8,750			11,000
			13,750			18,000
Less drawings			6,750			9,000
Closing capital			7,000			9,000

Note: Interest paid on the bank overdraft in 1997 was £250.

Prepare a cash flow statement for the year ended 31 December 1997; explain to John Smith the main points highlighted by the statement.

5.2 Martin Jackson is a shareholder in Retail News Limited, a company that operates a chain of newsagents throughout the West Midlands. Martin comments that, whilst the company is making reasonable profits, the bank balance has fallen quite considerably. He provides you with the following information for Retail News Limited:

BALANCE SHEET AS AT 31 DECEMBER

		1994		1995		1996
	£000	£000	£000	£000	£000	£000
Fixed assets at cost		252		274		298
Add additions during year		22		24		26
		274		298		324
Less depreciation		74		98		118
		200		200		206
Current assets						
Stock	50		64		70	
Debtors	80		120		160	
Bank	10		–		–	
	140		184		230	
Less Current liabilities						
Creditors	56		72		78	
Bank	–		10		46	
Proposed dividends	16		20		16	
Corporation tax	4		5		8	
	76		107		148	
Working capital		64		77		82
NET ASSETS		264		277		288
FINANCED BY						
Ordinary share capital		200		210		210
Retained profits		64		67		78
SHAREHOLDERS' FUNDS		264		277		288

Note: Interest paid on the bank overdraft was: £3,000 in 1995, and £15,000 in 1996.

Prepare a cash flow statement for the years ended for 1995 and 1996 and comment on the main points highlighted by the statements.

5.3 Discussion topics:

(a) Explain the difference between

- cash flow statement
- profit and loss account
- balance sheet

(b) Explain the difference between profit and cash. Discuss the relative merits of a business which:

- either is making profits
- or has cash in the bank

(c) At the beginning of the current financial year, the company for which you work has purchased a new computer system at a cost of £100,000. How will this be recorded in each of this year's financial statements?

(d) What are the limitations of the cash flow statement to the user of financial statements?

6 PUBLISHED ACCOUNTS OF LIMITED COMPANIES

this chapter covers ...

- *the financial statements required by the Companies Act*
- *the reasons for, and the layout of, published accounts*
- *the interpretation of the auditors' report*
- *the accounting policies followed by a particular company*
- *the purpose of consolidated accounts*
- *bonus issues and rights issues of shares*

INTRODUCTION

All limited companies have shareholders and many of the largest companies have many thousands of shareholders. Each shareholder owns a part of the company and, although they do not take part in the day-to-day running of the company (unless they are also directors), each is entitled to know the financial results of the company.

Every limited company, whether public or private, is required by law to publish financial statements, which are also available for anyone to inspect if they so wish. We need to distinguish between the *statutory accounts* and the *report and accounts*. The statutory accounts are those which are required to be produced under company law, and a copy of these is filed at Companies House. Smaller companies can file abbreviated accounts. The report and accounts, a copy of which is available to every shareholder, must include the statutory accounts, but usually also contains more information about the activities of the company. The report and accounts of large well-known companies are often presented in the form of a glossy booklet, well illustrated with photographs and diagrammatic presentations. Some companies, with the agreement of the shareholders, issue a simpler form of annual review, including a *summary financial statement*, the full report and accounts being available on request.

Company law not only requires the production of financial statements, but also states the detailed information that must be disclosed. The financial statements of all public limited companies and larger private companies must be audited (ie professionally checked) and the Auditors' Report included in the statements. All these legal requirements are detailed in the relevant sections of the Companies Act 1985 (as amended by the Companies Act 1989).

STATEMENTS REQUIRED BY THE COMPANIES ACT

The financial statements required by the Companies Act are:

- profit and loss account
- balance sheet
- directors' report

When producing financial statements, companies also have to bear in mind the requirements of the various Statements of Standard Accounting Practice (SSAPs) and Financial Reporting Standards (FRSs). As we have seen earlier (page 50), these are issued by the Accounting Standards Board and lay down acceptable accounting methods for various topics. Of particular note is FRS1, which requires larger limited companies to include a cash flow statement as part of the published accounts.

The reporting procedures of smaller companies call for simpler and less detailed disclosure requirements.

PROFIT AND LOSS ACCOUNT

The profit and loss account does not detail every single expense incurred by the company but, instead, summarises the main items. However, the Companies Act requires that certain items must be detailed either in the profit and loss account itself, or in separate notes.

The profit and loss account must follow one of two standard formats set out in the Act, and the example which follows shows the one that is most commonly used by trading companies. (The other format is appropriate for manufacturing companies.) Specimen figures have been shown – amounts in brackets are deducted and the presentation is in vertical style.

XYZ PLC

Profit and loss account

for the year ended 31 December 1997

	£000s
Turnover (sales)	27,000
Cost of sales	(16,500)
Gross profit	10,500
Distribution costs	(3,250)
Administrative expenses	(3,000)
Other operating income (eg rent received)	500
Income from investments	100
Interest payable	(200)
Profit on ordinary activities before tax	4,650
Tax on profit on ordinary activities	(2,000)
Profit on ordinary activities after tax	2,650
Dividends paid and proposed	(1,350)
Transfer to reserves	(500)
Retained profit for the financial year	800

In the notes to the profit and loss account must be disclosed details of:

- hire charges of plant and machinery
- auditors' fees
- rent receivable
- depreciation amounts
- the total of directors' emoluments (ie earnings)
- the highest paid director's emoluments (only required to be shown by companies quoted on the Stock Exchange, and where total directors' emoluments exceed £200,000 per year)
- the average number of employees, together with details of costs of wages and salaries, national insurance and pensions.

Fig 6.1 shows a recent profit and loss account for The Body Shop International PLC.

CONSOLIDATED PROFIT AND LOSS ACCOUNT

	Note	1999 £m	1998 £m
Turnover	2	303.7	293.1
Cost of sales		(127.7)	(115.9)
Gross profit		176.0	177.2
Operating expenses – excluding exceptional costs	3	(151.4)	(139.1)
– exceptional costs	3	(4.5)	–
Operating profit	2,3	20.1	38.1
Restructuring costs	4	(16.6)	–
		3.5	38.1
Interest payable (net)	5	(0.1)	(0.1)
Profit on ordinary activities before taxation		3.4	38.0
Taxation on profit on ordinary activities	7	(8.0)	(15.2)
(Loss)/profit for the financial year	8	(4.6)	22.8
Dividends paid and proposed	9	(10.9)	(10.8)
Retained (loss)/profit	21	(15.5)	12.0
Basic earnings per ordinary share	10	(2.4p)	11.8p
Earnings per ordinary share before exceptional and restructuring costs	10	7.0p	11.8p
Diluted earnings per ordinary share	10	(2.4p)	11.7p

Fig 6.1 Profit and loss account of Body Shop plc

(note that, for comparison, figures for both the current year and last year are shown)

continuing and discontinued operations

Limited company profit and loss accounts are also required (by Financial Reporting Standard No 3, entitled "Reporting Financial Performance") to show the financial results of any changes to the structure of the company, eg the purchase of another company, or the disposal of a section of the business. To this end the company must distinguish between:

- *continuing operations* – the profit and loss amounts relating to those activities of the company which continue in business at the end of the year; shown separately under this heading will be amounts relating to any *acquisitions*, ie businesses bought during the year

- *discontinued operations* – the amounts relating to activities which have now been sold or terminated during the year

As well as the above, there must be disclosed any *exceptional items* – large, usually one-off transactions, but which form part of normal trading activities. The following such transactions must be disclosed under FRS3:

- profits or losses on the sale or termination of part of the business
- costs of a fundamental reorganisation or restructuring
- profits or losses on the disposal of fixed assets

Finally, there must be disclosed any *extraordinary items* – large, one-off transactions which are outside normal trading activities.

The objective of these requirements is to give more information to users and to encourage them to seek a deeper understanding of the accounts.

A layout for the profit and loss account (with sample figures) which is commonly used is as follows:

ABC PLC

Profit and loss account for the year ended 31 December 1996

	Continuing operations	*Acquisitions*	*Discontinued operations*	*Total*
	£	£	£	£
Turnover (sales)	50	10	5	65
Cost of sales	(25)	(6)	(3)	(34)
Gross profit	25	4	2	31
Operating expenses	(15)	(2)	(1)	(18)
Operating profit	10	2	1	13
Profit on sale of an operation			5	5
Cost of restructuring	(4)			(4)
Profit on disposal of fixed assets	2			2
Profit on ordinary activities before interest	8	2	6	16
Interest payable				(3)
Profit on ordinary activities before taxation				13
Tax on profit on ordinary activities				(4)
Profit on ordinary activities after taxation				9
Extraordinary item (net of tax)				3
Profit for the financial year				12
Dividends paid and proposed				(6)
Retained profit for the financial year				6

BALANCE SHEET

The Companies Act 1985 sets out the standard formats for balance sheets. The example below is presented in the layout most commonly used. As with the profit and loss account, extra detail is often shown in the notes to the balance sheet.

XYZ PLC

BALANCE SHEET

as at 31 December 1997

	£000s	£000s
Fixed assets		
Intangible assets (eg goodwill)		50
Tangible assets (eg buildings, machinery)		3,750
Investments		1,000
		4,800
Current assets		
Stock	900	
Debtors	1,300	
Bank/cash	100	
	2,300	
Current liabilities		
Creditors	(800)	
Working capital		1,500
		6,300
Less Long-term liabilities		
Bank loan		1,500
NET ASSETS		4,800
FINANCED BY		
Capital and reserves		
Called up share capital		2,800
Reserves		1,200
Profit and loss account		800
SHAREHOLDERS' FUNDS		4,800

The notes to the balance sheet must include:

- fixed assets: cost, depreciation to date, net book value
- when fixed assets have been revalued, the date of revaluation and valuation amount
- investments: current market value and book value
- stock: where appropriate, amounts of raw materials, work in progress and finished goods
- creditors: amount payable within one year shown as a current liability
- creditors: amount payable in more than one year shown as a long-term liability, details to include repayment terms, interest rates, and security, if any given
- share capital, showing authorised and issued share capital and giving details of number of shares, nominal values (eg 25p, 50p, £1), and types of shares (ordinary, preference)
- reserves: details and movements on reserves

Fig 6.2 shows a recent balance sheet for The Body Shop International PLC.

DIRECTORS' REPORT

The directors' report must contain details of the following:

- review of the activities of the company over the past year and in the future
- directors' names and their shareholdings
- proposed dividends
- transfers to reserves
- significant changes in fixed assets
- political and charitable contributions
- policy on employment of disabled people
- health and safety at work of employees

CASH FLOW STATEMENTS

All but the smaller limited companies must include, as part of their published accounts, a cash flow statement, which we described in detail in Chapter 5. Such a statement shows where the funds (money) have come from during the course of a financial year, and how such funds have been used. The statement also provides a direct link between the previous year's balance sheet and the current one. Fig 6.3 on page 96 shows a recent cash flow statement for The Body Shop International PLC.

BALANCE SHEETS

	Note	GROUP 27 Feb 1999 £m	GROUP 28 Feb 1998 £m	COMPANY 27 Feb 1999 £m	COMPANY 28 Feb 1998 £m
Fixed assets					
Intangible assets	11	13.1	–	–	–
Tangible assets	12	71.3	78.4	47.0	50.7
Investments	13	3.4	2.0	57.6	50.5
		87.8	80.4	104.6	101.2
Current assets					
Stocks	15	38.6	47.7	23.5	28.5
Debtors	16	40.3	47.0	51.1	59.5
Cash at bank and in hand		34.0	29.6	21.0	21.3
		112.9	124.3	95.6	109.3
Creditors: amounts falling due within one year	17	82.6	70.4	66.5	59.3
Net current assets		30.3	53.9	29.1	50.0
Total assets less current liabilities		118.1	134.3	133.7	151.2
Creditors: amounts falling due after more than one year	18	2.1	2.9	–	–
Provisions for liabilities and charges					
Deferred taxation	19	1.7	1.1	1.9	1.9
		114.3	130.3	131.8	149.3
Capital and reserves					
Called up share capital	20	9.7	9.7	9.7	9.7
Share premium account	21	42.8	42.8	42.8	42.8
Profit and loss account	21	61.8	77.8	79.3	96.8
Shareholders' funds		114.3	130.3	131.8	149.3

These financial statements were approved by the Board on 12 May 1999 and signed on its behalf by:

TG RODDICK
Director

Fig 6.2 Balance sheet of The Body Shop International PLC.

(note that both the 'group' and 'company' balance sheets are shown – see also consolidated accounts on page 99)

CONSOLIDATED CASH FLOW STATEMENT

	Note	£m	1999 £m	£m	1998 £m
Net cash inflow from operating activities	22a		50.0		41.5
Returns on investments and servicing of finance					
Interest received		1.3		1.5	
Interest paid		(1.4)	(0.1)	(1.6)	(0.1)
Taxation			(13.7)		(16.6)
Capital expenditure					
Purchase of tangible fixed assets		(12.0)		(11.6)	
Purchase of EST shares		(1.4)		(1.5)	
Sale of tangible fixed assets		1.1	(12.3)	0.1	(13.0)
Acquisitions and disposals					
Cash consideration	14	(16.1)		(18.3)	
Cash acquired		1.7		(0.7)	
Cash received on disposal		–	(14.4)	0.3	(18.7)
Equity dividends paid			(10.9)		(9.7)
Cash outflow before use of liquid resources and financing			(1.4)		(16.6)
Management of liquid resources					
Short term deposits			5.1		5.3
Financing					
Issue of ordinary share capital		–		0.7	
Syndicated loans		7.1		18.3	
Loan repayments		(1.0)	6.1	(20.3)	(1.3)
Increase/(decrease) in cash	22b		9.8		(12.6)

Fig 6.3 Cash Flow Statement of The Body Shop International PLC.

AUDITORS' REPORT

Larger companies must have their accounts audited by external auditors, who are appointed by the shareholders to check the accounts. The audit report, which is printed in the published accounts, is the culmination of their work. The three main sections of the auditors' report are:

- *respective responsibilities of directors and auditors*, ie the directors are responsible for preparing the accounts, while the auditors are responsible for forming an opinion on the accounts
- *basis of opinion*, ie the framework of Auditing Standards (issued by the Auditing Practices Board) within which the audit was conducted, other assessments, and the way in which the audit was planned and performed
- *opinion*, ie the auditors' view of the company's accounts

An *'unqualified'* auditors' opinion will read as follows:

> *"In our opinion the financial statements give a true and fair view of the state of affairs of the Company at .... 19.., and of the profit, and cash flows of the Company for the year then ended, and have been properly prepared in accordance with the Companies Act 1985."*

A *qualified* auditors' report will raise points that the auditors consider have not been dealt with correctly in the accounts. Where such points are not too serious, the auditors will use phrases such as "except for ...." or "subject to .... the financial statements give a true and fair view." Much more serious is where the auditors' statement says that the accounts "do not show a true and fair view" or "we are unable to form an opinion ....". These indicate a major disagreement between the company and the auditors, and a person involved with the company – such as an investor or a creditor - should take serious note.

Note that companies are exempt from audit requirements if their turnover (sales) for the year is below a certain figure (£350,000 at the time of writing).

ACCOUNTING POLICIES

Accounting policies are the specific accounting bases that the directors of a company choose to follow; for example, whether to depreciate fixed assets using the straight-line method or the reducing balance method, and at what rate. Companies include a statement of their accounting policies in the published accounts. Fig 6.4 on the next page shows an extract from the accounting policies of The Body Shop International PLC.

ACCOUNTING POLICIES

The financial statements have been prepared under the historical cost convention and in accordance with applicable accounting standards. Under the Companies Act 1985, the Company has taken advantage of the exemption from presenting its own profit and loss account.

Accounts are prepared to the Saturday nearest to the end of February in each year. The principal accounting policies are:

BASIS OF CONSOLIDATION The consolidated accounts incorporate the financial statements of The Body Shop International PLC and all of its subsidiary undertakings made up to 27 February 1999. The Group uses the acquisition method of accounting to consolidate the results of subsidiary undertakings and the results of subsidiary undertakings are included from the date of acquisition to the date of disposal. The holding company's accounting policies have been applied consistently in dealing with items which are considered material in relation to the consolidated accounts.

GOODWILL Goodwill arising on the acquisition of a subsidiary or business is the difference between the consideration paid and the fair value of the assets and liabilities acquired. Goodwill arising on acquisitions prior to 28 February 1998 was set off directly against reserves and has not been reinstated on implementation of FRS 10.

Positive goodwill arising on acquisitions from 1 March 1998 is capitalised, classified as an asset on the balance sheet and amortised on a straight line basis over its useful economic life up to a presumed maximum of 15 years. It will be reviewed for impairment at the end of the first full financial year following the acquisition and in other periods if events or changes indicate that the carrying value may not be recoverable. Any goodwill previously eliminated to reserves will be charged/credited to the profit and loss account upon disposal of the related business.

VALUATION OF INVESTMENTS Investments held as fixed assets are stated at cost less any provision for a permanent diminution in value.

DEPRECIATION Depreciation is provided to write off the cost, less estimated residual values, of all tangible fixed assets, except for freehold land, over their expected useful lives.

It is calculated using the following rates:

Freehold buildings	– Over 50 years
Leasehold property	– Over the period of the respective leases
Plant and equipment	– Over 3 to 10 years.

STOCKS Stocks are valued at the lower of cost and net realisable value. Cost is calculated as follows:

Raw materials	– Cost of purchase on first-in first-out basis
Work in progress and finished goods	– Cost of raw materials and labour together with attributable overheads.

Net realisable value is based on estimated selling price less further costs to completion and disposal.

Fig 6.4 Extract from the accounting policies of The Body Shop International PLC.

CONSOLIDATED ACCOUNTS

Over the last twenty or thirty years many companies have been taken over by other companies to form groups. Each company within a group maintains its separate legal entity, and so a group of companies may take the following form:

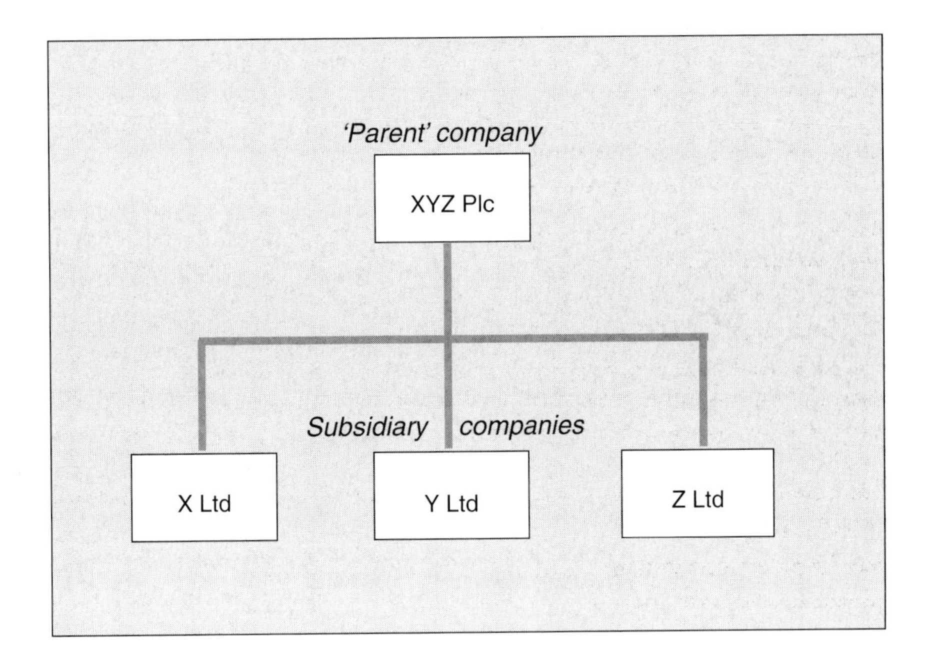

The Companies Act 1985 makes various provisions concerning groups of companies, including:

- A parent company and subsidiary company relationship exists where a parent company owns more than 50% of another company's share capital, or controls the composition of its board of directors.
- A parent company is required to produce *group published accounts.*
- Group accounts must include a consolidated profit and loss account and a consolidated balance sheet. (Such *consolidated accounts* are designed to show the position of the group as a whole to the outside world.)
- A parent company, which produces a consolidated profit and loss account, is not legally obliged to produce its own profit and loss account.

It is quite likely that, when you are studying a set of published accounts, you will find that you need to use the consolidated accounts for the group.

BONUS ISSUES AND RIGHTS ISSUES

Limited companies – and particularly plcs – quite often increase their capital by means of either *bonus issues* or *rights issues* of shares. Whilst both of these have the effect of increasing the number of shares in issue, they have quite different effects on the structure of the company balance sheet.

bonus issues

A bonus issue is made when a company issues free shares to existing shareholders; it does this by using reserves that have built up and capitalising them (ie they are turned into permanent share capital). The bonus issue is distributed on the basis of existing shareholdings – for example, one bonus share for every two shares already held.

With a bonus issue no cash flows in or out of the company. The shareholders are no better off: with more shares in issue the stock market price per share will fall in proportion to the bonus issue, ie the company's net assets are now spread among a greater number of shares.

Bonus issues are made in order to acknowledge the fact that reserves belong to shareholders. Often a build-up of reserves occurs because a company hasn't the cash to pay dividends, so a bonus issue is a way of passing the reserves to shareholders.

Note that capital or revenue reserves can be used for bonus issues. If there is a choice, then the capital reserve is used first – this is because it is one of the few uses of a capital reserve, which cannot be used to fund the payment of dividends.

rights issues

A rights issue is used by a company seeking to raise further finance through the issue of shares. Instead of going to the considerable expense of offering additional shares to the public, it is cheaper to offer shares to existing shareholders at a favourable price (usually a little below the current market price). As with a bonus issue the extra shares are offered in proportion to the shareholders' existing holding. The shareholder may take up the rights by subscribing for the shares offered; alternatively the rights can often be sold on the stock market.

BONUS ISSUES AND RIGHTS ISSUES

situation

The following are the summary balance sheets of Severn plc and Wye plc:

	Severn	*Wye*
	£	£
Fixed assets	300,000	300,000
Current assets (including bank)	100,000	100,000
	400,000	400,000
Ordinary shares of £1 each	200,000	200,000
Reserves (capital and revenue)	200,000	200,000
	400,000	400,000

Severn is planning a one-for-two bonus issue.
Wye is seeking finance for a capital expenditure programme through a one-for-two rights issue at a price of £1.80 per share (the current market price is £2.10).

solution

After the issues, the balance sheets appear as:

	Severn	*Wye*
	£	£
Fixed assets	300,000	300,000
Current assets (including bank)	100,000	280,000
	400,000	580,000
Ordinary shares of £1 each	300,000	300,000
Reserves	100,000	200,000
Share premium account (capital reserve)	–	80,000
	400,000	580,000

The changes are:

Severn Reserves are reduced by £100,000, whilst share capital is increased by the same amount; the ordinary share capital is now more in balance with fixed assets; no cash has been received.

Wye The bank balance has increased by £180,000, being 100,000 shares (assuming that all shareholders took up their rights) at £1.80; share capital has increased by £100,000, whilst 80p per share is the share premum, ie £80,000 in total. The company now has the money to finance its capital expenditure programme. There are also significant reserves which could be used for a bonus issue in the future.

- The Companies Act 1985 requires a considerable amount of detail to be disclosed in the published accounts of limited companies.
- The Act requires all limited companies to produce:
  - a profit and loss account
  - a balance sheet
  - a directors' report
- The Act lays down formats for profit and loss account and balance sheet.
- Besides the requirements of the Companies Act, companies must also abide by the Statements of Standard Accounting Practice (SSAPs) and Financial Reporting Standards (FRSs), as laid down by the Accounting Standards Board.
- Most companies also include in their published accounts a cash flow statement which shows where the funds (money) has come from during the course of the financial year, and how it has been used.
- For larger companies, external auditors report to the shareholders on the state of affairs of the company.
- The directors establish the accounting policies which the company will follow.
- Consolidated accounts are prepared for groups of companies.
- Bonus issues and rights issues increase the number of shares in issue – only the latter brings in cash to the company.

This chapter concludes the section of the book on *Financial Statements*; we have looked at the presentation of the profit and loss account, balance sheet and cash flow statement for businesses ranging from sole traders through to public limited companies. In the next section we will interpret the financial statements – by the use of accounting ratios and other means – so as to be able to monitor financial performance.

statutory accounts — financial statements required by law, a copy of which is filed at Companies House, where it can be inspected

report and accounts — the statutory accounts, together with additional information, sent to the shareholders of a company

summary financial statement — a shorter version of the statutory accounts which, by agreement with individual shareholders, can be sent in place of the report and accounts

exceptional items — costs (or revenues) relating to the trading activities of the company; need to be disclosed separately in the profit and loss account because of their size

extraordinary items	one-off transactions which are outside the company's normal trading activities
auditors' report	gives the auditors' opinion on the company's financial statements as to whether they give a true and fair view of the state of affairs of the company
accounting policies	the specific accounting bases that the directors of a company choose to follow
subsidiary company	where more than 50% of the shares are owned by another company; alternatively, where another company controls composition of its board of directors
consolidated accounts	group accounts for a holding company and its subsidiary companies
bonus issue	the capitalisation of reserves – either capital or revenue – in the form of free shares issued to existing shareholders in proportion to their holdings; no cash flows into the company
rights issue	the raising of cash by offering shares to existing shareholders, in proportion to their holdings, at a favourable price

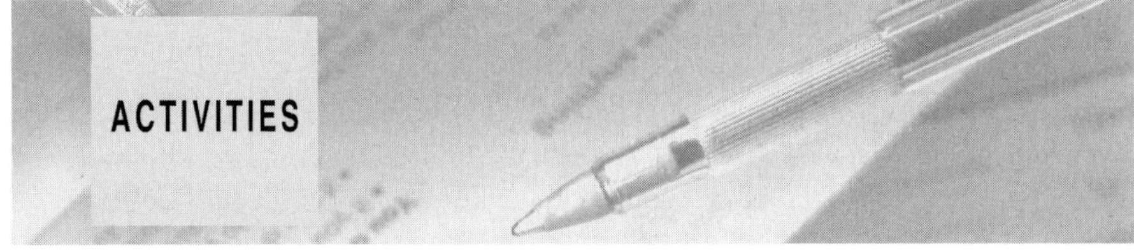

6.1 Select a public limited company of your choice and obtain the latest set of published accounts. (Either write to the company asking for a set; alternatively some financial newspapers offer a 'report and accounts service' whereby accounts for the larger plcs can be sent on request.)

Read the report and accounts and, from the financial statements, extract the following information for the current and previous year (if there is a choice of figures, use those from the consolidated accounts):

profit and loss account

- turnover
- profit on ordinary activities before taxation
- profit for the financial year
- earnings per share

balance sheet

- total of fixed assets
- total of current assets

- total of current liabilities (often shown as 'creditors: amounts falling due within one year')
- total of long-term liabilities (often shown as 'creditors: amounts falling due after one year')
- capital employed

cash flow statement

- cash flow from operating activities (noting any significant amounts)
- cash flow from
  - returns on investments and servicing of finance
  - taxation
  - capital expenditure and financial investment
  - acquisitions and dispersals
  - financing

  (note any significant amounts)

auditors' report (current year only)

- does it state that the financial statements show a 'true and fair view'?
- are there any 'qualifications' to the report

accounting policies (current year only)

- what method is used for valuing stocks?
- what depreciation policies are used?

Compile a short report – from the point of view of a private investor – which contains:

- an introduction to the selected plc; its structure, size, products, position in its own industry
- the information extracted from the published accounts
- a portfolio of your observations from the report and accounts, eg
  - is the company expanding/declining/remaining static?
  - has money been spent on major capital expenditure?
  - have the shareholders received higher/lower dividends?
- an assessment of the influence of external factors on the selected plc and any other significant developments

6.2 Discuss the following statements (some aspects may need additional research):

(a) "The company is planning a two-for-one bonus issue of shares; this means that any shareholding will be worth twice as much."

(b) "We are going to revalue the property this year; this will help us to show a healthy profit."

(c) "The accounting standards say that we must depreciate most fixed assets; however the methods we choose are up to us to decide. Therefore, I suggest we change the method from that used last year so as to charge as much as possible to profit and loss account; this will reduce our profit and so reduce the tax we pay."

(d) "Retained profit for the year is £5m, so that means we can afford to finance our £4m capital expenditure programme next year."

(e) "We need to raise some cash to pay for new capital expenditure. What are the merits of a rights issue?"

Section 3

monitoring financial performance

In this section we look at how the financial statements are analysed using accounting ratios and other techniques in order to assess the financial performance of the business.

profitability

liquidity

solvency

use of assets

investment performance

7 INTERPRETATION OF FINANCIAL STATEMENTS

this chapter covers ...

- *the importance of interpretation of financial statements*
- *the main accounting ratios*
- *a commentary on trends shown by the main accounting ratios*
- *how to report on the overall financial situation of a business*
- *limitations in the interpretation of accounts*

INTRODUCTION

The financial statements – profit and loss account, balance sheet, and cash flow statement – of businesses are often interpreted by interested parties for decision making, planning and control purposes. Interpretation of accounts is much more than the mechanical process of calculating a number of ratios; it should be approached as a five-stage process:

- *read* the accounts in order to understand the business
- *calculate* the main ratios, percentages and performance indicators
- *identify* the main strengths and weaknesses of the business
- *draw* conclusions as to how the business has performed
- *forecast* future business development

In this chapter we will examine the main themes within the business of:

- *profitability*, the relationship between profit and sales turnover, assets and capital employed
- *solvency/liquidity*, which considers the stability of the business on both a short-term and long-term basis
- *asset utilisation*, the effective and efficient use of assets
- *investment ratios*, which examine the returns to shareholders in companies

Note that the general term 'accounting ratios' is usually used to describe the calculations aspect of the interpretation of accounts. The term *ratio* is, in fact, partly misleading because the performance indicators include percentages, time periods, as well as ratios in the strict sense of the word.

MAKING USE OF ACCOUNTING RATIOS

It is important when examining a set of financial statements and calculating accounting ratios to relate them to reference points or standards. These points of reference might be to:

- establish trends from past years, to provide a standard of comparison
- benchmark against other businesses in the same industry
- compare with standards assumed to be satisfactory by the interested party, eg a bank

Above all, it is important to understand the relationships between ratios: one ratio may give an indication of the state of the business, but this needs to be supported by other ratios. Ratios can indicate symptoms, but the cause will then need to be investigated.

Another use of ratios is to estimate forward the likely profit or balance sheet of a business. For example, it might be assumed that the same gross profit percentage as last year will also apply next year; thus, given an estimated increase in sales, it is a simple matter to estimate gross profit. In a similar way, by making use of ratios, net profit and the balance sheet can be forecast.

Whilst all of the ratios calculated in this chapter use figures from the profit and loss account and balance sheet, the cash flow statement is important too. It assists in confirming the views shown by the accounting ratios and provides further evidence of the position. Look first at fig 7.1 on the following two pages.

Gross profit/sales percentage $= \dfrac{\text{Gross profit}}{\text{Sales}} \times \dfrac{100}{1}$

Expense/sales percentage $= \dfrac{\text{Specified selling expenses}}{\text{Sales}} \times \dfrac{100}{1}$

Operating profit/sales percentage $= \dfrac{\text{Operating profit*}}{\text{Sales}} \times \dfrac{100}{1}$

* profit before interest and tax

Net profit/sales percentage $= \dfrac{\text{Net profit}}{\text{Sales}} \times \dfrac{100}{1}$

Return on capital employed $= \dfrac{\text{Profit*}}{\text{Capital employed}} \times \dfrac{100}{1}$

* net profit or operating profit – see text

Return on net assets employed $= \dfrac{\text{Net profit}}{\text{Net assets*}} \times \dfrac{100}{1}$

* defined (for ratio analysis) as:
fixed assets + current assets – current liabilities

OTHER PROFITABILITY RATIOS (explained in the text):

- return on equity
- return on net assets employed
- primary ratio

Wyvern Trading Company Limited

PROFIT AND LOSS ACCOUNT

for the year ended 31 December 1997

	£000s	£000s
Sales		1,430
Opening stock	200	
Purchases	1,000	
	1,200	
Less Closing stock	240	
Cost of sales		960
Gross profit		470
Overheads		
Selling expenses	150	
Administration expenses	140	
		290
Operating profit		180
Less: Debenture interest		10
Net profit for year before taxation		170
Less: Corporation tax		50
Profit for year after taxation		120
Less:		
preference dividend paid	25	
ordinary dividend proposed	75	
		100
Retained profit for the year		20
Add balance of retained profits at beginning of year		180
Balance of retained profits at end of year		200

BALANCE SHEET (extract)

Net assets employed (fixed assets + current assets – current liabilities)	1,550
Capital employed (share capital + reserves + long-term liabilities)	1,550

Notes:

- *For ratio analysis, capital employed and net assets employed are the same amount*
- *Items used in the ratios on the opposite page are shown in bold type on a grey background*

Fig 7.1 Key accounting ratios: profitability

PROFITABILITY

One of the main objectives of a business is to make a profit. Profitability ratios examine the relationship between profit and sales turnover, assets and capital employed. Before calculating the profitability ratios, it is important to read the profit and loss account in order to review the figures.

The key profitability ratios are illustrated on the previous two pages. We will be calculating the accounting ratios from these figures in the Case Study (pages 125-130).

gross profit percentage

This expresses, as a percentage, the gross profit (sales minus cost of sales) in relation to sales. For example, a gross profit percentage of 20 per cent means that for every £100 of sales made, the gross profit is £20.

The gross profit percentage should be similar from year-to-year for the same business. It will vary between organisations in different areas of business, eg the gross profit percentage on jewellery is considerably higher than that on food. A significant change from one year to the next, particularly a fall in the percentage, needs investigation into the buying and selling prices.

Gross profit percentage, and also net profit percentage (see next page), needs to be considered in context. For example, a supermarket may well have a lower gross profit percentage than a small corner shop but, because of the supermarket's much higher turnover, the *amount* of profit will be much higher. Whatever the type of business, gross profit – both as an amount and a percentage – needs to be sufficient to cover the overheads, and then to give an acceptable return on capital.

expense/sales percentage

A large expense item can be expressed as a percentage of sales: for example, the relationship between advertising and sales might be found to be 10 per cent in one year, but 20 per cent the next year. This could indicate that an increase in advertising had failed to produce a proportionate increase in sales.

Note that each expense falls into one of three categories of cost:

- fixed costs, or
- variable costs, or
- semi-variable costs

Fixed costs remain constant despite other changes. Variable costs alter with changed circumstances, such as increased output or sales. Semi-variable costs combine both a fixed and a variable element, eg hire of a car at a basic (fixed) cost, with a variable cost per mile. It is important to appreciate the nature of costs when interpreting accounts: for example, if sales this year are twice last year's figure, not all expenses will have doubled. (We shall look in more detail at the nature of costs in Chapter 9).

operating profit percentage

Net profit percentage is calculated after loan and bank interest has been charged to profit and loss account. Thus it may be distorted when making comparisons are made between two different businesses where one is heavily financed by means of loans, and the other is financed by owner's capital. The solution is to calculate the *operating profit percentage* which uses profit before interest and tax.

net profit percentage

As with gross profit percentage, the net profit percentage should be similar from year-to-year for the same business, and should also be comparable with other firms in the same line of business. Net profit percentage should, ideally, increase from year-to-year, which indicates that the profit and loss account costs are being kept under control. Any significant fall should be investigated to see if it has been caused by

- *either* a fall in gross profit percentage
- *and/or* an increase in one particular expense, eg wages and salaries, advertising, etc

return on capital employed (ROCE)

This expresses the profit of a business in relation to the owner's capital. For this calculation, the capital at the start of the year should, ideally, be used; if this is not known, the year-end capital figure can be used. The percentage return is best thought of in relation to other investments, eg a building society might offer a return of five per cent, or a bank might offer three per cent on a deposit account. A person running a business is investing a sum of money in that business, and the profit is the return that is achieved on that investment. However, it should be noted that the risks in running a business are considerably greater than depositing the money with a building society or bank, and an additional return to allow for the extra risk is needed.

For limited companies, the calculation of return on capital employed must take note of their different methods of financing. It is necessary to distinguish between the ordinary shareholders' investment (the *equity*) and the capital employed by the company, which includes preference shares and debentures/long-term loans:

	Ordinary share capital
add	Reserves (capital and revenue)
equals	Equity
add	Preference share capital
add	Debentures/long-term loans
equals	Capital Employed

The reason for including preference shares and debentures/long-term loans in the capital employed is that the company has the use of the money from these contributors for the foreseeable future, or certainly for a fixed time period. These different definitions of capital employed give further accounting ratios:

return on equity

Percentage return on equity (also known as Return on owners' equity) =

$$\frac{\textit{Net profit for year - preference dividend (if any)}}{\textit{Ordinary share capital + reserves}} \times \frac{100}{1}$$

Note that the net profit is *after* deduction of the preference dividend (if any), ie it is the profit available for the ordinary shareholders, *before* deduction of corporation tax.

return on capital employed

Percentage return on capital employed =

$$\frac{\textit{Net profit for year + interest on debentures/long-term loans}}{\textit{Ordinary share capital + reserves + preference share capital + debentures/long-term loans}} \times \frac{100}{1}$$

Note that, here, the profit is *before* interest on debentures/long-term loans, ie it is the profit available to the providers of capital (shown as the divisor in the calculation), and before deduction of corporation tax.

primary ratio

Return on capital employed is perhaps the most effective ratio used in financial analysis. It is often known as the primary ratio, since it can be broken down into the two secondary factors of:

- net (or operating) profit percentage (see page 111)
- asset turnover ratio (see page 119)

The relationship between the three is:

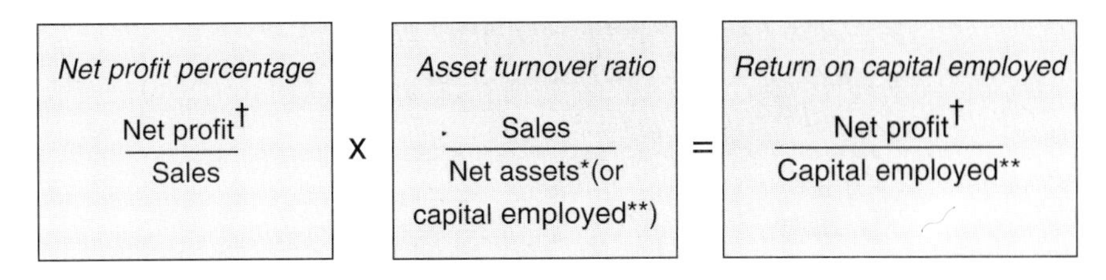

† net profit *or* operating profit

* Net assets: defined (for ratio analysis) as fixed assets + current assets – current liabilities

** Capital employed: defined as capital/share capital + reserves + long-term liabilities

For example, if a business has a net profit of £50,000, sales of £500,000 and net assets and capital employed of £250,000, the three figures are:

$$\frac{£50,000}{£500,000} \times \frac{£500,000}{£250,000} = \frac{£50,000}{£250,000}$$

$$10\% \times 2 \text{ times} = 20\%$$

The primary ratio is used to help us appreciate that the same return on capital employed can be achieved in different ways, depending on the type of business. Thus, one business may have a net profit percentage of 10 per cent, but an asset turnover of 2 times, while for a different business the respective values might be 2 per cent and 10 times: for both the return on capital employed is 20 per cent. These examples illustrate why, for example, an engineering firm and a supermarket could be equally profitable.

return on net assets employed

Percentage return on net assets =

$$\frac{\text{Net profit for year}}{\text{Net assets*}} \times \frac{100}{1}$$

*fixed assets + current assets – current liabilities

This is an important ratio as it relates the profitability of the business to the value of the net assets in use. It is another way of expressing return on capital employed, but relating profit to assets.

SOLVENCY/LIQUIDITY

Solvency/liquidity ratios measure the financial stability of the business, ie the ability of the business to pay its way – both on a short-term and long-term basis. For the short-term we focus our attention on the current assets and current liabilities sections of the balance sheet; for the long-term we look at long-term liabilities and the 'financed by' sections.

The key solvency/liquidity ratios are shown as part of fig 7.2, which are linked to the balance sheet of Wyvern Trading Company Limited. The ratios are calculated in the Case Study (pages 125-130).

working capital

Working capital = Current assets – Current liabilities

Working capital is needed by all businesses in order to finance day-to-day trading activities. Sufficient working capital enables a business to hold adequate stocks, allow a measure of credit to its customers (debtors), and to pay its suppliers (creditors) as payments fall due.

There is more on the management of working capital in Chapter 8.

working capital ratio (or current ratio)

Working capital ratio = Current assets : Current liabilities

Working capital ratio uses figures from the balance sheet and measures the relationship between current assets and current liabilities. Although there is no ideal working capital ratio, an accepatble ratio is about 2:1, ie £2 of current assets to every £1 of current liabilities. However, a business in the retail trade may be able to work with a lower ratio, eg 1.5:1 or even less, because it deals mainly in sales for cash and so does not have a large figure for debtors. A working capital ratio can be *too* high: if it is above 3:1 an investigation of the make-up of current assets and current liabilities is needed: eg the business may have too much stock, too many debtors, or too much cash at the bank, or even too few creditors.

liquid ratio (or quick ratio, or acid test)

$$\text{Liquid ratio} = \frac{\text{Current assets} - \text{stock}}{\text{Current liabilities}}$$

The liquid ratio uses the current assets and current liabilities from the balance sheet, but stock is omitted. This is because stock is the most illiquid current asset: it has to be sold, turned into debtors, and then the cash has to be collected from the debtors. Also, some of the stock included in the balance sheet figure may be unsaleable or obsolete. Thus the liquid ratio provides a direct comparison between debtors/cash/bank and short-term liabilities. The balance between liquid assets, that is debtors and cash/bank, and current liabilities should, ideally, be about 1:1, ie £1 of liquid assets to each £1 of current liabilities. At this ratio a business is expected to be able to pay its current liabilities from its liquid assets; a figure below 1:1, eg 0.75:1, indicates that the firm would have difficulty in meeting pressing demands from creditors. However, as with the working capital ratio, some businesses are able to operate with a lower liquid ratio than others.

capital gearing

Capital gearing percentage =

$$\frac{\textit{Long-term loans (including any preference shares)}}{\textit{Capital (ordinary shares + reserves)}} \times \frac{100}{1}$$

Whilst the working capital and liquid ratios focus on whether the business can pay its way in the short-term, capital gearing is concerned with long-term financial stability. Here we measure how much of the busines is financed by debt (including preference shares) against capital (ordinary shares plus reserves). The higher the gearing percentage, the less secure will be the equity capital of the business and, therefore, the future of the business. This is because debt is costly in terms of interest payments (particularly if interest rates are variable). It is difficult to set a standard for an acceptable gearing ratio: in general terms most investors (or lenders) would not wish to see debt exceeding equity, ie a gearing percentage of greater than 100% is undesirable.

Capital gearing can also be expressed as a ratio, ie debt:equity. Thus a gearing percentage of 100% is a ratio of 1:1.

interest cover

$$\frac{\textit{Net profit + interest (ie operating profit)}}{\textit{Interest}} = \textit{Interest cover}$$

The interest cover ratio, linked closely to gearing, considers the safety margin (or cover) of profit over the interest payable by a business. For example, if the operating profit of a business was £10,000, and interest payable was £5,000, this would give interest cover of 2, which is a low figure. If the interest was £1,000, this would give interest cover of 10 which is a higher and much more acceptable figure. Thus, the conclusion to draw is that the higher the interest cover, the better (although there is an argument for having some debt).

SOLVENCY/LIQUIDITY RATIOS

Working capital ratio = $\frac{\text{Current assets}}{\text{Current liabilities}}$

Liquid ratio = $\frac{\text{Current assets} - \text{stock}}{\text{Current liabilities}}$

Capital gearing percentage = $\frac{\text{Long-term loans (including preference shares)}}{\text{Capital (ordinary shares + reserves)}} \times \frac{100}{1}$

ASSET UTILISATION RATIOS

Stock turnover (days) = $\frac{\text{Average stock*}}{\text{Cost of sales}} \times 365 \text{ days}$

* usually taken as: (opening stock + closing stock) ÷ 2; alternatively, if opening stock figure not available, use closing stock in calculation

Debtors' collection period (days) = $\frac{\text{Debtors}}{\text{Credit sales}} \times 365 \text{ days}$

Creditors' payment period (days) = $\frac{\text{Trade creditors}}{\text{Credit purchases}} \times 365 \text{ days}$

Asset turnover ratio = $\frac{\text{Sales}}{\text{Net assets*}}$

* defined (for ratio analysis) as:
fixed assets + current assets – current liabilities

other ratios

solvency/liquidity – interest cover ratio*

asset utilisation – proprietary ratio*

*explained in the text

Wyvern Trading Company Limited

BALANCE SHEET

as at 31 December 1997

Fixed assets	*Cost*	*Dep'n to date*	*Net*
	£000s	£000s	£000s
Premises	850	–	850
Fixtures and fittings	300	120	180
Vehicles	350	100	250
	1,500	220	1,280
Current assets			
Stock		240	
Debtors		150	
Bank/cash		135	
		525	
Less **Current liabilities**			
Creditors	130		
Proposed ordinary dividend	75		
Corporation tax	50		
		255	
Working capital			270
			1,550
Less Long-term liabilities			
10% Debentures			100
NET ASSETS			1,450
FINANCED BY			
Authorised and Issued Share Capital			
1,000,000 ordinary shares of £1 each, fully paid			1,000
250,000 10% preference shares of £1 each, fully paid			250
			1,250
Revenue reserve			
Profit and loss account			200
SHAREHOLDERS' FUNDS			1,450

PROFIT AND LOSS ACCOUNT (extract)

Cost of sales	960
Credit sales	1,430
Credit purchases	1,000

Note: Items used in ratios are shown in bold type with a grey background.

Fig 7.2 Key accounting ratios for solvency/liquidity and asset utilisation

ASSET UTILISATION

Asset utilisation measures how effectively management controls the current aspects of the business – principally stock, debtors and creditors (see fig 7.2). This section covers the main accounting ratios; in the next chapter (Chapter 8) we will focus on the importance of efficient management of working capital.

stock turnover

$$\frac{\textit{Average stock}}{\textit{Cost of sales}} \times 365 \textit{ days}$$

Stock turnover is the number of days' stock held on average. This figure will depend on the type of goods sold by the business. For example, a market trader selling fresh flowers, who finishes each day when sold out, will have a stock turnover of one day. By contrast, a jewellery shop – because it may hold large stocks of jewellery – will have a much slower stock turnover, perhaps sixty or ninety days, or longer. Nevertheless, stock turnover must not be too long, bearing in mind the type of business, and a business which is improving in efficiency will have a quicker stock turnover comparing one year with the previous one, or with the stock turnover of similar businesses.

Stock turnover can also be expressed as number of times per year:

$$\textit{Stock turnover (times per year)} = \frac{\textit{Cost of sales}}{\textit{Average stock}}$$

A stock turnover of, say, twelve times a year means that about thirty days' stock is held. Note that stock turnover can only be calculated where a business buys and sells goods; it cannot be used for a business that provides a service.

debtors' collection period

$$\frac{\textit{Debtors}}{\textit{Credit sales}} \times 365 \textit{ days}$$

This calculation shows how many days, on average, debtors take to pay for goods sold to them by the business. The figure of *credit sales for the year* may not be disclosed in the profit and loss account, in which case the sales figure should be used. Some businesses make the majority of their sales on credit but others, such as shops, will have a considerably lower proportion of credit sales.

The debt collection time can be compared with that for the previous year, or with that of a similar business. In Britain, most debtors should make payment within about 30 days; however, sales made abroad will take longer for the proceeds to be received. A comparison from year-to-year of the collection period is a measure of the firm's efficiency at collecting the money that is due to it.

creditors' payment period

$$\frac{\textit{Trade creditors}}{\textit{Credit purchases}} \times 365 \textit{ days}$$

This calculation is the opposite aspect to that of debtors: here we are measuring the speed it takes to pay creditors. While creditors can be a useful temporary source of finance, delaying payment too long may cause problems. This ratio is most appropriate for businesses that buy and sell goods; it cannot be used for a business that provides a service; it is also difficult to interpret when a business buys in some goods and, at the same time, provides a service, eg an hotel. Generally, though, we would expect to see the creditor days period longer than the debtor days, ie money is being received from debtors before it is paid out to creditors.

Note that there is invariably an inconsistency in calculating both debtors' collection and creditors' payment periods: the figures for debtors and creditors *include* VAT, while sales and purchases *exclude* VAT. Strictly, therefore, we are not comparing like with like; however, the comparison should be made with reference to the previous year, or a similar company, calculated on the same basis from year-to-year.

asset turnover ratio

$$\frac{\textit{Sales}}{\textit{Net assets}}$$

This ratio measures the efficiency of the use of net assets in generating sales. An increasing ratio from one year to the next indicates greater efficiency. A fall in the ratio may be caused either by a decrease in sales, or an increase in net assets – perhaps caused by the purchase or revaluation of fixed assets, or increased stockholding, or increased debtors as a result of poor credit control.

Different types of businesses will have very different asset turnover ratios. For example a supermarket, with high sales and relatively few assets, will have a very high figure; by contrast, an engineering business, with lower sales and a substantial investment in fixed and current assets, will have a much lower figure. As we have seen in the primary ratio (page 112), asset turnover and net profit percentage are the two factors which go to making up return on capital employed; therefore, although different types of businesses will have differing asset turnover ratios, they could have the same return on capital employed.

proprietary ratio

The proprietary ratio, which may also be expressed as a percentage, indicates the proportion of owners' funds to the tangible assets (tangible fixed assets + current assets) of the business. It is calculated as follows:

$$\frac{\textit{Ordinary shareholders' (or owners') funds}}{\textit{Tangible assets*}}$$

* *Tangible assets:* assets which have material substance, unlike intangible assets, such as goodwill

As a guideline a ratio of around 0.5:1, or 50 per cent, should be considered as the minimum desirable figure. This shows that half of the tangible assets are owned by the ordinary shareholders or owners, and half by contributors of other types of share and loan capital and by creditors. Intangible assets, such as goodwill, are excluded from this calculation because they would, most probably, be worthless in the event of the forced sale of the business.

INVESTMENT RATIOS

Investment ratios are used by business people and investors who intend to buy either a whole business, or holdings of shares in limited companies. The ratios will help to assess the performance of the company in which they wish to invest.

dividend yield

$$\frac{\textit{Ordinary share dividend (in pence)}}{\textit{Market price of ordinary share (in pence)}} \times \frac{100}{1}$$

Investors in companies which are quoted on the stock market can obtain this information from the share price pages of the financial press. The dividend yield gives the investor the annual percentage return paid on a quoted share. However, dividend yield is an inadequate measure because it ignores the overall profits – or 'earnings' – available for the ordinary shareholders; retained profits (ie that part of profits not paid as dividends) should help to boost the share price, so giving investors capital growth rather than income.

earnings per share

$$\frac{\textit{Net profit, after corporation tax and preference dividends}}{\textit{Number of issued ordinary shares}}$$

Earnings per share (or EPS) measures the amount of profit *earned* by each share, after corporation tax and preference dividends. Comparisons can be made with previous years to provide a basis for assessing the company's performance.

earnings yield

$$\frac{\textit{Earnings per ordinary share (in pence)}}{\textit{Market price of ordinary share (in pence)}} \times \frac{100}{1}$$

This compares, in percentage terms, the earnings per ordinary share (after corporation tax and preference dividends) with the market price per share. It is an important calculation for investors because it shows the return earned by the company on each ordinary share. Some part of the earnings will, most likely, have been paid to investors, while the rest will have been retained in the company and should help to increase the capital value of the shares.

price/earnings ratio

$$\frac{\textit{Market price of ordinary share (in pence)}}{\textit{Earnings per ordinary share (in pence)}} = \textit{Price/earnings ratio}$$

The price/earnings ratio (or P/E ratio, as it is often abbreviated) compares the current market price of a share with the earnings (after corporation tax) of that share. For example, if a particular share has a market price of £3, and the earnings per share in the current year are 30p, then the P/E ratio is 10. This simply means that a person buying the share for £3 is paying ten times the last reported earnings of that share.

Investors use the P/E ratio to help them make decisions as to the 'expensiveness' of a share. In general, high P/E ratios (ie a higher number) indicate that the stock market price has been pushed up in anticipation of an expected improvement in earnings: therefore, the share is now expensive. The reason for a low P/E ratio is usually that investors do not expect much (if any) growth in the company's earnings in the foreseeable future.

P/E ratio is simply a reciprocal of the earnings yield (see above). Thus a P/E ratio of 10 is the same as an earnings yield of 10 per cent; a P/E ratio of 20 is the same as an earnings yield of 5 per cent.

dividend cover

$$\frac{\textit{Net profit, after corporation tax and preference dividends}}{\textit{Ordinary dividends}}$$

This figure shows the margin of safety between the amount of profit a company makes and the amount paid out in dividends. The figure must be greater than 1 if the company is not to use past retained profits to fund the current dividend. A figure of 5 as dividend cover indicates that profit exceeds dividend by five times – a healthy sign. The share price pages in the financial press quote the figure under the column headed 'cover' or 'cvr'.

economic value added (EVA) principles

An increasing number of financial analysts and investors are turning to the use of *economic value added* (EVA) principles to see if shareholder value has increased.

EVA principles value a company on the basis of cash flows from operating activities after taking into account the cost of capital. Cost of capital is the return that shareholders and lenders require to persuade them to invest in, or lend to, the company; it will be higher when there is greater risk. Shareholder value is added where cash flows are greater than the cost of capital; it is reduced where cash flows are less than the cost of capital. EVA focuses on cash beacuse it is seen as being more important than profit or balance sheet values – both of which can be subjective.

From time-to-time financial newspapers produce EVA tables which show the performance of a number of companies. Using EVA principles, comparisons can be made within the same sector to see which companies are successful in enhancing shareholder value.

OTHER PRESENTATIONS

Financial information is often presented to the users of financial statements in a visual format, such as

- bar chart
- pie chart
- line graph

These and other techniques are looked at in more detail in Chapter 19. For the moment, though, we can say that they show financial results on a year-by-year basis in a way that is easy to understand.

Illustrated on the opposite page are extracts from the report and accounts of The Body Shop International PLC.

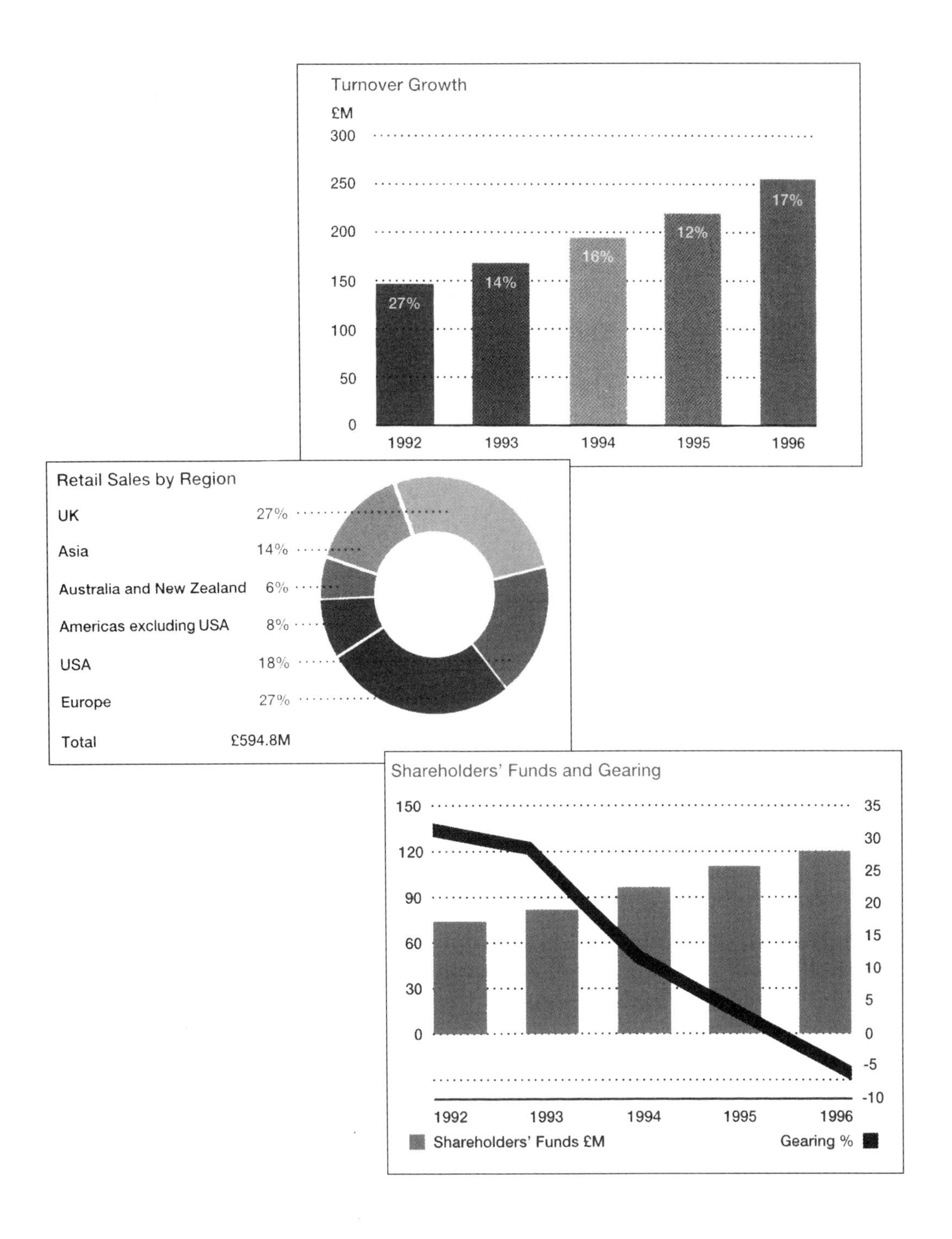

Fig 7.3 Visual presentation of financial data from the report and accounts of The Body Shop International PLC.

ANALYTICAL REVIEW

The interpretation of financial statements requires a full examination of both ratios and trends/changes from one accounting period to the next, together with a comparison between other companies in the same line of business. The objective is to obtain an understanding of the company and to highlight unusual trends and other items. The techniques involved are:

- *initial reading* – to gain an overview of the company's accounts and an understanding of the industry in which it operates
- *horizontal analysis* – where figures from the current financial statements are compared on a line-by-line basis with those from previous accounting periods
- *vertical analysis* – where the figures from the financial statements of a particular accounting period are studied to see how they link in with one another; figures can also be expressed as percentages, eg the percentage of expenses to sales
- *trend analysis* – where the figures from several accounting periods are compared to establish a trend, eg the percentage increase in sales over the period, compared with the percentage increase in expenses; trends can also be analysed in the form of indices, eg if a base year with an index of 100 is established, we could see how the index for, say, sales for the current year varies from the base (see also Chapter 19, page 348).
- *ratio analysis* – a common method of interpreting financial statements, which enables monitoring of performance from one accounting period to another, and comparisons with other companies by means of an inter-company analysis

WYVERN TRADING COMPANY

At the start of this chapter we saw that interpretation of financial statements does not require the extraction of a long list of ratios from a set of accounts. Instead, it involves the analysis of the relationships between the figures in the accounts and the presentation of the information gathered in a meaningful way to interested parties.

In this Case Study, we look at the set of accounts of a limited company. For clarity, one year's accounts are given although, in practice, two or more years' accounts should be used. The comments given indicate what should be looked for when analysing and interpreting a set of accounts.

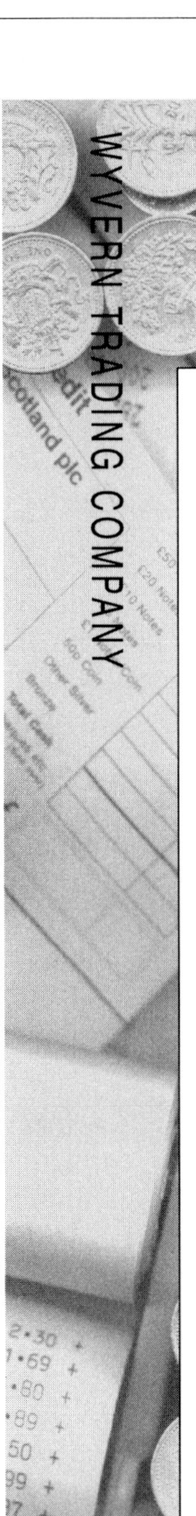

situation

The following are the accounts of Wyvern Trading Company Limited. The business trades in office supplies and sells to the public through its three retail shops in the Wyvern area; it also delivers direct to businesses in the area from its modern warehouse on a local factory estate.

Wyvern Trading Company Limited

PROFIT AND LOSS ACCOUNT

for the year ended 31 December 1997

	£000s	£000s
Sales		1,430
Opening stock	200	
Purchases	1,000	
	1,200	
Less Closing stock	240	
Cost of sales		960
Gross profit		470
Less overheads:		
Selling expenses	150	
Administration expenses	140	
		290
Operating profit		180
Less: Debenture interest		10
Net profit for year before taxation		170
Less: Corporation tax		50
Profit for year after taxation		120
Less:		
preference dividend paid	25	
ordinary dividend proposed	75	
		100
Retained profit for the year		20
Add balance of retained profits at beginning of year		180
Balance of retained profits at end of year		200

WYVERN TRADING COMPANY

BALANCE SHEET
as at 31 December 1997

Fixed assets	*Cost*	*Dep'n to date*	*Net*
	£000s	£000s	£000s
Premises	850	–	850
Fixtures and fittings	300	120	180
Vehicles	350	100	250
	1,500	220	1,280
Current assets			
Stock		240	
Debtors		150	
Bank/cash		135	
		525	
Less Current liabilities			
Creditors	130		
Proposed ordinary dividend	75		
Corporation tax	50		
		255	
Working capital			270
			1,550
Less Long-term liabilities			
10% debentures			100
NET ASSETS			1,450
FINANCED BY			
Authorised and Issued Share Capital			
1,000,000 ordinary shares of £1 each, fully paid			1,000
250,000 10% preference shares of £1 each, fully paid			250
			1,250
Revenue Reserve			
Profit and loss account			200
SHAREHOLDERS' FUNDS			1,450

Note: the current market price of the ordinary shares is £1.25.

solution

We will now analyse the accounts from the point of view of a potential investor. All figures shown are in £000s.

PROFITABILITY

Gross profit percentage

$$\frac{£470}{£1,430} \times \frac{100}{1} = 32.87\%$$

Specified expense: selling expenses to sales

$$\frac{\pounds150}{\pounds1{,}430} \times \frac{100}{1} = 10.49\%$$

Operating profit percentage

$$\frac{\pounds180}{\pounds1{,}430} \times \frac{100}{1} = 12.59\%$$

Net profit percentage

$$\frac{\pounds170}{\pounds1{,}430} \times \frac{100}{1} = 11.89\%$$

Return on capital employed

$$\frac{\pounds170 + \pounds10}{\pounds1{,}000 + \pounds250 + \pounds200 + \pounds100} \times \frac{100}{1} = 11.61\%$$

Return on equity

$$\frac{\pounds170 - \pounds25}{\pounds1{,}000 + \pounds200} \times \frac{100}{1} = 12.08\%$$

Return on net assets* employed

$$\frac{\pounds170}{\pounds1{,}550} \times \frac{100}{1} = 10.97\%$$

* fixed assets + current assets – current liabilities

Primary ratio

12.59% (operating profit %) x 0.922 (asset t/o ratio) = 11.61%

The gross and net profit percentages seem to be acceptable figures for the type of business, although comparisons should be made with those of the previous accounting period. A business should always aim at least to hold its percentages and, ideally, to make a small improvement. A significant fall in the percentages may indicate a poor buying policy, poor pricing (perhaps caused by competition), and the causes should be investigated.

Selling expenses seem to be quite a high percentage of sales. As these are likely to be a relatively fixed cost, it would seem that the business could increase sales turnover without a corresponding increase in sales expenses.

The small difference between net profit percentage and operating profit percentage indicates that finance costs are relatively low.

Return on capital employed is satisfactory, but could be better.The primary ratio shows how return on capital employed has been held back by a sluggish asset turnover ratio (see page 129). At 11.61% return on capital employed is less than two percentage points above the ten per cent cost of the preference shares and debentures (ignoring the taxation advantages of issuing debentures). Return on equity is better at 12.08%, but needs to be compared with the gross returns available elsewhere. This is not to suggest that the directors (who may well own the majority of the shares) should sell up: the business is likely to provide them (and others) with employment – directors'

remuneration having been deducted before arriving at the net profit figure used in the calculations. The figure for return on net assets employed confirms the mediocre performance of the company in this area.

SOLVENCY/LIQUIDITY

Working capital ratio

$$\frac{£525}{£255} = 2.06:1$$

Liquid ratio

$$\frac{(£525 - £240)}{£255} = 1.12:1$$

Capital gearing

$$\frac{£250 + £100}{£1{,}000 + £200} \times \frac{100}{1} = 29\% \text{ or } 0.29:1$$

Interest cover

$$\frac{£170 + £10}{£10} = 18 \text{ times}$$

The working capital and liquid ratios are excellent: they are slightly higher than the expected 'norms' of 2:1 and 1:1 respectively (although many companies operate successfully with lower ratios); however, they are not too high which would be an indication of inefficient use of assets.

The capital gearing percentage is low: anything up to 100% (1:1) is often seen. With a low figure of 29% this indicates that the company could borrow more money if it wished to finance, say, expansion plans (there are plenty of fixed assets for a lender – such as a bank – to take as security for a loan). The interest cover figure of 18 is very high and shows that the company has no problems in paying interest.

All-in-all, the company is very solvent, with no solvency or liquidity problems.

ASSET UTILISATION

Stock turnover

$$\frac{(£200 + £240) \div 2}{£960} \times 365 = 83.6 \text{ days (or 4.36 times per year)}$$

Debtors' collection period

$$\frac{£150 \times 365}{£1{,}430} = 38.3 \text{ days}$$

Creditors' payment period

$$\frac{£130 \times 365}{£1{,}000} = 47.4 \text{ days}$$

Asset turnover ratio

$$\frac{£1{,}430}{£1{,}550^*} = 0.92:1$$

* fixed assets + current assets – current liabilities

Proprietory ratio

$$\frac{£1{,}000 + £200}{£1{,}280 + £525} = 0.66:1$$

This group of ratios shows the main weakness of the company: not enough business is passing through for the size of the company. Stock turnover is very low for an office supplies business: the stock is turning over only every 83 days – surely it should be faster than this. Debtors' collection period is not too bad on the face of it – 30 days would be better – but quite a volume of the sales will be made through the retail outlets in cash. This amount should, if known, be deducted from the sales turnover before calculating the debtors' collection period: thus the collection period is, in reality, longer than that calculated. Creditors' payment period is quite leisurely for this type of business – long delays could cause problems with suppliers in the future. The asset turnover ratio says it all: this type of business should be able to obtain a much better figure:

- either, sales need to be increased using the same net assets
- or, sales need to be maintained, but net assets reduced

The proprietory ratio is good: above the suggested minimum figure of 50 per cent, indicating that the ordinary shareholders are financing 66% of the tangible assets.

INVESTMENT RATIOS

Dividend yield*

$$\frac{£75}{(1{,}000 \times £1.25)} \times \frac{100}{1} = 6\%$$

* like a number of investment ratios, this can be calculated either per share, or on the total shares in issue (as above).

Earnings per share

$$\frac{(£170 - £50 - £25)}{1{,}000} = 9.5 \text{ pence per share}$$

Earnings yield

$$\frac{9.5p}{125p} \times \frac{100}{1} = 7.6\%$$

Price/earnings ratio

$$\frac{125p}{9.5p} = 13.16 \text{ times}$$

Dividend cover

$$\frac{(£170 - £50 - £25)}{£75} = 1.27 \text{ times}$$

These ratios indicate that the company is not highly profitable for its shareholders (although shares are often bought for potential capital gains rather than income). The dividend yield is only 6 per cent, and the dividend is covered just 1.27 times: if profits were to fall, it is unlikely that the current level of dividend could be sustained. The lower price/earnings ratio seems appropriate for this company.

CASH FLOW STATEMENT

As well as the profit and loss account and balance sheet, we would need to see the company's cash flow statement to assist in confirming the views shown by the accounting ratios. In particular, we would be looking at:

- the cash inflow from operating activities
- the purchase of fixed assets, and how these have been financed
- the amount of dividends paid during the year
- the change in the bank and cash balances over the year

CONCLUSION

This appears to be a profitable business, although there may be some scope for cutting down somewhat on the profit and loss account selling expenses (administration expenses could be looked at too). The business offers a reasonable return on capital, although things could be improved.

The company is solvent and has good working capital and liquid capital ratios. Gearing is low – a good sign during times of variable interest rates.

The main area of weakness is in asset utilisation. It appears that the company could do much to reduce stock turnover and the debtors' collection period; at the same time creditors could be paid faster. Asset turnover is very low for this type of business and it does seem that there is much scope for expansion within the structure of the existing company. As the benefits of expansion flow through to the final accounts, the investment ratios will show an improvement from their present leisurely performance.

LIMITATIONS IN THE INTERPRETATION OF ACCOUNTS

Although accounting ratios can usefully highlight strengths and weaknesses, they should always be considered as a part of the overall assessment of a business, rather than as a whole. We have already seen the need to place ratios in context and relate them to a reference point or standard. The limitations of ratio analysis should always be borne in mind.

retrospective nature of accounting ratios

Accounting ratios are usually *retrospective,* based on previous performance and conditions prevailing in the past. They may not necessarily be valid for making forward projections: for example, a large customer may become insolvent, so threatening the business with a bad debt, and also reducing sales in the future.

differences in accounting policies

When the accounts of a business are compared, either with previous years' figures, or with figures from a similar business, there is a danger that the comparative accounts are not drawn up on the same basis as those currently being worked on. Different accounting policies, in respect of depreciation and stock valuation for instance, may well result in distortion and invalid comparisons.

inflation

Inflation may prove a problem, as most financial statements are prepared on an historic cost basis, that is, assets and liabilities are recorded at their original cost. As a result, comparison of figures from one year to the next may be difficult. In countries where inflation is running at high levels any form of comparison becomes practically meaningless.

reliance on standards

We have already mentioned guideline standards for some accounting ratios, for instance 2:1 for the working capital ratio. There is a danger of relying too heavily on such suggested standards, and ignoring other factors in the balance sheet. An example of this would be to criticise a business for having a low current ratio when the business sells the majority of its goods for cash and consequently has a very low debtors figure: this would in fact be the case with many well-known and successful retail companies. Large manufacturing businesses are able to operate with lower working capital ratios because of their good reputation and creditworthiness.

other considerations

Economic: The general economic climate and the effect this may have on the nature of the business, eg in an economic downturn retailers are usually the first to suffer, whereas manufacturers feel the effects later.

State of the business: The chairman's report for a limited company should be read in conjunction with the final accounts and cash flow statements to ascertain an overall view of the state of the business. Of great importance are the products of the company and their stage in the product life cycle, eg is a car manufacturer relying on old models, or is there an up-to-date product range which appeals to buyers?

Comparing like with like: Before making comparisons between 'similar' businesses (or, indeed, departments or divisions within the same business), we need to ensure that we are comparing 'like with like'. Differences, such as the acquisition of assets – renting premises compared with ownership, leasing vehicles compared with ownership – will affect the profitability of the business and the structure of the balance sheet; likewise, the long-term financing of a business – the balance between share capital/owner's capital and loans – will also have an effect.

CHAPTER SUMMARY

- Accounting ratios are numerical values – percentages, time periods, ratios – extracted from the financial statements of businesses.
- Accounting ratios can be used to measure:
  - profitability
  - solvency/liquidity
  - asset utilisation
  - investment potential
- Comparisons need to be made with previous financial statements, or those of similar companies.
- There are a number of limitations to be borne in mind when drawing conclusions from accounting ratios:
  - retrospective nature, based on past performance
  - differences in accounting policies
  - effects of inflation when comparing year-to-year
  - reliance on standards
  - economic and other factors

In the next chapter we will continue with the interpretation of financial statements by focussing on the importance of effective and efficient management of working capital.

KEY TERMS

A *help sheet* to assist with the key accounting ratios is given in Appendix A.

The key accounting ratios are summarised in this chapter on pages 108 and 116.

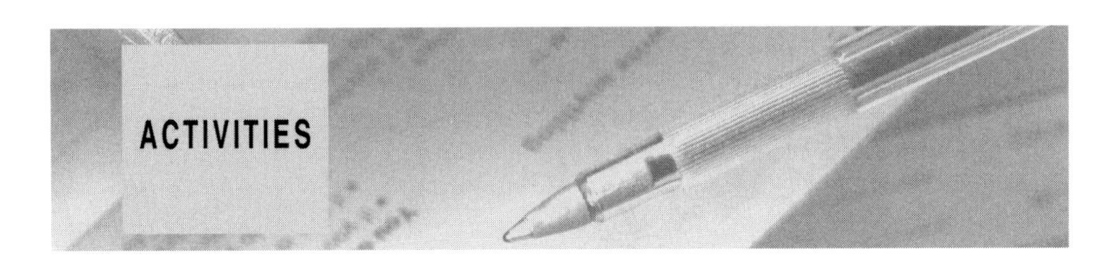

ACTIVITIES

7.1 The following information is taken from the profit and loss accounts of two plcs:

	A plc	*B plc*
	£m	*£m*
Sales	55.7	22.3
Cost of sales	(49.1)	(10.2)
GROSS PROFIT	6.6	12.1
Overheads	(4.4)	(6.3)
Interest paid	(0.6)	(1.1)
NET PROFIT BEFORE TAX	1.6	4.7
Note: Capital employed	£8.8m	£34.3m

For each company, calculate:

- gross profit percentage
- net profit percentage
- operating profit percentage
- return on capital employed

7.2 The following is taken from the balance sheets of two plcs:

	C plc	*D plc*
	£m	*£m*
Stock	3.8	4.1
Debtors	4.5	0.7
Bank/(bank overdraft)	(0.4)	6.3
Creditors	5.1	10.7
Long-term loans	3.2	2.1
Ordinary share capital	4.5	8.4
Reserves	1.4	4.7
Notes:		
Sales for year	43.9	96.3
Purchases for year	32.4	85.1
Cost of sales for year	33.6	84.7

For each company, calculate:

- working capital ratio
- liquid ratio
- debtors' collection period
- creditors' payment period
- stock turnover
- gearing ratio

One company runs department stores, the other is a chemical manufacturer. Which is which? Why is this?

7.3 The following is taken from the balance sheets of two plcs:

	ABC plc	*XYZ plc*
Ordinary dividend for year	£750,000	£1,250,000
Number of issued ordinary shares of £1 each	5,000,000	15,000,000
Current market price per share	£1.50	£6.00
Net profit after corporation tax and preference dividends	£1,500,000	£5,500,000

Note: both companies are in the same industry.

For each business, calculate:

- dividend yield
- earnings per share
- earnings yield
- price/earnings ratio
- dividend cover

In which company would you invest for (a) capital growth, (b) income?

7.4 The following information relates to two businesses, A and B:

	business A		business B	
	£000s	£000s	£000s	£000s
PROFIT AND LOSS ACCOUNT (EXTRACTS)				
Sales		3,057		1,628
Cost of sales		2,647		911
Gross profit		410		717
Overheads		366		648
Net profit		44		69

	business A		business B	
	£000s	£000s	£000s	£000s
SUMMARISED BALANCE SHEETS				
Fixed assets		344		555
Current assets				
Stock	242		237	
Debtors	6		269	
Bank	3		1	
	251		507	
Less Current liabilities	195		212	
Working capital		56		295
NET ASSETS		400		850
FINANCED BY				
Capital		400		850

One business operates a chain of grocery supermarkets; the other is a heavy engineering company.

- Calculate the following accounting ratios for both businesses:
  (a) gross profit percentage
  (b) net profit percentage
  (c) stock turnover (use balance sheet figure as average stock)
  (d) working capital ratio
  (e) liquid ratio
  (f) debtors' collection period
  (g) return on capital employed
- Indicate which company you believe to be the grocery supermarket chain and which the heavy engineering business. Briefly explain the reasons for your choice based on the ratios calculated and the accounting information.

7.5 The following accounting ratios have been calculated for a medium-sized plc in the printing industry. The company specialises in production of high-quality books, using colour printing.

	last year	*current year*
• gross profit percentage	42%	41%
• operating profit percentage	17%	11%
• net profit percentage	18%	8%
• return on capital employed	12%	6%
• working capital ratio	1.8:1	1.3:1
• liquid ratio	0.9:1	0.6:1
• capital gearing	10%	85%
• stock turnover	24 days	25 days
• debtors' collection period	35 days	34 days
• creditors' payment period	33 days	48 days

Use the accounting ratios to analyse and assess the profitability, liquidity and asset utilisation, and to present an overall report on the financial standing of the company.

7.6 The following summarised information is available to you:

J D ROWLES

PROFIT AND LOSS ACCOUNT (extracts)

for the year ended 30 April 1995 and 30 April 1996

	1995	1996
	£	£
Sales (all on credit)	120,000	200,000
Cost of sales	80,000	150,000
Gross profit	40,000	50,000
Overheads	10,000	15,000
Net profit	30,000	35,000

BALANCE SHEET (EXTRACTS) AS AT 30 APRIL 1995 AND 30 APRIL 1996

	1995			1996		
	£	£	£	£	£	£
Fixed assets			15,000			12,000
Current assets						
Stock		7,000			18,000	
Debtors		12,000			36,000	
Bank		1,000			–	
		20,000			54,000	
Less Current liabilities						
Creditors	6,000			15,000		
Bank overdraft	–			10,000		
		6,000			25,000	
Working capital			14,000			29,000
NET ASSETS			29,000			41,000
FINANCED BY						
Capital						
Opening capital			22,000			29,000
Add net profit			30,000			35 000
			52,000			64,000
Less drawings			23,000			23,000
Closing capital			29,000			41,000

Notes:

- there were no purchases or disposals of fixed assets during the year
- during 1995 and 1996 selling prices were reduced in order to stimulate sales
- assume that price levels were stable

Use accounting ratios to analyse and assess the profitability, solvency/liquidity and asset utilisation of the business over the two years.

7.7 Select a public limited company of your choice and obtain the latest set of published accounts.

Calculate accounting ratios for the last two years which examine:

- profitability
- solvency/liquidity
- asset utilisation
- investment ratios

Write a report which presents an overall assessment of the progress (or otherwise) made by the plc over the last two years.

Note: This activity could be expanded to include: share price movements over the last six months, consideration of the activities of the company within its industry and expectations for the future.

8 THE MANAGEMENT OF WORKING CAPITAL

this chapter covers ...

- *the need for working capital within a business*
- *the flow of working capital*
- *the importance of controls over the working capital items*
- *the calculation and interpretation, from a set of financial statements, of the working capital cycle*
- *the symptoms of overtrading and the dangers it can bring*

INTRODUCTION

In the previous chapter we used accounting ratios to assess the financial statements of a business. In this chapter we focus on working capital and the solvency and liquidity aspects. We will see that, without sufficient working capital, a business cannot survive for long.

Whilst accounting ratios usually look retrospectively at financial statements and show how the business performed in the past, with working capital we often assess what will happen in the future: will there be sufficient working capital? what happens to working capital if a particular course of action is taken?

WHAT IS WORKING CAPITAL?

As seen in the previous chapter, working capital is the excess of current assets over current liabilities, ie:

Working capital = Current assets – Current liabilities

Working capital can be described as the life-blood of a business because it must keep circulating for the business to survive. For example:

- creditors supply a stock of goods
- stock is sold to debtors (or cash sales, for a retailer)
- debtors make payment (cash or bank)
- payment (cash or bank) made to creditors

Fig 8.1 shows the flow of working capital in a business. From this, note that external funds may flow *into* working capital, for example, new or increased capital/loans, and the sale of fixed assets will increase the cash/bank balance and, consequently, the amount of working capital. An outflow of funds for the purchase of fixed assets, repayment of capital/loans, dividends/drawings, and payment of expenses and tax will reduce the cash/bank balance and, consequently, the amount of working capital.

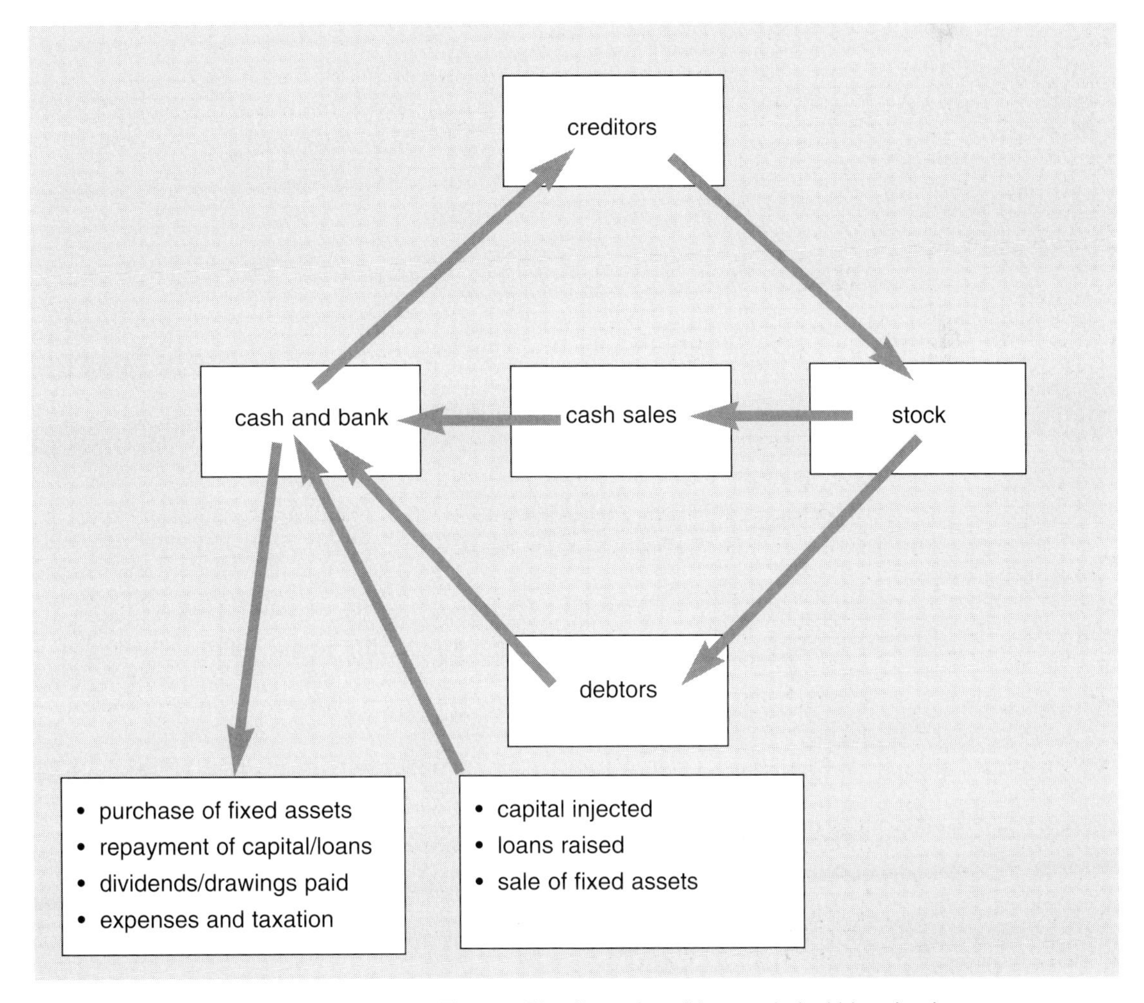

Fig 8.1 The flow of working capital within a business

how much working capital?

The *amount* of working capital required will vary from business to business depending on:

- *the nature of the business* – a shop is likely to need less working capital than an engineering business, because a shop has few, if any, debtors and less requirement for fixed assets
- *the size of the business* – a small corner shop will need less working capital than a large department store

working capital ratios

Because the amount of working capital varies between businesses, we calculate *ratios* which measure the relationship between current assets and current liabilities:

- working capital ratio (or current ratio)
- liquid ratio

Working capital ratio, as we saw in the previous chapter, measures the relationship between

CURRENT ASSETS : CURRENT LIABILITIES

Liquid ratio uses current assets and current liabilities, but omits stock (the least liquid of the current assets). It is calculated as:

(CURRENT ASSETS – STOCK) : CURRENT LIABILITIES

We have seen that the accepted standards are around 2:1 and 1.5:1 for working capital ratio, and around 1:1 for the liquid ratio. However, it is important to apply the ratios to the type of business being analysed: retailers usually work to lower ratios than these.

With both current and liquid ratios (and indeed with any ratio) it is important to note *trends* for the same business, or to make comparisons with similar types of business. Also, the different size of any business used in comparison needs to be considered: for example, a corner shop may have higher ratios than those of a major retailer (one reason being that the larger retailer will be able to negotiate longer credit terms from suppliers).

WORKING CAPITAL: WYVERN PACKAGING LIMITED

situation

Samantha Jones is the managing director of Wyvern Packaging Limited. The company has six employees and makes plastic mailing envelopes and other plastic packing materials which are sold in bulk to office stationery firms and mailing houses. Knowing that you have some knowledge of finance, Samantha asks you to help interpret the company's balance sheet which has just been prepared by the accountant. In particular, she mentions her concern at never seeming to have much cash to take out for her own salary. Samantha tells you that the bank overdraft limit is currently £10,000 and that she is to meet the bank manager next week at a regular six-monthly meeting to review the overdraft facility.

As a first analysis, you decide to look at the working capital position and the figures you extract are:

	last year	this year
	£	£
Stock	5,870	7,210
Debtors	14,290	17,340
Bank overdraft	3,830	9,680
Creditors	7,380	13,320

From the above, calculate working capital, liquid capital, working capital ratio and liquid ratio. Comment on the figures.

solution

	last year	this year
• working capital	£8,950	£1,550
• liquid capital	£3,080	(£5,660)
• working capital ratio	1.80:1	1.07:1
• liquid ratio	0.27:1	0.75:1

Working capital has decreased, and the liquid capital position has also worsened; both working capital and liquid ratios have declined markedly. Urgent action needs to be taken in order to prevent the situation overwhelming the company and forcing it out og business. In particular, if any of the creditors are pressing hard for settlement, it will be difficult to pay them without going over the current overdraft limit.

The following should be discussed with Samantha:

- Stock has increased during the year. Was the increase necessary?
- Debtors, also, have increased. Are any of the accounts overdue? Will there be any bad debts? As most or all of the company's customers are other businesses, it should be possible to factor the debts (ie use the debts to obtain finance from a factoring company). However, if this is done, the bank will wish to reduce, or eliminate, the overdraft facility.

- Creditors have, presumably, increased because of the lack of cash with which to pay them. If they aren't paid, they may well refuse to supply further goods and materials, which would jeopardise the survival of the business.
- The bank overdraft is very close to the current limit of £10,000. It seems unlikely that the bank will be prepared to increase this and, indeed, will be looking for reductions.

Overall, the company's short-term finances are in a bad way, with working capital and liquid ratios well below accepted norms. Samantha will need to exercise considerable control over the working capital items. During the last year all the figures have gone the wrong way, and it is not surprising that there is a shortage of cash to pay her salary. The next few months will prove a critical period for the survival of the company.

CONTROL OF WORKING CAPITAL ITEMS

The major working capital items are:

- stock
- debtors
- cash/bank
- creditors

We will now consider each in turn to see how they can best be managed by a business.

stock

Stock, for manufacturing businesses, consists of up to three categories: raw materials, work-in-progress, and finished goods. For a wholesale or retail business, it will consist only of goods that have been bought in for resale. In the financial statements, stock is usually valued at either cost price or, if lower, selling price (this valuation method forms the sentence usually found in accounts that "stock is valued at the lower of cost and net realisable value").

For most businesses, the problem is in maintaining a balance between the disadvantages of holding too much stock and of holding too little stock.

disadvantages of holding too much stock

- cash has been paid out early to finance extra stock – the money could have been put to better use in the business
- some of the stock may deteriorate or become obsolete, and so have to be written off
- a large stock may need a larger warehouse or premises than is necessary, and stockholding costs will be higher

disadvantages of holding too little stock

- erratic deliveries of stock could mean that items are out of stock
- sales will usually be lost if an item is out of stock because the customer will go elsewhere
- in a manufacturing business, to be out of stock of a small component could bring production to a halt

the middle course

A balance needs to be maintained between holding too much stock, and too little stock. This is usually achieved by:

- setting maximum and minimum stockholding quantities for each item of stock
- establishing appropriate re-order quantities
- the establishment of *just-in-time* (JIT) stock deliveries

Much routine stock control work can be carried out by a computer accounting system using a stock control program.

There are plenty of examples of good stock control: one that is particularly interesting is the *just-in-time (JIT)* method favoured by manufacturing businesses. Here supplies of components are delivered to the production line just as they are needed. For JIT to operate effectively, quality suppliers are needed who can be contracted to deliver goods in accordance with manufacturing schedules. In this way, stock levels are kept very low, with consequent savings in stockholding costs.

Stock turnover, as seen in the previous chapter, measures the number of days' stock held on average. It is calculated as follows:

$$\text{Stock turnover (in days)} = \frac{\text{Average stock}}{\text{Cost of sales}} \times 365$$

Comparisons of stock turnover need to be made for a business over a number of accounting periods, and also with similar businesses. Clearly different types of businesses will have different stock turnover figures. The more efficient business will be reducing the number of days' stock held. Stock control is one of those applications where the 'famous' 80:20 rule invariably applies: 80% of customers buy from 20% of the stock lines.

debtors

The control of debtors is the vital administrative task of ensuring that:

- credit references are obtained for all new customers
- credit limits are established for each debtor

- a credit agreement – setting out the terms of payment – is signed by each debtor
- invoices, and month-end statements are processed promptly
- action is taken swiftly to chase overdue debts and, where necessary, legal action is pursued
- goods are not sold to debtors who have reached their credit limit, or who are unlikely to pay up

A measure of the efficiency of debtor collection is to calculate the time it takes the debtors to pay.

$$\textit{Debtors' collection period (in days)} = \frac{\textit{Debtors}}{\textit{Credit sales}} \times 365 \textit{ days}$$

The debtor collection time can be compared with that for the previous year, or for a similar business.

One way to encourage debtors to pay faster is to offer a cash discount for quick settlement, and a business' terms of sale might be:

2.5% cash discount for settlement within seven days; normal terms thirty days.

Assuming that such terms encourage debtors to pay in seven days, instead of thirty days, this means that, on a debt of £100, it is costing £2.50 to have the use of £97.50 for twenty three. This is a very high rate of interest – an APR (annual percentage rate) of around 45%! It follows that a firm's cash discount policy needs to be looked at carefully – it may be costing more than it is worth. Also, many debtors are likely to deduct the 2.5% cash discount and continue to settle at their usual time!

To help with credit control, many firms produce an *aged schedule of debtors* (fig. 8.2) at the end of each month. This analyses individual debtor balances

COMPUTER SHOP LTD — Sales Ledger - Account Balances (Aged) — Date: 010397

A/C	Account Name		Turnover	Credit Limit	Balance	Current	30 Days	60 Days	Older
201	Able, Baker & Clark		370.00	1000.00	164.50	164.50	0.00	0.00	0.00
202	Hitech Trading Co		320.00	750.00	376.00	376.00	0.00	0.00	0.00
204	Sixth Form College	*	1730.00	1000.00	1632.75	799.00	833.75	0.00	0.00
205	Teleservice	*	2025.00	1500.00	1926.88	1880.00	46.88	0.00	0.00
208	Stone, Wall Ltd		425.00	750.00	499.38	499.38	0.00	0.00	0.00
	Totals :		4870.00	5000.00	4599.51	3718.88	880.63	0.00	0.00

Fig 8.2 Aged debtors' schedule
(an asterisk indicates debtors whose balances are above the credit limit)

into the time that the amount has been owing. Thus it shows the long outstanding debts that are, potentially, bad debts, against whom early action is necessary. An aged schedule is easily produced using a computer accounting system.

debt factoring

Factoring provides short-term finance by using the amounts owed by debtors: the factoring company effectively buys the debts, so releasing the valuable financial resource tied up in debtors.

Factoring companies will:

- provide finance by making advance payments in respect of money owing to the business by those debtors considered by the factoring company to be creditworthy
- manage the debtors of a business (ie handle the book-keeping records of sales made, and collect amounts due)
- insure against non-payment of debts by approved debtors

Charges for factoring comprise:

- a commission fee of between 1%-3% of sales turnover
- interest on finance provided at rates similar to a bank overdraft

The amount financed will be up to 85% of the invoice amount, with the balance (less commission fee and interest) being paid at an agreed future date – often in three months' time.

Factoring is only suitable where a business sells to other businesses on a regular basis – it cannot be used for retailers selling on credit terms to the general public. Normally, factoring is only available to businesses of a reasonable size: the factoring company will look for certain minimum turnover amounts.

When a company has a bank overdraft and starts to use a factoring company for finance, the bank will normally expect to reduce the overdraft by the amount factored.

cash/bank

Estimates of future inflows and outflows of cash can be made, as we shall see in Chapter 16, by means of a cash budget. In this way, overdrafts can be anticipated and arranged in advance, while surplus cash can be invested.

As with any budget, it is important to ensure that things are going according to plan and to investigate major variances – perhaps debtors are not paying as quickly as expected, or new fixed assets have had to be purchased earlier than originally thought.

creditors

Creditors are the amounts owed to suppliers, and we can measure the time it takes to pay creditors.

$$\text{Creditors' payment period (in days)} = \frac{\text{Trade creditors}}{\text{Credit purchases}} \times 365 \text{ days}$$

Certainly creditors can be a useful source of short-term finance, delaying payment for too long may cause problems, eg suppliers may refuse to deliver until the current amount due has been paid. There are moves to introduce a law to prevent large companies from deliberately delaying payment to suppliers (together with the possibility of allowing suppliers to charge interest on overdue debts).

An aged creditors' schedule is used by many businesses. This analyses individual creditors' balances into the time that the amount has been owing; thus the business can decide which creditors should be paid. The overall objectives of creditor management are to ensure that:

- creditors are paid within the timescales of company policy
- where cash discounts are offered, payment is made within the period covered by the cash discount *where it is financially attractive to do so*
- continuity of supplies to the business is not jeopardised by late payment to creditors

link between debtor and creditor days

As a general rule, there should be a clear link between debtor and creditor days: it would be most unusual to see a manufacturing business with a debtors' collection period of three days and a creditors' payment period of fifty days, or vice-versa. For most businesses, the time periods will be similar: however, in the absence of special circumstances, good working capital management will ensure that debtor days are less than creditor days, ie money is collected before it is paid out.

CASE STUDY

WORKING CAPITAL MANAGEMENT: JAMES BROWN

situation

James Brown operates a wholesale health-food business. He buys in bulk from manufacturers and producers, packages the goods, and then sells to health-food shops in smaller quantities.

James has prepared estimates for the next twelve months, and asks you to help him with certain aspects of these. He provides you with the following budgeted information:

- sales for the year expected to be £240,000
- purchases for the year expected to be £180,000
- net profit for the year expected to be £20,000

Note: both sales and purchases take place at an even rate throughout the year.

A summary of his forecast balance sheet at the end of the year is:

James Brown
Forecast Balance Sheet as at 31 December 19..

	£	£	£
Fixed assets			30,000
Current assets			
Stock		20,000	
Debtors		20,000	
		40,000	
Less Current liabilities			
Creditors	15,000		
Bank overdraft	5,000		
		20,000	
Working capital			20,000
NET ASSETS			50,000
FINANCED BY			
Capital			45,000
Add net profit			20,000
			65,000
Less drawings			15,000
Closing capital			50,000

First, James asks you to calculate and comment on:

- working capital ratio
- liquid ratio
- debtors' collection period
- creditors' payment period

He then asks you what the effect of implementing certain proposals will be:

- on his forecast net profit
- on his bank balance/overdraft
- on the working capital ratio
- on the liquid ratio

These proposals, which are to be considered separately, are:

(a) James wishes to increase depreciation by an extra £5,000 this year.

(b) A number of his customers have asked if they can have two months in which to pay, instead of the current terms.

(c) He has wondered if he could take one-and-a-half months' credit from his suppliers.

(d) He would like to buy new fixed assets at a cost of £30,000 (no depreciation on these fixed assets will be charged in the year of purchase).

solution

- working capital ratio 2:1
- liquid ratio 1:1

Both of these ratios are 'about right'.

- debtor collection time: 1 month or 30 days
- creditor payment time: 1 month or 30 days

Very good figures for any business.

proposal	net profit	bank/ (overdraft)	working capital ratio	liquid ratio
(a)	£15,000	(£5,000)*	2:1*	1:1*
(b)	£20,000*	(£25,000)	1.5:1	1:1*
(c)	£20,000*	£2,500	1.9:1	1:1*
(d)	£20,000*	(£35,000)	0.8:1	0.4:1

* indicates figures unchanged from original forecasts

points to note

Proposal (a): Net profit is reduced by £5,000 because of extra depreciation. The bank overdraft remains unchanged, because depreciation is a non-cash expense. Both working capital and liquid ratios are unchanged because depreciation forms no part of working capital.

Proposal (b): Net profit is unchanged because total sales are not affected, only the timing of the receipt of those sales. The bank balance is an extra £20,000 overdrawn because an additional £20,000 of debtors has to be financed.
The working capital ratio is £60,000 (£20,000 + £40,000) ÷ £40,000 (£15,000 + £25,000) = 1.5:1.
The liquid ratio is £40,000 ÷ £40,000 = 1:1.

Proposal (c): Net profit is unchanged because only the timing of the payment for the purchases is altered, not the total. Creditors now become £22,500 and the bank balance benefits from the extra credit received to become £2,500.
The working capital ratio is £42,500 (£20,000 + £20,000 + £2,500 bank) ÷ £22,500 (creditors) = 1.9:1.
The liquid ratio is £22,500 ÷ £22,000 = 1:1.

Proposal (d): Net profit is unaffected. The bank overdraft is £35,000 after purchase of the new fixed assets. Both working capital and liquid capital are reduced by £30,000. Working capital ratio is £40,000 (£20,000 + £20,000) ÷ £50,000 (£15,000 + £35,000) = 0.8:1.

The liquid ratio is £20,000 ÷ £50,000 = 0.4:1.

summary

Changes in the pattern of trading, for example allowing longer credit terms to debtors, or taking longer to pay creditors, have an effect on the bank balance and the working capital ratio. Transactions such as the purchase of fixed assets reduce the working capital of a business (unless the fixed assets are financed by long-term loans or an increase in capital) and have a significant effect on working capital and liquid ratios. Changes in depreciation affect net profit but, because they are non-cash, do not alter the bank balance or working capital and liquid ratios.

The general conclusion is that the working capital of a business is not a fixed amount but changes according to the nature of business transactions.

WORKING CAPITAL CYCLE

A further use of ratios covering the working capital items, ie the turnover of stock, debtors and creditors, is to calculate the *working capital cycle* (sometimes known as the cash operating cycle). This shows the period of time between the payment for goods received into stock and the collection of cash from customers in respect of their sale. The shorter the length of time between the initial outlay and the ultimate collection of cash, the lower the amount of working capital to be financed by the business.

The length of the working capital cycle is calculated in three stages, by calculating:

1. the time that goods are in stock
2. the time that debtors take to pay
3. deduct from 1 + 2 the period of credit received from suppliers

The working capital cycle calculations can take the following format (with example figures):

Working capital cycle	**Days**
Time period that goods are in stock	
Stock turnover: (average stock ÷ cost of sales) x 365	37
Time period that debtors take to pay	
Debtors' collection period: (debtors ÷ sales) x 365	40
	77
Less: Period of credit received from suppliers	
Creditors' payment period: (creditors ÷ purchases) x 365	30
WORKING CAPITAL CYCLE	47

Like all accounting ratios, a comparison needs to be made – either with the figure for the previous year, or with a similar firm. The working capital cycle is likely to show either an overall position that is better, ie the cycle has been reduced, or one that is worse, where the total time has been increased. There are three ways in which the cycle can be reduced:

- reducing stocks (which will lower the number of days that stock is held)
- speeding up the rate of debtor collection (ie less time is allowed to debtors to pay)
- slowing down the rate of creditor payment (ie taking longer to pay the creditors)

Any one of these actions will achieve the result of reducing the working capital cycle. However, it may not always be possible to put them into practice, or they may have unexpected consequences for a particular business. For example:

- reducing stocks might mean that a poorer service is offered to customers, who may take their business elsewhere
- giving debtors less time to pay may cause customers to seek alternative suppliers who are offering better terms
- taking extra credit from suppliers may be difficult, and they might decline to supply goods unless immediate payment is forthcoming

OVERTRADING – A DANGER

We have just looked at the working capital cycle and seen how this can be timed, and steps taken to reduce its timing. Profits are made when sales are made to debtors (or in cash), so the faster the cycle can be made to operate, the faster profits will accumulate.

But a business that has too little working capital is likely to get into financial difficulties. The working capital may become depleted, perhaps because of losses, or excessive dividends/drawings. A rapidly expanding business which experiences a rising demand for its products or services may have to buy larger premises, or buy new fixed assets in order to satisfy the demand. Unless the business has adequate reserves of working capital, it may find that little is left after the additional fixed assets have been bought. The only recourse may be heavy borrowing with resultant interest charges, or reliance on extended trade credit in order to purchase stocks of goods and supplies of services. If creditors start to demand repayment, the only way to repay the debts may be to sell some of the fixed assets.

This is a downward spiral towards bankruptcy or liquidation, as no business can continue to operate without a full complement of fixed assets. A business trying to manage with too little working capital is said to be *overtrading*.

Overtrading is often evidenced by the following:

- a rapid increase in sales
- a considerably increased bank overdraft
- a rapid increase in creditors

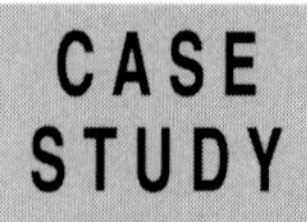

DANGERS OF OVERTRADING

situation

Joyce Banner has recently opened a fashion shop in rented premises in the centre of a university town. After twelve months of trading, and sales of £50,000, she has made satisfactory profits. Her balance sheet appears as:

Joyce Banner
Balance Sheet as at 30 June 1996

	£	£
Fixed assets		10,000
Current assets		
Stock	24,000	
Debtors	6,000	
Bank	2,000	
	32,000	
Less Current liabilities		
Creditors	8,000	
Working capital		24,000
NET ASSETS		34,000
FINANCED BY		
Capital		30,000
Add net profit		15,000
		45,000
Less drawings		11,000
Closing capital		34,000

From the above balance sheet, working capital is £24,000, with the ratio at 4:1. The liquid ratio is 1:1.

Joyce is keen to expand the business and wishes to open a new shop in the university area of town. She has already seen suitable premises to rent and has estimated the cost of fitting them out at £20,000. To stock the new shop she will need to buy stock at a cost of £24,000: half of this will have to be paid for in cash, the other half can be bought on one month's credit.

To help her make a final decision she asks you to draft her balance sheet as it will appear immediately after these transactions have taken place.

DANGERS OF OVERTRADING

solution

Joyce Banner
Balance Sheet

	£	£	£
Fixed assets £10,000 + £20,000			30,000
Current assets			
Stock		48,000	
Debtors		6,000	
		54,000	
Less Current liabilities			
Creditors £8,000 + £12,000	20,000		
Bank £2,000 - £20,000 - £12,000	30,000		
		50,000	
Working capital			4,000
NET ASSETS			34,000
FINANCED BY			
Capital			34,000

Working capital is now only £4,000, with a ratio of 1.1:1 and a liquid ratio of just 0.1:1. This is a very different position from that illustrated before the expansion. Joyce and her business will face a number of problems:

- considerable support will be required from the bank to assist with the venture
- creditors will soon be pressing for payment and it is unlikely that the bank will wish to see a further increase in the overdraft
- the working capital that has been used to purchase fixed assets, £20,000, will only be replaced gradually as profits are made and, in addition, some of this profit must be used to pay interest on the bank overdraft
- if stock is not turned over quickly there will be no money with which to pay the creditors (there is now little working capital to fall back on) and an unpaid creditor could force the business into insolvency

Expansion on such a scale would be better financed by an increase in permanent capital: perhaps Joyce could go into partnership. Of course it does not follow that every business will come to an end if it tries to expand: if the fall in working capital is replaced quickly by extra profits coming in from increased trade, then all will be well. Steady expansion of a business is not usually a hazard; the danger comes when the expansion is too rapid and the working capital is inadequate.

CHAPTER SUMMARY

- Working capital can be described as the life-blood of a business.
- A working capital ratio of about 2:1 is often considered to be ideal, although many businesses, particularly those in the retail sector, can operate on lower ratios, eg 1.5:1, or even less.
- A liquid ratio of 1:1 is the ideal.
- Both the working capital and liquid ratios can be too high, indicating too many current assets or too few current liabilities.
- A change in each of the main working capital components of stock, debtors and creditors will have a direct effect on the bank balance.
- The turnover figures for stock, debtors' collection period, and creditors' payment period are all measures of the efficiency of the working capital management of a business: they can be used to time the working capital cycle.
- A business that tries to expand too fast with too little working capital is said to be *overtrading*.

KEY TERMS

working capital	current assets minus current liabilities
liquid capital	(current assets – stock) minus current liabilities
stock turnover	a measure of the number of days' stock held on average
debtors' turnover	a measure of the efficiency of debtor collection; expresses the number of days that debtors take to pay on average
creditors' turnover	a measure of the time period it takes to pay creditors
aged debtors' or creditors' schedule	an analysis of the individual debtor or creditor balances into the time period that the amounts are outstanding
working capital cycle	time period between paying creditors for goods and services, and the collection of cash from debtors; also known as the *cash operating cycle*
overtrading	a symptom of a business that is expanding rapidly but with too little working capital

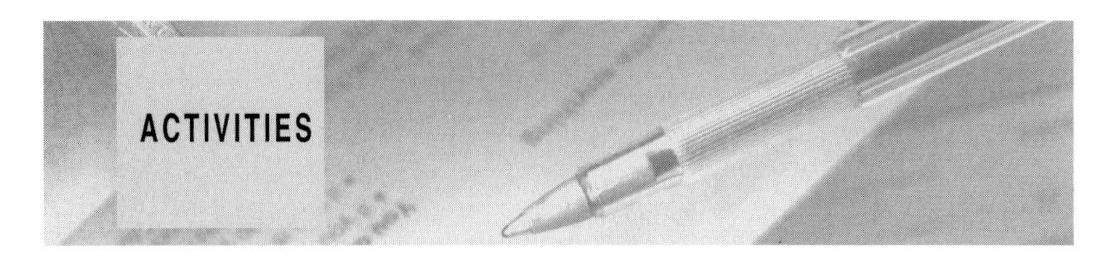

8.1 At 31 December 1996, George Harvey's business, a newsagents shop, had the following assets:

	£
Premises	71,000
Fixtures and fittings	7,000
Stock	13,700
Debtors	3,375
Cash	790
Capital and liabilities were:	
Capital account	24,500
Loan: mortgage on premises	50,900
Creditors	17,300
Bank overdraft	3,160

(a) State the amount of his current assets, current liabilities, working capital and liquid capital

(b) Calculate the working capital ratio and liquid ratio

(c) During the first week of 1997, he sells 10% of his stock for £2,200, receiving cheques for £1,760 and cash of £440 in payment; he also receives cheques totalling £1,450 from his debtors. All cheques are banked as soon as they are received. He pays creditors of £4,100 by cheque.

Calculate the amount of his working capital and liquid capital at the end of the week, together with the ratios. Discuss any changes that have taken place.

8.2 The following statement shows the working capital of OS Limited, a wholesaler of office stationery and other supplies:

	£
Stock	138,000
Debtors	110,000
Bank	8,000
	256,000
Less Creditors	80,000
	176,000

The directors are considering the following separate proposals:

(a) buying a further £20,000 of stock on credit

(b) selling goods in stock which had cost £6,000, for £10,000 on credit

(c) issuing a further 40,000 shares at £1.50 each

(d) paying a dividend of £16,000

(e) selling fixed assets for £10,000

- Alter the working capital statement for each proposal (treat each proposal separately)
- Calculate for each proposal:
  (a) working capital ratio
  (b) liquid ratio
- Discuss your findings

8.3

- Obtain the financial statements of two businesses – eg two plcs in the same or different type of business.
- Calculate, and comment upon, the working capital and liquid ratios of each business.
- Calculate the number of days' stock turnover, debtors' collection and creditors' payment for each business. Comment on the policies adopted by the two businesses – are they appropriate for the type of business?
- Calculate, and comment upon, the working capital cycle for each business – is it appropriate for the type of business?
- Comment on any other aspects of working capital management that you have observed from the financial statements.

8.4 The following figures have been extracted from the accounts of Builders Merchants Limited:

	1995	1996
	£	£
Sales	685,400	722,300
Purchases	372,700	450,500
Cost of sales	360,750	342,400
Average debtors	45,500	70,350
Average creditors	37,250	63,050
Average stock	62,750	75,400

All purchases and sales are made on credit, and transactions occur at an even rate throughout the year.

(a) For each year, calculate stock turnover in days, debtors' collection period in days, creditors' payment period in days (take each of your calculations to the nearest day)

(b) Calculate the working capital cycle for each year

(c) Discuss your findings and suggest possible ways in which the situation might be improved

8.5 You are a director of Mercia Limited, a manufacturer of office and commercial furniture, with a factory in the West Midlands.

Just over a year ago, in Autumn 1996, a new sales director was appointed. During the last twelve months, the sales director has followed a policy of reducing selling prices and offering extended credit terms to customers in order to stimulate sales and increase profit. This required a major investment in new machinery in early 1997 in order to meet the growing demand that the change in sales policy brought about.

The financial statements for the year to 31 December 1997 are now available and are shown below and on the next page, together with the statements for 1996 (ignore taxation aspects).

Mercia Limited

Profit and loss accounts for the year to 31 December

	1996	1997
	£000s	£000s
Sales (all on credit)	1,800	5,840
Less cost of sales	720	3,431
Gross profit	1,080	2,409
Less overheads:		
Selling expenses	300	640
Depreciation	116	435
Bad debts	36	290
Interest	24	414
Net profit for year	604	630
Retained profit brought forward	654	1,258
Retained profit carried forward	1,258	1,888

Mercia Limited: Balance sheets as at 31 December

	1996		1997	
	£000s	£000s	£000s	£000s
Fixed assets				
Factory premises		900		882
Machinery		980		3,582
		1,880		4,464
Current assets				
Stocks	60		486	
Debtors	166		1,166	
Bank	24		–	
	250		1,652	
Less Current liabilities				
Creditors	72		350	
Bank	–		22	
	72		372	
Working capital		178		1,280
		2,058		5,744
Less Long-term liabilities				
Loans		200		3,200
NET ASSETS		1,858		2,544
FINANCED BY				
Share capital (£1 ordinary shares)		600		656
Reserves		1,258		1,888
SHAREHOLDERS' FUNDS		1,858		2,544

(a) There is to be a directors' meeting tomorrow to discuss the financial performance of the company in 1997. You are to outline the financial points you will wish to discuss.

(b) The finance director is under pressure from the bank to avoid the necessity for short-term overdrafts. Various proposals have been suggested to the finance department, including to:

- reduce the debtors' collection period to 45 days
- make a 2 for 1 bonus issue of shares
- reduce stockholding to 40 days
- have a rights issue of shares, at a price of £1.50 each, on the basis of one new share for every two held

You are to evaluate these proposals, and to show how much cash will be generated by each.

8.6 Just over a year ago Jeff Judge bought a small bookshop called Spa Books in Walvern, a spa town in the 'shire' counties. The previous owner of the bookshop had been ill for some time and business had remained at a fairly low level.

During the first year of business Jeff has been 'learning the ropes' and getting to know the area. His balance sheet at the end of the first year is as follows:

Balance Sheet as at 30 June 1997

	£	£
Fixed assets		
Premises at cost		100,000
Fixtures and fittings	4,000	
Less depreciation to date	800	
		3,200
		103,200
Current assets		
Stock	7,000	
Debtors	1,100	
Bank	1,200	
	9,300	
Less Current liabilities		
Creditors	3,300	
Working capital		6,000
		109,200
Less Long-term liabilities		
Mortgage loan		90,000
NET ASSETS		19,200
FINANCED BY		
Capital		18,000
Add net profit		10,800
		28,800
Less drawings		9,600
Closing Capital		19,200

Jeff is now actively trying to build up the business. Walvern has a number of private schools and he has obtained contracts to supply a number of them with books and stationery. In order to persuade these schools to leave their present supplier, Jeff has offered two months' credit on all purchases they make from him.

Jeff asks if you will look at his plan to increase sales in this way and to point out any 'snags' (if any). As he says,

"I am going to make good profits on this deal because I always mark up my buying prices by 50%, and the schools haven't asked for any discount; I just can't lose."

His plan is as follows:

July	He will buy the books and stationery on one month's credit at a cost of £20,000
August	He will deliver the goods, with invoices to the schools
September	He will pay his creditors
October	Payment will be received from the schools

You are to

- Prepare working capital summaries at the end of July, August, September and October (for the purpose of this, ignore transactions from his 'normal' trading).
- Calculate appropriate working capital and liquid capital ratios at the end of July, August, September and October.
- Advise him of any practical points he should do before entering into this transaction; also, point out any dangers in the transaction itself.

Section 4

costing

In this section we turn our attention to management accounting. We see how costing systems and methods assist with the financial decision making, planning and control of the business.

Customer

Product or Service

sales

minus

costs

equals

profit

material

labour

expenses

Inputs

9 INTRODUCTION TO COST AND COSTING SYSTEMS

this chapter covers ...

- *the role of costing in assessing performance and in decision making*
- *cost units and cost centres*
- *the categories into which costs can be classified*
- *the difference between direct and indirect costs*
- *the main costing systems and their purposes*

INTRODUCTION

Management accounting is concerned with providing the management of a business with financial recommendations, based on costing information, in order to enable day-to-day decisions and longer-term plans to be made. This is different from much of what we have studied so far, which has been concerned with financial transactions and statements that have *already taken place.* Management accounting uses information from past transactions as an aid to financial decision making, planning and control *for the future.*

The management of a business needs information from which to work. It needs to know accurate costs of individual products or services, together with the total costs of running the business: such information is found from the costing records. The use of costing information to make decisions is of great importance in enabling businesses to maximise profits and public sector organisations to provide value for money services. To this end, many businesses have specialist costing sections: the information provided by the costing system will enable managers to assess performance and make decisions which will affect what the business does in the future, such as:

- to manufacture more of one product than another
- to provide one service in preference to another
- to reduce costs
- to review selling prices
- to manufacture a new product, or provide a new service
- to close one department or division of the business

In later chapters we shall see how cost accounting is used in decision making and in the budgeting process; before this, though, we need to look at certain techniques of cost accounting, including the *classification of costs* and *costing systems.* Costing and its use in decision making and the budgeting process applies equally to manufacturing businesses and those which provide a service:

- "at what point do we break-even?" is applicable to manufacturing a product as well as to ticket sales at a swimming pool
- "shall we close down X?" is applicable to a manufacturer looking at production lines as well as to a large store considering the financial viability of different departments

S & T MANUFACTURING COMPANY

This Case Study shows how a basic understanding of cost accounting enables the management of a business to have better information about its activities.

situation

The following information is given for S & T Manufacturing Company, a two-product (S and T) company, for the year 1996:

			£	£
Sales:	S			100,000
	T			200,000
				300,000
Less:	Cost of materials	S	50,000	
		T	95,000	
	Labour costs	S	40,000	
		T	50,000	
	*Overheads	S	20,000	
		T	30,000	
				285,000
Profit				15,000

* Overheads include factory rent, depreciation of machinery, and other costs.

How would you present this information in a way which will be of more use to the management of the business? What conclusions do you draw for this business?

solution

The information is best presented in a way which analyses the profit of each product of S&T Manufacturing Company:

	S	T	Total
	£	£	£
Cost of materials	50,000	95,000	145,000
Labour costs	40,000	50,000	90,000
Overheads	20,000	30,000	50,000
Cost of sales	110,000	175,000	285,000
Sales	100,000	200,000	300,000
Less Cost of sales	110,000	175,000	285,000
Profit/(Loss)	(10,000)	25,000	15,000

On the basis of this information, product S should be discontinued because it is making a loss. However, this may be a simplistic solution, and other factors will have to be considered, eg sales of product T may be linked to sales of S; the overheads of T are likely to increase if S is discontinued.

This Case Study brings out two important functions of costing:

- to find out the costs (in this case of each product)
- to give responsibility to someone for those costs (here for the manager of product S to investigate the reasons for the loss of £10,000)

COST UNITS AND COST CENTRES

Before we begin our study of costing we need to understand the terms: cost units and cost centres.

Cost units are units of output to which costs can be charged.

A cost unit can be

- *either* a unit of production from a factory such as a car, a television, an item of furniture
- *or* a unit of service, such as a passenger-mile on a bus, a transaction on a bank statement, an attendance at a swimming pool, a call unit on a telephone

Care should be taken in choosing the appropriate cost unit. Within a business – particularly in the service industry – there may well be several cost units that can be used. For example, in an hotel the cost units in the restaurant will be meals; for the rooms, the cost units will be guest nights.

Cost centres are sections of a business to which costs can be charged

A cost centre in a manufacturing business, for example, is a department of a factory, a particular stage in the production process, or even a whole factory. In a college, examples of cost centres are the teaching departments, or particular sections of departments such as the school or college administrative office. In a hospital, examples of cost centres are the hospital wards, operating theatres, specialist sections such as the X-ray department, pathology department.

The structure of the cost centres will vary according to the information needs of different levels of management. For example, in a large company, the chief executive, the factory manager, and the supervisor each have different information needs from the cost centres: the supervisor requires detailed information, the manager needs a less-detailed report, while the chief executive requires an overall summary.

CLASSIFICATION OF COSTS

Within any business, whether it manufactures a product or provides a service, there are certain costs involved at various stages to produce the units of output. The diagram which follows (fig 9.1) shows the costs of a manufacturing business which are incurred by the three main sections of the business, ie the factory, the warehouse, the office.

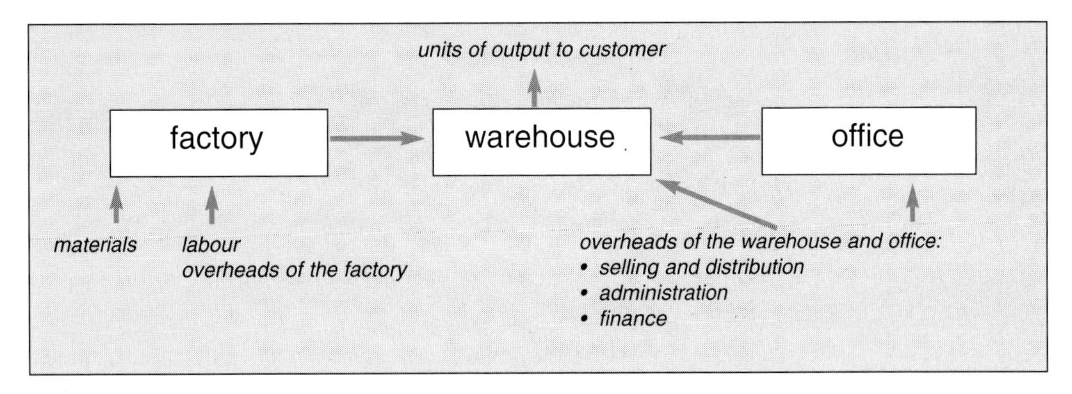

Fig 9.1 Costs incurred in a manufacturing business

Note that although the above diagram shows the costs of a manufacturing business, it can be adapted easily to fit non-manufacturing organisations, such as a shop, a hospital, a school or college, a church, a club. While the units of output of these organisations differ from those of a manufacturer, nevertheless they still incur costs at various stages of the 'production' process.

Having identified costs for each main section of a business, we can now *classify the costs*. This can be done in three ways:

- by element
- by function
- by nature

classification of costs by element

The diagram in fig 9.1 shows that there are three elements of cost:

- materials, ie the cost of goods used
- labour, ie the cost of employees' wages and salaries
- expenses, ie other costs, mainly the overheads

Each of the cost elements can be categorised between:

- direct costs – those costs that can be identified directly with each unit of output
- indirect costs – all other costs, ie those that cannot be identified directly with each unit of output

Thus the cost elements for a manufacturing business can be shown as:

MATERIALS	**direct**	materials from which the finished product is made
	indirect	other materials used in the factory, eg grease for machines, cleaning materials, etc

LABOUR	**direct**	wages paid to those who work the machinery on the production line or who are involved in assembly of the product
	indirect	wages and salaries paid to those who are not directly involved in production, eg supervisors, maintenance staff, etc

EXPENSES	**direct**	expenses which can be attributed to units of production, eg royalties payable to the designer of a product, special items bought in for a particular product
	indirect	other expenses, such as rent, rates, telephone, lighting, heating, which cannot be attributed directly to production

Note that the *indirect* costs of materials, labour and expenses form the *overheads* of the business:

indirect materials + *indirect labour* + *indirect expenses* = *overheads*

classification of costs by function

Each section of a business, eg factory, warehouse, office, retail outlet, performs a *function*. Thus, for example, the office provides an administrative function. In carrying out these functions, costs are incurred and can be classified by function. For a manufacturing business the main functions are:

- factory, or production
- selling and distribution
- administration
- finance

Other functions can be added to suit the needs of a particular business. For example, a company might spend large sums of money in researching and developing new products – the costs incurred by this function will be classified under the research and development heading.

Non-manufacturing organisations – such as a hospital or a college – will use some of the same functions listed above, and will add other, specialist, functions. Both direct and indirect costs can be classified by function. It is important to note that, when costs are classified by function, they are the same costs used in classifying by element, but are presented in a different way.

classification of costs by nature

It is important in cost accounting to appreciate the nature of costs – in particular to appreciate that not all costs increase or decrease directly in line with increases or decreases in output. By nature, costs are:

- fixed, or
- variable, or
- semi-variable

Fig 9.2 shows the differences between these.

We shall see in Chapter 11 "Cost behaviour and break-even analysis" how a knowledge of the nature of costs helps with decision making.

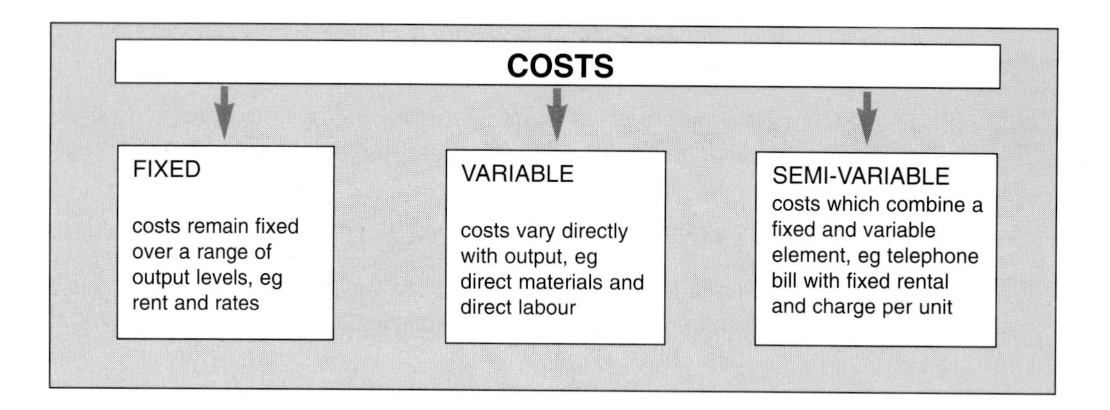

Fig 9.2 Classifying costs by nature

reasons for classifying costs

The question might be asked, "Why classify costs in three ways?" The answer is that we can see the same business from three different viewpoints – this will help management to run the business better:

- ***by element***

  looking for the high cost elements in order to make savings, eg labour costs might be identified as being too high

- ***by function***

  looking at the different departments to see which are the high-spending departments – perhaps savings can be made

- ***by nature***

  identifying the costs as being fixed, variable, or semi-variable; this will help with decision making – the business might be able to alter the balance between fixed and variable costs in order to increase profits

CALCULATING THE COST OF GOODS AND SERVICES

Using the principles of costing will help the owner of a business to calculate the cost of a product – whether goods or services. Only when the cost of producing each unit of output is known, can a business make decisions about the selling price.

The steps towards calculating the cost of goods and services are:

- ***identify the unit of output***

  The cost units for a particular business must be identified. As we have seen earlier, these are the units of output to which costs can be charged.

Only by recovering costs through the sale of output can a business make a profit.

- ***calculate the number of units of output for a particular time period***

  Once the unit of output is identified, the business is then able to calculate how many units can be produced or provided in a given time period, such as a day, week, month, quarter or year. For example, a garage will work out how many hours of mechanics' time are available, or a car manufacturer will calculate how many cars it can produce in a year.

- ***calculate the direct costs for a particular time period***

  Having established the number of units of output for a particular time period, the next task is to calculate the direct costs for that time period. As we have seen earlier in this chapter, the direct costs comprise:

direct materials	identifiable with the product
direct labour	the wages paid to those who make the product
direct expenses	attributable to the product

  The amounts of the three direct costs are added together to give the total direct costs of the output for the time period:

  direct materials + *direct labour* + *direct expenses*

- ***calculate the indirect costs for a particular time period***

  The indirect costs, or overheads, of the product or service must be calculated for the particular time period. Indirect costs comprise:

indirect materials	materials used that are not attributed directly to production
indirect labour	wages and salaries paid to those who are not directly involved in production
indirect expenses	expenses of the business not attributed directly to production

  Once the indirect costs have been calculated, we must then ensure that their total cost is charged to the cost of the units of output for a particular time period. Only by including indirect costs in the total cost of the output can a business recover their cost from the sales made.

  The amounts of the indirect costs are added together to give the total indirect costs (overheads) for the time period.

- ***calculate the total cost of a unit of output***

  Once the direct and indirect costs for a time period are known, the total cost of a unit of output can be calculated, as follows:

  $$\frac{\textit{direct costs + indirect costs}}{\textit{units of output}} = \textit{total costs of a unit}$$

  The total cost is also referred to as the *absorption cost* – because it absorbs, or includes, both the direct costs and the indirect costs. Once total cost is known, the business can use the information to help it make pricing and other decisions – these topics are covered fully later in the book.

- ***calculate the cost – a summary***

  The process of calculating the cost of output is illustrated in fig 9.3 below.

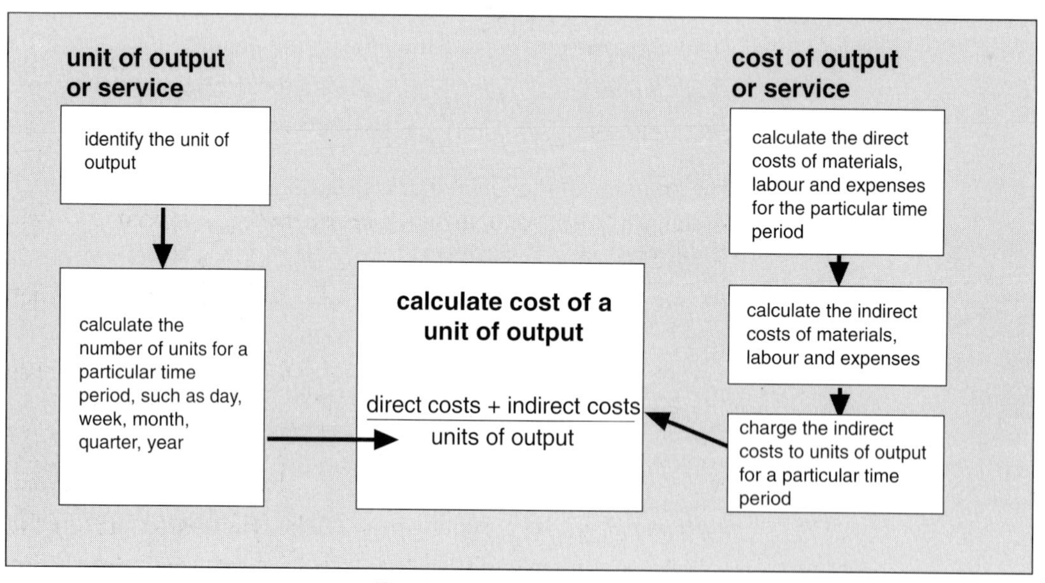

Fig 9.3 Calculating the cost of a unit of output

TOTAL COST STATEMENT

The total cost statement brings together all the costs involved in producing the output of a business. It can be prepared on the basis of:

- a single cost unit, eg the cost of making one car in a car factory
- a batch, eg the cost of making 1,000 'limited edition' cars

- the whole factory, eg the cost of all the car factory's output for a given time period

The total cost statement is prepared as follows:

			£
	Direct materials		x
add	Direct labour		x
add	Direct expenses		x
equals	PRIME COST		x
add	Factory overheads		x
equals	PRODUCTION COST		x
add	Selling and distribution costs	office overheads	x
add	Administration costs	office overheads	x
add	Finance costs	office overheads	x
equals	TOTAL COST		x

Note that:

- *prime cost* is the direct cost of manufacturing products, before the addition of factory overheads
- *production cost* is the factory cost of manufacturing the products, ie prime cost plus factory overheads
- *total cost* is production cost plus office overheads; note that total cost plus profit of the business equals the selling price of the products

The cost structure above is especially appropriate for a manufacturing business; indeed a separate *manufacturing account* – which shows costs through to production cost - is prepared prior to the profit and loss account. Production cost is used as the basis for valuing stocks of finished goods.

By taking total cost away from sales revenue we can create a profit statement. This shows the profitability of the business after all costs have been taken into account. The profit statement is:

		£
	Sales	x
less	Total cost	x
equals	PROFIT	x

COSTING SYSTEMS

The main costing systems used by the management accountant include:

- absorption costing
- marginal costing
- activity based costing
- standard costing

Fig 9.4 below, shows the purpose of each of these costing systems. The use of each costing system is dependent on the information needs of the business:

- do we require a figure for profit? (use absorption costing)
- why are the overheads so high for the production line making 'Product X'? (use activity based costing)
- can we afford to sell 1,000 units each month to Megastores Limited at a discount of 20 per cent? (use marginal costing)
- how much will it cost us to make 'Product Y' next month? (use standard costing)

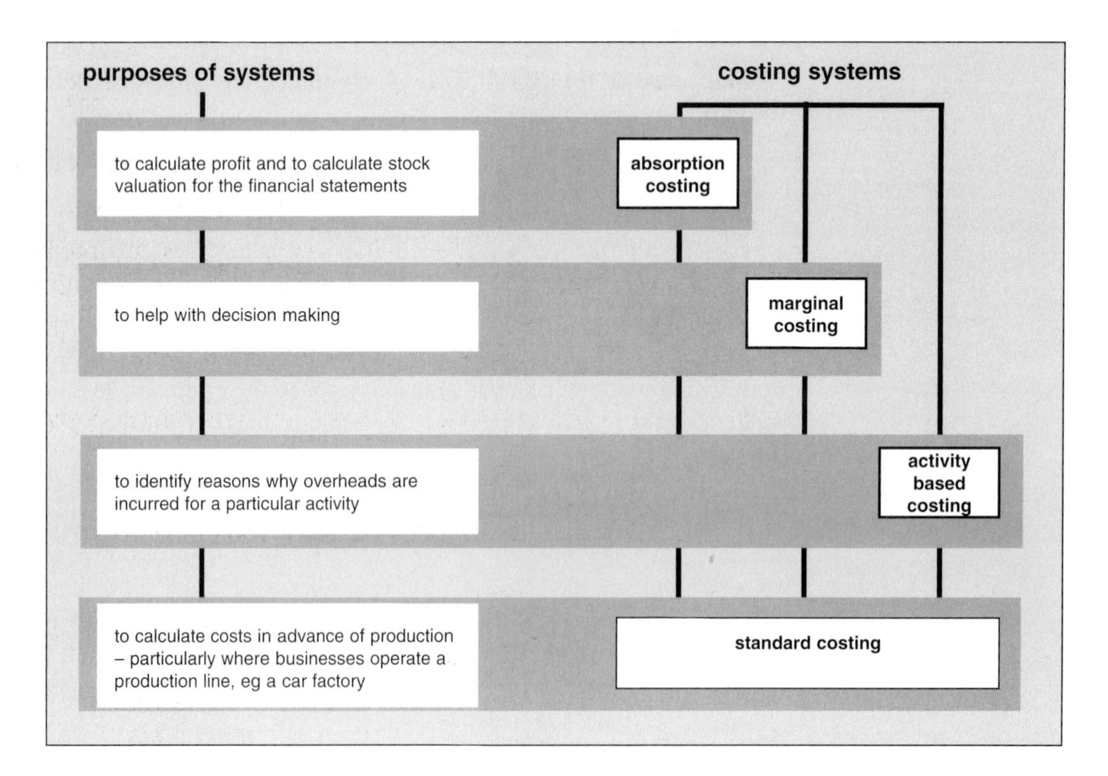

Fig 9.4 Costing systems and their purposes

Note that absorption costing, marginal costing, and activity based costing are all systems that can be used in conjunction with standard costing, if required.

The remainder of this chapter considers each costing system in more detail.

ABSORPTION COSTING

Absorption costing absorbs the total costs of the whole business into each cost unit. Absorption costing answers the question, "What does it cost to make one unit of output?"

The absorption cost of a unit of output is made up of the following costs:

		£
	direct materials	x
add	direct labour	x
add	direct expenses	x
add	overheads (fixed and variable)	x
equals	ABSORPTION COST	x

Notes:

- The overheads of a business comprise both the factory and the office costs of indirect materials, indirect labour, and indirect expenses.
- Under some circumstances, absorption costing includes only production costs, ie it excludes all costs beyond production, such as selling and distribution costs, administration costs, and finance costs.

Example

The Wyvern Bike Company makes 100 bikes each week, and its costs are as follows:

Weekly costs for producing 100 bikes

	£
direct materials (£20 per bike)	2,000
direct labour (£25 per bike)	2,500
PRIME COST	4,500
overheads (fixed)	3,500
TOTAL COST	8,000

Notes:

- there are no direct expenses incurred by the company
- the selling price of each bike is £100, which gives a profit statement of:

		£
	selling price (100 bikes x £100)	10,000
less	total cost	8,000
equals	PROFIT	2,000

The absorption cost of producing one bike is:

$$\frac{\text{total cost (direct and indirect costs)}}{\text{units of output}} = \frac{£8,000}{100 \text{ bikes}} = £80 \text{ per bike}$$

As the above example shows, each cost unit bears an equal proportion of the costs of the overheads of the business. Because of its simplicity, absorption costing is a widely used system which tells us how much it costs to make one unit of output. It works well where the cost units are identical, eg 100 identical bikes, but is less appropriate where some of the cost units differ in quality, eg 100 bikes, of which 75 are standard models and 25 are handbuilt to the customers' specifications. It also ignores the effect of changes in the level of output on the cost structure. For example, if the bike manufacturer reduces output to 50 bikes a week:

- will direct materials remain at £20 per bike? (buying materials in smaller quantities might mean higher prices)
- will direct labour still be £25 per bike? (with lower production, the workforce may not be able to specialise in certain jobs, and may be less efficient)
- will the overheads remain fixed at £3,500? (perhaps smaller premises can be used and the factory rent reduced)

MARGINAL COSTING

Marginal costing is the cost of producing one extra unit of output

As seen earlier in this chapter costs, by nature, are:

- *fixed,* ie they do not vary with changes in the number of units of output produced

  or

- *variable,* ie they vary in line with the amount of activity, eg number of units produced

  or

- *semi-variable,* ie they combine both a fixed and a variable element

For most purposes, marginal costing is not concerned with fixed costs (such as the rent of a factory); instead, it is concerned with variable costs – direct materials, direct labour, direct expenses, and variable factory overheads – which increase as production increases. For most decision making, the marginal cost of a unit of production is, therefore, the prime cost of making one more unit.

Example

Continuing with the example of the Wyvern Bike Company, the marginal cost per unit is:

	£	
direct materials	20	per bike
direct labour	25	per bike
MARGINAL COST	45	per bike

It therefore costs £45 to produce one extra bike.

Knowing the marginal cost of a unit enables the management of a business to focus their attention on the *contribution* provided by each unit. The contribution is the amount of money coming in to the business from sales after marginal costs have been paid.

The contribution in the case of the Wyvern Bike Company is:

		£
	selling price of one bike	100
less	marginal cost of producing one bike	45
equals	CONTRIBUTION per bike	55

The contribution, as its name implies, contributes to the costs of the overheads (running expenses) of the business. Once these are covered, the remainder of contribution is profit. Thus the calculation for the Wyvern Bike Company's weekly production of 100 bikes is:

		£
	selling price	10,000
less	marginal cost	4,500
equals	CONTRIBUTION	5,500
less	overheads (fixed)	3,500
equals	PROFIT	2,000

Note that absorption costing and marginal costing give two different costs per bike for the Wyvern Bike Company: under absorption costing it is £80 per bike, while marginal costing gives £45. At a level of production of 100 bikes per week, both costing systems show a profit of £2,000. You might say, "What is the difference between the two systems?" Supposing that the owner of the Wyvern Bike Company, as a friend, says to you, "I'll make one extra bike next week for you, and you can have it at cost price." Which price do you think you should pay: £80 or £45? The answer is, of course, at the marginal cost of £45. (If you prefer to pay £80, try reworking the cost statement, on the previous page, based on 101 bikes, and then calculate the profit.) Knowing the marginal cost of production helps with management decision making. In Chapter 12, we shall come back to marginal costs and see how they are used in making pricing decisions for 'special orders' and in other situations.

ACTIVITY BASED COSTING

Activity based costing (ABC) charges overheads to output on the basis of activities.

Activity based costing is a relatively new costing system which adopts a different approach to charging overheads to output from absorption costing. ABC relates overheads to output, rather than simply charging total overheads for a particular period.

Traditional costing systems usually charge overheads to output on the basis of direct labour hours (or labour cost), or machine hours. For example, for each labour hour – or machine hour – required by the output, £x of overheads is charged through an *overhead absorption rate* (see Chapter 10). While this method may be suitable for industries which are labour intensive, or where production requires the use of heavy machinery, it is not always appropriate for today's capital intensive, low-labour industries, as the example which follows will show.

Example

A company manufactures two products, X and Y. Product X is produced on a labour-intensive production line, using basic machinery; product Y is produced using the latest 'state of the art' computer-controlled machinery, which requires few employees.

The company's elements of cost are:

direct materials, total	£500,000
– product X	£250,000
– product Y	£250,000
direct labour, total	£250,000
– product X	£200,000
– product Y	£50,000
overheads (fixed), total	£250,000

– a major proportion of these relate to maintenance and depreciation of the computer controlled machinery used to make product Y

The company uses labour cost as the basis by which to charge overheads to production. Therefore, the overhead will be split between the two products as:

overhead for product X = four-fifths of total overheads of £250,000 = £200,000

overhead for product Y = one-fifth of total overheads of £250,000 = £50,000

Thus, the majority of the overhead is charged to the labour-intensive production line (product X), and relatively little to the capital intensive line (product Y). As a major proportion of the costs relates to product Y, this has the effect of undercosting this product (and overcosting product X). Instead, a more appropriate costing system is needed.

the use of cost drivers

Cost drivers are activities which cause costs to be incurred.

In the example looked at above, the cost driver used to charge overheads to output was – inappropriately – labour costs. Instead of using a cost driver linked to the volume of business (as above), activity based costing uses cost drivers linked to the *way in which business is conducted*: this concept is illustrated in the example which follows:

Example

A company manufactures two products, A and B. Product A is produced in batches of 500 units of output; product B is produced in batches of 100 units of output. Each unit of production – whether A or B – requires one direct labour hour.

Production of each batch of A and B requires the following overheads:

- the machinery to be set-up at a cost of £400 per batch (to cover the engineer's time, test running of the machinery, etc)
- quality inspection at a cost of £200 per batch (to cover the inspector's time, cost of rejects, etc)

In a typical week the company produces 500 units of product A, ie one batch of 500 units, and 500 units of product B, ie five batches of 100 units. Thus the set-up and quality inspection costs for the week will be:

6 set-ups at £400 each	=	£2,400
6 quality inspections at £200 each	=	£1,200
TOTAL		£3,600

Note: each 'box' represents one set-up and one quality inspection

As each unit of output requires one direct labour hour, ie product A 500 hours, product B 500 hours, the overhead costs of set-ups and quality inspection, using traditional costing systems, will be charged to output as follows:

product A	=	£1,800
product B	=	£1,800
TOTAL		£3,600

We can see that this is an incorrect basis on which to charge overheads to output, because product A required just one set-up and one quality inspection, while product B took five set-ups and five quality inspections. By using the system of activity based costing, with set-up and inspection as cost drivers, we can charge overheads as follows:

product A

1 set-up at £400	=	£400
1 quality inspection at £200	=	£200
TOTAL		£600

product B

5 set-ups at £400	=	£2,000
5 quality inspections at £200	=	£1,000
TOTAL		£3,000

By using the activity based costing system, there is a more accurate reflection of the cost of demand on the support functions of set-up and quality inspection: it reduces the cost of 500 units of product A by £1,200 (ie £1,800 – £600) and increases the cost of 500 units of product B by £1,200 (ie from £1,800 to £3,000). This may have implications for the viability of product B, and for the selling price of both products.

other cost drivers

Cost drivers must have a close relationship with an activity, which can then be related to output. In the example, we have seen the cost of set-ups and quality inspections used as cost drivers. Examples of other activities and their cost drivers include:

activity	cost driver
• processing orders to suppliers	• number of orders
• processing invoices received from suppliers	• number of invoices
• processing orders to customers	• number of orders
• processing invoices issued to customers	• number of invoices

As has been seen in the example above, by using activity based costing, the emphasis is placed on which activities cause costs. It answers the question why costs are incurred, instead of simply stating the amount of the cost for a given period. By using ABC, the responsibility for the cost is established and so steps can be taken to minimise it for the future.

STANDARD COSTING

Standard costing sets a pre-determined cost for materials, labour and overheads in advance of production.

All businesses need methods of controlling the costs of materials, labour and overheads that go to make up the finished product (we shall see, in later chapters, how budgets can be set and controlled). Imagine a car factory where the cost and amount of materials to make the car is not known; where the hours of work and rates of pay are not known, where the cost of overheads is not known. Under such circumstances, the costs could not be controlled, and it would be impossible to quote a price for the product to a customer. Therefore many businesses establish a standard cost for their output. Thus a standard cost can be calculated for things as diverse as a product manufactured in a factory, a hospital operation, servicing a car, a meal in a restaurant.

The standard cost for units of output is calculated in advance of production and working on the assumption of either an *ideal standard* (ie no poor quality material, no idle time, no machine breakdowns), or an *attainable standard*, which allows for a pre-determined amount of loss or wastage and a given level of efficiency.

Standard costs are set for:

- ***materials***

  The quantity and quality of each type of material to be used in production, and the price of such materials is pre-determined. Standard materials cost is the expected quantity and quality of materials multiplied by expected material price.

- ***labour***

  The labour hours required to manufacture a quantity of goods, and the cost of the labour is pre-determined. Standard labour cost is the expected labour hours multiplied by expected wage rates.

- ***overheads***

  The expected quantity of output within a time period divided into the expected overheads will determine the standard overhead cost.

Once a standard cost has been established, it can be used as a method of cost control through variance analysis (see Chapter 17), and also for making pricing decisions (see Chapter 13). Note that standard costing is used in conjunction with the other costing systems, ie the standard cost is set in advance of production using either absorption costing or marginal costing systems, or activity based costing systems.

setting standards

In standard costing, it is important that care should be taken over the setting of standards. Poorly set standards will be of no help to the management of a business when the figures are used in further analysis.

The main departments within an organisation which can provide information to enable standards to be set are:

- ***Purchasing***

  The buying department of a business will be able to determine prices, and their expected trends, of materials used.

- ***Personnel***

  This department will have current wage and salary rates, together with bonus and overtime details, of the various grades of employees; forecasts of changes can also be ascertained.

- ***Management services***

  Often called work study, this department will determine the standard amount of time that each work-task in the production process should take.

- ***Production***

  This department has overall responsibility for production and will know the quantities of raw materials required for each unit of production, and the value of production will be linked to the overhead costs.

CASE STUDY

AMC ENGINEERING LIMITED

situation

This company manufactures car bumper mouldings. It has been asked by its major customer, Okassa (Japan) Limited to prepare a quotation for mouldings for a new car, which is code-named "OK10". The elements of cost for 100 mouldings have been calculated by AMC Engineering as:

materials:	polycarbonate (of specified quality), 200 kilos at £1.10 per kilo
	matt black finishing material, 10 litres at £5.40 per litre
labour:	10 hours at £5.75 per hour
	3 hours at £8.50 per hour
overheads:	13 hours at £20 per hour

What is the standard cost of producing 100 bumper mouldings?

solution

	£	£
materials		
polycarbonate: 200 kilos at £1.10 per kilo	220.00	
finishing material: 10 litres at £5.40 per litre	54.00	
		274.00
labour		
10 hours at £5.75 per hour	57.50	
3 hours at £8.50 per hour	25.50	
		83.00
		357.00
overheads		
13 hours at £20 per hour		260.00
STANDARD COST		617.00

This standard cost will then be used by AMC Engineering to help establish the selling price to the customer, ie: standard cost + profit = selling price

Pricing decisions are covered in Chapter 13

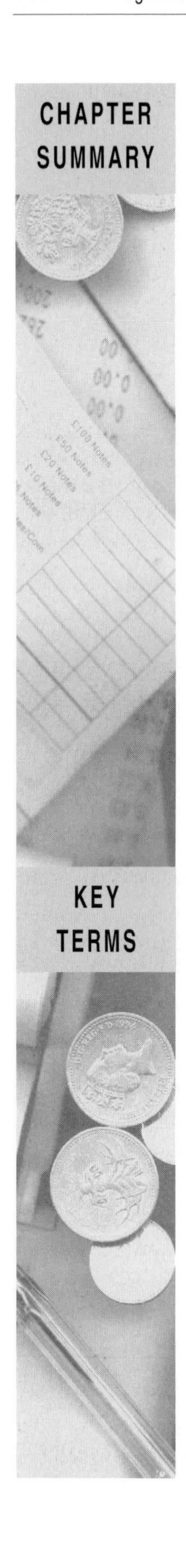

CHAPTER SUMMARY

- Costing calculates how much it costs to produce a unit of goods or services.
- Costs can be classified by element, by function and by nature.
- The main elements of cost are
  - materials
  - labour
  - expenses

  Each of these can be direct or indirect.
- Costs can be classified by function, eg factory or production, selling and distribution, administration, finance.
- By nature, costs are fixed, or variable, or semi-variable.
- A total cost statement lists all the direct costs and the overheads involved in producing the output of a business. Sales revenue minus total cost equals profit.
- Costing systems include
  - absorption costing
  - marginal costing
  - activity based costing
  - standard costing

KEY TERMS

cost unit — unit of output to which costs can be charged

cost centre — section of a business to which costs can be charged

unit of output — the output of the business expressed in terms of units

direct costs — those costs that can be identified directly with each unit of output

indirect costs — all other costs, ie those that cannot be identified directly with each unit of output

overheads — the indirect costs of materials, labour and expenses

fixed costs — costs which remain fixed over a range of output levels

variable costs — costs which vary directly with activity

semi-variable costs — costs which combine a fixed and variable element

total cost statement — list of all the direct costs and overheads

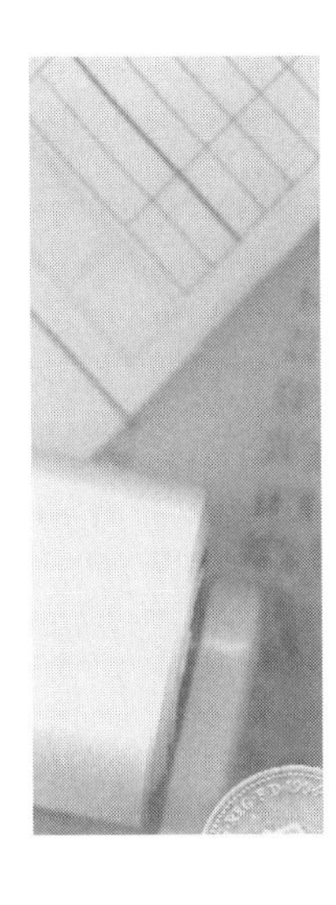

	involved in producing the output of the business
absorption costing	absorbs the total costs of the whole business into each cost unit
marginal cost	the cost of producing one extra unit of output
activity based costing	charges overheads to output on the basis of activities
cost drivers	activities which cause costs to be incurred
standard costing	a pre-determined cost for materials, labour and overheads in advance of production

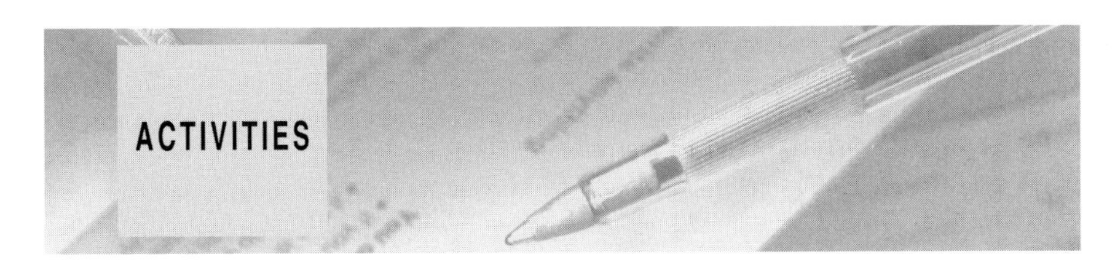

9.1 Select an organisation – either where you work, or another one with which you are familiar.

(a) Prepare a diagram, similar to that shown on page 165, identifying the main functions of the organisation and the costs incurred by each section.

(b) Describe the cost units and cost centres used by the organisation. Discuss whether or not you consider these to be appropriate.

9.2 (a) Why is it important to analyse costs in different ways, eg by element, by function and by nature?

(b) Classify each of the following costs by nature (ie fixed, or variable, or semi-variable):

- raw materials
- factory rent
- telephone
- direct labour, eg production workers paid on a piecework basis
- indirect labour, eg supervisors' salaries
- commission paid to sales staff

Taking the costs in turn, explain to a friend, who is about to set up a furniture manufacturing business, why you have classified each as fixed, or variable, or semi-variable. Answer the comment, "What difference does it make anyway, they are all costs that have to be paid."

9.3 Severn Manufacturing Limited makes chairs for school and college use. The chairs have plastic seats, and tubular steel legs. The firm's management accountant asks you to help her classify the manufacturing costs into:

- direct materials
- indirect materials
- direct labour
- indirect labour
- direct expenses
- indirect expenses

The costs to be classified are:

COST	CLASSIFICATION (write your answer)
Tubular steel	
Factory supervisor's salary	
Wages of employee operating the moulding	
Machine which produces the chair seats	
Works canteen assistant's wages	
Rates of factory	
Power to operate machines	
Factory heating and lighting	
Plastic for making chair seats	
Hire of special machinery for one particular order	
Cost of oil for the moulding machine	
Depreciation of factory machinery	
Depreciation of office equipment	

If you believe alternative classifications exist, argue the case and state if you need further information from the company.

9.4 Eveshore Pottery Limited manufactures a range of 'souvenir' mugs, cups and saucers, plates, etc, which sell well to visitors from abroad who are seeking a memento of 'Olde England'. A number of different costs have been incurred during the last month, and you are asked to classify them into:

- direct materials
- indirect materials
- direct labour
- indirect labour
- direct expenses
- indirect expenses

The costs are:

(a) cleaning materials for the machines

(b) wages of factory supervisor

(c) clay from which the 'pots' are made

(d) 10p royalties payable to the designer for each 'Eveshore Plate' made

(e) salary of office clerk

(f) electricity used to heat the kilns

(g) rates of factory

(h) depreciation of office equipment

(i) wages of production line workers

(j) salesperson's salary

(k) interest charged on bank overdraft

If you believe alternative classifications exist, argue the case and state if you need further information from the company.

Of the overhead costs, ie indirect materials, indirect labour, and indirect expenses, you are to indicate which would be classified as:

- factory overheads
- selling and distribution overheads
- administration overheads
- finance overheads

9.5 The following figures relate to the accounts of Hughes Limited, a manufacturing business, for the year ended 31 December 1996:

	£
Raw materials used in the factory	118,830
Rent and business rates	16,460
Factory wages	117,315
Factory power	3,825
Factory heat and light	1,185
Factory expenses and maintenance	4,095
Office salaries and wages	69,350
Advertising	11,085
Office expenses	3,930
Depreciation of factory plant and machinery	3,725
Sales revenue	426,350

(a) Prepare a total cost statement for the year which shows:

- prime cost
- production cost
- total cost

Discuss any assumptions that you make and state if you need further information from the company.

(b) Prepare a profit statement for the year (on the assumption that all the goods manufactured have been sold).

9.6 John Walker Limited manufactures high quality training shoes (trainers). The management of the company is considering next year's production and has asked you to help with certain financial decisions.

The following information is available:

wholesale selling price (per pair)	£40
direct materials (per pair)	£15
direct labour (per pair)	£12
overheads (fixed)	£245,000 per year

The company is planning to manufacture 25,000 pairs of trainers next year.

(a) calculate the absorption cost per pair of trainers

(b) calculate the marginal cost per pair of trainers

(c) prepare a profit statement to show the profit or loss if 25,000 pairs of trainers are sold

9.7 Rowcester Engineering Limited makes engine castings for a major car manufacturer. The castings are made in the foundry and are then sent to the machine shop for machining to the customer's specifications.

As a cost clerk, you have been asked to prepare a standard cost based on production of 100 castings. The following information is available to you:

- materials for 100 castings
  - 550 kg of ordinary steel at £3.50 per kg
  - 200 kg of high tensile steel at £10.00 per kg
- labour for 100 castings
  - 60 hours of foundry-workers' wages at £10.50 per hour
  - 155 hours in the machine shop at £12.75 per hour
- overheads (factory and office)
  - 210 hours at £25 per hour

What is the standard cost of producing 100 castings?

9.8 Mereford Manufacturing Limited makes two products, A and B. Product A is made in batches of 10,000 units, and Product B is made in batches of 1,000 units. Each batch has the following set-up and quality inspection costs:

- set-up £250
- quality inspection £150

Each week, the company produces 50,000 units of A and 50,000 units of B. At present the company charges overheads to output on the basis of labour hours which are 500 hours per week for A and 500 hours for B.

(a) calculate the overheads charged to A and B each week, on the basis of labour hours

(b) calculate the overheads charged to A and B each week, using activity based costing with the cost drivers of set-up and quality inspection

(c) advise the management of Mereford Manufacturing Limited which is the more appropriate method of charging overheads to output

10 OVERHEAD ANALYSIS AND METHODS OF COSTING

this chapter covers ...

- *the need to recover overheads through the units of output*
- *the process of allocating and apportioning the cost of overheads – including those of service departments – into the units of output*
- *bases of apportionment of overheads*
- *the main overhead absorption rates and their relative merits in given circumstances*
- *the main methods of costing and their use in particular industries*

INTRODUCTION

The overheads of a business are the indirect materials, indirect labour and indirect expenses. These costs do not relate to particular units of output but must, instead, be shared amongst all the cost units to which they relate. In this chapter we shall look at ways in which overheads are charged to production, and some of the difficulties that may occur.

The important point to remember is that all the overheads of a business, together with the direct costs (materials, labour and expenses) must be covered by money flowing in from sales.

Overheads are usually classified by *function* under headings such as:

- *factory, or production,* eg factory rent and rates, indirect labour, indirect materials, heating and lighting of factory
- *selling and distribution,* eg salaries of sales staff, packing costs, vehicle costs

- *administration,* eg office rent and rates, office salaries, heating and lighting of office
- *finance,* eg bank interest

In order to determine how much has been spent on overheads, it will be necessary to use the financial records: for example, the amount for rent, rates, salaries, wages, heating, lighting, vehicle costs, etc. Some figures, such as those for wages, and for purchases, will need to be analysed to see which part of the total cost is a direct expense (to be charged directly to the appropriate cost units), and which is the indirect expense (to be charged to overheads).

Once the various overheads have been classified, they are then either *allocated* or *apportioned* to cost centres.

ALLOCATION AND APPORTIONMENT OF OVERHEADS

Allocation of overheads is the charging to a cost centre of those overheads that have been directly incurred by that cost centre.

For example, in a large organisation a whole factory might be a cost centre and so the rent and rates of that factory will be allocated to it as a separate cost centre. Another example would be where a department is the cost centre; here the costs of a supervisor working solely within one department would be allocated to that department.

Apportionment of overheads is where cost centres are charged with a proportion of overheads.

For example, a department which is a cost centre within a factory will be charged a proportion of the factory rent and rates. Another example is where a supervisor works within two departments, both of which are separate cost centres: the indirect labour cost of employing the supervisor will be shared or apportioned between the two cost centres.

With apportionment, a suitable basis must be found to apportion overheads between cost centres. Different methods might be used for each overhead, as shown in the Case Study which follows.

LASER ENGINEERING LIMITED

situation

A friend of yours, Natalie Wood, runs Laser Engineering Limited. The company uses some of the latest laser equipment in one department, while another section of the business continues to use traditional machinery. You have been helping Natalie with financial aspects of the business and she asks you which overheads of the business should be allocated or apportioned. Details of the factory are as follows:

> *Department A* is a 'hi-tech' machine shop equipped with laser-controlled machinery which has cost £80,000. This department has 400 square metres of floor area. There are three machine operators: the supervisor spends one-third of the time in this department.
>
> *Department B* is a 'low-tech' part of the factory equipped with machinery which has cost £20,000. The floor area is 600 square metres. There are two workers who spend all their time in this department: the supervisor spends two-thirds of the time in this department.

The overheads to be allocated or apportioned are as follows:

1 Factory rates, £12,000

2 Wages of the supervisor, £21,000

3 Factory heating and lighting, £2,500

4 Depreciation of machinery, £20,000

5 Buildings insurance, £2,000

6 Insurance of machinery, £1,500

7 Specialist materials for the laser equipment, £2,500

How would you suggest each of these should be allocated or apportioned to each department?

solution

The recommendations are:

1 Factory rates – apportioned on the basis of floor area, ie 40% to Department A, and 60% to Department B.

2 Supervisor's wages – apportioned on the basis of time spent, ie one-third to Department A, and two-thirds to Department B. If the time spent was not known, an alternative basis could be based on the number of employees.

3 Factory heating and lighting – apportioned on the basis of floor area.

4 Depreciation of machinery – apportioned on the basis of machine value, ie four-fifths to Department A, and one-fifth to Department B.

5 Buildings insurance – apportioned on the basis of floor area.

6 Insurance of machinery – apportioned on the basis of machine value.

7 Specialist materials for the laser equipment – allocated to Department A, the cost centre which directly incurred the cost.

It is important to note that there are no fixed rules for the apportionment of overheads – the only proviso is that the basis used should be equitable, ie that a fair proportion of the overhead, matching cost with responsibility for cost, is charged to the department.

The apportionment for Laser Engineering Co Limited would take place as follows:

Cost	Basis of apportionment	Total £	Dept A £	Dept B £
Factory rates	Floor area	12,000	4,800	7,200
Wages of supervisor	Time spent	21,000	7,000	14,000
Heating and lighting	Floor area	2,500	1,000	1,500
Dep'n of machinery	Machine value	20,000	16,000	4,000
Buildings insurance	Floor area	2,000	800	1,200
Machinery insurance	Machine value	1,500	1,200	300
Specialist materials	Allocation	2,500	2,500	–
		61,500	33,300	28,200

SERVICE DEPARTMENTS

Many businesses have departments which provide services within the business; for example, maintenance, transport, stores or stationery, etc. Each service department is likely to be a cost centre, to which a proportion of overheads is charged. As service departments do not themselves have any cost units to which their overheads may be charged, the costs of each service department must be *re-apportioned* to the production departments (which do have cost units into which overheads can be absorbed). A suitable basis of re-apportionment must be used, for example:

- the overheads of a maintenance department might be re-apportioned to production departments on the basis of value of machinery or equipment, or on the basis of time spent in each production department
- the overheads of a stores department could be re-apportioned on the basis of value of goods issued to production departments, or on the number of requisitions
- the overheads of a subsidised canteen could be re-apportioned on the basis of the number of employees

Fig 10.1 summarises the ways in which overheads are allocated or apportioned to production cost centres, together with the re-apportionment of the service department's costs.

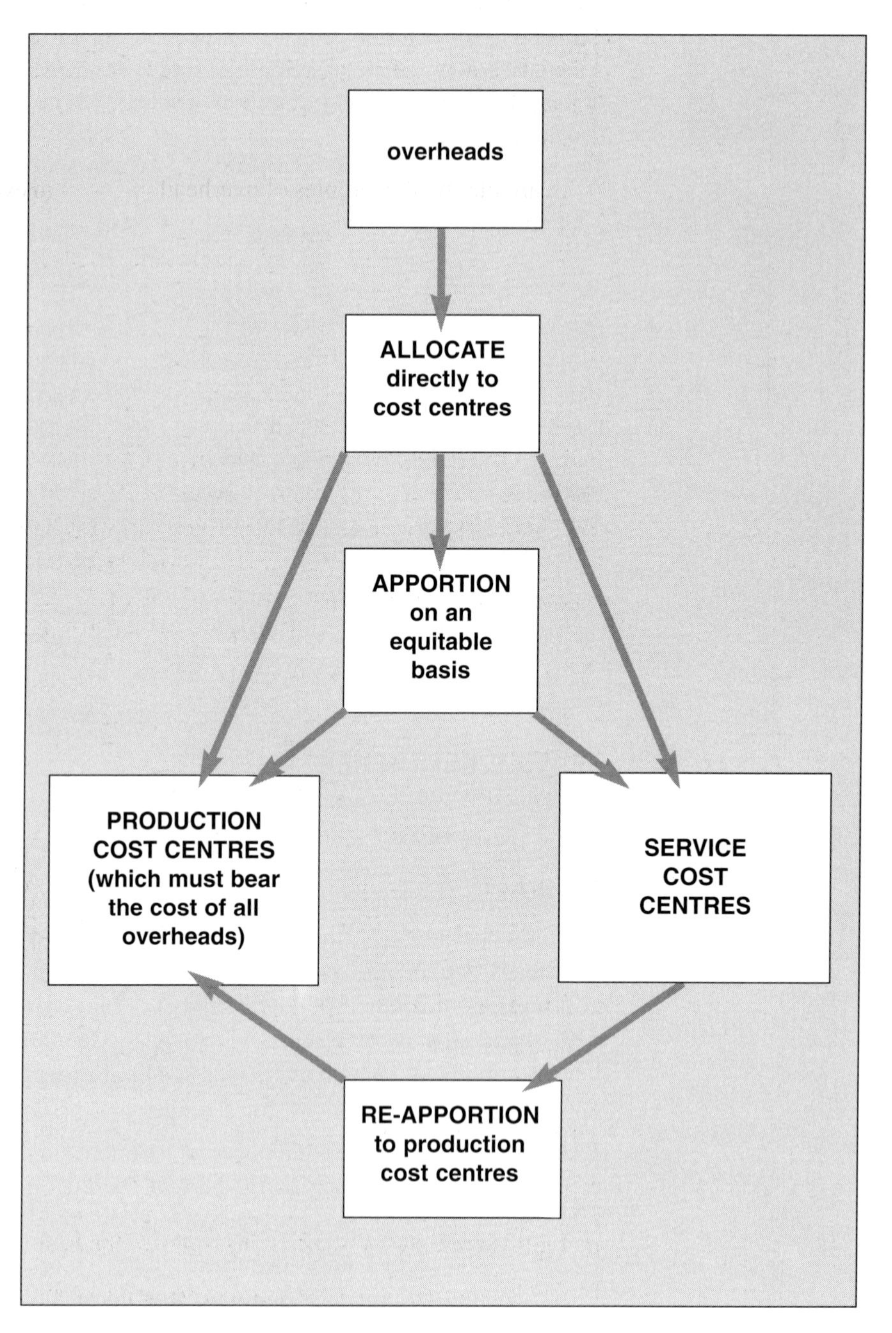

Fig 10.1 Allocation and apportionment of overheads

OVERHEAD ABSORPTION

Once overheads have been allocated or apportioned to production cost centres, the final step is to ensure that the overheads are charged to cost units. In the language of costing this is known as *absorption*, ie the cost of overheads is charged to the cost units which pass through that particular production department.

There are plenty of examples of overhead recovery in everyday life – it is not something used solely by factories. For example, if you take a car to be repaired at a garage, the bill will be presented as follows:

Parts	£70.00
Labour: 3 hours at £30 per hour	£90.00
Total	£160.00

Within this example bill are the three main elements of cost: materials (parts), labour and overheads. The last two are combined as labour – the garage mechanic is not paid £30 per hour; instead the labour rate might be £10 per hour, with the rest, ie £20 per hour, being a contribution towards the overheads of the garage. Other examples are accountants, solicitors, etc who charge a 'rate per hour', part of which is used to contribute to the cost of overheads.

In order to absorb the overheads of a department, there are two steps to be followed:

1 calculation of the overhead absorption rate

2 application of this rate to cost units

Although there are a variety of methods available to a business, three traditionally used (and still popular) overhead absorption methods are:

- units of output
- direct labour hour
- machine hour

UNITS OF OUTPUT

Using this method overhead is absorbed on the basis of each unit of output.

1 *Calculation of the overhead absorption rate:*

$$\frac{\text{total cost centre overheads}}{\text{total cost units}}$$

2 *Application of the rate:*

cost units x overhead absorption rate

Example

Department A: total cost centre overheads for year, £100,000
expected total output for year, 20,000 units
output in March, 1,500 units

1 Overhead absorption rate:

$\frac{£100,000}{20,000}$ = £5.00 per unit

2 Application of the rate:

1,500 x £5.00 = £7,500 of overhead absorbed in March

DIRECT LABOUR HOUR

With this method, overhead is absorbed on the basis of the number of direct labour hours worked.

1 ***Calculation of the overhead absorption rate:***

$$\frac{\text{total cost centre overheads}}{\text{total direct labour hours (in cost centre)}}$$

2 ***Application of the rate:***

direct labour hours worked x overhead absorption rate

Example

Department B: total cost centre overheads for year, £40,000
expected direct labour hours for year, 5,000
actual direct labour hours in March, 450

1 Overhead absorption rate:

$\frac{£40,000}{5,000}$ = £8 per direct labour hour

2 Application of the rate:

450 direct labour hours x £8 = £3,600 of overhead absorbed in March

MACHINE HOUR

Here the overhead is absorbed on the basis of machine hours.

1 ***Calculation of the overhead absorption rate:***

$$\frac{\text{total cost centre overheads}}{\text{total machine hours (in cost centre)}}$$

2 ***Application of the Rate:***

cost units x overhead absorption rate

Example

Department C: total cost centre overheads for year, £216,000

expected machine hours for year, 36,000

actual machine hours in March, 3,500

1 Overhead absorption rate:

$$\frac{£216{,}000}{36{,}000} = £6 \text{ per machine hour}$$

2 Application of the rate:

3,500 machine hours x £6 = £21,000 of overhead absorbed in March

WHICH METHOD TO USE?

Only one overhead absorption rate will be used in a particular department, and managers must choose the method that suits their particular business.

Where units of production are identical, the units of output method is appropriate. However, it would be entirely unsuitable where different types and sizes of products pass through the same department, because each unit would be charged the same rate.

The direct labour hour method is a very popular method (eg the garage mentioned earlier) because overheads are absorbed on a time basis. Thus the cost unit that requires twice the direct labour of another cost unit will be charged twice the overhead. However this method will be inappropriate where some units are worked on manually while others quickly pass through an automated process and require little direct labour time.

A machine hour rate is particularly appropriate where expensive machinery is used in the department. However, it would be unsuitable where some products pass through the machine while others are worked on by hand: in the latter case, no overheads would be charged to the cost units.

It is important to select the best method of overhead absorption for the particular business, otherwise wrong decisions will be made on the basis of the costing information. As overheads are often incurred on a time basis, they are traditionally absorbed in this way. The use of *activity based costing* (pages 176 to 179) is one way of linking activities to costs by identifying the appropriate cost drivers. Overheads can be linked to the cost drivers and then charged to the cost units depending on the number of transactions generated for the cost driver. This approach to absorption costing is now used by a number of businesses.

Alternative overhead absorption methods can be based on a percentage of certain costs, eg direct labour costs.

PRE-DETERMINED OVERHEAD RATES

Overhead absorption rates are set *in advance* by making forecasts of production and costs. The making of forecasts is known as *budgeting,* and this topic is discussed fully in Chapters 15-17. It is quite likely that actual overhead absorbed will be different from the estimates made at the beginning of the year. Thus overhead will be either *under-absorbed*, or *over-absorbed*; under-absorption means that less overhead has been recovered than has been incurred; over-absorption means that more overhead has been recovered than incurred.

Example

Department D: overhead absorption rate (based on units of output), £6.00 per unit

expected total output for year, 6,000 units

actual output in year, 6,300 units

- Total overheads for the department are 6,000 units x £6.00 per unit = £36,000
- Actual overhead absorbed: 6,300 units x £6.00 per unit = £37,800
- Over-absorption of overhead: £37,800 - £36,000 = £1,800

The management of a business will constantly monitor actual production and will seek reasons for variances between this and budgeted production. While over-absorption of overheads, on first impressions, seems to be a 'bonus' for a business – profits will be higher – it should also be remembered that the overhead rate may have been set too high. As a consequence, sales might have been lost because the selling price has been too high.

METHODS OF COSTING

We have seen how overheads are absorbed by cost units. In this part of the chapter we shall look at the *costing methods* used by businesses in order to calculate the total cost of their output.

These costing methods are

- *for specific orders*
  - job costing
  - batch costing
  - contract costing
- *for continuous operations*
  - process costing
  - service costing

Each of these is used in conjunction with absorption costing to recover the cost of overheads; they can also be used with marginal costing (see Chapter 12) to help with specific problems. However, it is important to remember that businesses must recover their overheads in the total price charged to their customers – this applies both to manufacturing businesses and service industries – such as banks, shops, transport companies. Only when the full cost of overheads has been recovered can a business give thought to the application of marginal costing techniques.

JOB COSTING

Job costing is used where:

- each job can be separately identified from other jobs
- costs are charged to the job

Thus the job becomes the *cost unit* to which costs are charged. Examples of job costing include engineering firms that produce 'one-offs' to the customer's specifications, printing businesses, vehicle repairs, jobbing builders, painters and decorators, etc.

Fig 10.2 shows the main steps involved in job costing. The important points are:

- each job is given a number, in order to identify it
- a separate *job cost sheet* is prepared for each job, listing the estimates of direct materials, direct labour, and overheads
- the actual costs incurred are compared with the estimated costs, and variances between the two are analysed (there is more on *variance analysis* in Chapter 17); action can then be taken to correct the variances, which will help when preparing future estimates

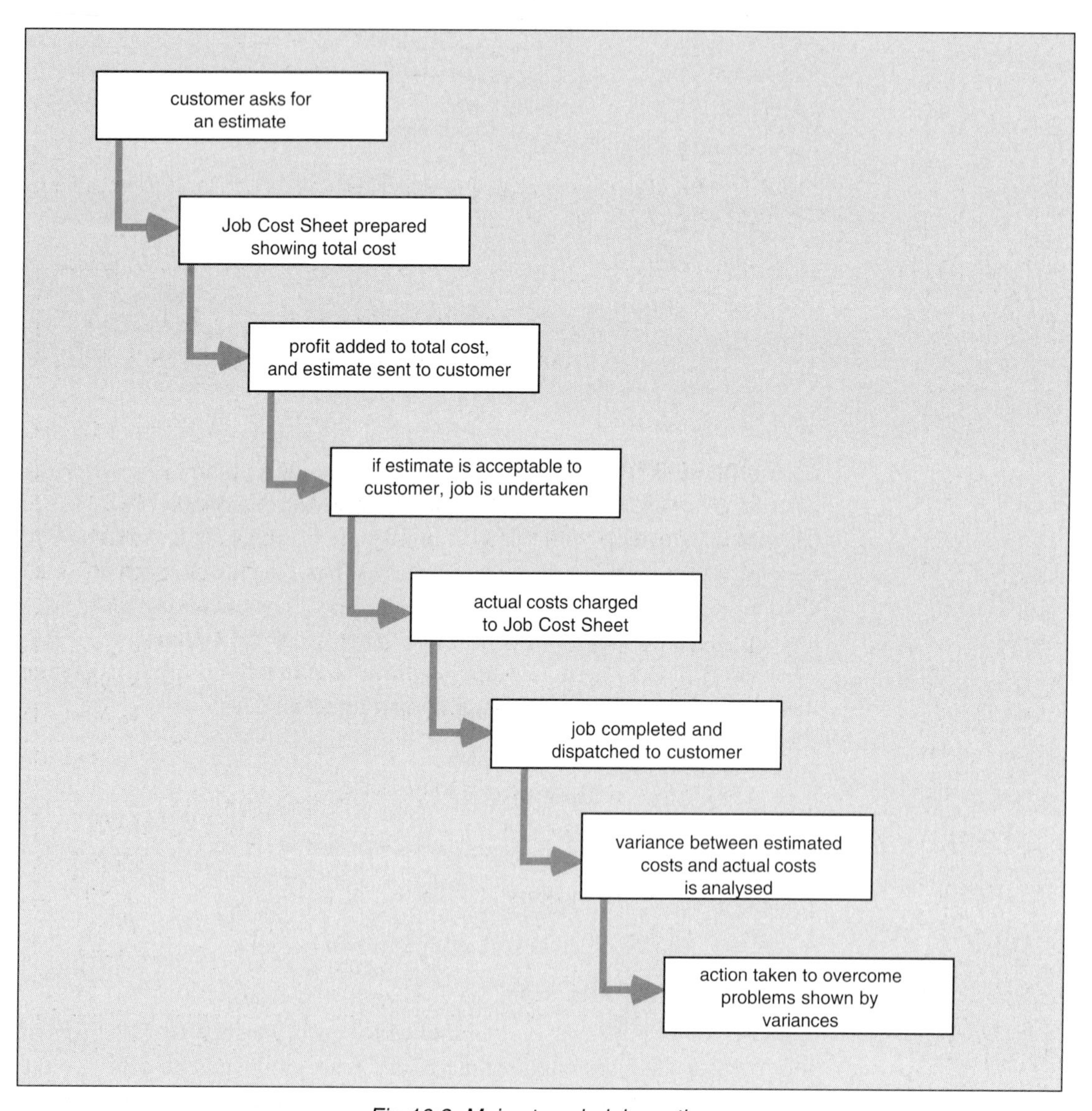

Fig 10.2 Main steps in job costing

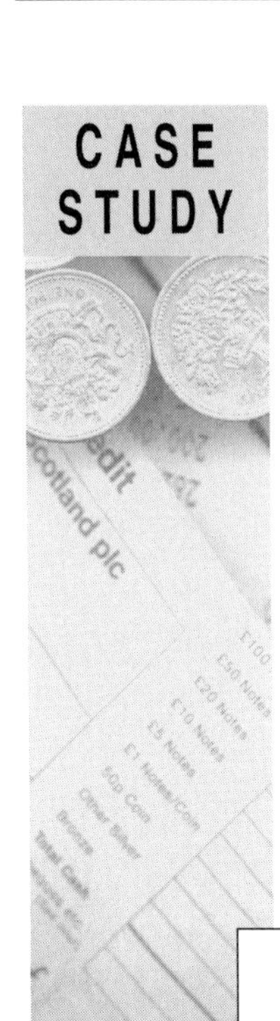

'FASHIONAID' – A CHARITY PROGRAMME

situation

The youth group at a local church has decided to organise an evening fashion show, to be called *'FashionAid'*. The objective of the show is to raise money to send to a children's charity working in Central Africa. Your daughter/son is one of the organisers and has asked for your help in arranging the printing of a programme for the evening's events. You approach Pearshore Printers for an estimate of the cost of printing 750 copies of a sixteen page programme.

solution

From their point of view, Pearshore Printers will allocate a number to the job. They prepare the costs of the job as follows:

JOB NO. 6789

'FashionAid' Programme: 750 copies

	£
Direct materials	
Paper: text: white glossart paper 135g (per square metre)	82.00
Paper: cover: coated board 200g (per square metre)	55.00
Printing plates	15.00
Direct labour	
Printing: 5 hours at £10.00 per hour	50.00
Finishing: 2 hours at £9.00 per hour	18.00
Overheads (based on direct labour hour)	
7 hours at £20.00 per hour	140.00
Total Cost	360.00
Profit (15% of total cost)	54.00
Total price	414.00

Assuming that the price is acceptable, the job will go ahead and Pearshore Printers will charge the actual costs to the job, and will calculate any variances, as follows:

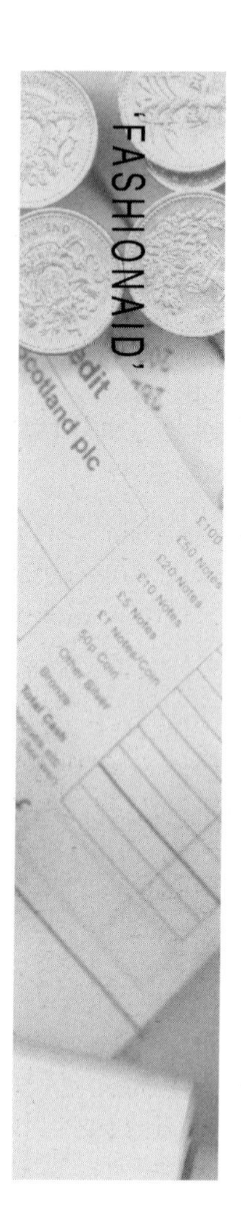

JOB NO. 6789

'FashionAid' Programme: 750 copies

	ESTIMATE	ACTUAL	VARIANCE*	
	£	£	£	
Direct materials				
Paper: text	82.00	90.00	8	ADV
Paper: cover	55.00	50.00	5	FAV
Printing plates	15.00	15.00	–	
Direct labour				
Printing: actual 6 hours at £10.00 per hour	50.00	60.00	10	ADV
Finishing: actual 2 hours at £9.00 per hour	18.00	18.00	–	
Overheads				
8 hours at £20.00 per hour	140.00	160.00	20	ADV
Total cost	360.00	393.00	33	ADV
Profit	54.00	21.00	33	ADV
Total price	414.00	414.00	–	

* The variances are either *adverse* or *favourable:*

- a favourable variance is where the actual cost is lower than the estimate
- an adverse variance is where the actual cost is higher than the estimate

Pearshore Printers would need to analyse the reason for the variances (see Chapter 17), and to take corrective steps to overcome the problems caused by them.

BATCH COSTING

This form of costing is used where the output consists of a number of identical items which are produced together as a batch. Examples include a bakery producing a batch of standard white loaves, and then a batch of croissants; or a clothing factory producing a batch of jackets, and then a batch of trousers. Each batch is the cost unit to which the costs are charged. Once the batch has been produced, the cost per unit is calculated as follows:

$$\frac{\textit{total batch cost}}{\textit{number of units of output}} = \textit{cost per unit}$$

In essence, batch costing is very similar to job costing – in a batch a number of identical units are produced.

CONTRACT COSTING

Contract costing is used by the construction industry and major engineering companies to cost large, complex projects which last for long periods of time (usually more than a year). The principles followed are those of job costing but the length and complexity of contract work causes financial differences:

- a large contract will often itself comprise a considerable number of smaller jobs (some of which may be sub-contracted) to be costed
- invariably building contracts are based at the construction site – this means that many costs that would otherwise be indirect become direct costs, eg supervisors' wages, site power and telephones, fuel for vehicles, depreciation of equipment
- as many contracts run for longer than one year, there is a need to calculate the profit or loss on the contract at the end of the financial year of the construction company, and to value the contract for balance sheet purposes; the contract is valued at either:
  - *if an overall profit is expected,* costs to date plus attributable profit (depending on how far through the contract is); or
  - *if an overall loss is expected,* costs to date, less the whole of the expected loss

Clearly the costing of a contract is a major task and one which can go spectacularly wrong as a number of companies have found in the past.

PROCESS COSTING

While job, batch, and contract costing are suitable for specific orders, process costing is used where a factory or a production line makes a particular product using a continuous process.

The objective of process costing is to find the cost per unit produced.

There are many examples of process costing in manufacturing industry, for example, the cost of making a bar of soap, or a car, or a litre of petrol, or a packet of cereal.

Where a product passes through a number of separate operations, before it is completed, the costs of each process can be calculated.

Example: The cost of producing 2,000 identical units of a product is:

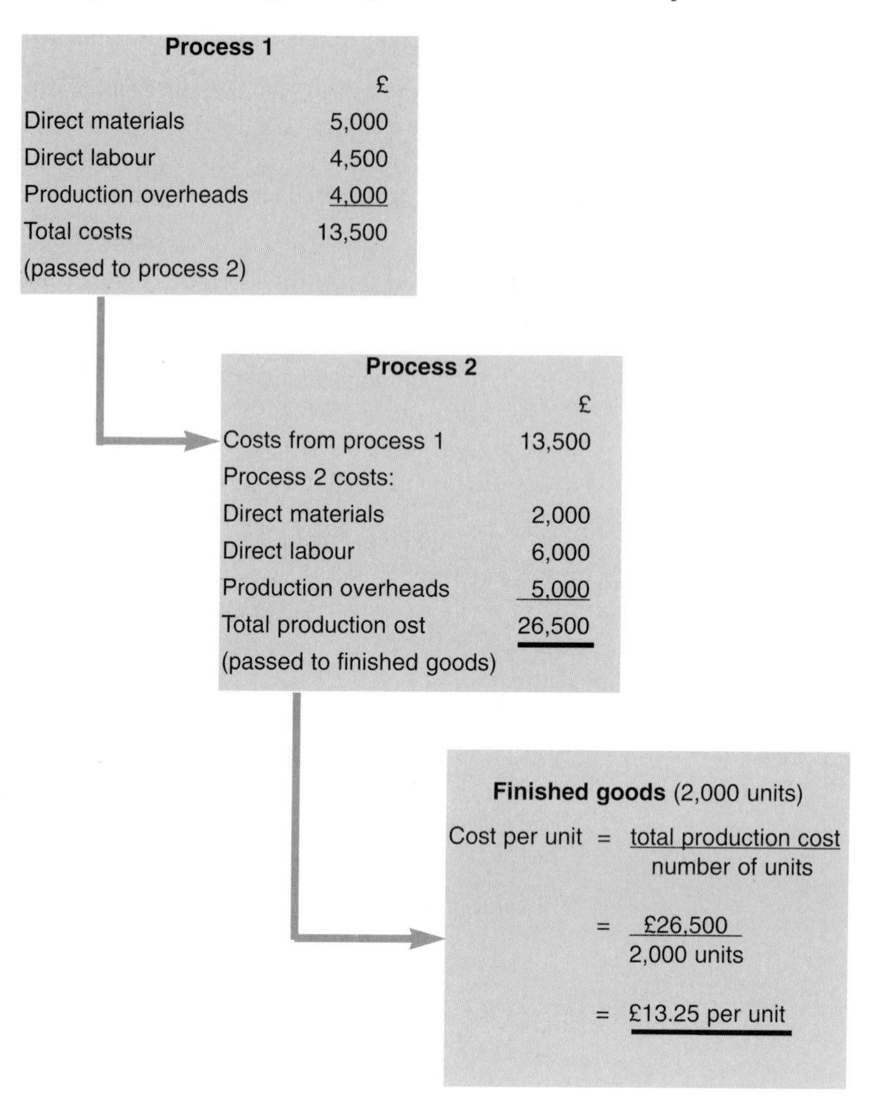

In many processes there is some loss of product during the various operations: for example, in the process of distilling whisky and other spirits there is a considerable shortfall between the volume at the start and the volume at the end! The reason for such a difference is evaporation, together with the need to take regular samples. *Normal process losses* are expected and their cost is included in the cost per unit. *Abnormal process losses or gains* fall outside expected differences and losses may be caused by machine failure, poor quality materials, inefficient working practices, etc. Abnormal losses or gains, ie the excess over normal losses, are not charged or allowed to production but, instead, are transferred to profit and loss account; clearly the reason for such gains or losses will need to be investigated by management.

WORK-IN-PROGRESS

With most manufacturing processes it is likely that, at any one time, there will be some units which are partly completed. For example, the production line at a car factory will always have cars which vary from being only just started, to those nearing the end of the line which are almost complete.

In calculating the cost per unit, it is necessary to take into account the degree of completeness of the work-in-progress. This is done by making equivalent unit calculations:

Number of units in progress x percentage of completeness = equivalent units.

Thus, 100 units which are exactly 40% complete are equal to 40 completed units.

The formula for calculating the cost per unit now becomes:

$$\frac{\textit{total cost of production}}{\textit{number of units of output + equivalent units-in-progress}} = \textit{cost per unit}$$

Example

The Cradley Cider Company brews a popular local cider at its cider house in rural Herefordshire. The figures for the first month of the new season's production of its award-winning 'Five Crowns' variety are:

total cost of production	£8,500
units completed	800 barrels
units in progress	100 barrels

The units in progress are exactly half-finished. The equivalent units-in-progress, and the cost per barrel, for the month are as follows:

completed units		= 800 barrels
equivalent units	100 x 50%	= 50 barrels
cost per unit	$\frac{£8,500}{800 + 50}$	= £10 per barrel

work-in-progress: different cost elements

Although in the example above, it was assumed that the work-in-progress was exactly half-finished, this may well not be the case for all the elements of cost. For example, while direct materials might be 100% complete, direct labour, and overheads might be 50% complete. Allowance has to be made for these differences in the calculation of the valuation of work-in-progress, and the layout used in the example below is one way in which the calculations can be made.

Example

The Toy Manufacturing Company makes a plastic toy called a 'Humber-Wumber'. The figures for the first month's production are:

direct materials	£6,600
direct labour	£3,500
production overheads	£4,000
units completed	900
units in progress	200

The units in progress are complete as regards materials, but are 50% complete for direct labour and production overheads.

Cost element	Costs	Completed Units	Work-in-progress			Total Equivalent Units	Cost per Unit	WIP valuation
			Units	% complete	Equivalent Units			
	A	B	C	D	E	F	G	H
					C x D	B + E	A ÷ F	E x G
	£						£	£
Direct materials	6,600	900	200	100	200	1,100	6.00	1,200
Direct labour	3,500	900	200	50	100	1,000	3.50	350
Production overheads	4,000	900	200	50	100	1,000	4.00	400
Total	14,100						13.50	1,950

Note: columns are lettered to show how calculations are made

The cost per unit of the first month's production, and the month-end valuation figure for work-in-progress (WIP) is as follows:

900 completed units at £13.50 each	= £12,150
work-in-progress valuation	= £ 1,950
total costs for month	= £14,100

opening work-in-progress

When there is opening work-in-progress, the values of the different cost elements are added to the input costs of the period. For example, if in the month which follows the example above, direct labour costs are £4,000, the figure shown in the column *costs* for direct labour will be:

work-in-progress at start	=	£ 350
input costs for the month	=	£4,000
total costs for the month	=	£4,350

The calculation of costs per unit and work-in-progress valuation at the month-end can then be made as follows:

$$\frac{\textit{opening work-in-progress} + \textit{input costs for period}}{\textit{number of units of output} + \textit{equivalent units-in-progress}} = \textit{cost per unit}$$

SERVICE COSTING

This method of costing uses the principle of process costing and applies it to service industries. In this way, the cost per passenger mile of a bus or train service, the cost of clearing a cheque, and the cost per student hour at a school or college can be calculated. (However, a bus company quoting for a trip to the seaside for a pensioners' group, or a college tendering for an in-house course, would use job costing.)

Example

A nursing home has capacity for twenty residents at any one time. The home achieves an occupancy rate of 90%, ie an average of eighteen beds are occupied at any one time. Costs for last year were:

	£
direct costs	
food and other supplies	27,290
nursing and medical staff	116,340
other support services	22,650
indirect costs	
overheads	29,410
	195,690

The cost per day per resident is calculated as follows:

- The occupancy in days is (20 residents x 365 days) x 90% = 6,570 days
- Cost per day per resident is:

$$\frac{\text{total cost}}{\text{number of days}} = \frac{£195,690}{6,570} = £29.79 \text{ per day}$$

CHAPTER SUMMARY

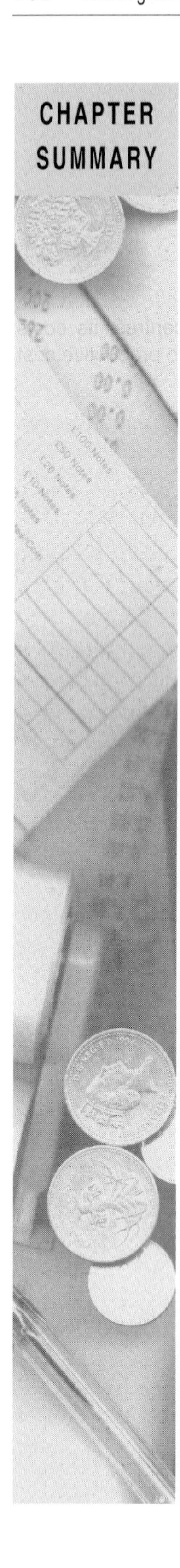

- Overheads are the indirect costs of a business which do not relate to particular units of output:
  - where a cost centre has directly incurred the overheads, they are *allocated* to that cost centre
  - other overheads are *apportioned* between cost centres, using an equitable basis

- Cost centre overheads are charged to cost units by means of an *overhead absorption rate* such as
  - units of output
  - direct labour hour
  - machine hour

  The objective of overhead absorption is to ensure that overheads are recovered by the cost units which pass through the cost centre.

- With pre-determined overhead absorption rates, there may be either under-absorption or over-absorption of overheads.

- Methods of costing include:

  for specific orders
  - job costing
  - batch costing
  - contract costing

  for continuous operations
  - process costing
  - service costing

- Each of the methods of costing enables the calculation of a cost per unit of output.

This chapter concludes the section covering the fundamentals of costing systems and methods. In the next section we move on to looking at how costing can be used as an aid to decision making.

overheads	indirect costs of a business
allocation of overheads	charging to a cost centre those overheads that have been directly incurred by that cost centre
apportionment of overheads	the charging to a cost centre of a proportion of overheads
service department	cost centre of a business that provides services to other cost centres; its costs must be re-apportioned to productive cost centres
overhead absorption	the method by which overheads are charged to cost units
job/batch/contract costing	a form of specific order costing which applies costs to jobs/batches/contracts
process costing	a form of costing for continuous operations; costs are averaged to find the cost per unit
service costing	a form of costing for service industries; costs are averaged to find the cost per unit

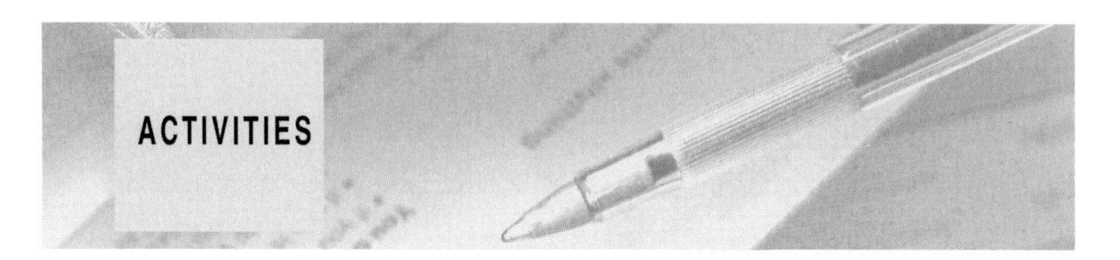

10.1 (a) Select an organisation – either where you work, or another one with which you are familiar – and investigate the methods of costing used.

(b) Discuss the method of costing that would be appropriate for:

- an oil refinery
- an accountant
- a bus company
- a baker
- a sports centre
- an hotel

10.2 Wye Engineering Limited offers specialist engineering services to the car industry. It has two production departments – machinery and finishing – and a service department which maintains the machinery of both departments. Expected costs for the forthcoming year are:

	£
Rent and rates	5,520
Buildings insurance	1,320
Insurance of machinery	1,650
Lighting and heating	3,720
Depreciation of machinery	11,000
Supervisory salaries	30,000
Maintenance department salary	16,000
Factory cleaning	4,800

The following information is available:

	Machinery	*Finishing*	*Maintenance*
Floor area (square metres)	300	200	100
Number of employees	6	3	1
Value of machinery	£40,000	£15,000	–

The factory works a 35-hour week for 47 weeks each year.

(a) Prepare an analysis of overheads showing the basis of allocation and apportionment to the three departments of the business.

(b) Re-apportion the service department overheads to production departments on the basis of value of machinery.

(c) Calculate an overhead absorption rate based on direct labour hours for each of the two production departments.

(d) Discuss alternative overhead absorption rates that the company could use.

10.3 Rossiter and Rossiter is a firm of chartered accountants, with two partners. Overhead costs for next year are estimated to be:

Office rent	£10,000
Secretarial salaries	£30,000
Rates	£4,800
Heating and lighting	£2,400
Stationery	£2,000
Postage and telephone	£5,100
Car expenses	£5,600

The two partners plan to work for 47 weeks next year. They will each be in the office for 40 hours per week, but will be working on behalf of their clients for 35 hours per week.

(a) What is the overhead absorption rate per partner hour?

(b) If each partner wishes to earn a salary of £30,000 per year, what is the combined hourly rate per partner, which includes overheads and their salaries?

(c) If both partners actually work on their clients' behalf for 37 hours per week, what will be the total over-recovery of overheads for the year?

10.4 A friend of yours is about to start in business making garden seats. She plans to make two different qualities – 'standard' and 'de luxe'. Costs per unit for direct materials and labour are expected to be:

	Standard	*De Luxe*
Direct materials	£12.50	£20.00
Direct labour:		
3 hours at £8.00 per hour	£24.00	–
3.5 hours at £10.00 per hour	–	£35.00
	£36.50	£55.00
Machine hours	1	2.5

Factory overheads are expected to be £1,000 per month.

Production (per month) is expected to be 80 'standard' seats and 40 'de luxe' seats.

(a) Suggest three different methods by which overheads can be absorbed.

(b) Calculate the factory cost of each of the two qualities of garden seats using the three different methods of overhead absorption.

(c) Compare the results of your calculations and suggest to your friend the most appropriate method of overhead absorption for this business.

10.5 OB Printers has been asked by John Dun, a local poet, to quote for the cost of printing a small book of poetry. John Dun is not sure how many copies to order, and has asked for quotations for 500, 1,000 and 2,000 copies.

The estimates by OB Printers are as follows:

Setting up the printing machine: 6 hours at £10.00 per hour

Artwork: 7 hours at £12.00 per hour

Typesetting: 20 hours at £15.00 per hour

Paper (for 500 copies): £100.00

Other printing consumables (for 500 copies): £50.00

Direct labour (for 500 copies): 5 hours at £13.00 per hour

Overheads: 80% of direct labour costs

Profit: 25% on cost price

(a) Prepare quotations for 500, 1,000 and 2,000 copies.

(b) Calculate the cost per book to the author at each of the three different production levels.

(c) Respond to John Dun who, on seeing the quotations, says:

"Why is the price per copy so high for 500 copies? I am a starving poet, and I can't afford to have a large quantity printed. If the book sells well I shall regret not having had 2,000 copies printed."

10.6 Agchem Limited is a manufacturer of specialist chemicals for the agricultural industry. One of its products is called 'Oxytone' and passes through three manufacturing processes: 1, 2 and 3. The following information covers a week's production during which 25,000 litres were completed:

	Process 1	Process 2	Process 3
	£	£	£
Direct materials	3,350	1,170	825
Direct labour	1,200	800	1,000
Direct expenses	750	–	220

Production overheads for the week were £1,860 and are apportioned to each process on the basis of direct labour costs.

There was no loss during processing; nor was there any opening or closing work-in-progress.

(a) Calculate the cost per litre for each process

(b) Calculate the total cost of one litre of 'Oxytone'

10.7 At the beginning of January, Processing (Rowcester) Limited had 5,000 units in process. The costs of this work-in-progress were made up as follows:

	£
Direct materials	18,200
Direct labour	7,350
Production overheads	8,500

During January a further 20,000 units were put into the process, with additional costs of:

	£
Direct materials	79,100
Direct labour	36,300
Production overheads	42,200

At the end of January, 18,000 units had been fully processed, and 7,000 units remained in process. The closing work-in-progress was complete as regards direct materials, and 50% complete as regards direct labour and overheads.

(a) Tabulate the month's production and cost figures

(b) Calculate the cost per unit for completed output in January

(c) Calculate the value of work-in-progress at the end of January

10.8 City Transit plc is a small train operating company which runs passenger rail services on a commuter line in a large city. The line links the docks area, which has been redeveloped with flats and houses, with the city centre, and then runs on through the suburbs. An intensive service is operated from early morning to late at night carrying people to and from work, schoolchildren, shoppers and leisure travellers.

The tracks that City Transit uses are leased from the track owner, Trakrail plc. The modern fleet of six diesel trains are owned and maintained by City Transit.

The following information is available in respect of last year's operations:

	cost	*life*
Diesel trains	£650,000 each	20 years

Depreciation is on a straight-line basis, assuming a residual value of £50,000 for each train.

Leasing charges for track	£500,000 pa
Maintenance charges for trains	£455,000 pa
Fuel for trains	£105,000 pa
Wages of drivers and conductors	£240,000 pa
Administration	£260,000 pa

There were 2.5 million passenger journeys last year with an average distance travelled of five miles.

Calculate the cost per passenger mile of operating the railway for last year.

Section 5

decision making

In this section we see how costing systems and methods provide the information for decision making by business owners and managers. In particular, we look at the techniques of

- ***break-even analysis***
- ***marginal costing***
- ***pricing decisions***
- ***capital investment appraisal***

where is the market?

what will the costs be?

what will the profit be?

11 COST BEHAVIOUR AND BREAK-EVEN ANALYSIS

this chapter covers ...

- *the behaviour of fixed, variable and semi-variable costs*
- *the concept of break-even, including the calculation, table and graph methods*
- *the interpretation of break-even*
- *the limitations of break-even analysis*
- *the application of margin of safety and contribution to sales ratio*
- *the uses of break-even analysis*

INTRODUCTION

This chapter looks at the behaviour of costs – fixed, variable, semi-variable – in relation to changes in the level of activity. We shall study the relationship between costs in break-even analysis, which is the point at which a business makes neither a profit nor a loss.

In the chapter we look at:

- the nature of costs, and their behaviour in relation to activity
- the numerical and graphical aspects of break-even analysis
- the use of break-even as a decision making tool
- the limitations of break-even analysis

FIXED AND VARIABLE COSTS

We have already seen (Chapter 9, page 166) the main elements of total cost for most businesses comprise:

- materials
- labour
- overheads

We know that, by nature, costs are:

- fixed, or
- variable, or
- semi-variable

FIXED COSTS

Fixed costs remain constant over a range of output levels, despite other changes – for example, insurance, rent, rates. In the form of a graph, they appear as follows:

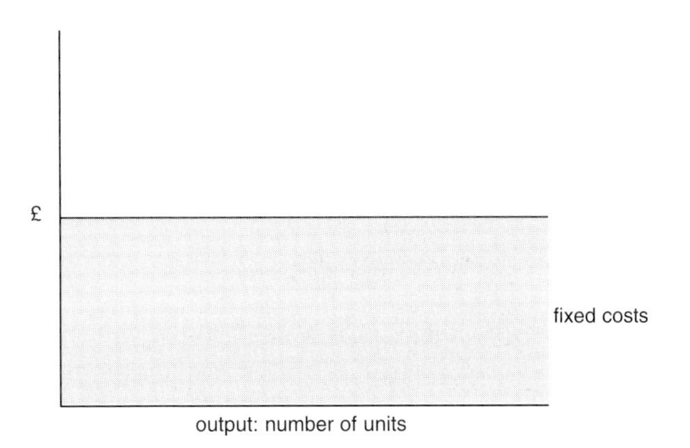

Note: money amounts shown on the vertical axis; units of output shown on the horizontal axis.

For fixed costs, the *cost per unit* falls as output increases, as follows:

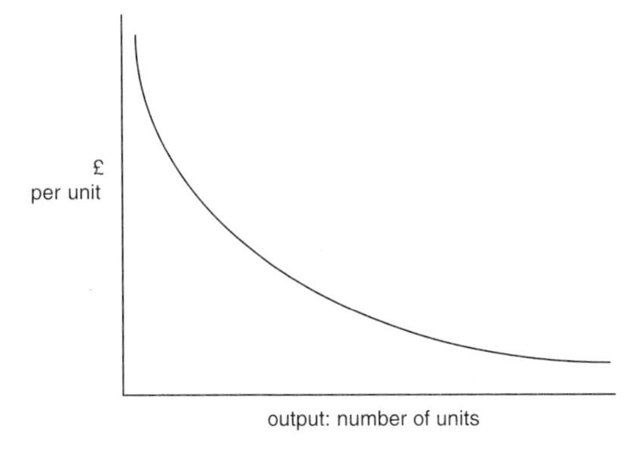

For example, with rent of £40,000 per year:

- at output of 4,000 units, equals £10 per unit
- at output of 10,000 units, equals £4 per unit

Whilst it is sensible to seek to achieve maximum output in order to reduce the cost per unit, fixed costs do not remain fixed at all levels of production. For example, a decision to double production is likely to increase the fixed costs – an increase in factory rent, for example. Fixed costs are often described as *stepped fixed costs*, because they increase by a large amount all at once; graphically, the cost behaviour is shown as a step:

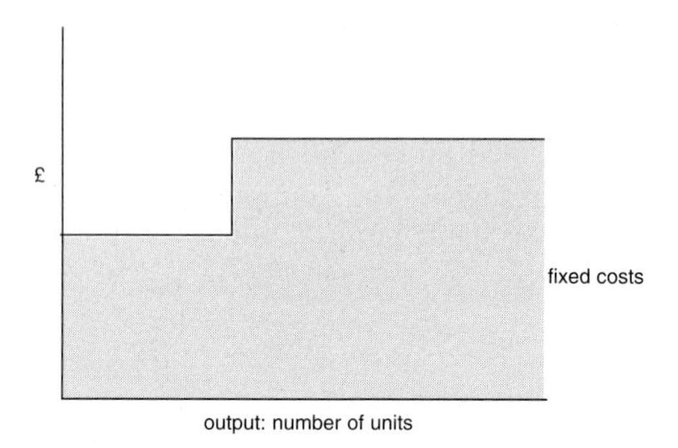

VARIABLE COSTS

Variable costs vary directly with changes in output levels, ie as activity increases, then the cost increases. Examples include direct materials, direct labour, royalties. Graphically, variable costs appear as follows:

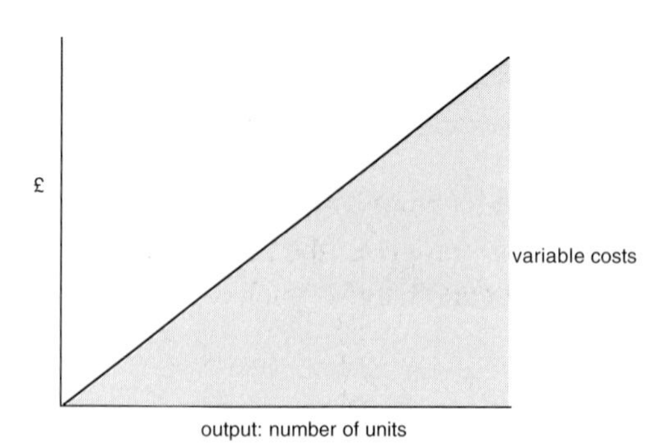

For example, a record company paying a royalty of £1 for each compact disc (CD) produced:

- at output of 1,000 CDs, equals variable cost of £1,000
- at output of 10,000 CDs, equals variable cost of £10,000

The cost per unit remains constant at all levels of output, as follows:

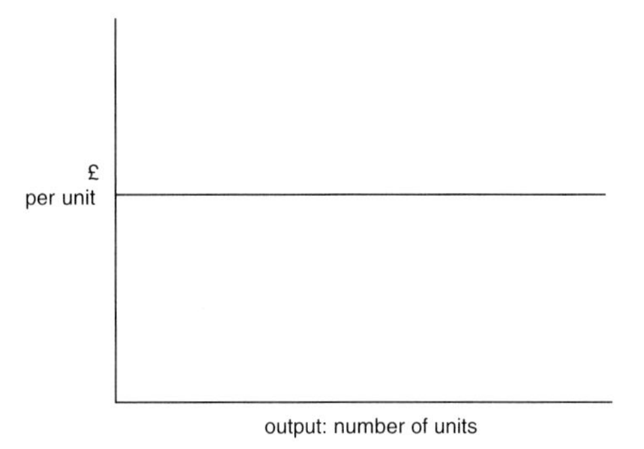

In reality, of course, as output increases more of the item is being bought and it is usually possible to obtain quantity discounts. This means that the cost per unit is slightly reduced at higher levels. Thus, in practice, the variable cost forms a curvilinear line on the graph, as follows:

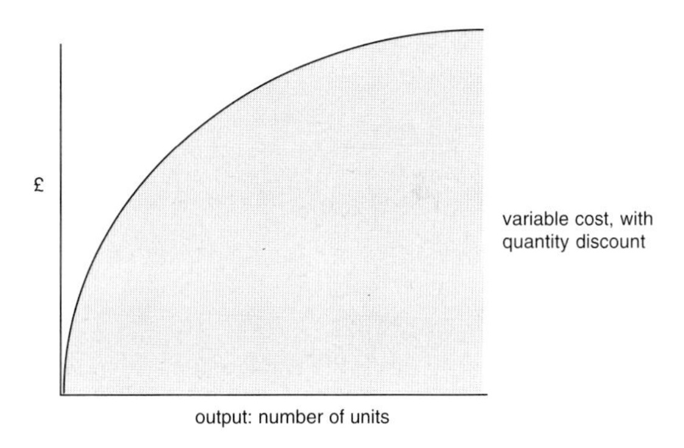

SEMI-VARIABLE COSTS

These combine both a fixed and a variable element. For example, a telephone bill comprises the fixed rental for the line, together with the variable element of call charges. Such a *mixed cost* is expressed graphically as:

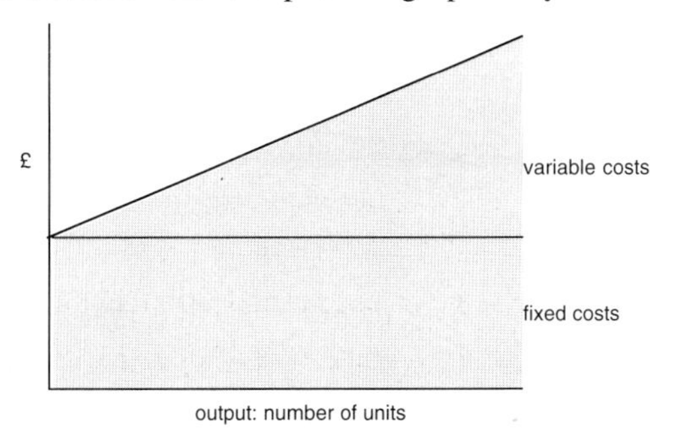

Mixed costs sometimes incorporate a variable element which does not commence until a certain point has been reached. For example, the daily rate for hiring a car might include, say, 100 'free' miles with an additional cost per mile thereafter; or the monthly rental of a photocopier might allow for, say, 10,000 copies with a further charge thereafter. This type of mixed cost is expressed graphically as:

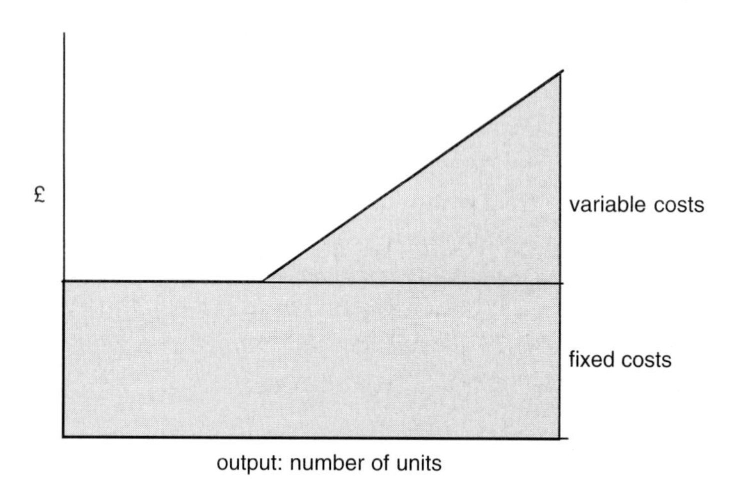

For the purposes of break-even analysis – and also for decision making – we need to distinguish between fixed and variable costs, and to be able to identify from semi-variable costs the amounts of the fixed and variable elements.

BREAK-EVEN POINT

Break-even is the point at which neither a profit nor a loss is made.

In order to use break-even analysis, we need to know:

- selling price (per unit)
- costs of the product
  - variable costs (such as materials, labour) per unit
  - overhead costs, and whether these are fixed or variable
- limitations, such as maximum production capacity, maximum sales

FLUFFY TOYS LIMITED - BREAK-EVEN

situation

Fluffy Toys Limited manufactures soft toys, and is able to sell all that can be produced. The variable costs (materials and direct labour) for producing each toy are £10 and the selling price is £20 each. The fixed costs of running the business are £5,000 per month. How many toys need to be produced and sold each month for the business to cover its costs, ie to break-even?

solution

This problem can be solved by calculation, by constructing a table, or by means of a graph. Which method is used depends on the purpose for which the information is required:

- the *calculation method* is quick to use and is convenient for seeing the effect of different cost structures on break-even point
- the *table method* shows the amounts of fixed and variable costs, sales revenue, and profit at different levels of production
- the *graph method* is used for making presentations – for example, to the directors of a company – because it shows in a visual form the relationship between costs and sales revenue, and the amount of profit or loss at different levels of production

Often the calculation or table methods are used before drawing a graph. By doing this, the break-even point is known and suitable scales can be selected for the axes of the graph in order to give a good visual presentation.

calculation method

The contribution per unit is:

Selling price per unit	£20
Less variable costs per unit	£10
Contribution per unit	£10

Each toy sold gives a contribution (selling price, less variable costs) of £10. This contributes towards the fixed costs and, in order to break-even, the business must have sufficient £10 'lots' to meet the fixed costs. Thus, with fixed costs of £5,000 per month, this business must sell £5,000 ÷ £10 = 500 toys each month. The break-even formula is:

$$\frac{\text{fixed costs (£)}}{\text{contribution per unit (£)}} = \text{break-even point (number of units)}$$

table method

units of production	*fixed costs* A	*variable costs* B	*total cost* C	*sales revenue* D	*profit/(loss)*
			A + B		D – C
	£	£	£	£	£
100	5,000	1,000	6,000	2,000	(4,000)
200	5,000	2,000	7,000	4,000	(3,000)
300	5,000	3,000	8,000	6,000	(2 000)
400	5,000	4,000	9,000	8,000	(1,000)
500	5,000	5,000	10,000	10,000	nil
600	5,000	6,000	11,000	12,000	1,000
700	5,000	7,000	12,000	14,000	2,000

graph method

A graphical presentation uses money amounts as the common denominator between fixed costs, variable costs, and sales revenue.

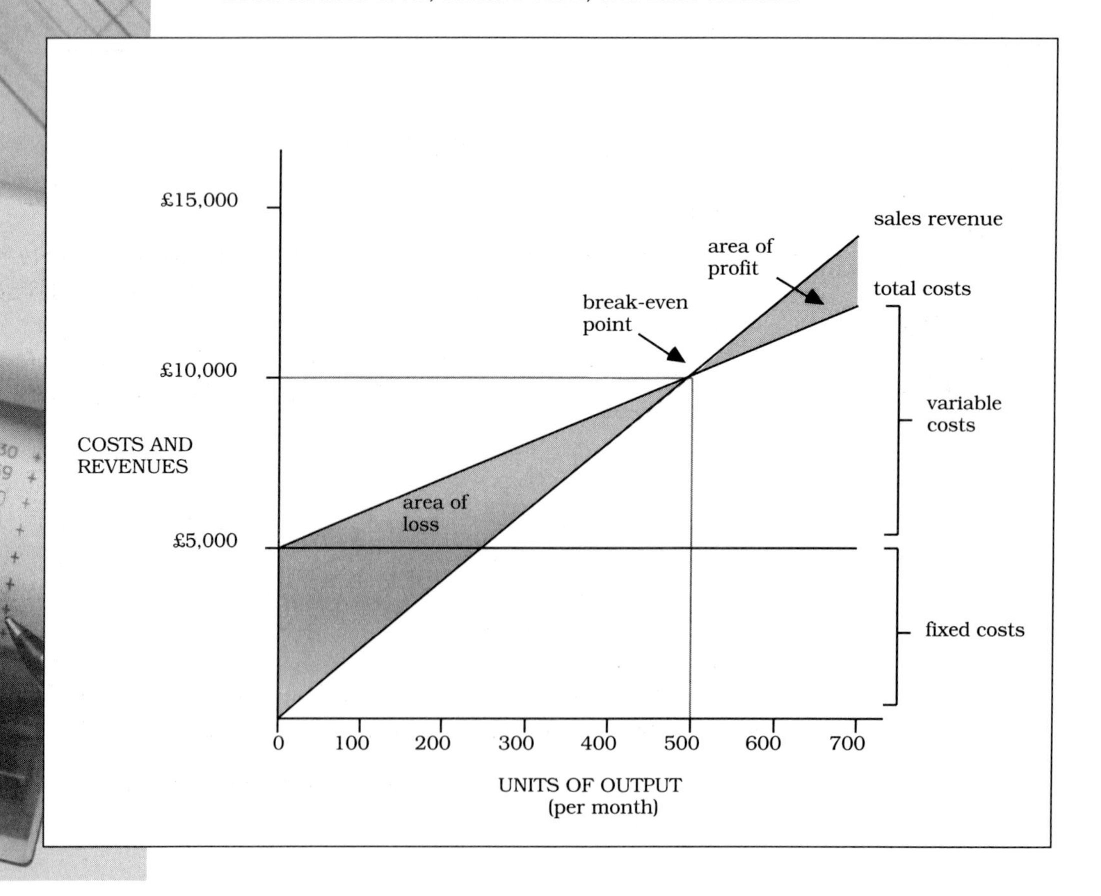

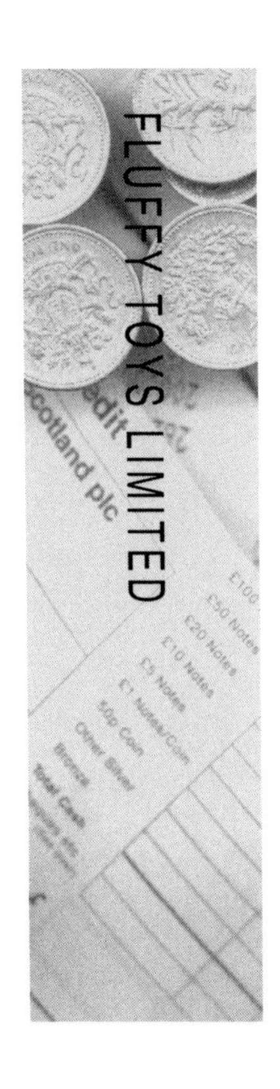

notes to the graph

- With a break-even graph, it is usual for the vertical axis to show money amounts; the horizontal axis shows units of output/sales.
- The fixed costs are unchanged at all levels of output, in this case they are £5,000.
- The variable costs commence, on the vertical axis, *from the fixed costs amount*, not from 'zero'. This is because the cost of producing zero units is the fixed costs.
- The fixed costs *and* the variable costs form the *total costs line.*
- The point at which the total costs and sales revenue lines cross is the break-even point.
- From the graph we can read off the break-even point both in terms of units of output, 500 units on the horizontal axis, and in sales value, £10,000 on the vertical axis.
- The 'proof' of the break-even chart is:

	£
Sales revenue (500 units at £20 each)	10,000
Less variable costs (500 units at £10 each)	5,000
Contribution	5,000
Less fixed costs	5,000
Profit/loss	nil

HINTS FOR DRAWING A BREAK-EVEN GRAPH

- In most break-even charts *all lines are straight.* This means that only two points need be plotted for each line; for example, with sales, choose a number that is fairly near to the maximum expected, multiply by the selling price per unit, and this is the point to be marked on the graph. As the sales line always passes through zero, there are now two points along which to draw a straight line.

- When drawing a break-even graph it is often difficult to know what total value to show on each axis, ie how many units, and/or how much in costs and revenues. As a guide, look for a maximum output or sales level that will not be exceeded: this will give the horizontal axis. Multiply the maximum sales, if known, by the unit selling price to give the maximum sales revenue for the vertical axis. If the figure for maximum sales is not known, it is recommended that the break-even point is calculated before drawing the graph so that the extent of the graph can be established.

- A common error is to start the variable costs from the zero point instead of the fixed costs line.

INTERPRETATION OF BREAK-EVEN

When interpreting break-even, it is all too easy to concentrate solely on the break-even point. The graph, for example, tells us much more than this: it also shows the profit or loss at any level of output/sales contained within the graph. To find this, simply measure the gap between sales revenue and total costs at a chosen number of units, and read the money amounts off on the vertical axis (above break-even point it is a profit; below, it is a loss). For example, the graph in the Case Study above shows a profit or loss at:

- 700 units = £2,000 profit
- 650 units = £1,500 profit
- 400 units = £1,000 loss

Break-even analysis, whether by calculation, by table, or by graph, can be used by all types of businesses and organistions. For example, a shop will wish to know the sales it has to make each week to meet costs; a sports centre will wish to know the ticket sales that have to be made to meet costs; a club or society might wish to know how many raffle tickets it needs to sell to meet the costs of prizes and of printing tickets.

Once the break-even point has been reached, the *additional* contribution forms the profit. For example, if the business considered in the Case Study above was selling 700 toys each month, it would have a total contribution of 700 x £10 = £7,000; of this the first £5,000 will be used to meet fixed costs, and the remaining £2,000 represents the profit (which can be read off the break-even graph). This can be shown by means of a financial statement as follows:

MONTHLY PROFIT STATEMENT

	£
Sales revenue (700 units at £20 each)	14,000
Less variable costs (700 units at £10 each)	7,000
Contribution (to fixed costs and profit)	7,000
Less monthly fixed costs	5,000
Profit for month	2,000

A further use of the break-even concept is where a business wishes to know how many units it needs to make and sell to give a certain amount of profit. This is calculated as follows:

$$\frac{\textit{fixed costs (£) + target profit (£)}}{\textit{contribution per unit (£)}} = \textit{number of units}$$

Thus, if the business in the Case Study above required a profit of £2,000, the calculation is:

$$\frac{£5,000 + £2,000}{£10} = 700 \text{ units, with a sales value of } £14,000 \text{ (700 units at } £20 \text{ each)}$$

See also *contribution to sales ratio* on the next page.

LIMITATIONS OF BREAK-EVEN ANALYSIS

The problem of break-even analysis is the assumption that the relationship between sales revenue, variable costs and fixed costs, remains the same at all levels of production. This is a rather simplistic view because, for example, in order to increase sales, a business will often need to offer bulk discounts, so reducing the sales revenue per unit at higher levels. The limitations of break-even analysis can be summarised as follows:

- The assumption is made that all output is sold. There is no point in preparing the cost data, calculating the break-even point, and estimating the profits to be made if the product will not sell in sufficient quantities. However, break-even analysis is useful for a new business in order to establish the level of sales that must be achieved to reach break-even point. The feasibility of reaching that level of sales must then be considered by the owners of the business.
- All costs and revenues are expressed in terms of straight lines. However, this relationship is not always so. As indicated above selling prices may vary at different quantities sold; in a similar way, as we have seen earlier in the chapter, variable costs alter at different levels as a business takes advantage of lower prices to be gained from bulk buying, and/or more efficient production methods.
- Fixed costs do not remain fixed at all levels of production; instead, as we have seen, they are stepped fixed costs.
- It is not possible to *extrapolate* the graph or calculation; by extrapolation is meant extending the lines on the graph beyond the limits of the activity on which the graph is based. For example, in the Case Study, the graph cannot be extended to, say, 1,000 units of output and the profit read off at this point. The relationship between sales revenues and costs will be different at much higher levels of output – different methods of production might be used, for example.
- The profit or loss shown by the graph or calculations is probably only true for figures close to current output levels – the further away from current figures, the less accurate will be the expected profit or loss.

- A further disadvantage of break-even analysis is that it concentrates too much attention on the break-even point. While this aspect is important to a business, other considerations such as ensuring that the output is produced as efficiently as possible, and that costs are kept under review, are just as important.

BREAK-EVEN: MARGIN OF SAFETY

The margin of safety is the amount by which sales exceed the break-even point. Margin of safety can be expressed as:

- a number of units
- a sales revenue amount
- a percentage, using the following formula

$$\frac{\text{current output} - \text{break-even output}}{\text{current output}} \times \frac{100}{1} = \text{percentage margin of safety}$$

Example

In the Case Study earlier in this chapter, if current output is 700 units, while the break-even point is 500 units, the margin of safety is:

- 200 units (ie 700 – 500)
- £4,000 of sales revenue (ie 200 units at £20 each)
- 29 per cent, ie $\frac{700 - 500}{700} \times \frac{100}{1}$

In interpreting this margin of safety we can say that production/sales can fall by these values before the business reaches break-even point and ceases to make a profit.

Margin of safety is especially important in times of recession as it expresses to management the amount of the 'cushion' which current production/sales gives beyond the break-even point.

CONTRIBUTION TO SALES RATIO

The contribution to sales (or C/S) ratio, or percentage, expresses the amount of contribution in relation to the amount of the selling price:

$$\frac{\text{contribution (£)}}{\text{selling price (£)}} = \text{contribution to sales ratio}$$

The ratio, or percentage, can be calculated on the basis of a single unit of production or for the whole business.

In break-even analysis, if fixed costs are known, we can use the C/S ratio to find the sales value at which the business breaks-even, or the sales value to give a target amount of profit.

Example

Referring back to the Case Study (Fluffy Toys Limited), the C/S ratio (on a per unit basis) is:

$$\frac{\text{contribution (£)}}{\text{selling price (£)}} = \frac{\text{£10*}}{\text{£20}} = 0.5\text{, or }50\%$$

* selling price (£20) – variable costs (£10) = contribution £10

Fixed costs are £5,000 per month, so the sales revenue needed to break-even is:

$$\frac{\text{fixed costs (£)}}{\text{C/S ratio}} = \frac{\text{£5,000}}{\text{0.5 (see above)}} = \underline{\text{£10,000}}$$

If the directors of Fluffy Toys Limited wish to know the sales revenue that must be made to achieve a target profit of £2,000 per month, the C/S ratio is used as follows:

$$\frac{\textit{(fixed costs + target profit)}}{\textit{C/S ratio}} = \textit{required level of sales}$$

$$\frac{\text{(£5,000 + £2,000)}}{0.5} = \underline{\text{£14,000}}$$

WHEN TO USE BREAK-EVEN ANALYSIS

Break-even analysis is often used:

before starting a new business

The calculation of break-even point is important in order to see the level of sales needed by the new business in order to cover costs, or to make a particular level of profit. The feasibility of achieving the level can then be considered by the owner of the business, and other parties such as the bank manager. Break-even analysis will be included in the business plan (see Chapter 20).

when making changes to a business

The costs of a major change in a business will need to be considered by the owners and/or managers. For example, a large increase in production will, most likely, affect the balance between fixed and variable costs. Break-even analysis will be used as part of the planning process to ensure that the business remains profitable.

to measure profits and losses

Within the limitations of break-even analysis, profits and losses can be estimated at different levels of output from current production. (Remember that this can be done only where the new output is close to current levels and where there is no major change to the structure of costs – ie it is not possible to extrapolate.)

to answer 'what if?' questions

Questions such as 'what if sales fall by 10 per cent?' and 'what if fixed costs increase by £1,000?' can be answered – in part at least – by break-even analysis. The effect on the profitability of the business can be seen, subject to the limitations noted earlier. A question such as 'what if sales increase by 300 per cent?' is such a fundamental change that it can only be answered by examining the effect on the nature of the fixed and variable costs and then re-calculating the break-even point.

to evaluate alternative viewpoints

There are often different ways of production; this is particularly true of a manufacturing business. For example, a product could be made:

- either, by using a labour-intensive process, with a large number of employees supported by basic machinery
- or, by using expensive machinery in an automated process with very few employees.

In the first case, the cost structure will be high variable costs (labour) and low fixed costs (depreciation of machinery). In the second case, there will be low variable costs and high fixed costs. Break-even analysis can be used to examine the relationship between the costs which are likely to show a low break-even point in the first case, and a high break-even point in the second. In this way, the management of the business is guided by break-even analysis; management will also need to know the likely sales figures, and the availability of money with which to buy the machinery.

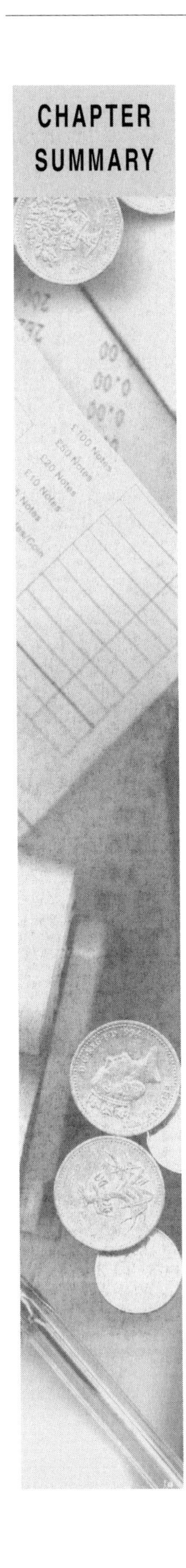

- Break-even analysis distinguishes between fixed costs and variable costs.

- The relationship between sales revenue, and fixed costs and variable costs is used to ascertain the break-even point, by means of a calculation, a table, or a graph.

- The break-even calculation is:

$$\frac{\textit{fixed costs (£)}}{\textit{contribution per unit (£)}} = \textit{break-even point (number of units)}$$

- Break-even analysis can show:
  - break-even point in units of production
  - break-even point in value of sales
  - profit or loss at a given level of output/sales

- The limitations of break-even analysis are that:
  - the assumption is made that all production is sold
  - costs and revenues are expressed in straight lines
  - fixed costs do not remain fixed at all levels of output
  - it is not possible to extrapolate the break-even graph or calculation
  - the profit or loss is probably only true for figures close to current output levels
  - it concentrates too much on break-even point

- Break-even analysis is often used:
  - before starting a new busines
  - when making changes to a business
  - to measure profits or losses
  - to answer 'what if?' questions
  - to evaluate alternative viewpoints

In this chapter we have used contribution as part of the calculation of break-even. We shall see further uses of contribution in the next chapter which focuses on marginal costing in decision making.

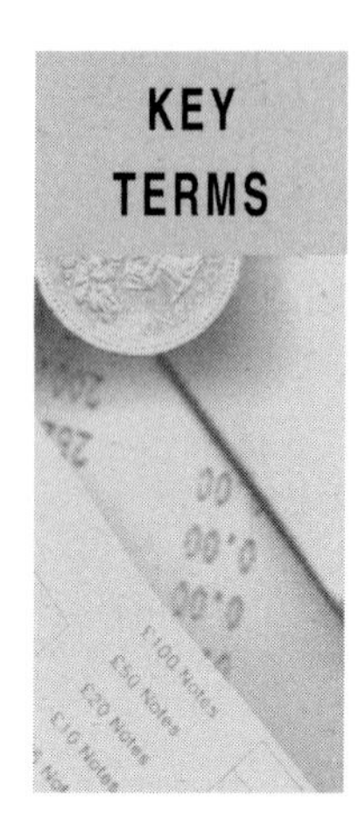

cost behaviour	the way in which costs respond to changes in the level of units of output
break-even	the point at which neither a profit nor a loss is made
contribution	selling price minus variable costs
margin of safety	the amount by which sales exceed the break-even point: expressed as a number of units, an amount of sales revenue, or as a percentage
contribution to sales ratio	expresses the amount of contribution in relation to the amount of the selling price

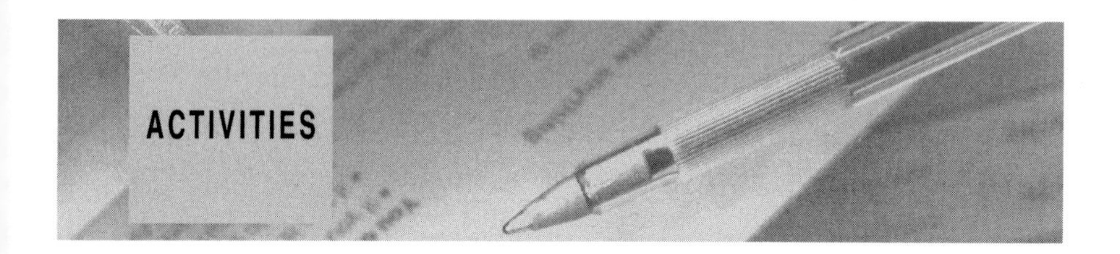

11.1 Select an organisation – either where you work or another one with which you are familiar. For one section of the organisation:

(a) Identify the fixed, variable, and semi-variable costs. How would these be affected if the output of the organisation was to double?

(b) Report on an application of the concept of break-even, and explain how it was used to make decisions.

11.2 Using a product or service with which you are familiar, you are to:

(a) (i) identify the costs as fixed or variable or semi-variable

(ii) subdivide the semi-variable costs between the fixed and variable elements

(iii) identify the selling price

(b) Demonstrate the concept of break-even by means of

(i) the calculation method

(ii) the table method

(iii) the graph method

(c) Calculate the margin of safety.

(d) Discuss the implications of your findings.

11.3 Mike Etherton, a manufacturer of cricket bats, has the following monthly costs:

material cost	£ 8 per bat
labour cost	£12 per bat
selling price	£35 per bat
overheads (fixed)	£12,000

You are to:

- Prepare a table showing costs, sales revenue, and profit or loss for production of bats in multiples of 100 up to 1,200.
- Draw a graph showing the break-even point.
- Prove your answer by calculation.
- Read off the graph the profit or loss if 200 bats, and 1,200 bats are sold each month: prove the answer by calculation.
- If production is currently 1,000 bats per month, what is the margin of safety, expressed in units and as a percentage?

11.4 Bert Peters is the owner of a petrol filling station which has the following weekly costs:

Cost of petrol from oil company	60p per litre
Selling price	65p per litre
Overheads (fixed)	£750

You are to:

- Prepare a table showing costs, sales revenue, and profit or loss for sale of petrol in multiples of 1,000 litres up to 20,000 litres.
- Draw a graph showing the break-even point.
- Prove your answer by calculation.
- Read off the graph the profit or loss if 12,000 litres, and 18,000 litres are sold each week: prove the answer by calculation.
- If sales are currently 18,000 litres each week, what is the margin of safety, expressed in litres and as a percentage?

11.5 Peter Parkinson is a central heating engineer who has designed a special type of thermostatic valve for use in heating systems. He has decided to set up in business to manufacture the product and he has carried out market research which suggests that demand for the product will be between 9,000 units and 20,000 units per annum. Accordingly he has produced the following estimated costs at different levels of production:

budgeted sales (number of units)	9,000	12,000	15,000	20,000
direct materials (£)	27,000	36,000	45,000	60,000
direct labour (£)	9,000	12,000	15,000	20,000
production overheads (£)	48,000	54,000	60,000	70,000
administration, selling and distribution expenses (£)	18,000	18,000	18,000	18,000

Each thermostatic valve will sell for £10.

Peter asks you to help him interpret the results, and in particular he wishes to know:

(a) the profit or loss he will make at each level of production

(b) the break-even point

(c) the fixed amount of production overheads

One market-research survey suggested that a level of sales of 25,000 units per annum might be achieved. Peter asks you to rework the budget at this level of production and to calculate the net profit or loss which will be achieved. He asks you to advise him of any limitations to the usefulness of your figures at this level.

11.6 The research department of Castlemayne Limited, a design and engineering business, has recently developed a new type of electronic dispenser for serving exact quantities of beers and lagers. The company has taken the decision to manufacture the product but has not yet decided which one of two methods of manufacture should be used. Method 1 would involve the purchase of expensive computer-controlled machinery; method 2 would use more traditional machinery but would require more materials and direct labour. Details are as follows:

Method 1: an investment of £240,000 would be required, made up of:

- £200,000 of machinery with an estimated life of five years and a nil scrap value
- £40,000 of working capital requirements

Fixed overheads (excluding depreciation) would amount to £60,000 per annum, and variable costs per unit would be £35.

Method 2: an investment of £120,000 would be needed made up of:

- £80,000 of machinery with an estimated life of five years and a nil scrap value
- £40,000 of working capital requirements

Fixed overheads (excluding depreciation) would amount to £29,000 per annum, and variable costs per unit would be £45.

The product is to be marketed at £60 per unit, and the maximum feasible production capacity under either method is 10,000 units per annum. The company depreciates plant on the straight-line basis. A target rate of return on capital invested of 20% is applied to all projects by the company.

(a) Calculate the number of units which must be produced and sold under either method each year in order to achieve a return of 20 per cent on the capital invested.

(b) Discuss the two alternative production methods, advising the circumstances under which one is preferable to the other.

12 MARGINAL COSTING

this chapter covers ...

- *the importance of marginal costing techniques to management decision making*
- *the application of the concept of marginal costing to*
  - *decisions about products/departments that do not make a profit*
  - *the use of spare capacity for special orders*
  - *make or buy decisions*
  - *the allocation of scarce resources*
- *the effect of marginal costing on other aspects of the business*

INTRODUCTION

We have already seen in Chapter 9 (page 174) that the marginal cost is the cost of producing one extra unit of output. Marginal costing techniques recognise that fixed costs vary with time rather than activity. For example, the rent of premises relates to a certain time period – such as a week, month or year – and remains unchanged whether there are 100 units of output or 300 (always assuming that the capacity of the premises is at least 300 units). By contrast, one extra unit of output will incur an increase in the variable costs – such as direct materials and direct labour – this increase is the *marginal cost.* Within an accounting period every business which seeks to make profits must cover its costs and make a profit from the selling price it charges for its output. However, a knowledge of marginal costing techniques can help with decision making in the forms of:

- contribution to sales ratio, rather than profit margin
- use of spare capacity for special orders
- make or buy decisions
- allocation of scarce resources

The key to all of these, as we shall see shortly, is the *contribution* from the sale of units of output. Contribution is calculated as:

	unit selling price
minus	unit marginal cost
equals	contribution to fixed costs and profit

We have already seen, in the previous chapter, how contribution is used as part of the calculation for break-even.

CONTRIBUTION TO SALES (C/S) RATIO

The C/S ratio (see page 224) can be used, in place of gross and net profit margins, to measure the contribution of departments or products of a business. It will help management to answer questions such as:

- are all departments/products giving a contribution?
- what happens if one department/product line is closed?

CASE STUDY

WYVERN FURNITURE LIMITED – CONTRIBUTION AND CONTRIBUTION TO SALES RATIO

situation

Wyvern Furniture Limited is a large store with three departments: furniture, carpets, curtains. Last year's profit and loss account shows the following:

	furniture	*carpets*	*curtains*	*total*
	£000s	*£000s*	*£000s*	*£000s*
Sales	3,000	1,500	1,000	5,500
Materials (variable)	1,500	1,050	300	2,850
Labour (variable)	300	250	100	650
Overheads (fixed)*	600	300	300	1,200
TOTAL COSTS	2,400	1,600	700	4,700
PROFIT/(LOSS)	600	(100)	300	800

* apportioned on the basis of floor area

The managing director says that, in view of the loss made by the carpet department, it should be closed. The management accountant disagrees ...

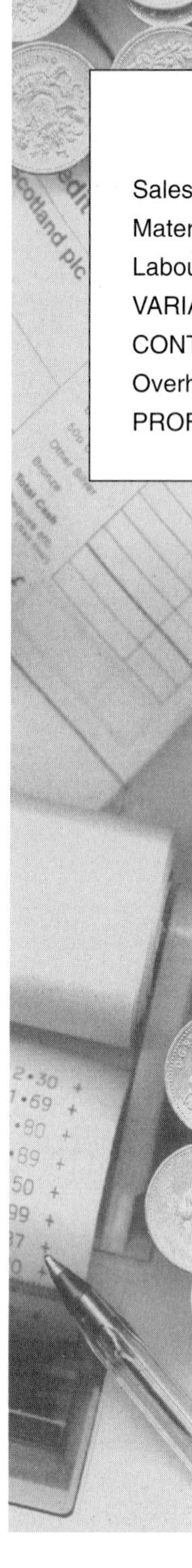

solution

The management accountant presents the financial results of Wyvern Furniture Limited in a different way in order to show the contribution made by each department:

	furniture	*carpets*	*curtains*	*total*
	£000s	*£000s*	*£000s*	*£000s*
Sales	3,000	1,500	1,000	5,500
Materials	1,500	1,050	300	2,850
Labour	300	250	100	650
VARIABLE COSTS	1,800	1,300	400	3,500
CONTRIBUTION	1,200	200	600	2,000
Overheads (fixed)				1,200
PROFIT				800

This shows that each department makes a contribution towards the fixed overheads of the business. The contribution/sales ratios are:

furniture	$\frac{£1,200}{£3,000}$	= 0.4 or 40%
carpets	$\frac{£200}{£1,500}$	= 0.13 or 13%
curtains	$\frac{£600}{£1,000}$	= 0.6 or 60%

A number of questions need to be considered before taking the decision about closing the carpet department. These include:

- As the carpet department contributes £200,000 towards fixed overheads, its closure means that profits of the store will fall to £600,000 (assuming that the fixed overheads do not reduce in the short-term).
- Closure of the carpet department may well have implications for sales in the other departments – for example, customers will often wish to buy carpets and curtains at the same time, or furniture and carpets together.
- The floor space currently occupied by the carpet department could be used for other retailing purposes. Will this give a higher contribution than £200,000?

Before taking a decision about the carpet department, the managing director needs to review the contribution of this section of the business. The contribution/sales ratio of each department should be discussed with departmental managers to look at ways of increasing the percentage. Additionally, the level of fixed overheads should be studied to see if there are ways in which they can be reduced.

Thus the Case Study provides important facets of decision making:

- it establishes the contribution of each department to overall fixed costs
- it shows the contribution/sales ratio of each department and gives individual responsibility to the managers for improvements
- it measures performance and provides a benchmark for future improvements

USE OF SPARE CAPACITY

Once a business is profitable at its current level of output, it can make additional sales at a selling price above marginal cost, but below absorption cost, and so increase its profits. The proviso is that the additional sales must be spare capacity within, for example, the factory: if, in order to sell 100 extra units, a new factory has to be bought with a capacity of one million units, then it seems unlikely that the additional sales will prove to be profitable! The key to increasing profit from additional sales is to ensure that a contribution to profit is made from the special order: the Case Study (below) illustrates this principle.

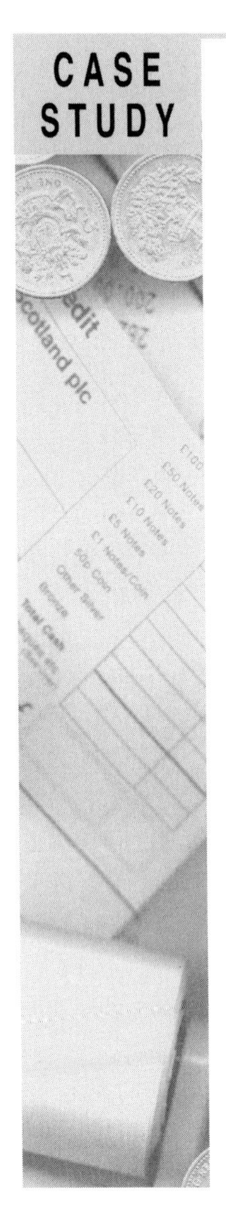

WYVERN BIKE COMPANY

situation

The Wyvern Bike Company produces 100 bikes a week, and sells them for £100 each. Its costs are as follows:

weekly costs for producing 100 bikes

	£
Direct materials (£20 per bike)	2,000
Direct labour (£25 per bike)	2,500
PRIME COST	4,500
Overheads (fixed)	3,500
TOTAL COST	8,000

The management of the company has been approached by a mail order warehouse which wishes to buy:

- *either* 50 bikes each week at a price of £60
- *or* 100 bikes each week at a price of £40

The bikes can be produced in addition to existing production, with no increase in overheads. The special order is not expected to affect the company's existing sales. How would you advise the management?

solution

The *absorption cost* of producing one bike is £80 (£8,000 ÷ 100 bikes). The mail order warehouse is offering either £60 or £40 per bike. On the face of it, with an absorption cost of £80, both orders should be rejected. However, as there will be no increase in overheads, we can use *marginal costing* to help with decision making.

The *marginal cost* per bike is £45 (direct materials £20, plus direct labour £25 per

bike), and so any contribution, ie selling price less marginal cost, will be profit:

- ***50 bikes at £60 each***

  Although below absorption cost, the offer price of £60 is above the marginal cost of £45 and increases profit by the amount of the £15 extra contribution, ie (£60 – £45) x 50 bikes = £750 extra profit.

- ***100 bikes at £40 each***

  This offer price is below absorption cost of £80 and marginal cost of £45; therefore there will be a fall in profit if this order is undertaken of (£40 – £45) x 100 bikes = £500 reduced profit.

weekly profit statements

	Existing production	Existing production + 50 units @ £60 each	Existing production + 100 units @ £40 each
	£	£	£
Sales revenue (per week):			
100 bikes at £100 each	10,000	10,000	10,000
50 bikes at £60 each	–	3,000	–
100 bikes at £40 each	–	–	4,000
	10,000	13,000	14,000
Less production costs:			
Direct materials (£20 per unit)	2,000	3,000	4,000
Direct labour (£25 per unit)	2,500	3,750	5,000
Overheads (fixed)	3,500	3,500	3,500
PROFIT	2,000	2,750	1,500

The conclusion is that the first special order from the mail order warehouse should be undertaken, and the second declined. The general rule is that, once the fixed overheads have been recovered, provided additional units can be sold at a price above marginal cost, then profits will increase.

MAKE OR BUY DECISIONS

A make or buy decision is a management decision whether to make a product, or supply a service, 'in-house', or to buy in the product/service from an outside supplier.

Examples of make or buy decisions include:

- a car manufacturer needing many different components to make the car –

some components will be manufactured in-house while others will be bought from outside suppliers

- a local authority facing the decision whether to provide a payroll accounting service itself, or to buy in the service from an outside contractor

Whilst there are a number of considerations before taking a make or buy decision, the costs involved in the decision and the effect on profit – both financial aspects – are usually uppermost in the mind of management.

the effect on fixed and variable costs

Make or buy decisions affect the cost structure of the business, particularly the relationship between fixed and variable costs. For example, a business seeking to increase output can:

- either expand its own production facilities – which will mainly affect its fixed costs (ie rent of premises, depreciation of new machinery and equipment), with a smaller effect on variable costs
- or buy in from outside suppliers – which will mainly affect its variable costs (ie bought in units are classed as direct materials), with a smaller effect on fixed costs

The first course of action takes a long-term view and assumes that the increase in production can be sustained for a number of years. The second course of action is rather more flexible (ie the number of units bought in can be varied to meet demand) and could be either a long-term arrangement, or for the short-term with, perhaps, the possibility of expanding in-house production facilities in the future.

the use of marginal costing

When considering make or buy decisions, comparisons need to be made between:

- the marginal cost of the product from in-house supply

  and

- the price quoted by the outside supplier

The lower price is, in financial terms, the better choice; however there may well be non-financial aspects to consider, such as quality, reliability, etc.

opportunity cost

Opportunity cost is the benefit that is foregone when a particular course of action is taken.

In make or buy decisions we must consider the resources used (eg factory or office space, machines and equipment) when goods or services are provided in-house. The use of these resources may cause other work to be lost or curtailed. The loss of contribution from this other work needs to be added to the marginal cost in order to make the decision. The make or buy decision is expressed now as a comparison between:

- the marginal cost of making the product in-house, *plus* the contribution from lost or curtailed work

  and

- the price quoted by the outside supplier

The lower price is the better choice in financial terms.

CASE STUDY

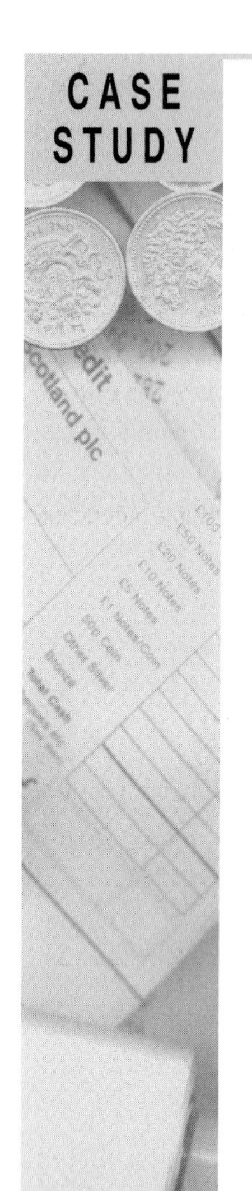

WYVERN ALARMS LIMITED – MAKE OR BUY

situation

Wyvern Alarms Limited manufactures high quality security alarms called 'Wyvern Super'. These are sold to alarm companies who install and maintain them.

Until now, Wyvern Alarms has been proud of its in-house production line – materials are bought in, and all manufacturing and assembly is carried out at its factory in Wyvern. With the rise in crime rates, the company is finding that demand for its products is increasing. The point has been reached when decisions must be taken about buying in components from outside suppliers.

The management accountant of Wyvern Alarms has obtained a price from a potential supplier for control boxes, detailed below.

control boxes

These comprise a metal box with a hinged, lockable cover. The box is spray painted in white, with the company logo applied by means of a transfer. It is not considered that quality will be compromised if this item is bought in from an outside supplier.

These are the two alternatives:

1 The cost of making each control box in-house at the current level of 5,000 units each year is:

	£
direct materials	2.50
direct labour	5.50
variable overheads	1.50
fixed overheads	5.50
total cost	15.00

There is no other use for the specialist production machinery required to make this product.

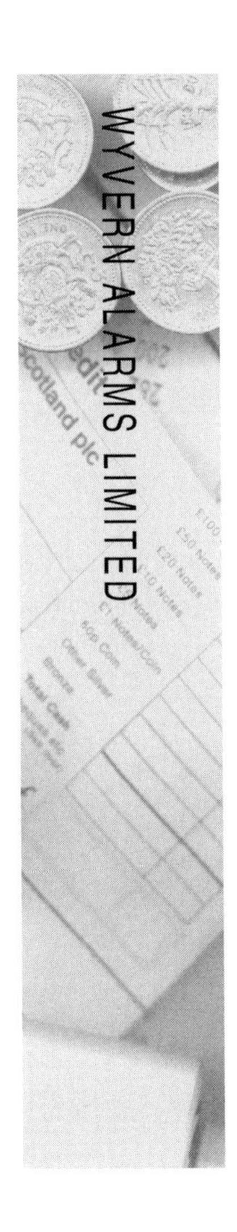

2 An outside supplier has quoted a price of £10 per unit (based on Wyvern's requirements of 5,000 units each year).

Should the management of Wyvern Alarms 'make' or 'buy' ?

solution

The marginal cost of producing each control box is:

	£
direct materials	2.50
direct labour	5.50
variable overheads	1.50
marginal cost	9.50

The comparison is then:

- marginal cost of in-house manufacturer, £9.50 x 5,000 units = £47,500
- price quoted by outside supplier, £10 x 5,000 units = £50,000

As there is no other use for the production machinery currently being used, the decision should be to continue making this component in-house.

Note that if there was an alternative use for the production machinery, the comparison then becomes:

- marginal cost of in-house manufacture, *plus* contribution from alternative work
- price quoted by outside supplier

In this Case Study, a contribution of more than £2,500 per year from the production machinery, would make the buy-in a better financial proposition.

ALLOCATION OF SCARCE RESOURCES

Scarce resources, or *limiting factors*, are those aspects of a business which prevent further expansion. Examples include:

- availability of materials
- availability of skilled labour
- factory or office space
- finance
- the quantity of the output which can be sold – whether a manufactured product or a service

At any one time there is usually one main limiting factor. It is essential to minimise its effect by optimising resources and maximising profit. After one limiting factor has been dealt with, another one then affects the business – for example, once a shortage of materials has been resolved, the limiting factor might well become a lack of skilled labour.

Where a business sells more than one product, under normal circumstances it will be best to switch output to the product that gives the highest contribution in relation to sales. For example, a company makes two products for which the selling prices and contributions are:

	product X	product Y
selling price	£100	£200
contribution	£40	£60

With no limiting factors, the company should concentrate on making and selling product X. The reason for this is that the contribution/sales percentage is 40 per cent when compared with product Y, where it is 30 per cent.

Where there is a limiting factor, for example the availability of skilled labour, a business will switch production to the product which gives the highest contribution from each unit of the limiting factor (eg contribution per direct labour hour). The Case Study which follows illustrates this concept.

CASE STUDY

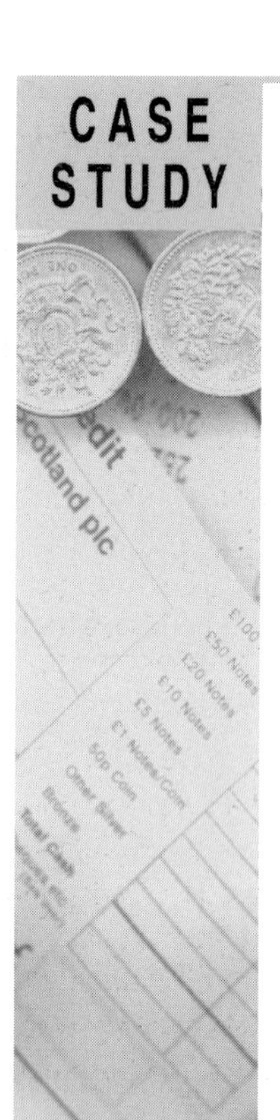

SOUND SYSTEMS LIMITED – LIMITING FACTORS

situation

Sound Systems Limited is a small company which makes reproduction radios to 1930s' designs (but with year 2000 sound quality!). Two models are made – the 'Windsor' and the 'Buckingham'. Both products require skilled direct labour which cannot be increased in the short-term. Demand for the company's products is increasing rapidly and, while the company is taking steps to train new employees, the production manager is unsure of the 'mix' of products that should be produced each week.

The information available is:

	Windsor	Buckingham
selling price per unit	£50	£100
contribution per unit	£20	£30
direct labour hours per unit	2	2

- the number of direct labour hours each week is 240
- the weekly fixed overheads of the business are £2,000
- all of the company's output can be sold

Give the production manager your recommendations for next week's production, supporting your views with a forecast profit statement.

solution

Ignoring, for the moment, the limiting factor of direct labour, the better model for the company to produce is the Windsor, because this gives a higher contribution sales percentage:

- Windsor: £20 contribution on £50 of sales = 40 per cent
- Buckingham: £30 contribution on £100 of sales = 30 per cent

However, as direct labour is the limiting factor, the company should maximise the contribution from each hour of direct labour:

- Windsor: contribution per direct labour hour £20 ÷ 2 hours = £10
- Buckingham: contribution per direct labour hour £30 ÷ 2 hours = £15

Therefore, the company should utilise fully its direct labour hours in production of the Buckingham, ie 120 units will be made (240 hours ÷ 2 hours per unit).

The forecast weekly profit statement will be as follows:

forecast weekly profit statement

	£
Sales of Buckingham (120 units x £100)	12,000
Contribution (120 units x £30)	3,600
Less overheads (fixed)	2,000
Profit	1,600

Note however that, by taking this action, no Windsor models will be produced the marketing director will not be too keen on this as it may be difficult to re-establish the Windsor in the market when production of this model can be restarted following the completion of training for new employees. In practice, it is likely that both models will be made, but with preference being given to the Buckingham. The problem is that often customers want availability of all products and, if one isn't available, they won't buy the others (think of the store closing its carpet department and the effect on sales in the furniture department).

MARGINAL COSTING: OTHER POINTS

We have seen how marginal costing techniques can be useful in decision making. Nevertheless, there are a number of points that must be borne in mind:

- ***fixed costs must be covered***

  A balance needs to be struck between the output that is sold at above marginal cost and the output that is sold at absorption cost. The overall contribution from output must cover the fixed costs of the business and provide a profit for the owners. Overall output should be sold at a high enough price to provide a contribution to fixed costs.
- ***separate markets for marginal cost***

  It is sensible business practice to separate out the markets where marginal cost is used. For example, a business would not quote a price based on absorption cost to retailer A and a price based on marginal cost to retailer B, when A and B are both in the same town! It would be better to seek new markets – perhaps abroad – with prices based on marginal cost.
- ***effect on customers***

  One of the problems of using marginal cost pricing to attract new business is that it is difficult to persuade the customer to pay closer to, or above, absorption cost later on. Thus one of the dangers of using marginal cost is that profit margins can be squeezed quite dramatically if the technique is used too widely.
- ***problems of product launch on marginal cost basis***

  There is great temptation in business to launch a new product at the keenest possible price – below absorption cost (but above marginal cost). If the product is highly successful, it could well alter the cost structure of the business. However, it could also lead to the collapse of sales of older products so that most of the company's sales are derived from output priced on the marginal cost basis – it may then be difficult to increase up prices to above absorption cost levels.
- ***special edition products***

  Many businesses use marginal costing techniques to sell off older products at a keen price. For example, car manufacturers with a new model due in a few months' time will package the old model with 'special edition' bodywork and sell it at a low price (but above marginal cost)

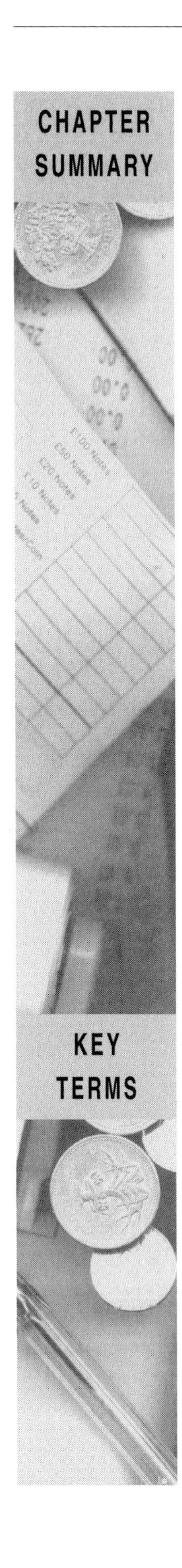

CHAPTER SUMMARY

- Marginal costing techniques can help with decision making.
- Contribution/sales ratio is used to measure the contribution of departments or products of a business.
- Spare capacity is used for output which can be sold as 'special orders' at a price above marginal cost, but below absorption cost – always provided that the fixed costs are covered by the contribution from normal sales.
- Make or buy decisions compare the marginal cost of the product from in-house supply with the price quoted by the outside supplier.
- Scarce resources – or limiting factors – should be allocated to the output which gives the highest contribution/sales percentage.
- Using marginal costing techniques, decision makers must bear in mind:
  - separate markets for marginal cost
  - effect on customers
  - problems of product launch on a marginal cost basis
  - special edition products

In the next chapter we look at how costs can be used to make pricing decisions and to work out the selling price to the customer.

KEY TERMS

marginal cost	the cost of producing one extra unit of output
make or buy decisions	whether to make a product/supply a service 'in-house' or to buy in the product/service from an outside supplier
opportunity cost	the benefit that is foregone when a particular course of action is taken
limiting factor	some aspect of a business which prevents further expansion

12.1 Select an organisation – either where you work, or another with which you are familiar.

(a) Investigate the limiting factor(s) currently affecting the organisation. Suggest possible solutions.

(b) Identify the opportunities for using marginal costing to increase sales.

12.2 Investigate applications of marginal costing in a service industry, for example:

- hotel
- transport
- cinema or theatre
- holiday companies

- Identify the benefits and possible restrictions to customers
- Identify the benefits and potential problems for the supplier

12.3 Planter Pete's Garden Centre Limited has four departments: shrubs and trees, plants, hardware, and a coffee shop. Last year's profit and loss account shows the following:

	shrubs and trees	*plants*	*hardware*	*coffee shop*	*total*
	£000s	*£000s*	*£000s*	*£000s*	*£000s*
Sales	150	200	100	60	510
Materials (variable)	50	60	45	30	185
Labour (variable)	35	40	15	20	110
Overheads (fixed)*	45	60	30	18	153
TOTAL COSTS	130	160	90	68	448
PROFIT/(LOSS)	20	40	10	(8)	62

* apportioned on the basis of sales values

The managing director is meeting with the heads of department tomorrow. She is considering the closure of the coffee shop but seeks your advice as to any points she should bear in mind before the meeting.

12.4 Wyvern Airways is a local airline which flies to short-haul destinations within the UK and Europe. The costs of flight WA 005 to Rome, which uses a 100 seater aircraft are as follows:

direct materials	£12.50 per passenger
direct labour	£10.00 per passenger
direct expenses	£2.50 per passenger
fixed overheads	£3,500 per flight

For next week's flight, sixty seats have been sold at a standard-class fare of £100 each.

You are to calculate:

- the absorption cost per seat on this flight with sixty seats sold
- the marginal cost per seat
- the profit or loss if no further tickets are sold for this flight

The marketing manager thinks it unlikely that any further standard-class fares will be sold. There are two possibilities that she must consider:

- to release the surplus seats to a firm that sells cheap flights: the airline will receive £45 for each seat sold and, from past experience, the marketing manager expects thirty seats to be sold
- to sell all forty spare seats to a local newspaper, which will offer them as prizes for a 'spot-the-ball' competition: the newspaper will pay £35 per seat

Advise the marketing manager whether either of these possibilities should be considered; explain your reasoning, and illustrate your answer with profit statements.

12.5 The Last Company is famous for its 'Snowdon' range of hill-walking boots. The management of the company is considering the production for next year and has asked for help with certain financial decisions.

The following information is available:

wholesale selling price (per pair)	£60
direct materials (per pair)	£20
direct labour (per pair)	£18
overheads (fixed)	£200,000 per year

The company is planning to manufacture 12,500 pairs of boots next year.

You are to calculate:

- the absorption cost per pair
- the marginal cost per pair
- the profit or loss if 12,500 pairs of boots are sold

A mail order company, Sales-by-Post Limited, has approached The Last Company with a view to selling the 'Snowdon' boot through its catalogue. Sales-by-Post offers two contracts:

- either 2,500 pairs of boots at £45 per pair
- or 5,000 pairs of boots at £37 per pair

As The Last Company usually sells through specialist shops, it is not expected that 'normal' sales will be affected. These 'special orders' are within the capacity of the factory, and overheads will remain unchanged. You are to advise the management as to whether these offers should be accepted; illustrate your answer with profit statements.

12.6 Dean Limited makes two products – A and B. Both products are made from the same type of direct materials. These materials are currently in short supply. At present the company can obtain only 500 kilos of the direct materials each week. The production manager seeks your guidance as to the 'mix' of products that should be produced each week. The information available is:

	A	B
selling price per unit	£150	£200
contribution per unit	£30	£50
kilos of direct materials per unit	2	4

The weekly fixed overheads of the business are £4,000.

You are to give the production manager your recommendations for next week's production, supporting your views with a forecast profit statement.

12.7 Sesame Shoes Limited manufactures shoes at its factory in Wyvern. A company in the Far East has offered to manufacture one particular style of shoe – the 'Paris' design – at a cost of £20 per pair.

The management accountant of Sesame Shoes has prepared the following cost statement (per pair of shoes) – based on current production levels – for the 'Paris' design:

	£
direct materials	10.00
direct labour	5.00
variable overheads	3.00
fixed overheads	5.00
total cost	23.00

There is currently no other use for the factory space and production machinery used to make the 'Paris' design.

Advise the management of Sesame Shoes whether or not, in financial terms, the shoes should be bought from the Far Eastern manufacturer.

Apart from financial data, what other aspects should the management of Sesame Shoes consider before making a final decision?

12.8 Pentland Pumps Limited manufactures electric pumping equipment used in industry and agriculture. At present all parts are made in-house from raw materials. The company is considering buying in pump motors from an outside supplier in order to release facilities for a new product, an 'olde worlde' handpump for decorative (and practical) use.

The following information is available:

- the cost of making each pump motor in-house at the current level of production of 3,500 pumps per year is:

	£
direct materials	40.00
direct labour	25.00
variable overheads	20.00
fixed overheads	15.00
total cost	100.00

- an outside supplier has quoted a price of £95 per motor
- if pump motors are bought in from an outside supplier, the company will be able to make 750 'olde worlde' handpumps each year, with a selling price of £250 per unit and variable costs of £150 per unit

You are to advise the management of Pentland Pumps Limited whether or not, in financial terms, the motors should be bought in from the outside supplier.

13 PRICING DECISIONS

this chapter covers ...

- *the importance of relevant costs when making pricing decisions*
- *the factors to consider when determining price*
- *the main pricing strategies of cost-plus, market led, and marginal cost/contribution pricing*
- *the objective of establishing a transfer price and the more common ways in which this can be done*

INTRODUCTION

In studying costing so far we have considered the techniques used to calculate the cost of output – either making a product or providing a service. In this chapter we see how the selling price to the customer is worked out by looking at a number of pricing strategies:

- *cost-plus* – cost price, plus profit (often a percentage of cost price) equals selling price
- *market led* – the selling price is determined largely by what other suppliers of similar products or services are charging
- *marginal cost/contribution pricing* – the selling price for special orders is above marginal cost but below absorption cost
- *transfer pricing* – the price at which products are sold in internal markets within the business or organisation

Before turning to each of these in more detail we need to be sure that a business is using the *relevant costs* on which to base its pricing decisions.

RELEVANT COSTS

Relevant costs are those that are appropriate to a specific management decision.

Not only for pricing but also for other management decisions, it is essential for the manager to have available the right information. We have already seen in the previous chapter how a knowledge of marginal costing gave information so that more informed decisions could be taken between different courses of action.

How does a manager decide which costs are relevant and which are non-relevant? The following gives some guidance:

sunk costs

These are past costs which are not taken into account in decision making. As the money has been spent in the past, the costs have no relevance (other than in providing a guide as to what future costs might be). Therefore, it is *future* costs (and revenues) that must be used in decision making.

notional costs

These are an allowance for a benefit received for which no cost is incurred. For example, if a business owns its own premises (rather than renting), then it must allow a notional cost for rent in its cost calculations. The notional rent is a relevant cost and to ignore it would undercost its output. Applying the same principle, a whisky producer will need to allow for notional interest as a cost for the period during which its product is maturing.

opportunity costs

We have already touched on opportunity cost in the previous chapter (page 237). The opportunity cost is the benefit that is foregone when a particular course of action is taken. For example, if we make product X, then we can't make product Y: the opportunity cost is the contribution derived from output of product Y. Opportunity cost is a relevant cost where there are scarce resources or other limiting factors.

differential costs

When comparing alternative courses of action it is only those costs (and revenues) which change as a result of the decision that are important. Many costs remain the same for different alternatives, eg the fixed costs may well be constant. Thus, the decision makers will focus on those costs that are changed – the differential costs. We have already used this technique with marginal costing (see page 175); the reason for concentrating on differential costs is because the costs that remain unchanged cancel each other out and can be ignored in the choice between alternatives.

cost benefit analysis

A wider view of costing is to use cost benefit analysis to measure the resources used in a particular course of action and to compare these with the value of the benefits to the business or organisation.

In the public sector, cost benefit analysis is often used to allocate scarce resources to the project that will give the most benefit to the community, eg shall we spend money on a dog warden, or shall we employ a gardener? In business, cost benefit analysis enables a view to be taken which goes beyond the costing information. The market that the business is in can be considered: for example, is it product led, or market led? Are there cheaper alternatives to our product? How can we add more value to our products? And at what cost?

FACTORS WHICH DETERMINE PRICE

A price is the amount of money that is agreed between a buyer and a seller which enables the exchange of a product – goods or a service – to take place.

There are three main factors that a business must consider when deciding the price at which to sell its goods:

- *the need to make a profit* – in the long-term, selling price must be higher than total cost
- *prices of competing products* – the selling price is determined largely by what other suppliers of the product are charging
- *under-used capacity* – selling some of the output at a cut price, eg selling unsold tickets cheaply at a theatre just before the performance

For each of these factors which determine price, there is a related pricing strategy:

- *the need to make a profit* – the pricing strategy is *cost-plus pricing*
- *prices of competing products* – the pricing strategy is *market led pricing*
- *under-used capacity* – the pricing strategy is *marginal cost/contribution pricing*

We will now look at each of these in more detail.

COST-PLUS PRICING

The calculation for cost-plus pricing is:

cost price + *profit* = *selling price*

Cost is usually calculated on the basis of absorption cost (see page 173), which adds together all the costs of each cost unit.

Profit can be calculated:

- *either* as a percentage mark-up on cost price (ie the profit, being a percentage of cost price, is added to cost price to give selling price)
- *or* to give a percentage return on capital employed (ie the money invested in the business)

The Case Study which follows illustrates the ways in which a company can use cost-plus pricing to determine the selling price for its products.

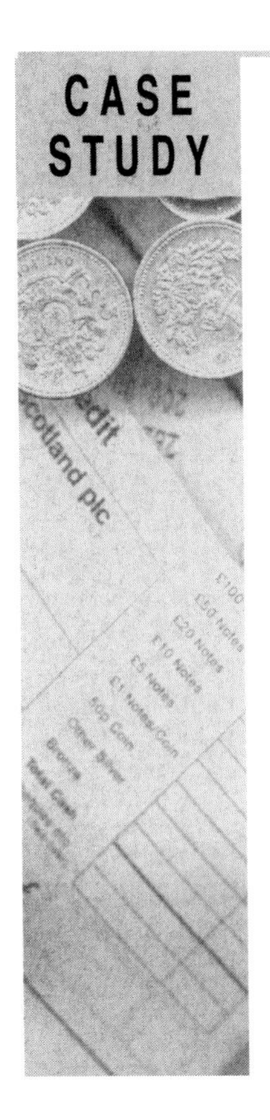

LEATHERCRAFT LIMITED

situation

Leathercraft Limited makes high-quality 'executive' chairs. Each year, at its factory in Mereford, it makes 2,000 chairs and its costs are as follows:

annual costs for producing 2,000 chairs

	£
Direct materials (£100 per chair)	200,000
Direct labour (£70 per chair)	140,000
PRIME COST	340,000
Overheads (fixed)	100,000
TOTAL COST	440,000

The company is currently reviewing its selling prices and is considering cost-plus pricing based on:

- *either* a 40 per cent mark-up on cost price (ie profit is 40 per cent of cost price, which is added to cost price to give selling price)
- *or* a 20 per cent return on capital employed

Leathercraft Limited has capital employed of £1,000,000.

solution – using cost-plus pricing

percentage mark-up method

selling price is calculated as:	£
total costs	440,000
40 per cent mark-up (40% x £440,000)	176,000
selling price	616,000

Using percentage mark-up, the selling price per chair will be:
£616,000 ÷ 2,000 chairs = £308 per chair

percentage return on capital employed method

Return on capital employed is a performance measure, expressed as a percentage, which compares profit with the capital needed to run the business (see page 111). It is expressed as:

$$\frac{\textit{profit}}{\textit{capital employed}} \times \frac{100}{1} = \textit{percentage return on capital employed}$$

For Leathercraft Limited the capital employed is £1,000,000. A 20 per cent return on capital employed is the target return set by the company. Thus, the profit required is:

capital employed	x	*percentage return*	= *profit*
£1,000,000	x	20%	= £200,000

Selling price is calculated as:	£
total costs	440,000
20 per cent return on capital employed (see above)	200,000
selling price	640,000

Using percentage return on capital employed, the selling price per chair will be: £640,000 ÷ 2,000 chairs = £320 per chair.

conclusion

The two methods of cost-plus pricing used in the case study give different selling prices per cost unit:

- percentage mark-up: £308 per chair
- percentage return on capital employed: £320 per chair

Whilst both methods meet the target requirements of mark-up and return on capital employed, it does not follow that Leathercraft Limited will be able to sell its chairs at either price. It might be that its customers will find a supplier who is able to produce chairs of the same quality but at a cheaper price; in other words, the price Leathercraft will charge is *market led.*

MARKET LED PRICING

When a business has a product or service for which there is considerable demand and over which it has sole rights, it may be able to set and maintain its own price level (subject to government intervention on the grounds of monopoly pricing). Most businesses, however, must set their prices in comparison with other suppliers of the same or similar products and services. In the economy of the free market, buyers will tend to buy from the supplier than can produce the product, or supply the service, at least cost. Thus, in an ideal world (but not always in reality), inefficient suppliers will be forced out of the market and, in order to re-establish themselves, will have to look carefully at their costings and/or production techniques.

There are many examples of market led pricing, some of which (but not all) benefit the buyer:

- ***the price of similar products***

  Supermarket shelves, as an example, often contain 'rival' brands of the same product, eg tins of baked beans, cans of cola drink. Whilst each manufacturer will always tell you that their product is infinitely superior to that of their rivals, market led pricing means that there is little, if any, difference in price. Whilst supermarket 'own brand' products are usually cheaper, the pricing is still market led, ie a smaller margin below the price of branded goods.

- ***the price of seasonal products, such as fresh fruit***

  Usually the market leads the price, eg a supplier of strawberries cannot charge significantly more than the competitors.

- ***price cutting***

  In recent years there have been many examples of price cutting started by one retailer and then spreading across the whole industry, ie the price cutting has been market led. Examples include newspapers,and holidays – see the Case Study which follows.

- ***summary***

  With market led pricing:

  – selling prices are determined largely by what others charge for the same product

  – where competition exists, the buyer will tend to buy from the cheapest seller

HOLIDAY 'PRICE WARS' – MARKET LED PRICING

situation

This Case Study looks at examples of market led pricing in the holiday industry.
Until recently, whenever you booked a holiday through a travel agent, the price you paid was that shown in the tour operator's brochure – the only exception being if the holiday was a special offer, such as a 'late availability'. Nowadays most travel agents offer discounts – one company led the way, and the others followed. Take a look at the offers available from travel agents, both in your local shopping centre, or by telephone:

"Book early and save up to 25%"

"Great discounts on every overseas holiday we offer"

"Massive discounts – great summer deals"

"Up to 25% off overseas summer and next winter's holidays"

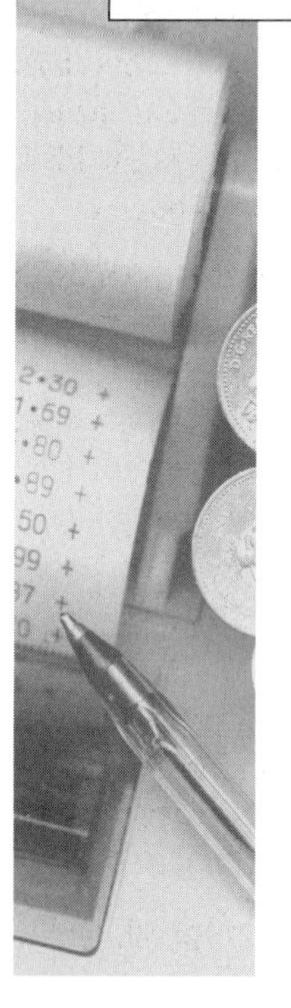

It should be pointed out that such offers are not available all of the time and there are usually some restrictions, eg from particular brochures, or a certain minimum holiday price. Offers are usually advertised when the new season's brochures are published so as to encourage early booking; also, if holidays are not selling well, the offers will be made in an attempt to boost trade.

With holiday offers like this, there is usually some 'small print' – for example, the requirement to buy the travel agent's own travel insurance. This often proves to be more expensive than that available from other insurers but, on balance, there is likely to be a saving on the holiday overall.

conclusion

Market led pricing has reduced the price of holidays to the customer. Holiday companies have all acted in response to a move by one of the larger companies in the industry. The others have followed in order to be able to maintain market share – their profitability is likely to have been affected but, with lower prices, it is hoped that more people will be tempted to go on holiday, so increasing the volume of business.

MARGINAL COST/CONTRIBUTION PRICING

In the long term, every business that seeks to make profits, must cover its costs and make a profit from the selling prices of its output. As we have seen earlier in the chapter, traditionally this involves cost-plus pricing techniques which add a percentage to absorption cost. However, it is common to use marginal cost when pricing 'special orders' which utilise spare capacity (as already discussed in Chapter 12, pages 235 to 236). However, remember that marginal cost pricing must be used with care: if an increasing percentage of output is priced in this way, there will be a considerable downturn in profits. Overall, if the business is to be profitable, the selling prices used must give sufficient contribution to meet the fixed costs and provide an acceptable level of profit.

TRANSFER PRICES

The pricing strategies that we have looked at so far are those which are used when selling the output to external customers of the business. However, many large company groups and other organisations sell some or all of their output to companies within the group, or to other sections of the organisation; in other words an internal market exists. Output sold on an internal market may comprise not only manufactured goods, but also services such as photocopying, payroll, hospital operations, maintenance, forensic services, etc. The problem with such internal markets is to establish the price (known as the *transfer price*) at which the output is to be sold.

The range of possibilities for establishing a transfer price is almost endless; for example, it can be based on:

- marginal cost
- full cost
- market price
- negotiation

The objective of establishing a transfer price is to allow the producer of the output to be paid by the recipient for the cost and effort incurred by production. Note that, whatever price is charged, whether high or low, it has no effect on the overall profitability of the group of companies or the organisation: the goods and the money paid are kept within the company/organisation.

Transfer prices are used in order to enable the performance of the supplying company/section to be assessed against targets set for profitability, return on capital, etc; in this way, management and staff are given independence to ensure the most efficient use of resources in producing the output. However, the objectives of the group of companies/organisation must take overall preference: for example, too high a transfer price for a sub-assembly which is to be used in a finished product, could lead to a high price being charged to the final customer, who may well look around for cheaper alternatives.

For international companies, the problem of establishing a transfer price becomes even more complex. There may well be particular countries where the market-led price to the final customer is higher than others; in order to avoid the accusation of excess profits being made in that market, the transfer price charged to the supplying subsidiary in that market is set high. Equally, transfer prices can be set so that subsidiaries in low-tax economies make more profits than those in high-tax countries.

The issue of transfer prices is rarely mentioned in the notes to financial statements of public limited companies because, as seen earlier, it has no effect on overall profitability of the group. The policy followed within a company or organisation will seek to strike a balance between:

- establishing independence for the supplying company/section of the organisation
- setting financial and other performance targets
- offering the buyer a discount for costs saved on the internal transfer (eg reduced selling costs, administration, transport, packing)

WYVERN COUNTY COUNCIL – TRANSFER PRICES

situation

The payroll section of Wyvern County Council is soon to charge its services to the other departments of the Council following a reorganisation of service functions into commercial providers.

The accountant of the payroll section is seeking to establish an hourly charge out rate that can be made to other departments. The following information has been gathered on projected costs for next year:

	per hour
Variable costs (labour, materials, overheads)	£25
Fixed overheads	£15
TOTAL COST	£40
Cost charged by outside payroll company	£35

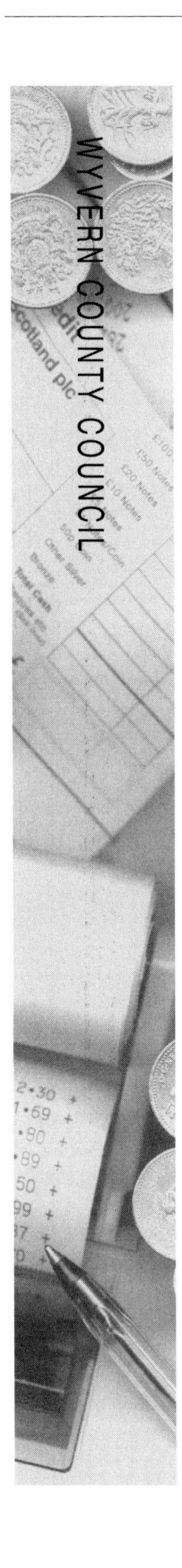

What transfer price should be charged for payroll services?

solution

- ***marginal cost***

  This method will charge the variable cost of £25 per hour. While this has the virtue of simplicity, there are a number of disadvantages:

  - the buyers of the payroll services have no way of knowing if £25 represents the most efficient variable costs; there could be scope for reductions
  - financial performance measures cannot be established for the payroll section in terms of profitability, return on capital employed
  - the fixed overheads of the payroll section will have to be apportioned in some acceptable way to the other departments of the Council

- ***full cost***

  This will charge £40 per hour, and a financial performance for the payroll section will be the requirement to break-even. Whilst the full cost may, as with marginal cost, hide inefficiencies, a major advantage is that the fixed overheads are charged to user departments on an equitable basis. The major disadvantage, in this example, is that the full cost price is higher than that charged by an outside payroll company.

  A variation of full cost is to use *cost plus*. Here a figure, often based on a percentage, is added to allow the section to make a profit. For example, here cost plus 10 per cent would give a price of £40 + £4 = £44 per hour. The use of a profit element gives a financial performance standard which will also encourage managers to seek economies in costs.

- ***market price***

  The payroll section could be encouraged to charge the market price of £35 per hour. Whilst this seemingly gives a loss of £5 per hour, it will establish a target for managers to seek to achieve by means of reductions in costs.

- ***negotiation***

  It is likely that the transfer price to be used will be established by negotiation. In this example, it might be that the price will be close to that charged by the outside payroll company, with the managers of the payroll section looking to reduce costs to at least £35 per hour.

- When making pricing and other management decisions, only relevant costs must be considered.
- The main factors that determine the selling price of a product are:
  - the need to make a profit
  - the prices of competing products
  - the availability of any under-used capacity
- The main pricing strategies are:
  - cost-plus pricing
  - market led pricing
  - marginal cost/contribution pricing
- Transfer prices are used when output is sold in internal markets, eg between companies within a group, or between sections of an organisation.
- Transfer prices are usually based on:
  - marginal cost
  - full cost
  - market price
  - negotiation

relevant cost	those costs that are appropriate to a specific management decision
sunk costs	past costs which are not taken into account in decision making
notional costs	allowance for a benefit received for which no cost is incurred
opportunity cost	the benefit that is foregone when a particular course of action is taken
differential costs	the costs that change when comparing alternative courses of action
cost benefit analysis	a comparison of the resources used in a particular course of action and the value of the benefits
price	the amount of money that is agreed between a buyer and a seller which enables the exchange of a product to take place
cost-plus pricing	cost price *plus* profit = selling price (with profit calculated as either a percentage mark-up on cost price, or to give a percentage return on capital employed)
market led pricing	selling price largely determined by what others charge for the same product
marginal cost/contribution pricing	where a product is sold at a price which is above marginal cost, but below absorption cost; used for pricing 'special orders' which take up under-used capacity
transfer price	the price at which products are sold in internal markets

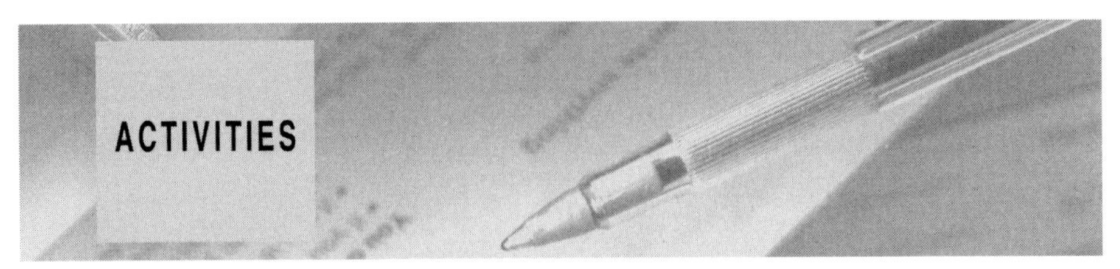

13.1 Research a management decision involving costs and revenues made recently in an organisation with which you are familiar:

- briefly outline the problem
- list the cost and revenues used to help the decision making
- state the decision
- comment on the relevance of the costs and revenues used in the decision
- if appropriate, indicate other costs and revenues that you think should have been considered

13.2 Prepare a briefing paper on pricing strategies which:

- explains the basic factors that influence the pricing of goods or services in an organisation with which you are familiar
- takes one particular good or service of your choice, and describes the related pricing strategy for that product

13.3 Wyvern Private Hospital Limited carries out a large number of minor operations for day patients. For next year it plans 2,500 operations based on the following costs:

annual costs for 2,500 minor operations

	£
Direct materials (£100 per operation)	250,000
Direct labour (£200 per operation)	500,000
PRIME COST	750,000
Overheads (fixed)	200,000
TOTAL COST	950,000

The hospital is reviewing its pricing policy for minor operations and is considering cost-plus pricing based on:

- either a 25 per cent mark-up on cost price
- or a 20 per cent return on capital employed

The capital employed for the minor operations section of the hospital is £1,000,000.
Calculate the price per minor operation using the two cost-plus pricing methods.

13.4
- What are the objectives of transfer pricing?
- Discuss the relevant costs and the method of transfer pricing to be used when the Department of Computing at a college runs an information technology course for the staff of the Department of Management.

14 CAPITAL INVESTMENT APPRAISAL

this chapter covers ...

- *the nature of a capital investment project*
- *the financial techniques of capital investment appraisal: payback, accounting rate of return, discounted cash flow*
- *differences between the capital main investment appraisal methods*
- *the calculation of internal rate of return and its application as a method of capital investment appraisal*

INTRODUCTION

In this chapter we look at the financial methods used to help with decision making about capital investment projects – for example, if we need a new photocopier, shall we buy a Toshiba or a Canon model? The main methods of capital investment appraisal are:

- payback
- accounting rate of return
- discounted cash flow

We look at what capital investment appraisal involves, and then study each of the three methods by means of a Case Study, and make comparisons between them. At the end of the chapter, we look at a further capital investment appraisal method called internal rate of return.

WHAT IS CAPITAL INVESTMENT APPRAISAL?

You will readily appreciate that, whether at home or at work, resources are limited in supply and, as a result, there is a need to use them in such a way as to obtain the maximum benefits from them. To do this it is necessary to choose between various financial alternatives available; for example, on a personal level, we have to make decisions such as:

Should I save my spare cash in a bank or in a building society?

Should I save up for a car, or should I buy on hire purchase?

Which make of car, within my price range, should I buy?

Should I rent a house or should I buy, taking out a mortgage?

While these decisions are personal choices, the management of businesses of all sizes are faced with making choices, as are other organisations, eg local authorities and central government.

The management of any business is constantly having to make decisions on *what* goods or services to produce, *where* to produce, *how* to produce, and *how much* to produce. For each major choice to be made, some method of appraisal has to be applied to ensure that, whatever decisions are taken, they are consistent with the objectives of the organisation. This means that it is necessary to look at all the alternatives available and to choose the one that is going to give the most benefit to the business. For example, a business may have to decide whether to replace its existing machinery with new, more up-to-date machinery. If it decides on new machinery, it then has to choose between different makes of machine and different models, each having a different cost and each capable of affecting output in a different way. At the same time a decision has to be made whether to pay cash outright, to buy on hire purchase, or to lease.

The objective of capital investment appraisal is to enable a business to decide whether or not to invest in a particular capital investment project and, where there are a number of viable alternatives, to decide in which of them to invest.

WHAT IS A CAPITAL INVESTMENT PROJECT?

A capital investment project is the spending of money now in order to receive benefits (or reduce costs) in future years; it is illustrated in fig 14.1 (on the next page).

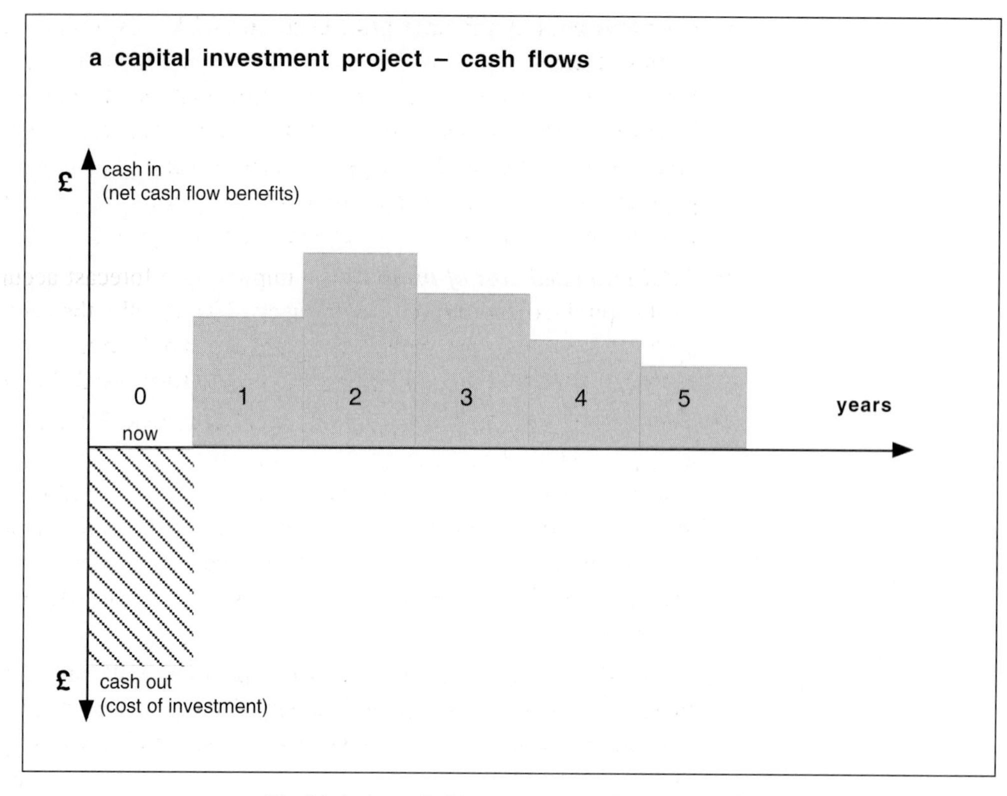

Fig 14.1 A capital investment project – cash flows in and out

Here the capital expenditure being spent now (often stated as 'year 0') brings benefits (or reduced costs) in future years. The business needs to apply capital investment appraisal methods to ensure that the investment decision is the correct choice.

INVESTMENT APPRAISAL IN CONTEXT

As well as the cash flows in and out for a capital investment project, a number of other factors need to be considered before a decision is made. These factors include:

- *Source of finance.* Where is the money coming from to finance the project? Is it from a cash surplus, an existing or new bank overdraft, loans? A large project may warrant a share or debenture issue to raise specific finance. Assets such as machinery, equipment and vehicles are often financed using hire purchase and leasing.

- *Cost of capital.* All finance has a cost – invariably expressed as a rate of interest. Cost of capital will be different for each source of finance – from the interest foregone on cash surpluses, to that which must be paid on bank overdrafts and loans. With ordinary shares, the cost of capital is the dividend that shareholders expect to receive. Hire purchase and leasing payments include the interest cost. Note that, with variable interest rates, cost of capital may well vary during the life of a project.
- *Total estimated cost of project.* It is important to forecast accurately the total capital expenditure cost of projects. Historically, the cost of large-scale projects has often been under-estimated and the final actual cost has been much higher than anticipated, leading to financial difficulties.
- *Taxation implications.* A project will usually include both tax allowances and payments. The allowances occur when new assets – such as machinery, equipment and vehicles – are purchased; called writing down allowances, these reduce the amount of tax to be paid. However, the cost savings or increasing profits of the investment project will increase overall profitability of the business and will lead to more tax being paid.
- *Working capital requirements.* Most projects will also require an investment in working capital – stock, debtors and creditors. Thus an amount of working capital is needed at the start, and throughout the project's life. It will only be disinvested at the end of the project.
- *Audit of project.* It is important to keep a regular check on costs to ensure that they are in line with the estimates. There are three separate phases that should be audited:

  – costs of bringing the project into commission

  – operational costs

  – decommissioning costs
- *Other considerations*

  Economic climate – recession or period of growth.

  Political implications – a possible change of government may affect investment decisions.

  Commissioning – the length of time that it will take for the project to be up and running.

  Training – the costs and implications of staff training.

  Location – where the project is to be located, and subsequent effects on the culture of the organisation.

  Capacity – effect on overall output of the organisation.

  Product life cycle – the implications on the project of the stage of the company's output in the product life cycle.

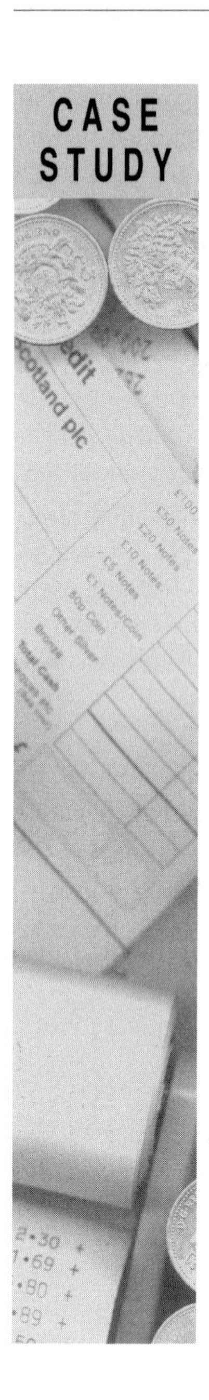

MAKING THE DECISION – WHICH PROJECT?

situation

A business is investing in a new project and has to make the choice between Project Aye and Project Bee. The initial cost and the net cash flow (income, less expenses but not depreciation) to the business have been calculated over five years for each project as follows:

	PROJECT AYE	PROJECT BEE
Initial cost	£20,000	£28,000
Net cash flow:		
Year 1	£8,000	£10,000
Year 2	£12,000	£10,000
Year 3	£5,000	£8,000
Year 4	£4,000	£9,000
Year 5	£2,000	£9,000

Only one project can be undertaken and, at the end of five years, it will have no value. To finance the selected project, the business can borrow money at 10 per cent per annum. Which project should be chosen?

solution

Three methods are commonly used to appraise a capital investment project such as this:

- payback
- accounting rate of return
- discounted cash flow

Each of these methods will be considered in this chapter in order to help the business to make its decision. At the end of the chapter we will also look at how the internal rate of return (or discounted cash flow yield) is used in order to make a direct comparison between projects which have different amounts of capital investment at the start.

PAYBACK

This method, as its name implies, sees how long it takes for the initial outlay to be repaid by the net cash flow coming in. Thus project Aye costs £20,000 and it is expected that the net cash flow over the first two years will equal the cost. The payback time for Project Aye is, therefore, two years, while that for

Project Bee is three years. So, using payback, Project Aye is preferable. The faster the payback the better, particularly where high technology or fashion projects are concerned – they may be out-of-date before they reach the end of their useful lives. Earlier cash flows are likely to prove more accurate estimates than later cash flows. Thus, if two projects have the same payback, the one with the greater cash flow in early years is preferred. For example, consider two projects with a payback of two years from the following cash flows:

	Wye	Zed
Year 1	£8,000	£12,000
Year 2	£12,000	£8,000

While both projects have the same payback period of two years, Zed is the preferred project under the payback method because of earlier cash flows.

advantages of payback

- it is easy to calculate
- it is easy to understand
- it places emphasis on the earlier cash flows, which are more likely to be accurate than later cash flows
- an ideal capital investment appraisal method for high technology projects

disadvantages of payback

- all cash flows after the payback period are ignored
- within the payback period it fails to take into account the timing of net cash flows, eg Project Aye would still have had a payback of two years even if the cash flows for years one and two had been reversed (as noted above, greater cash flows in earlier years are to be preferred)

ACCOUNTING RATE OF RETURN

The accounting rate of return method uses the profit over the life of the project to calculate the percentage rate of return, based on the average cost of the project. It is calculated as follows:

$$\frac{(\textit{Total estimated cash flow}^{*} - \textit{Initial cost})}{\textit{Estimated life of project}} \times \frac{100}{\textit{Average cost}}$$

* Scrap value or residual value, if any, at the end of the project would be taken into account.

Note that 'total estimated cash flow, minus initial cost' used in accounting rate of return is the calculation of profit over the project's life.

The preferred project will be the one that has the highest percentage accounting rate of return.

For Project Aye, the accounting rate of return is calculated as follows:

$$\frac{(£31,000 - £20,000)}{5 \text{ years}} \times \frac{100}{£10,000^*} = 22 \text{ per cent}$$

*£20,000 ÷ 2 = £10,000

For Project Bee, using the same formula, the accounting rate of return is 25.7 per cent; so, using this method, Project Bee is preferable.

advantages of accounting rate of return

- it is relatively easy to calculate
- all cash flows are used in the calculation of profit
- it is easy to understand the results

disadvantage of accounting rate of return

The timing of cash flows is completely ignored, ie the same result would have been reached if the cash flows for Project Aye had been £1,000, £1,000, £1,000, £1,000 for each of the first four years, and £27,000 in year five (as noted under payback, greater cash flows in earlier years are to be preferred).

DISCOUNTED CASH FLOW

Discounted cash flow (DCF) is a capital investment appraisal method which recognises that money has a time value. For example, supposing that today a friend asks you to lend her £1 and offers to repay you either tomorrow, or in one year's time, which will you choose? The answer is clear: you would want the money back sooner rather than later because, if you don't intend to spend it, you can always save it in a bank or building society, where it will earn interest. Thus the rate of interest represents the time value of money.

Using £1 as an example, if it is invested with a bank or building society at an interest rate of 10 per cent per year, it will increase as follows:

original investment	£1.00
interest at 10% on £1	£0.10
value at end of first year	£1.10
interest at 10% on £1.10	£0.11
value at end of second year	£1.21

This uses the technique of compound interest. So, with interest rates of 10 per cent per year, we can say that the future value of £1 will be £1.10 at the end of year one, £1.21 at the end of year two, and so on; thus £1 set aside now will gain in value so that, at some time in the future, we will have access to a larger sum of money. However, supposing that we were to receive £1 at the end of year one, what is it worth to us now? To find the answer to this, we need to carry out the following calculation:

$$£1 \times \frac{100}{110^*} = £0.91$$

* 100 per cent, plus the rate of interest (in this example, 10 per cent).

Therefore, if we had £0.91 now and invested it at 10 per cent per year, we would have £1 at the end of year one. We can say that the *present value* of £1 receivable in one year's time is £0.91. In the same way, £1 receivable in two years' time is £0.83, calculated as follows:

$$£1 \times \frac{100}{110} \times \frac{100}{110} = £0.83$$

We can build up a *table of factors* (for 10 per cent interest rate) as shown in fig 14.2 (below):

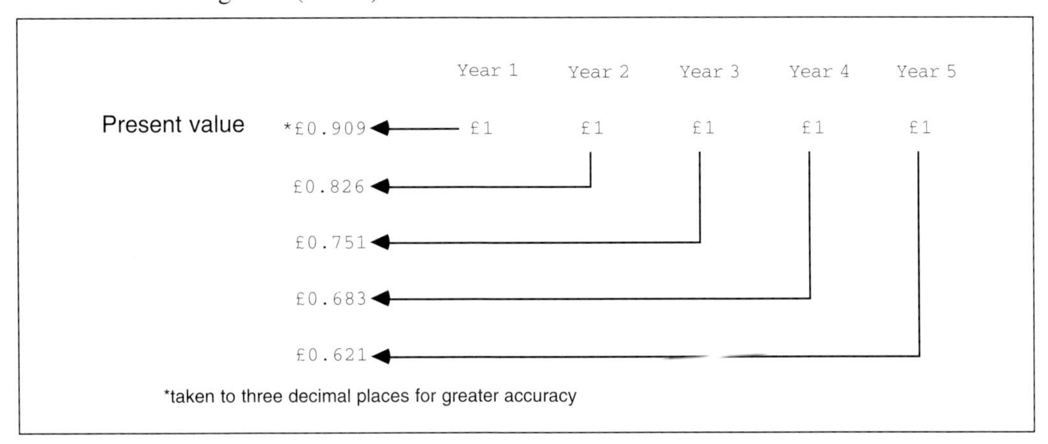

Fig 14.2 Table of present value factors for 10 per cent interest rate

The table of factors reminds us of the basic principle that *money has a time value* and, from this, the further into the future that we expect to receive money, then the lower is its *present value.* Thus the present value (or discount) factors relate to interest rates which represent the cost of capital (ie the rate of return that the business expects on its money, or the rate of interest it has to pay when borrowing).

Let us now return to the problem of the business which has to choose between Projects Aye and Bee. We will look at this assuming, firstly, a cost of capital of 10 per cent. For each project, the expected net cash flows are multiplied by the relevant factor to give the *discounted cash flow*; the difference between total discounted cash flow and the initial cost is the *net present value* of the project.

For Project Aye the calculations are:

	Cash Flow		Discount Factor		Discounted Cash Flow
	£				£
Year 0*	(20,000)	x	1.000	=	(20,000)
Year 1	8,000	x	0.909	=	7,272
Year 2	12,000	x	0.826	=	9,912
Year 3	5,000	x	0.751	=	3,755
Year 4	4,000	x	0.683	=	2,732
Year 5	2,000	x	0.621	=	1,242
			Net Present Value (NPV)	=	4,913

* Year 0 is the commencement of the project when the initial costs are paid.

Note that the initial cost is shown in brackets because it is a cost, whereas the net cash flows are positive amounts; net present value is the sum of all cash flows.

For Project Bee the figures are:

	Cash Flow		Discount Factor		Discounted Cash Flow
	£				£
Year 0	(28,000)	x	1.000	=	(28,000)
Year 1	10,000	x	0.909	=	9,090
Year 2	10,000	x	0.826	=	8,260
Year 3	8,000	x	0.751	=	6,008
Year 4	9,000	x	0.683	=	6,147
Year 5	9,000	x	0.621	=	5,589
			Net Present Value (NPV)	=	7,094

Here, with a cost of capital of 10 per cent, Project Bee is better, producing a considerably higher net present value than Aye. Note that both projects give a positive net present value at 10 per cent: this means that either project will be of benefit to the organisation but Bee is preferable; a negative NPV would indicate that a project should not go ahead.

Thus, using a discounted cash flow method, future cash flows are brought to their value now; this means that, the further on in time that cash flows are receivable, the lower is the net present value.

advantages of discounted cash flow

- all cash flows are used
- the timing of cash flows is taken into account
- using a table of factors the calculations are easy to make

disadvantages of discounted cash flow:

- the cost of capital rate is, in practice, difficult to ascertain and may also vary over the life of the project
- the meaning of net present value is not always clear to users of the information
- the project with the higher net present value does not always represent the better project for the business or organisation

CAPITAL INVESTMENT APPRAISAL: COMPARISON

It is unlikely that a business will rely on one investment appraisal method only; instead two or more criteria might be required before a capital project is given the go-ahead. Supposing, for example, that the business, having to choose between Projects Aye and Bee, applied the following criteria: "projects must have a payback period not exceeding two and a half years, and must have a positive net present value at a 10 per cent cost of capital." How do the two projects compare?

	Project Aye	*Project Bee*
Payback	2 years	3 years
NPV at 10 per cent	£4,913	£7,094

Under the criteria that the business has laid down, Aye would be chosen. However, Bee seems a better project on the net present value basis and is only rejected because it does not meet the payback requirement; also Bee has the better accounting rate of return (at 25.7 per cent, instead of 22 per cent for Aye). However, the capital expenditure required for Bee is £8,000 greater than Aye – something which NPV does not take fully into account. To obtain a better analysis, we need to use the method of *internal rate of return.*

INTERNAL RATE OF RETURN

The principles of discounted cash flow can be developed further in order to calculate the capital investment appraisal method of *internal rate of return* (IRR) – this method is also known as *DCF yield.* Note that internal rate of return is different from accounting rate of return which was discussed earlier.

The internal rate of return is the rate of cost of capital at which the present value of the cash inflows exactly balances the initial investment. In other words, it shows the cost of capital percentage at which the investment 'breaks-even', ie income equals expenditure, but still applying DCF principles.

IRR can be calculated in one of three ways:

- trial and error
- graphically
- interpolation

trial and error

To calculate IRR by trial and error we start with a cost of capital which gives a positive net present value – for example, 10 per cent cost of capital for Project Aye gives a NPV of £4,913. We increase the cost of capital by one or two percentage points each time until, eventually, it becomes negative. For example:

PROJECT AYE			
Cost of Capital	Present Value of Cash Flow	Capital Investment	Net Present Value
	£	£	£
10%	24,913	(20,000)	4,913
12%	23,946	(20,000)	3,946
14%	23,025	(20,000)	3,025
16%	22,177	(20,000)	2,177
18%	21,375	(20,000)	1,375
20%	20,619	(20,000)	619
22%	19,915	(20,000)	(85)
24%	19,242	(20,000)	(758)

The net present value that balances the present value of cash flow with the initial investment lies between 20% and 22% – closer to 22% than 20%, so we can call it approximately 22% (an answer to the nearest one or two percentage points is acceptable for most decisions).

graphically

Internal rate of return can be found by means of a graph (see fig 14.3 on the next page) and just two calculations.

The procedure is:

- select a low cost of capital percentage which gives a positive net present value figure
- select a high cost of capital percentage which gives a negative net present value figure
- prepare a graph with
  - on the vertical axis net present values (both positive and negative) for the range of the two calculations
  - on the horizontal axis cost of capital for the percentages used in the two calculations
- plot the positive and negative figures for net present values against their respective cost of capital percentages
- join the two points in a straight line
- read off the internal rate of return from the horizontal axis

Note: Whilst the graph in fig 14.3 shows a straight line, if more than two points were plotted, the line would be slightly curved and to the left of that shown. This has the effect of very slightly reducing the reading of internal rate of return from the graph: in practice the difference is unlikely to affect investment appraisal decisions.

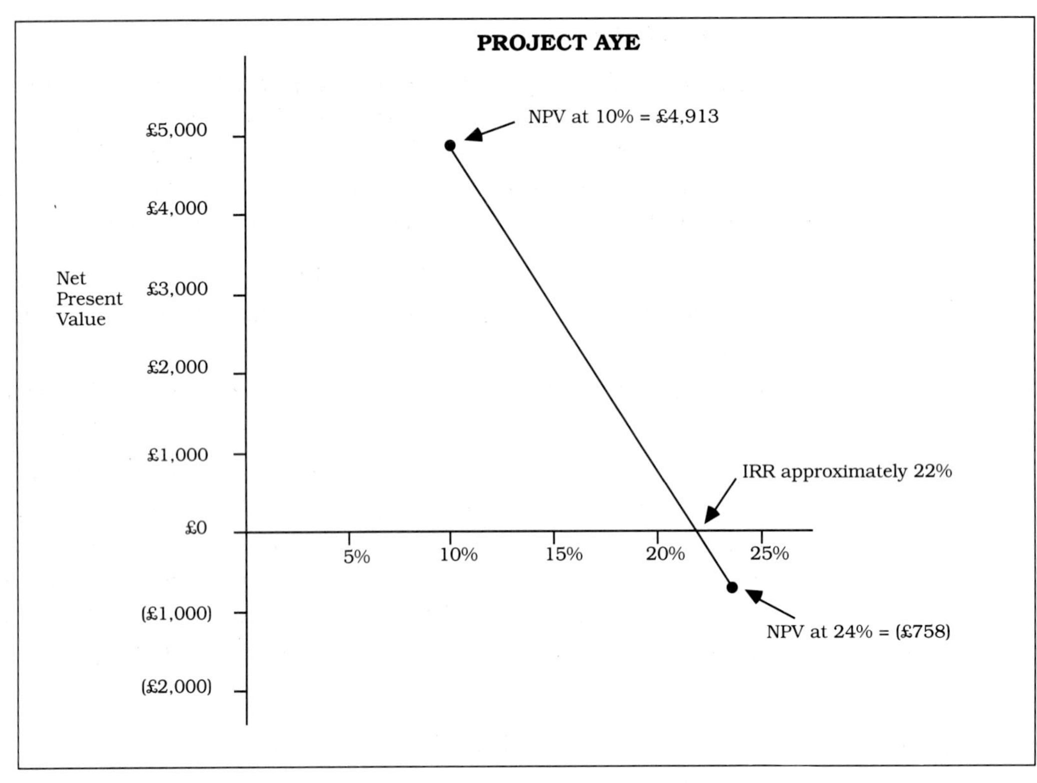

Fig 14.3 Internal rate of return graph for Project Aye

interpolation

Like the graphical method, interpolation uses two initial calculations:

- a low cost of capital percentage which gives a positive net present value figure
- a high cost of capital percentage which gives a negative net present value figure

This information can then be inserted into the following formula:

$$\text{low cost of capital \%} + \left(\frac{\text{NPV at lower \%}}{\text{NPV at lower \% } \textit{plus} \text{ NPV at higher \%}} \times \begin{array}{l}\text{difference between}\\ \text{high and low}\\ \text{cost of capital \%}\end{array} \right) = \text{IRR}$$

For example, with project Aye the figures are:

$$10 + \left(\frac{£4,913}{£5,671^{**}} \times 14^{*} \right) = 22.13\%$$

* 24 – 10 = 14
** £4,913 + £758 = £5,671

conclusion

Returning to the two projects, Aye and Bee, the IRR for Aye is approximately 22%; by following the calculations, Bee will be found to be approximately 20%. Thus, Aye gives a higher IRR and is the preferred capital investment. The reason for this is that Aye requires a lower capital expenditure, and the timing of the cash flows is weighted towards the earlier years.

The decision criteria when using IRR is to:

- accept the higher IRR, where there is a choice between different capital investments
- accept projects with an IRR greater than either the cost of borrowing (the cost of capital), or the rate of return specified by company policy

Thus, while IRR can be compared between two (or more) different capital investments, it can also be applied to cost of capital. In the example we have followed in this chapter, the cost of capital is 10%. The organisation could have gone ahead with either investment. However, if the cost of capital had been 20%, project Bee would have been rejected and Project Aye accepted – although the 2% margin above the cost of capital is very tight.

OTHER CONSIDERATIONS

As well as the numerical techniques that can be used for capital investment appraisal, an organisation must consider a number of other factors before making the final decision. These include:

- *Total implications.* The effect of the project on the organisation as a whole will include implications for
  - sales, with possible increases in output
  - output, with changes in techniques, eg a switch from labour-intensive to machine-intensive output
  - staff, with possible redundancies, training needs, pay structure
  - working capital required for the project
  - needs, such as premises, transport, materials
- *Cost of finance.* Possible changes in the cost of capital will have a direct effect on the viability of the project. For example, an increase in the general level of interest rates will reduce the project's overall profitability. Projects are often financed through fixed interest rate loans, or through hire purchase and leasing, thus establishing some part of the finance at fixed rates; however, invariably working capital is at variable rates.
- *Taxation considerations.* The project will include the implications of both tax allowances and charges. However, a change in the level of taxation –

including 'one-off' charges – will affect the viability of the project.

- *Forecasting techniques.* These can be used to answer 'what if?' questions: for example, "what if sales increase by 25 per cent?" or "what if materials costs fall by 5 per cent?" In this way, management can use *sensitivity analysis* to see how the project is affected by changes to any of the data used in the appraisal.

CHAPTER SUMMARY

- Capital investment appraisal uses a number of methods to help in management decision making.
- The main methods include payback, accounting rate of return and discounted cash flow.
- Businesses often use a combination of two or more appraisal methods before making decisions about major projects.
- Internal rate of return (also known as DCF yield) is used to rank projects, while still applying the principles of discounted cash flow.
- Before authorising a capital project, other considerations include:
  - total implications for the organisation
  - cost of finance, and effect of changes
  - taxation
  - forecasting techniques to answer 'what if?' questions

KEY TERMS

capital investment appraisal enables a business to decide whether or not to invest in a particular capital investment project and, where there are alternatives, to help to decide in which to invest

cost of capital The percentage cost of financing an investment – either the rate of return that the business expects on its money, or the rate of interest it has to pay when borrowing

payback time period for the initial outlay to be repaid by the net cash inflow

accounting rate of return uses profit to calculate the percentage rate of return, based on average cost of the project

discounted cash flow capital investment appraisal technique that uses cash flows and recognises the time value of money

net present value (NPV) the value of cash outflows and inflows for a project discounted to present-day amounts

internal rate of return (IRR) the rate of cost of capital at which the net present value of cash inflows equals the cost of the initial investment

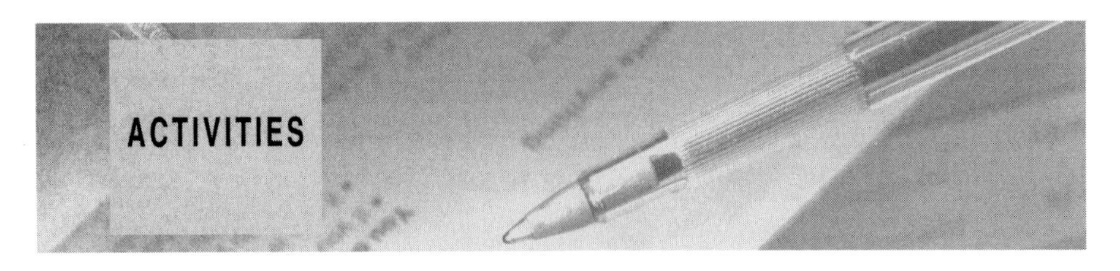

TABLE OF DISCOUNTED CASH FLOW FACTORS

Cost of capital	10%	12%	14%	16%	18%	20%	22%	24%
Year 1	0.909	0.893	0.877	0.862	0.847	0.833	0.820	0.806
Year 2	0.826	0.797	0.769	0.743	0.718	0.694	0.672	0.650
Year 3	0.751	0.712	0.675	0.641	0.609	0.579	0.551	0.524
Year 4	0.683	0.636	0.592	0.552	0.516	0.482	0.451	0.423
Year 5	0.621	0.567	0.519	0.476	0.437	0.402	0.370	0.341
Year 6	0.564	0.507	0.456	0.410	0.370	0.335	0.303	0.275

14.1 Select an organisation – either where you work, or another with which you are familiar. Identify a capital investment appraisal project – one that has been completed recently.

(a) Discuss the non-financial aspects of the project that were considered.

(b) Research and critically examine the investment appraisal methods used by the organisation.

(c) Report on how the investment appraisal methods were used for the particular project.

(d) How close have the actual results of the project been to the original estimates? Explain the reasons for any variances.

14.2 Robert Smith is considering two major capital investment projects for his business. Only one project can be chosen and the following information is available:

		Project Exe	Project Wye
		£	£
Initial capital outlay		80,000	100,000
Net cash inflows, year:	1	40,000	20,000
	2	40,000	30,000
	3	20,000	50,000
	4	10,000	50,000
	5	10,000	49,000

The initial capital outlay will occur immediately and you may assume that the net cash inflows will arise at the end of each year. Smith's estimated cost of capital over the five year period is 12 per cent per annum. Neither project will have any residual value at the end of five years.

To assist Robert Smith make his decision you are to:

- Produce numerical assessments of the two projects based on the following capital investment appraisal methods:
  (a) payback
  (b) net present value (NPV)
  (c) accounting rate of return
- Comment on the relative merits of the project appraisal methods, and advise Robert Smith which capital investment, if either, should be undertaken.

14.3 Ken Jones needs some equipment for his printing firm. He has to choose between the following methods of acquisition:

- purchase of the equipment for cash
- purchase under a hire purchase contract, involving an initial deposit and two annual payments
- hire of the equipment

The following information is available:

– cash price of equipment	£10,000
– period of use in Jones' firm	5 years
– scrap value at end of use	£1,000
– initial deposit under hire purchase contract	£4,000
– two annual hire purchase payments due at end of first year and end of second year	£4,000 each
– hire of equipment, five annual hire charge payments due at end of each year	£2,500 each

Jones' estimated cost of capital over the five year period is 10 per cent per annum.

To assist Ken Jones make his decision, you are asked to:

- produce numerical assessments of the three methods of acquisition using discounted cash flow methods
- advise Ken Jones of the best method of acquisition

14.4 Calculate the internal rate of return (DCF yield) by trial and error, and interpolation to the nearest two per cent for projects Exe and Wye in Activity 14.2. Prove your answer by means of a graph.

Comment on the IRR for both projects.

Section 6

budgeting and budgetary control

This section shows how a business plans its future financial performance by means of budgets, and then uses budgets as a control mechanism by comparing actual results against budgeted results.

Budget

Actual performance

Variance

Review

15 PRINCIPLES OF BUDGETING

this chapter covers ...

- *the nature of budgets*
- *the benefits of budgets*
- *the steps involved in budgetary planning*
- *the purpose of budgetary control*
- *the differences between fixed and flexible budgets*
- *the use of zero-based budgeting*

INTRODUCTION

Businesses and other organisations need to plan for the future. In large businesses such planning, usually known as *corporate planning*, is very formal while, for smaller businesses, it will be less formal. Planning for the future falls into three time scales:

- *long-term:* from about three years up to, sometimes, as far as twenty years ahead
- *medium-term:* one to three years ahead
- *short-term:* for the next year

Clearly, planning for these different time scales needs different approaches: the further on in time, the less detailed are the plans. In the medium and longer term, a business will establish broad *corporate objectives*. Such corporate objectives do not have to be formally written down, although in a large organisation they are likely to be; for smaller businesses, corporate objectives will certainly be thought about by the owners or managers. This is very similar to each one of us having personal objectives, which we are likely to think about, rather than write down.

In this chapter we are concerned with planning for the more immediate future, ie the next financial year. Such planning takes note of the broader corporate objectives and sets out how these are to be achieved in the form of detailed plans known as *budgets*.

The link between long-term and short-term planning is that short-term plans provide the means of achieving long-term goals. For example, the long-term objective of "we plan double sales volume in the next five years" may well be translated into a short-term plan of "we intend to increase sales volume by 15 per cent this year." The long-term view is *strategic planning*, which is taken at director level, and provides an overall view; the short-term view is *operational planning*, taken at senior manager level, and which sets out in a detailed budget how it will be achieved. The following diagram illustrates the link between long-term and short term plans:

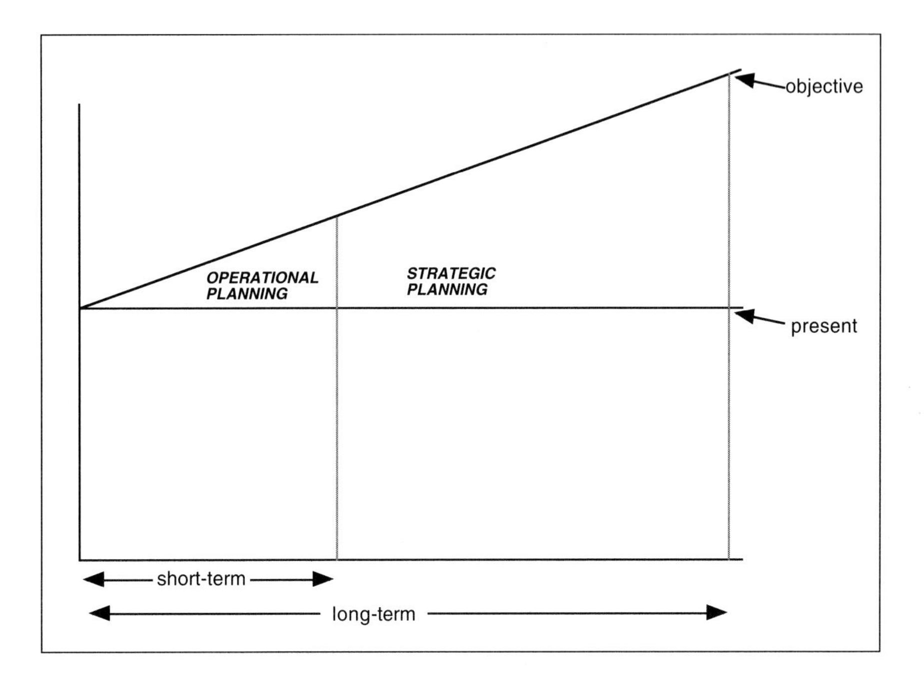

Thus the gap between the present level and the objective represents the expected achievement in the long-term, and how it is expected to be achieved in the short-term through detailed budgets. However, the short-term plan should not be seen as an end in itself; instead it needs to be reviewed regularly to see if targets are being met which will allow the long-term objective to be achieved.

WHAT IS A BUDGET?

A budget is a means of planning and control used by the management of a business or organisation to achieve stated objectives.

A budget is commonly set in financial terms, eg a sales revenue budget, but can also be expressed in terms of units, eg items produced, items sold, number of employees.

Budgets can be *income* budgets for money received, eg a sales budget, or *expenditure* budgets for money spent (eg an administration budget).

Most budgets are prepared for the next financial year (the *budget period*), and are usually broken down into shorter time periods, commonly four-weekly or monthly. This enables control to be exercised over the budget: over time the actual results can be monitored against the budget, and discrepancies between the two can be investigated and corrective action taken where appropriate.

BENEFITS OF BUDGETS

Budgets provide benefits both for the business, and also for its managers and other employees:

co-ordinating functions and departments

The budgets for each function and department of the business or organisation are co-ordinated so that each relates to all the other budgets. In this way the activities of the business are linked together in order to optimise the value of resources and to achieve the corporate objectives.

communicating

The process of preparing budgets provides a means for managers to communicate both upwards, downwards, and across the organisation. Once budgets have been prepared, they can be used as a means of communicating to the employees who will see how the objectives of the business affect their own job or department.

motivating employees

As a means of motivating employees, budgets are an example of *responsibility accounting*. Individuals are made responsible for their own budgets – by delegating budgets down the organisation – but, in order to have effective budgets, managers must participate in the budgeting process. As a method of motivation, budgets can be seen by employees as either a 'carrot' or a 'stick', ie as a form of encouragement to achieve the targets set by budgets, or as a form of punishment if targets are missed.

One possible problem that can occur is that employees in one department of the organisation may over-achieve against their budget and create problems elsewhere. For example, a production department might produce extra output that the sales department finds difficult to sell. In order to avoid such *disfunctional management*, budgets need to be set at realistic levels and linked across all departments within the organisation.

controlling performance

The process of *budgetary control* (see page 289) enables businesses to see how successful they are in meeting targets (eg sales, production) set by budgets. We shall see how budgets are controlled through variance analysis in Chapter 17.

FUNCTIONAL BUDGETS

The functional budget is a plan for a specific *function* within a business or organisation, eg:

- sales budget – which covers sales income to be received by the business
- production budget – which covers the number of items produced and their cost
- selling and distribution budget – which includes costs such as commission, advertising and delivery
- administration budget – which provides administrative support to the whole organisation

Within each functional budget, there will be a number of *subsidiary budgets*. For example, the production budget will have a number of subsidiary budgets, such as:

- materials budget
- labour budget
- direct expenses budget
- overheads budget

In this way, the managers and supervisors responsible for these areas are set their own budgets, ie they are *budget holders* for their section of the production function.

THE MASTER BUDGET

The end result of the budgeting process is the production of a *master budget* which takes the form of forecast financial statements – forecast profit and loss account and balance sheet at the end of the budget period. The master budget is the 'master plan' which shows how all the other budgets 'work together' towards achieving the objectives of the organisation. It brings together:

- functional budgets
- cash budget – which will show money paid in and out of the bank account
- capital expenditure budget – which will plan for purchases of fixed assets

Fig 15.1 on the next page, shows how all the budgets are linked to each other. Note, however, that some organisations see the cash budget as being part of the master budget.

In this chapter we will look in more detail at the sales and production budgets. The cash budget and master budget are discussed more fully in Chapter 16.

LIMITING FACTORS

All budgets are affected by *limiting factors*; these factors include:

- the quantity of output that can be sold – this principle applies to both products and services
- the availability of raw materials
- the availability of skilled labour
- factory or office space
- finance

It is essential to identify the limiting factor(s) and to minimise the effect of the constraint in order to best achieve the organisation's objectives (see Chapter 12, page 239).

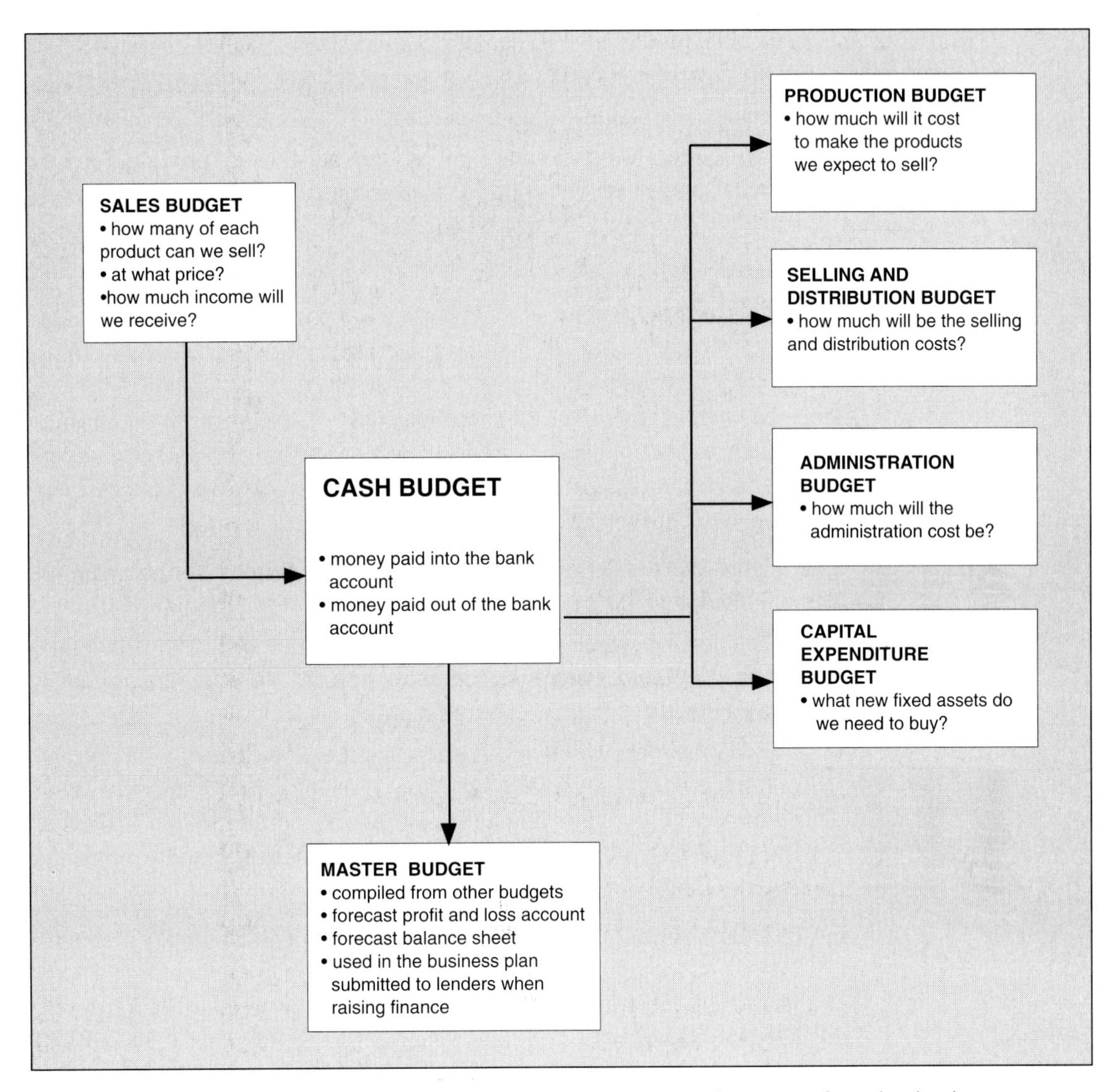

Fig 15.1 The budgeting process for a manufacturing business

For most businesses the limiting factor is *sales.* The starting point for the budgeting process is therefore normally the *sales budget.* Consequently the order in which the budgets will be prepared is often:

- *sales budget* – what can the business sell in the next 12 months?
- *production budget* – how can the business make/supply all the items which it plans to sell?
- *selling and distribution budget* – what resources will the business need to sell and distribute the product?
- *administration budget* – what administration expenses will be incurred?
- *capital expenditure budget* – what fixed assets (eg machinery, vehicles)

need to be purchased over the next 12 months?

- *cash budget* – what money will be flowing in and out of the bank account? – will an overdraft be needed?
- *master budget* – a summary of all the budgets to provide forecast financial statements, ie profit and loss account and balance sheet

BUDGETARY PLANNING

The planning of a budget is co-ordinated by a member of the finance department, often the management accountant. However, budget holders prepare budgets or subsidiary budgets for their own sections of the business and these must fit in with the overall objectives of the business.

Many large businesses and organisations take a highly formal view of planning the budget and make use of:

- *budget manual*, which provides a set of guidelines as to who is involved with the budgetary planning and control process, and how the process is to be conducted
- *budget committee*, which organises the process of budgetary planning and control; comprises representatives from the functions of the organisation – eg production, sales, selling and distribution, administration – together with a budget co-ordinator whose job is to administer and oversee the activities of the committee

Fig 15.2 (next page) shows a diagrammatic approach to budgetary planning. It is important, though, that the planning process begins well before the start of the budget period; this then gives time for budgets to be prepared, reviewed, redrafted, and reviewed again before being finally agreed and submitted to the directors for approval. For example, the planning process for a budget which is to start on 1 January might commence in the previous June, as follows:

- *June* Budget committee meets to plan next year's budgets
- *July* First draft of budgets prepared
- *August* Review of draft budgets
- *September* Draft budgets amended in light of review
- *October* Further review and redrafting to final version
- *November* Budgets submitted to directors for approval
- *December* Budgets for next year circulated to managers
- *January* Budget period commences

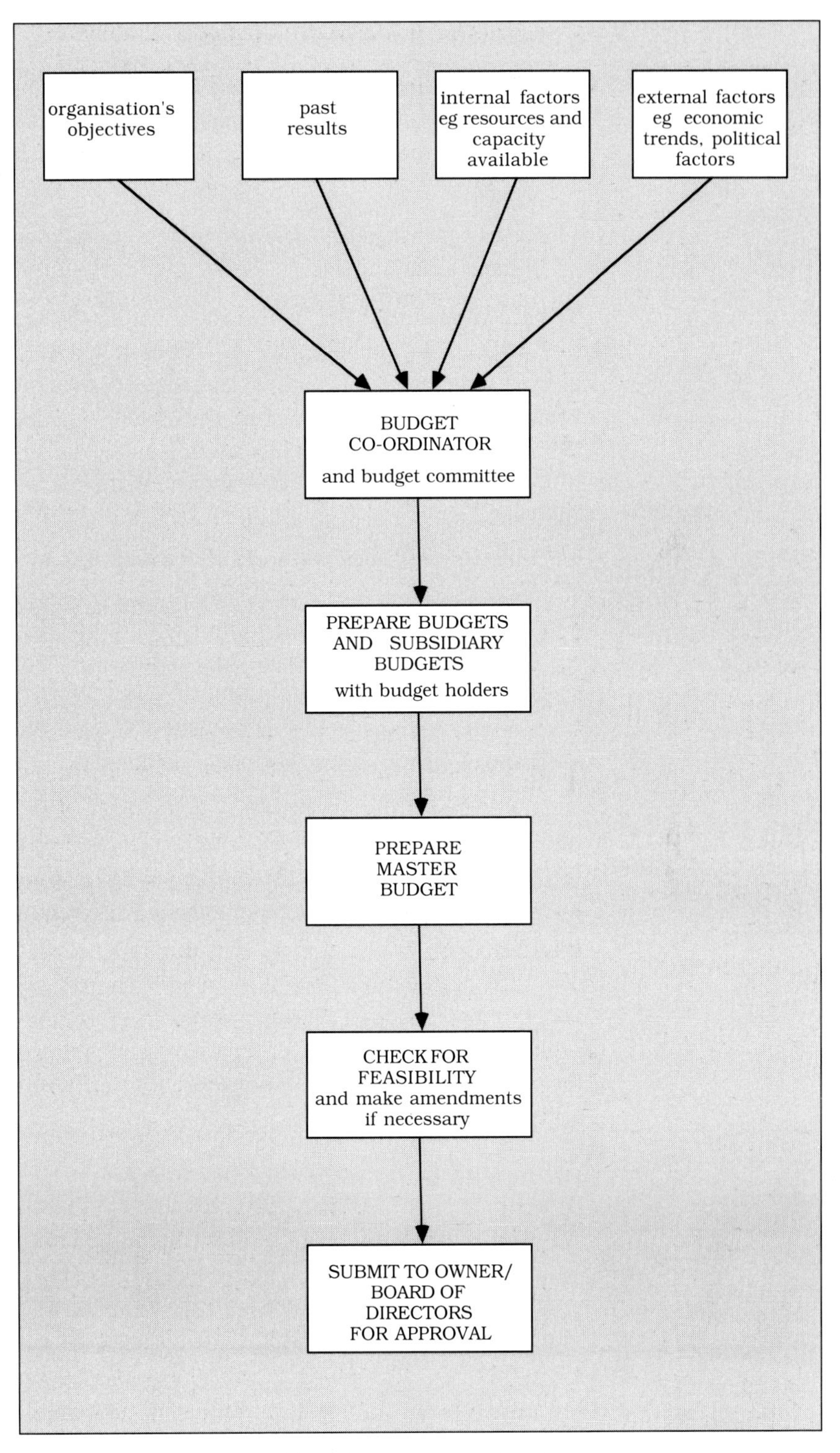

Fig 15.2 Budgetary planning

planning the sales budget

The sales budget is often the starting point for budgetary planning in any type of business. It is an annual plan which will project the sales of:

- products made by a *manufacturing* business, eg cars, CDs, breakfast cereals
- services provided by a *service* business, eg holidays, educational courses, bus and train journeys

The accuracy of the sales budget is critical for the success of the business. If a business overestimates sales, it will be left with unsold goods or under-utilised services; if sales are underestimated, then customers will be lost to competitors. Both overestimating and underestimating sales can lose money. While budgeting is not an exact science, and is unlikely to be 100% accurate, it is essential that as much accurate information as possible is gathered; this can include:

- details of past sales performance – available within the business
- present sales figures – up-to-date figures from sales representatives
- what the competition is doing – estimates of market share
- assessment of whether the market is expanding or declining
- forecasts made – by sales representatives and market researchers
- trading conditions and the economic climate

A sales budget will start off by estimating the number of units to be sold over the next year and then applying a selling price to produce an estimate of the income figure in money terms. There is no laid-down format for a sales budget: it can project sales in a number of different ways:

- by product
- by customer
- by geographical area

An example of a product-based sales budget follows:

sales budget by product (extract)

	January	February	March	April	May	June	Total
	£	£	£	£	£	£	£
product A	1,000	1,000	1,000	1,000	1,000	1,000	6,000
product B	1,500	1,500	1,500	1,500	1,500	1,500	9,000
product C	2,500	2,500	2,500	2,500	2,500	2,500	15,000
etc ...							

Note how the budget uses:

budget periods – the subdivision of the budget into monthly, four-weekly (which divides a 52-week year into 13 four-weekly periods), or weekly

budget headings – the subdivision of the budget by product (or other category of income or expense).

planning the production/operating budget

When a business has established its sales budget it is then in a position to work out its production budget (for a manufacturing business), or its operating budget (for a service).

When planning a production/operating budget, management must gather together information about the business' resources and consider a range of external factors in order to assess what can and cannot be achieved. These include:

- *timing* — When during the year are the products required? Are there any seasonal fluctuations (Christmas cards, fireworks) which will produce uneven demands on production facilities? Will the business need to hold stocks of products in advance?
- *capacity* — Can the existing production facilities cope with the expected demand? Will new fixed assets be needed? Should some work be subcontracted to other businesses?
- *labour cost* — Does the business have the right number of staff with the necessary skills? Will more staff be needed? Will there need to be training? Will overtime need to be worked, or is an additional shift required?
- *materials* — Can the right quality of materials be obtained at the right price?

When all of this information has been gathered and analysed, the business should then be in a position to prepare an annual production budget, taking into account:

- the projected monthly sales figures
- the finished products in stock at the beginning and end of each month

Once the production budget has been established then the subsidiary budgets can be prepared:

- materials budget – the cost of purchasing materials to make the goods
- labour budget – the wages of employees involved in the production process
- direct expenses – the cost of other direct production expenses

- overheads budget – the cost of the other expenses of production

By using a standard costing system (see page 179), a business can calculate the costs of output in advance of production – the details from the standard costing system are an important factor in the budgetary process.

FITTA HOMEGYM LIMITED – PRODUCTION BUDGET

situation

Jim Lewis is the production manager of Fitta Homegym Limited, manufacturers of the Fitta De Luxe Exercise Cycle. The sales manager has just presented Jim with the budgeted sales for the forthcoming twelve months, as follows:

January	150 units
February	150 "
March	200 "
April	400 "
May	400 "
June	400 "
July	500 "
August	300 "
September	200 "
October	200 "
November	700 "
December	425 "

Stock in the warehouse on 1 January at the start of the year is budgeted to be 100 units. Jim's problem is that the factory, working at normal capacity, can produce 350 units each month. More units can be made if overtime is paid, but the directors are not keen to see this happen, just as they do not like to see too much under-utilisation of the factory. Jim has to work out an even production budget – set in terms of units of production – which will keep the factory working at near or full capacity, but without incurring too much overtime. He has three other constraints:

- month-end stock must never fall below 100 units
- the warehouse is fairly small and cannot hold more than 600 units
- the factory is closed for half of August

solution

Jim plans the production budget as follows:

production budget for next year

UNITS	Jan	Feb	Mar	Apr	May	Jun	Jul	Aug	Sep	Oct	Nov	Dec
Opening stock	100	275	450	600	550	500	450	300	175	325	475	125
add Units produced	325	325	350	350	350	350	350	175	350	350	350	400
less Units sold	150	150	200	400	400	400	500	300	200	200	700	425
Closing stock	275	450	600	550	500	450	300	175	325	475	125	100

Note that Jim has been successful in meeting all of the limiting factors, except that:

- the factory could produce another 25 units in both January and February; however, the effect of this would be to take the warehouse beyond its capacity in March
- overtime will have to be paid for the production of 50 units in December

BUDGETARY CONTROL

Once the budgetary planning process has been completed, and the budget is approved by the owner or board of directors, the budget becomes the official plan of the business. During the period of the budget the process of *budgetary control* uses the budget as a control mechanism, as shown in fig 15.3 (on the next page).

The main aspect with which budgetary control is concerned is in comparing actual results with what was planned to happen in the budget. As the budget period progresses, separate budget reports are prepared monthly. The 'actual' and 'variance' columns are completed and the cumulative figures for the year-to-date are recorded. Invariably a computer spreadsheet is used for this task. An example of a budget report is shown below (the owner/directors should be pleased with the results shown).

Fitta Homegym Limited – sales budget report (extract)

	Income: December			*Income: Year-to-date*		
	budget	actual	variance	budget	actual	variance
	£	£	£	£	£	£
Retail sales	200,000	250,000	50,000 FAV	2,750,000	3,125,000	375,000 FAV
Mail order	225,000	200,000	25,000 ADV	1,275,000	1,350,000	75,000 FAV
Total sales	425,000	450,000	25,000 FAV	4,025,000	4,475,000	450,000 FAV

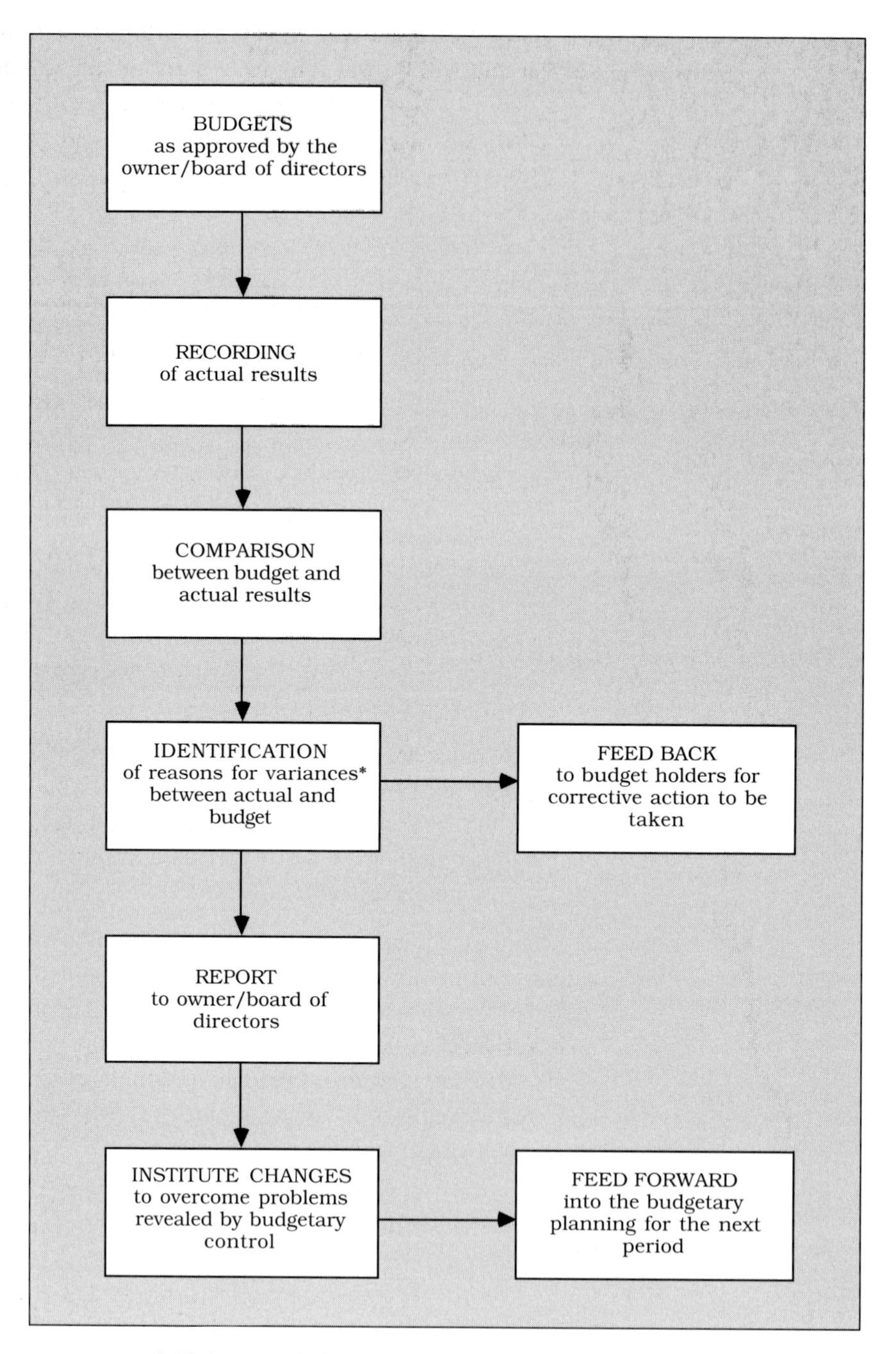

* Variance analysis will be considered in detail in Chapter 17

Fig 15.3 Budgetary control

The senior management of a business will be monitoring the budget during the year and will be watching closely for differences between the budgeted and actual figures – the *variances*. There are two types of variance:

- a *favourable variance* (FAV), where the results are better than expected
- an *adverse variance* (ADV), where the results are worse than expected

Details of variances are used to:

- *feed back* information to managers so that, where necessary, corrective action can be taken
- *feed forward* into the planning process for the next period's budgets

Variances are an example of *management by exception*: only those variances that are considered to be of significant size relative to the business need be drawn to the attention of senior management for further investigation. We will be looking in more detail at the analysis of variances in Chapter 17.

The management accountant will produce *budgetary control reports* which explain to directors and senior managers the reasons for variances and the corrective action taken. Such reports will be prepared in order to meet the needs of the organisation, ie they will:

- be produced promptly
- contain accurate information
- be prepared in a suitable format with the correct level of detail and the emphasis in the right areas

FIXED AND FLEXIBLE BUDGETS

fixed budgets

A fixed budget remains the same whatever the level of activity of the business.

So far we have taken a simple view of budgets. We have assumed that budgets have been set at the beginning of the financial year and then adhered to and monitored, whatever the circumstances – ie the budgeted figures do not change. This is the *fixed budget*. This type of budget will be useful in situations where circumstances are stable – for example a departmental budget for a school or a college, where a set amount of money is allowed for buying textbooks each year.

flexible budgets

A flexible budget changes with the level of activity and takes into account different cost behaviour patterns.

In reality, situations do change. For example, the sale of products can vary quite widely from the target figures in the budget: a new product can be more successful than expected – or it can be a complete disaster. In either case the budgeted figures for sales (and production costs too) will be wide of the mark. The answer is to use a *flexible budget*, which will vary in line with the level of activity of a business – ie with output of products sold or services provided.

A business may therefore prepare a flexible production budget assuming 100%, 90%, 80% and 70% of normal activity. If production is at 80% of capacity, the budget is 'flexed' so that the 80% option can be used, and appropriate variances calculated.

flexible budgets – fixed and variable costs

When calculating costs for a flexible budget, certain costs vary with the level of activity, eg

- materials costs for a manufacturing business
- direct labour costs – the production line wages bill

The other costs of making a product or providing a service, eg office rent, warehouse rent, fuel bills, insurance, office staff wages – the *overheads* – fall into two categories:

- fixed overheads, eg the rent of an office
- variable overheads, eg sales commission

The important point here is that when constructing a flexible budget, fixed overheads will normally remain the same, whatever the level of activity but variable overheads will change in line with activity.

CASE STUDY

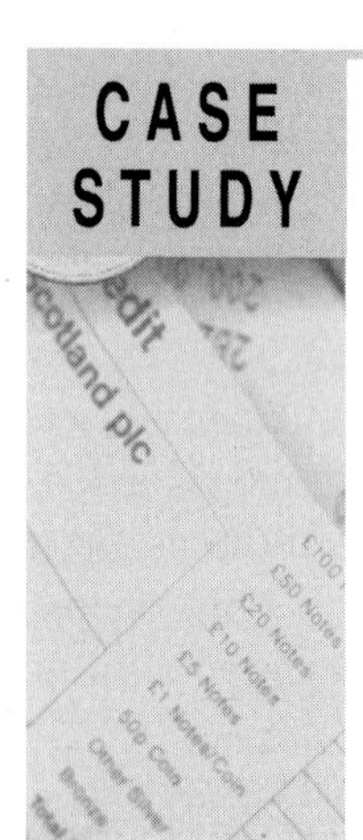

PITMAN PLASTICS – FIXED AND FLEXIBLE BUDGETS

situation

Pitman Plastics manufactures plastic kitchenware. The production manager has extracted the cost figures for last month's output and compares them with the budgeted figures:

	budget	*actual*
	£	£
materials	100,000	81,000
labour	50,000	42,000
variable overheads	25,000	18,000
fixed overheads	25,000	26,000
TOTAL	200,000	167,000

The results, on the face of it, look very encouraging – costs are £33,000 below budget. The manager knows, however, that sales have been depressed during the month and also that production has been running at 80% of normal capacity. The finance department produces a flexible budget at 80% of output.

solution

The fixed budget report based on the figures given shows a total favourable variance of costs, being £33,000 below budget. The production director knows that this is misleading.

fixed budget report

	budget	*actual*	*variance*	*trend*
output level	100%			
	£	£	£	
materials	100,000	81,000	19,000	FAV
labour	50,000	42,000	8,000	FAV
variable overheads	25,000	18,000	7,000	FAV
fixed overheads	25,000	26,000	1,000	ADV
TOTAL	200,000	167,000	33,000	FAV

The flexible budget report, based on costs for 80% output shows a total adverse variance of £2,000. This is a more realistic picture of performance, and is less encouraging. Note that while budgeted fixed overheads remain at £25,000 for 80% production, budgeted variable overheads have been reduced by 20% to £20,000.

flexible budget report – assuming 80% output for month

	budget	*budget*	*actual*	*variance*	*trend*
output level	100%	80%			
	£	£	£	£	
materials	100,000	80,000	81,000	1,000	ADV
labour	50,000	40,000	42,000	2,000	ADV
variable overheads	25,000	20,000	18,000	2,000	FAV
fixed overheads	25,000	25,000	26,000	1,000	ADV
TOTAL	200,000	165,000	167,000	2,000	ADV

SETTING NEW BUDGETS

When the time comes for budgets to be set for the *next* budget period there are two methods that can be used:

incremental budgets

In an *incremental budget* the previous budget figures are used as a basis and a small percentage added on (the 'increment') to allow for general rises in costs brought about by inflation. This type of budgeting works reasonably well in situations where the area budgeted for is stable – eg in local authorities – but has the major disadvantage that it does not analyse costs; thus inefficiences and overspending remain in the system.

zero-based budgeting

The other alternative when setting budgets is to 'start from scratch'. The budget starts from zero, and each item going into the budget has to be justified by the budget holder – normally the manager of the department. This ensures that inefficiencies and overspending are avoided. It is, however, a time-consuming procedure, and is hardly feasible every year. Some businesses therefore adopt the policy of using zero-based budgeting from time-to-time and incremental budgeting in the intervening years.

BUDGETING – FURTHER THOUGHTS

The main advantages of using budgets are that they:

- help the organisation to survive, and to achieve its long-term objectives
- co-ordinate the various functions – eg sales, production, selling and distribution, administration
- provide the benefits of planning
- establish performance targets
- enable comparison between budget and actual performance, thus allowing appropriate corrective action to be taken

Despite these clear advantages, for a budget to be useful to business, it has to be a realistic forecast of what can be achieved. If it is not, then the people who have to work to the budget will simply 'give up' and will not try to achieve the targets set. At the same time, the management of the business, starting at the top with the owner or directors, must be convinced of the usefulness of the budget. If budgeting is seen as a necessary chore to be undertaken without much enthusiasm, then this attitude will soon permeate down through the organisation.

Not all managers and supervisors will wish to be involved in the budgetary planning and control process. They may not be motivated by budgets and may consider that there are too many factors outside their control to enable budget targets to be achieved. Often the overall objectives of a large business or organisation are not fully understood by managers, who do not appreciate the role of their function or department in achieving these objectives.

The overall effectiveness of budgets will depend, amongst other factors, on:

- the effective communication of the organisation's overall objectives
- an achievable level of targets set in the budgets
- the favourable attitude of managers and supervisors to the budgetary planning and control process

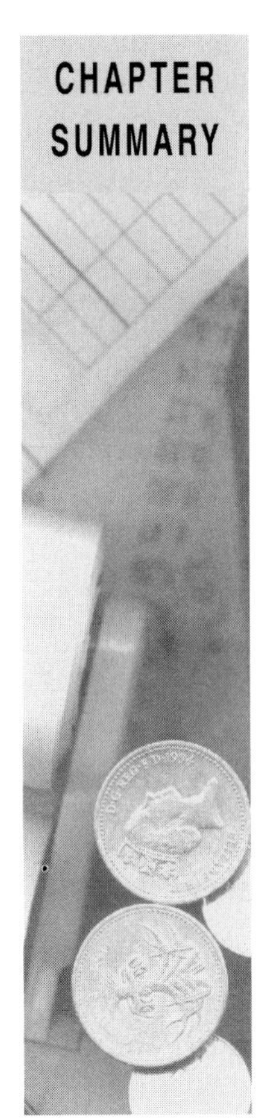

- Budgets are used by managers to plan and control the business or organisation in the short- and long-term.
- Functional budgets – for income or expenditure – are prepared for each section of the organisation.
- Individual budgets all contribute to the master budget.
- Budgets are affected by limiting factors, eg the quantity of a product that can be sold, availability of skilled labour, finance; the effect of the constraint should be minimised.
- Budgetary planning establishes the targets and, when approved by the owners/directors, the budget becomes the official plan of the organisation for the budget period.
- Budgetary control uses the budget to monitor actual results with budgeted figures.
- Responsibility for budgets is given to managers and supervisors – the budget holders – as part of what is known as *responsibility accounting.*
- Variances – the difference between actual and budgeted figures – should be investigated if they are significant; appropriate action can then be taken to correct the reason for the variance.
- Flexible budgets are a series of fixed budgets for different levels of activity of the business for a given budget period.
- Budgets for the next budget period can be set either on an incremental basis, or on a zero-based system.

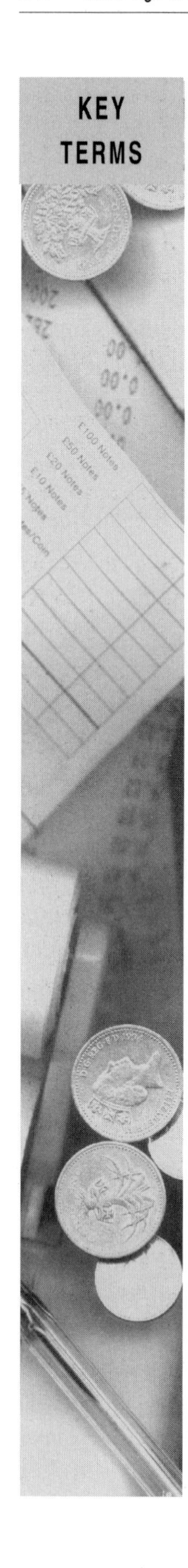

budget	a means of planning and control used by the management of a business or organisation to achieve stated objectives
functional budgets	a plan for a specific function within a business or organisation, eg sales, production, selling and distribution, administration
subsidiary budgets	budgets prepared for the separate activities within a function, eg materials, labour, direct expenses, overheads – all within the production function
master budget	forecast profit and loss account and balance sheet, compiled from the information in the budgets
budgetary planning	the process of establishing budgets relating to functions of the business or organisation
budgetary control	the process of monitoring actual results against budgeted figures with the intention of taking action to correct significant variances
fixed budget	remains the same whatever the level of activity of the business
flexible budget	changes with the level of activity and takes into account different cost behaviour patterns
budget holder	the person responsible for a particular budget
budget manual	guidelines of the budgetary planning and control process
budget committee	committee which organises the process of budgetary planning and control
feed back	the process of providing information on variances to the budget holders in order that, where appropriate, corrective action can be taken
feed forward	the process of carrying forward information about variances and any corrective action taken into the budgetary planning for the next period

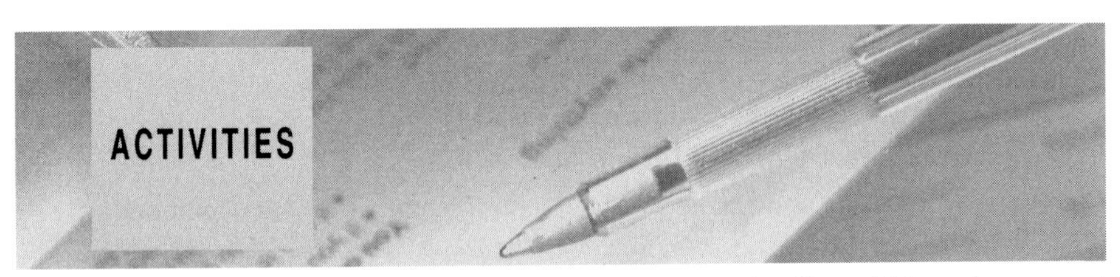

15.1 Identify an organisation with which you are familiar which makes use of budgets and consider the following:

- What are the long- and short-term objectives of the organisation? How does the budget process link to these objectives?
- What budgets does it use? Show the budgets (including master budget) in diagrammatic form, and provide a note of explanation on each budget.
- How is the budgetary planning process conducted? Which supervisors/managers are involved?
- How is the budgetary control process conducted? Look for and explain examples of *responsibility accounting* and *management by exception*. How does management identify significant variances between actual and budgeted figures?
- What system is used for preparing the budgets for the next budget period? Is there a case for using zero-based budgeting in a future budget period?

15.2 Discuss the following statements:

(a) "From the directors' viewpoint, we use budgets to motivate our employees."

(b) "As a supervisor I have no say in the budgets."

(c) "The budgets are set far too high for me, as a departmental manager, to achieve."

(d) "Budgets are a good example of responsibility accounting."

(e) "Senior managers aren't interested when we achieve the targets set by budgets; they only get involved when there is a significant variance."

(f) "We always prepare next year's expenditure budget by taking the current year's budget figures and adding the rate of inflation, plus one per cent."

(g) "Budgets should always be expressed in terms of quantities rather than monetary values."

15.3 Radionics Limited is a manufacturer of audio equipment for cars – radios, cassette and CD players. Most parts for the radios are bought in and assembled at the company's factory, which is situated on a modern industrial estate near Slough. The directors are currently planning the company's progress over the next twelve months.

Working in the finance department, you have been asked by the Finance Director to prepare a short paper for her to present at the next board meeting of the company which is to be held next week. The paper is to cover the following points:

- the different budgets that the company should prepare for the forthcoming year

- any limiting factors that the directors must bear in mind when considering budget proposals, and how such factors are likely to affect the company

15.4 Shades Limited manufactures quality sunglasses at its 'hi-tech' factory unit near Cambridge. Although there is some all-year round demand for sunglasses, highest demand is in late spring, and in summer. Because of the quality of the product, and the high skills needed from the workforce, there is little possibility of increasing production to meet peak demand; instead the company adopts a policy of keeping the factory working at full or near-full capacity throughout the year. The disadvantage of this policy is that completed stock needs to be warehoused until demand increases. Overtime can be worked to increase production by a maximum of 10%.

The sales director has been preparing a sales budget (in numbers of units of sunglasses) expected to be sold in the forthcoming year. Here is her budget:

January 5,500, February 4,500, March 3,500, April 4,000, May 7,000, June 12,500, July 15,000, August 10,000, September 2,000, October 3,000, November 5,000, December 5,000.

The production director now has to work out a production budget, taking into account the following:

- Stock at 1 January is 8,500 units
- Maximum monthly output without working overtime: 7,500 units. However, the factory is closed for one week in April (Easter), for two weeks in August (annual holiday), and for one week at Christmas. Each week of holiday loses one-quarter of that month's production.
- At the end of each month there must always be in stock two-thirds of the next month's budgeted sales.
- Overtime can be worked to produce a maximum increase in output of 10%.

(a) Prepare a month-by-month production budget for Shades Limited which also shows:
- when and how much overtime working will be necessary
- closing stock (in units) at each month-end

(b) What are the limiting factors of Shades Limited, from the point of view of both production and sales?

15.5 (a) Explain what is meant by:

- fixed budgets, and
- flexible budgets

What is the main objective of preparing flexible budgets?

(b) Seats Limited manufactures chairs which sell to schools and colleges throughout Britain. The company is currently producing budgets for the next year. The sales director is budgeting for sales of 90,000 chairs; the selling price is £10 each. Production costs are budgeted as being:

- materials £2.50 per chair
- labour £2.75 per chair
- variable overheads £0.50 per chair
- fixed overheads £242,000 per year

However, a general election was announced a few days ago, and conversation at today's board meeting of the company's directors goes as follows:

"The outcome of the election looks unpredictable".

"If the government is re-elected, they are committed to a 10% cut in education spending."

"On the other hand, if the opposition party win, they have pledged to increase education spending by 25%."

"Until we get further information we had better assume that our sales will be affected by the same percentages."

- Prepare the fixed budget for the year based on sales of 90,000 chairs, to show budgeted profit
- Prepare two flexible budgets based on the changes in educational spending proposed by each of the main political parties
- Write an explanation to the directors of the reason for the different budgeted profit figures

15.6 Greenlawn Limited manufactures a combined lawn weedkiller and fertiliser at its recently completed chemical works in Birmingham. Output last year was 1,000,000 litres which sold for £5 per litre. However, this is well below the production capacity of the works and it is planned to increase production, and reduce the selling price.

The company wishes to prepare flexible budgets for output of 1,500,000 litres, 2,000,000 litres, and 2,500,000 litres (which is the maximum capacity of the works).

The selling price is to be reduced by 50p per litre for each increase in output. Variable overheads are £2,000,000 at an output level of 1,000,000 litres; fixed overheads are £1,500,000; semi-variable overheads are £750,000 at the present capacity, and are expected to increase by equal increments to £1,500,000 at the maximum production level.

- Prepare a budget based on last year's level of output
- Prepare flexible budgets at the different production levels, showing budgeted profit
- Advise the management of Greenlawn Limited of the production level which they should set for next year

16 CASH BUDGETS AND MASTER BUDGETS

this chapter covers ...

- *the purpose of a cash budget*
- *the format of a cash budget*
- *preparation of a master budget*
- *the uses to which a cash budget and master budget can be put*
- *the development of a cash budget and master budget for a particular business*

INTRODUCTION

We saw in the previous chapter that the cash budget is the subsidiary budget that brings together financial information from all the other individual budgets. Once the cash budget (which is often known as a *cash flow forecast*) has been produced the *master budget* follows. The master budget takes the form of forecast financial statements:

- forecast profit and loss account
- forecast balance sheet

Both the cash budget and the master budget form an important part of a *business plan* (see Chapter 20). This is prepared by a business seeking finance from a lender or investor.

CASH BUDGET: PURPOSE

The purpose of a cash budget is to detail the expected cash/bank receipts and payments, usually on a month-by-month basis, for the next three, six or twelve months (or even longer), in order to show the estimated bank balance at the end of each month throughout the period.

From the cash budget, the managers of a business can decide what action to take when a surplus of cash is shown to be available or, as is more likely, when a bank overdraft needs to be arranged.

CASH BUDGET: FORMAT

A suitable format for a cash budget, with sample figures, is set out below:

Name ....Cash Budget for the .... months ending ....

	Jan £000	Feb £000	Mar £000	etc £000
Receipts				
eg from debtors	150	150	161	170
cash sales	70	80	75	80
Total receipts for month (A)	220	230	236	250
Payments				
eg to creditors	160	165	170	170
expenses	50	50	50	60
fixed assets		50		
Total payments for month (B)	210	265	220	230
Net cash flow (Receipts less Payments, ie A–B)	10	(35)	16	20
Add bank balance at beginning of month	10	20	(15)	1
Bank balance (overdraft) at end of month	20	(15)	1	21

A cash budget consists of three main sections:

- receipts for the month
- payments for the month
- summary of bank account

The *receipts* are analysed to show the amount of money that is expected to be received from cash sales, debtors, sale of fixed assets, issue of shares, etc.

Payments show how much money is expected to be paid in respect of cash purchases, creditors, expenses, purchases of fixed assets, repayment of shares and loans. Note that non-cash expenses (such as depreciation and bad debts) are not shown in the cash budget.

The summary at the bottom of the cash budget shows *net cash flow* (total receipts less total payments) added to the bank balance at the beginning of the month, and resulting in the estimated closing bank balance at the end of the month. An overdrawn bank balance is shown in brackets.

The main difficulty in the preparation of cash budgets lies in the *timing* of receipts and payments – for example, debtors may pay two months after date of sale, or creditors may be paid one month after date of purchase: it is important to ensure that such receipts and payments are recorded correctly. Note too that the cash budget, as its name suggests, deals only in cash/bank transactions; thus non-cash items, such as depreciation, are never shown. Similarly, where cash discounts are allowed or received, only the actual amount of cash expected to be received or paid is recorded.

CASE STUDY

MIKE ANDERSON, TRADING AS "ART SUPPLIES"

situation

A friend of yours, Mike Anderson, has recently been made redundant from his job as a sales representative for an arts and crafts company. Mike has decided to set up in business on his own selling art supplies to shops and art societies. He plans to invest £20,000 of his savings into the new business. He has a number of good business contacts, and is confident that his firm will do well. He thinks that some additional finance will be required in the short term and plans to approach his bank for this.

Mike asks for your assistance in producing estimates for his new business for the next six months. He provides the following information:

- The business will commence in January 1998.
- Fixed assets costing £8,000 will be bought in early January. These will be paid for immediately and are expected to have a five-year life, at the end of which they will be worthless.
- An initial stock of goods costing £5,000 will be bought and paid for at the beginning of January.
- Monthly purchases of stocks will then be made at a level sufficient to replace forecast sales for that month, ie the goods he expects to sell in January will be replaced by purchases made in January, and so on.
- Forecast monthly sales are:

January	£3,000
February	£6,000
March	£6,000

April	£10,500
May	£10,500
June	£10,500

- The selling price of goods is fixed at the cost price plus 50 per cent.
- To encourage sales, he will allow two months' credit to customers; however, only one month's credit will be received from suppliers of stock (but the initial stock will be paid for immediately).
- Running expenses of the business, including rent of premises, but excluding depreciation of fixed assets, are estimated at £1,600 per month.
- Mike intends to draw £1,000 each month in cash from the business.

You are asked to prepare a cash budget for the first six months of the business.

solution

Mike Anderson, trading as "Art Supplies"
Cash budget for the six months ending 30 June 1998

	Jan	Feb	Mar	Apr	May	Jun
	£	£	£	£	£	£
Receipts						
Capital introduced	20,000					
Debtors	–	–	3,000	6,000	6,000	10,500
Total receipts for month	20,000	–	3,000	6,000	6,000	10,500
Payments						
Fixed assets	8,000					
Stock	5,000					
Creditors	–	2,000	4,000	4,000	7,000	7,000
Running expenses	1,600	1,600	1,600	1,600	1,600	1,600
Drawings	1,000	1,000	1,000	1,000	1,000	1,000
Total payments for month	15,600	4,600	6,600	6,600	9,600	9,600
Net cash flow	4,400	(4,600)	(3,600)	(600)	(3,600)	900
Add bank balance (overdraft) at beginning of month	–	4,400	(200)	(3,800)	(4,400)	(8,000)
Bank balance (overdraft) at end of month	4,400	(200)	(3,800)	(4,400)	(8,000)	(7,100)

Reminder: No depreciation – a non-cash expense – is shown in the cash budget.

Notes:

- purchases are two-thirds of the sales values (because selling price is cost price plus 50 per cent)
- customers pay two months after sale, ie debtors from January settle in March

- suppliers are paid one month after purchase, ie creditors from January are paid in February

The cash budget shows that there is a need, in the first six months at least, for some bank finance. An early approach to the bank needs to be made.

Later in the chapter, we will see how the master budget is prepared for this business.

CASH BUDGETS: BENEFITS AND LIMITATIONS

The ***benefits*** of a cash budget include:

- it forms part of the planning process of the business or organisation
- it identifies in advance cash flow problems, so that steps can be taken to minimise borrowings and, thus, interest charges
- any surplus cash can be invested so as to maximise income from deposits
- it helps to identify overtrading (see Chapter 8, pages 151-153), which is often characterised by increasing cash deficits
- comparisons between actual and budget figures should be made so that variances can be investigated (indeed, to help with this, the layout of a cash budget can incorporate columns for both *projected* and *actual* figures)

The main ***limitations*** are that:

- the cash budget is only as good as the estimates on which it is based (eg optimistic figures for sales for the next six or twelve months will show an equally optimistic picture of the bank balance)
- a cash budget – like all budgets – that looks too far into the future will probably prove to be inaccurate in later months

A cash budget does not indicate the profits (or losses) being made by a business. It does not follow that a cash budget which reveals an increasing bank balance necessarily indicates a profitable business. The *master budget*, in the form of forecast final accounts, includes a forecast profit and loss account which will show profitability.

CASH BUDGETS AND 'WHAT IF?' QUESTIONS

A cash budget is prepared on the basis of certain assumptions, for example:

- debtors pay, in full, two months after the month of sale
- purchases from suppliers are paid for in the month following purchase

Often the managers or owner of a business will wish to change the assumptions on which the cash budget is based by saying 'what if?' For example:

- *What if* half our debtors take three months to pay?
- *What if* we buy a new machine three months earlier than planned?
- *What if* we take advantage of cash discounts offered by our creditors and pay within, say, 14 days of purchase?

Each of these examples will change the cash budget substantially, and any two of the three, or all three together, is likely to have a considerable effect on a previously calculated budget, and may lead to an increased bank overdraft requirement.

To answer *'what if?'* questions, the whole cash budget has to be reworked on the basis of the new assumptions. The reason for this is that, as the estimates of receipts and payments change each month, so the estimated closing month-end bank balances change. This is where a computer spreadsheet is ideal for the preparation of cash budgets: each change can be put in, and the computer can be used to rework all the calculations. A printout can be taken of each assumption and then passed to the owner/managers for consideration.

CASH: A LIMITING FACTOR

The cash budget may show, for certain months, a potential bank overdraft which is beyond the limits of the business. It might be unacceptably high for the business because of the interest cost, or the bank may not be prepared to allow such overdraft facilities. Thus a shortage of cash may be the *limiting factor* for a business, and it may have to rethink the other budgets in order to change its plans so as to work within its cash resources. After all, it is a shortage of cash that forces most companies into liquidation, even if they provide a good product or service: thus the efficient use of cash resources is one of the most important control aspects for the management of a business.

THE MASTER BUDGET

A *master budget* is the next logical step once all other budgets, including the cash budget, have been prepared.

A master budget takes the form of forecast financial statements, ie forecast profit and loss account, and balance sheet.

"ART SUPPLIES" (CONTINUED)

situation

Before visiting the bank to arrange finance, you help Mike Anderson to prepare a master budget for the first six months of his business.

solution

Mike Anderson, trading as "Art Supplies"
Forecast profit and loss account for the six months ending 30 June 1998

	£	£
Sales		46,500
Opening stock	5,000	
Purchases £46,500 x 2/3	31,000	
	36,000	
Less Closing stock	5,000	
Cost of sales		31,000
Gross profit		15,500
Less overheads:		
Running expenses	9,600	
Depreciation of fixed assets		
(68,000 ÷ 5 years) ÷ 2, ie six months	800	
		10,400
Net profit		5,100

Forecast balance sheet as at 30 June 1998

	£	£
Fixed assets		
At cost		8,000
Less depreciation to date		800
		7,200
Current assets		
Stock	5,000	
Debtors £10,500 x 2 months	21,000	
	26,000	
Less Current liabilities		
Creditors	7,000	
Bank overdraft	7,100	
	14,100	
Working capital		11,900
NET ASSETS		19,100
FINANCED BY		
Capital		
Opening capital		20,000
Add net profit		5,100
		25,100
Less Drawings		6,000
Closing capital		19,100

Points to note when preparing forecast final accounts:

- The sales figure used is the total amount of goods sold, whether paid for or not (sales made, but not yet paid for, are recorded as debtors in the balance sheet).
- Likewise, the figure for purchases is the total of goods bought, with amounts not yet paid for recorded as creditors in the balance sheet.
- Depreciation, which *never* appears in the cash budget, is shown amongst the overheads in the profit and loss account, and deducted from the cost of the fixed asset in the balance sheet. (Note that, in the example above, depreciation is for a period of six months.)

Master budget of Mike Anderson

There are a number of points that Mike Anderson's bank manager will wish to discuss. Some general points are listed in the next section; we will turn our attention to Mike Anderson's business in Activity 16.2 (page 309).

USES OF THE CASH BUDGET AND MASTER BUDGET

After the cash budget and master budget have been prepared they are used by a busines in a number of ways. However, it is vitally important that the subsidiary budgets used in their preparation are accurate, as anything that follows will be thrown by an inaccurate budget.

commentary on business plans

The owner, or a potential lender (see also *business plan*, below) will wish to review the business' plans in the light of the financial figures from the cash budget and master budget.

The following are some of the questions that might be asked by the owner or a lender:

- Will bank finance be needed at any time during the period covered by the cash budget? If so, how long will it take to repay such borrowing?
- Is there a build-up of cash that needs to be invested on a short-term basis?
- Is the business expected to be profitable?
- Are the credit terms allowed to debtors similar to those received from creditors?
- How much is the owner taking out of the business in relation to the forecast net profit?
- If the purchase of fixed assets creates a large overdraft, could other forms of finance be considered, eg hire purchase, or leasing?

In addition to these points, ratio analysis (see Chapter 7) can be used to analyse the forecast final accounts, and comparisons can be made with what was achieved by the same business in the previous year or half-year (assuming it was then trading).

the 'business plan' for a lender

The master budget, together with the cash budget, form the basis of the financial section of a business plan (see Chapter 20) – the document which will be prepared by the business when it wishes to raise money from a lender or investor. The financial element of the plan is central to the case which the business will present to a bank, or other lender. A business may have an excellent product and a growing market share, but without financial forecasts to back up its plans, it will have difficulty in convincing the potential lender of its financial integrity.

monitoring

Both the cash budget and the master budget will be monitored, usually on a monthly basis. Reports will be produced and the actual results compared with the budgeted figures. Variances will be identified, and action taken where appropriate or possible. The cash budget and master budget enable the owner(s) to see how the business is expected to progress. Without the benefit of these budgets, the business could be running into problems of which the owner/managers could be quite unaware.

- A cash budget (or cash flow forecast) is a subsidiary budget which records the expected cash receipts and payments, usually on a monthly basis, for a period ahead of up to one year.
- The bank summary section on a cash budget shows the expected month-end bank balance. From this it is possible to see if short-term overdraft facilities need to be arranged.
- The master budget is compiled from the subsidiary budgets of a business.
- The master budget comprises:
  - forecast profit and loss account
  - forecast balance sheet
- The master budget enables the owner/managers of the business to plan effectively over the budget period and to monitor the success (or otherwise) of the business.
- The master budget, together with the cash budget, form the basis of the financial section of the business plan which will be presented to a potential lender or investor when the business wants to raise money.

cash budget (cash flow forecast) — a budget of expected cash/bank receipts and payments

net cash flow — difference between expected cash receipts and payments

master budget — forecast profit and loss account and balance sheet

business plan — document submitted to a potential lender or investor which sets out in detail the plans for the business, usually over the next twelve months

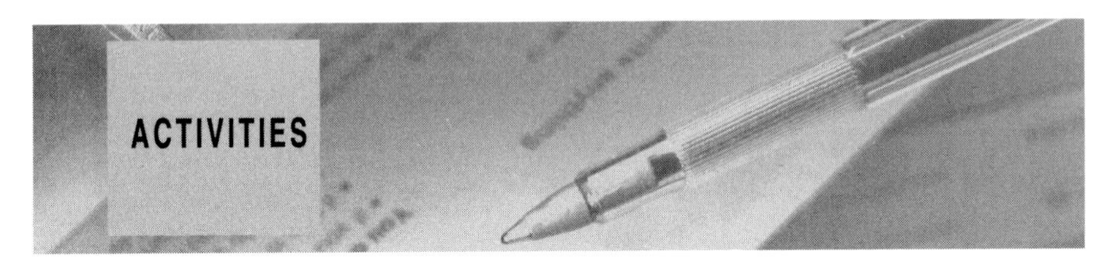

16.1 For the section or department of the organisation where you work:

- prepare a cash budget for the next six months
- over the coming months, compare actual results against the budget
- investigate and discuss the possible reasons for any variances

16.2 Refer back to the cash budget and master budget for "Art Supplies" (pages 303 and 306).

As a potential bank lender, prepare an assessment of Mike Anderson's forecasts and financial requirements for the six months to 30 June 1998. What questions would you wish to ask him about the financial aspects of the business?

16.3 You are preparing the cash budget of Wilkinson Limited for the first six months of 1998. The following budgeted figures are available:

	Sales	*Purchases*	*Wages and salaries*	*Other expenses*
	£	£	£	£
January	65,000	26,500	17,500	15,500
February	70,000	45,000	18,000	20,500
March	72,500	50,000	18,250	19,000
April	85,000	34,500	18,500	18,500
May	65,000	35,500	16,500	20,500
June	107,500	40,500	20,000	22,000

The following additional information is available:

- Sales income is received in the month after sale, and sales for December 1997 amounted to £57,500
- 'Other expenses' each month includes an allocation of £1,000 for depreciation; all other expenses are paid for in the month in which they are incurred
- Purchases, and wages and salaries are paid for in the month in which they are incurred
- The bank balance at 1 January 1998 is £2,250
- Stock at 1 January 1998 is valued at £15,500 and, at 30 June 1998, is expected to have a value of £17,350

You are to prepare:

(a) a month-by-month cash budget for the first six months of 1998

(b) a forecast profit and loss account for the six months ending 30 June 1998

16.4 Jim Smith has recently been made redundant; he has received a redundancy payment and this, together with his accumulated savings, amounts to £10,000. He has decided to set up his own business selling computer stationery and this will commence trading with an initial capital of £10,000 on 1 January. On this date he will buy a van for business use at a cost of £6,000. He has estimated his purchases, sales, and expenses for the next six months as follows:

	Purchases	*Sales*	*Expenses*
	£	£	£
January	4,500	1,250	750
February	4,500	3,000	600
March	3,500	4,000	600
April	3,500	4,000	650
May	3,500	4,500	650
June	4,000	6,000	700

He will pay for purchases in the month after purchase; likewise, he expects his customers to pay for sales in the month after sale. All expenses will be paid for in the month they are incurred.

Jim realizes that he may need bank overdraft facilities before his business becomes established. He asks you to help him with information for the bank and, in particular, he asks you to prepare:

(a) a month-by-month cash budget for the first six months

(b) a forecast profit and loss account for the first six months – for this he tells you that his closing stock at 30 June is expected to have a value of £3,250, and that he wishes to depreciate the van at 20% per annum

(c) a forecast balance sheet as at 30 June

16.5 Mayday Limited was recently formed and plans to commence trading on 1 June 1998. During May the company will issue 200,000 ordinary shares of £1 each at par (ie nominal value) and the cash will be subscribed at once. During the same month £130,000 will be spent on plant and £50,000 will be invested in stock, resulting in a cash balance on 1 June of £20,000.

Plans for the twelve months commencing 1 June 1998 are as follows:

- Stock costing £40,000 will be sold each month at a mark-up of 25%. Customers are expected to pay in the second month following sale.
- Month-end stock levels will be maintained at £50,000 and purchases will be paid for in the month following delivery.
- Wages and other expenses will amount to £6,000 per month, payable in the month during which the costs are incurred.
- Plant will have a ten-year life and no scrap value. Depreciation is to be charged on the straight line basis.

You are to prepare:

(a) a month-by-month cash budget for Mayday Limited for the year to 31 May 1999

(b) the company's forecast profit and loss account for the year ending 31 May 1999, together with a forecast balance sheet at that date.

17 BUDGET MONITORING AND VARIANCE ANALYSIS

this chapter covers ...

- *the principles of budgetary control systems*
- *the role of a budgetary control report as an aid to investigating variances*
- *the main variances and sub-variances for materials and labour*
- *the use of variance analysis for overheads and sales*
- *variances revealed by operating statements*

INTRODUCTION

The previous two chapters have covered budgeting in some detail. We have seen already

- the way in which budgets are planned
- the framework for budgetary controls
- the uses of the master budget
- the need for accuracy in subsidiary budgets

In this chapter, we shall study the budgetary control systems that are set up by a business to monitor budgets. Budgetary control systems show how well planned performance targets are being met and, if they are not, help us to find out why, so that action can be taken as necessary.

An important aspect of budgetary control is linked to standard costing: this costing system (page 179) enables a business to calculate the cost of output in advance of production. Standard costing is used as a method of cost control by comparing standard cost with the actual cost of the output in order to establish the variance, ie

standard cost	*minus*	actual cost	*equals*	variance

BUDGETARY CONTROL SYSTEMS

responsibility for budgets

The setting of budgets for different departments – the budget centres – within an organisation implies that an individual – normally the departmental manager – is responsible for the budget as a *budget holder*. He or she will seek to achieve the various targets. These targets might include costs (for a production department) or income (for a sales department). This accountability for budgets (known as *responsibility accounting*) should motivate the manager and the supervisors to achieve the required level of performance. Some businesses give managers and supervisors incentives and bonuses for meeting targets, or improving upon them.

monitoring results – variances

The budget, once it is set for the financial year, is monitored by comparing budgeted figures with actual results. Any differences between the two are known as *variances*. Significant variances will need to be investigated.

management by exception

The budgetary control system of a business will set down procedures for acting on variances, but only significant variances. This type of system is known as *management by exception*, ie acting on variances that are exceptional. Departmental managers will normally work to *control limits* imposed on costs. A control limit is an acceptable percentage variation on the budgeted cost. If the cost exceeds the control limit, the variance will be significant and investigative action will need to be taken. For example the labour cost for a production department may be budgeted at £50,000 a month, with a control limit of 5 per cent set. If labour costs in any one month exceed £50,000 x 5%, ie a variance of £2,500, action will have to be taken and the cause investigated – see fig 17.1.

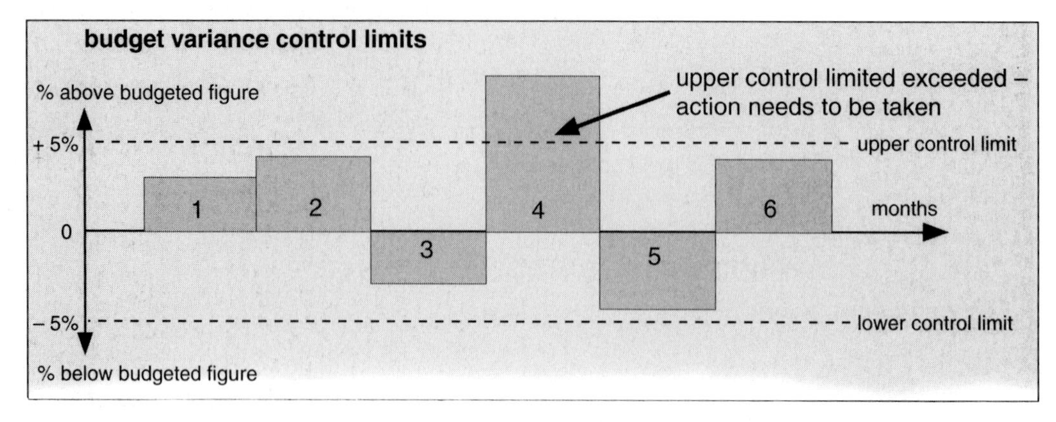

Fig 17.1 Control limits for budget variances

who needs to know about variances?

Variances in budgets need to be reported to the *appropriate* level of management within the business or organisation. This level will depend on the significance of the variance, as shown in the two extreme examples which follow:

- *The sales department office has spent £50 over budget on stationery.*

The managing director is unlikely to be interested – it will be up to the office supervisor to sort out the problem.

- *Sales of one product exceed the sales budget by 50% – a runaway success!*

This is a matter to bring to the attention of higher management and the directors of the company: production patterns, purchasing and staffing will have to be re-organised so that production of that item can be increased.

reporting variances

Budget holders base their decisions on budget reports. Such budget reports are likely to be produced on a computer printout by the finance department and circulated to managers for comment and action. The reports are very detailed and list every item of expenditure and income. Less significant variances are dealt with by the manager and supervisors; significant variances need to be referred to a higher management level. Many variances do not need reporting: the overspending on stationery mentioned above being an example. Summarised reports – including the master budget – are circulated to higher management to provide a picture of how the business is meeting its targets.

Fig 17.2 sets out the format of a typical budget report for a sales department. Note that the illustration shows only an extract from the report; in reality many more products would be shown, and possibly also a breakdown of sales by area and sales reprentative. The details shown are:

- the budget centre (sales department) and the budget holder (manager) responsible
- budget, actual and variance figures for the current period (here October 1997
- year-to-date figures
- the variance trend: FAV (favourable) – better than budget, or ADV (adverse) – worse than budget
- comments – the column here would suffice for simple reasons, a more detailed report would be needed for significant variances

BUDGETARY CONTROL REPORT

budget centre Sales Dept **date** 07.11.1997

budget holder R Brunson **period** October 1997

	current period			*year-to-date*			*comments*
	budget £000s	actual £000s	variance £000s	budget £000s	actual £000s	variance £000s	
PRODUCT A	200	250	50 FAV	2,750	3,125	375 FAV	
PRODUCT B	225	200	25 ADV	1,275	1,150	125 ADV	
PRODUCT C	425	450	25 FAV	4,025	4,475	450 FAV	
etc ...							

Fig 17.2 Format of a budget report (extract only)

investigating variances

changes in income

The sale of products or services provides the main income for most businesses. It comprises the number of items sold, or units of service provided, multiplied by the price of the item. The sales income will, therefore, vary according to the number of items sold and the price charged.

A rise in sales income is clearly desirable and if a business has a number of different products, the successful items should be identified and efforts made to increase sales of them further.

A fall in sales income might be brought about by:

- *overpricing* – if the item is priced too highly when compared with the competition, the price may need to be reduced to stimulate demand
- *price-cutting* – this is sometimes necessary when there is a lot of competition amongst providers, eg petrol prices at supermarkets and garages
- *slack consumer demand* – if the level of spending in the economy is low, or interest rates are high, consumer demand could be stimulated by 'special offers'

changes in expenditure

Expenditure costs comprise:

- purchase of goods for stock – in a shop, for example
- purchase of materials for a manufacturing business
- overheads of the business

A *fall* in costs is generally considered to be an acceptable variance (although sales income may also have fallen).

A *rise* in costs can come about from a number of factors:

- a rise caused by a general price rise, or by buying from a different supplier, or in smaller (more expensive) quantities
- a rise in the cost of imported items following adverse exchange rate fluctuations
- wastage of materials in a manufacturing process (perhaps caused by poor quality materials)

Note also that one cost in a budget may increase, but could lead to a reduction in another cost. For example, a switch from a manual to a computer accounting system will increase the equipment and expenses budget headings (new computers and software have to be purchased) for the accounts department, but should reduce the staff budget headings (as fewer staff will be needed).

controllable and non-controllable costs

When investigating variances, it is important to appreciate that not all of the costs in an expenditure budget can be controlled directly by the budget holder. For example, in a production budget, the cost of rent paid on the premises is outside the control of the production manager – the rent being negotiated by the property services manager. Nevertheless, the proportion of rent charged to production department will be an item on the budget. Thus we can distinguish between:

- *controllable costs* – costs which can be influenced by the budget holder
- *non-controllable costs* – costs which cannot be influenced by the budget holder

Note that all costs are controllable on somebody's budget within the business or organisation: it is that they will be non-controllable on some budgets.

There are a number of ways of dealing with these costs in budgetary control reports:

- to show only the controllable costs of the budget holder
- to show both controllable costs and non-controllable costs, but to distinguish between them
- to show both controllable costs and non-controllable costs, without distinguishing between them

The second and third versions have the merit that the total costs of the department are shown, ie the budget holder appreciates the full costs of his or her department of the business. The main purpose of a budgetary control report, though, is that it must highlight aspects of the costs that merit further investigation.

virement

Sometimes an overspend under one budget heading can be set-off against an underspend under another heading: this technique is known as *virement.* Although not all organisations allow virement, it does give budget holders some leeway to manage the total spending within their budgets.

BUDGETARY CONTROL AND STANDARD COSTING

A business using the standard costing system (see pages 179-181) will monitor the outcomes by comparing the standard costs set with the results that actually occurred. An outline of the monitoring process is shown in fig 17.3 which follows on the next page.

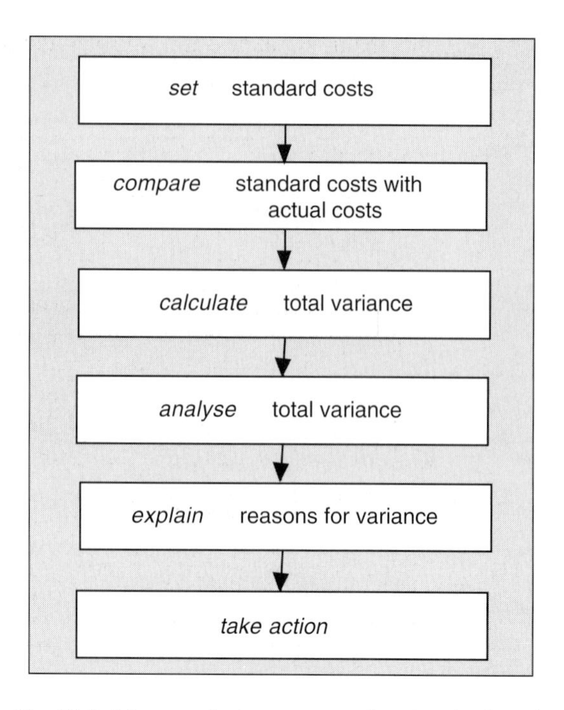

Fig 17.3 The monitoring process for standard costs

VARIANCES AND SUB-VARIANCES

The full amount by which the actual cost of a product differs from the standard cost is known as the total cost variance. It is calculated by deducting actual cost from standard cost, for example:

costs of making 1,200 garden walling blocks

	£	
standard cost	1,000	
actual cost	980	
TOTAL COST VARIANCE	20	FAV

The total cost variance is made up of the variances for each of the main elements of cost:

- materials
- labour
- overheads

The variance for each element can be further analysed into a number of sub-variances which are used to identify the *reasons* for the variance.

The main variances and sub-variances for a manufacturing business are shown in fig 17.4 below.

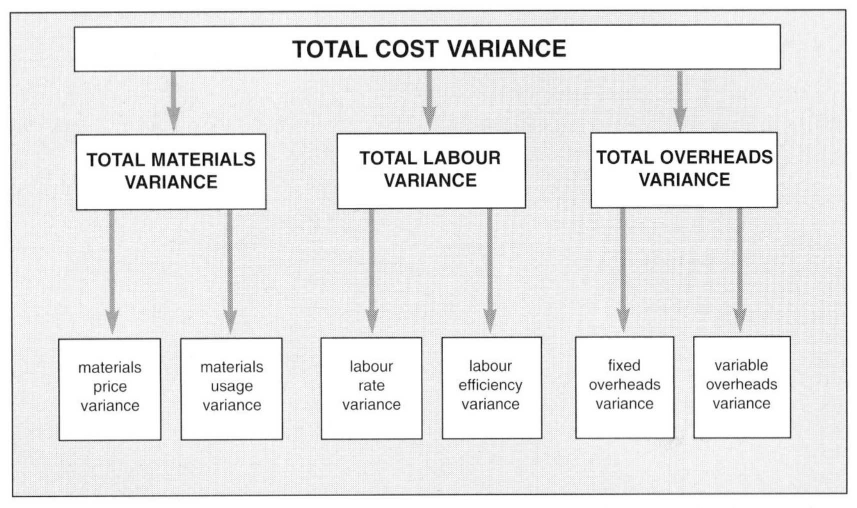

Fig 17.4 Variances and sub-variances for a manufacturing business

As fig 17.4 shows, the total cost variance can result from a combination of different factors:

- ***total materials variance***
  - price variance, caused by a price rise (or price fall) in the cost of materials
  - usage variance, caused by a change in the amount of materials used
- ***total labour variance***
  - rate variance, caused by a rise in pay rates, or the need to use a different grade of employee (at a higher or lower wage rate)
  - efficiency variance caused by a higher or lower output than expected
- ***total overheads variance***
  - fixed overhead variance, caused by a change in fixed costs, such as an increase in the rent of the factory
  - variable overhead variance, caused by a change in the cost or use of a variable overhead, such as electricity

Later in the chapter we will see how these variances – or sub-variances – can be identified and calculated. The principle of variance analysis is that variances and sub-variances are identified and calculated until they can be seen to be the responsibility of an individual employee, or small section within the business. For example, a materials price variance, where the cost of materials is different from the standard cost, is the responsibility of the buying department; it is this department that will have to explain to management the reason(s) for any variance. Note that a variance can only identify that a problem exists; it is for the appropriate section of the business to identify the cause of the variance.

STANDARD COST REPORT AND MONITORING VARIANCES

The variances for each cost element are summarised on a standard cost report, which takes a similar format to the budgetary control report already seen (page 315). An example of a standard cost report is shown in fig 17.5 which follows:

STANDARD COST REPORT

product 1,200 garden walling blocks **date** 07.11.1997

supervisor Richard Stone **period** October 1997

	current period			*comments*
	standard cost	**actual cost**	**variance**	
	£	£	£	
materials	300	270	30 FAV	
labour	300	325	25 ADV	
overheads:				
fixed	300	275	25 FAV	
variable	100	110	10 ADV	
TOTAL COST	1,000	980	20 ADV	

Fig 17.5 Format of a standard cost report

The standard cost report shows the variances for each cost element. A favourable variance is a positive amount, eg for materials £300 – £270 = £30

FAV. Because actual costs are lower than standard, a favourable variance increases profits. By contrast, an adverse variance, eg labour £300 – £325 = £25 ADV, adds to costs and so reduces profits.

Management of the business must decide which variances are significant and need further investigation.

In order to calculate the sub-variances for materials and labour we need to know the make-up of both the standard and the actual cost in terms of

- materials: price and usage
- labour: rate and efficiency

Sub-variances can also be calculated for overheads, although we shall not be covering them in detail.

Fig 17.6 illustrates how the standard cost report for 1,200 garden walling blocks (on the previous page) can be developed to show the sub-variances. The specific calculations for these sub-variances will be shown in the Case Studies which follow each of the next two sections.

	standard cost		*actual cost*		*sub-variances*			
		£		£		£	£	
materials	1,200 kilos		900 kilos		price	45		ADV
	at 25p per kilo	300	at 30p per kilo	270	usage	75		FAV
							30	FAV
labour	50 hours		65 hours		rate	65		FAV
	at £6.00 per hour	300	at £5.00 per hour	325	efficiency	90		ADV
							25	ADV
overheads								
fixed		300		275			*25	FAV
variable		100		110			*10	ADV
TOTAL COST		1,000		980			20	FAV

* sub-variances not calculated here

Fig 17.6 Standard cost report, showing sub-variances for materials and labour

From the report, the materials and labour sub-variances will certainly cause the management to investigate the reasons for both the favourable and adverse variances.

THE CALCULATION OF MATERIALS VARIANCES

As we have seen in fig 17.4, the variances and sub-variances for materials costs are:

variance

- total materials variance, *which is caused by*

sub-variances

- materials *price* variance – the price paid
- materials *usage* variance – the amount used

The money amounts of these are calculated from the areas indicated in the diagram set out below. Note that, for clarity of presentation, both the actual price and the actual quantity used are *greater* than standard, ie they are adverse variances.

The variances are calculated as follows:

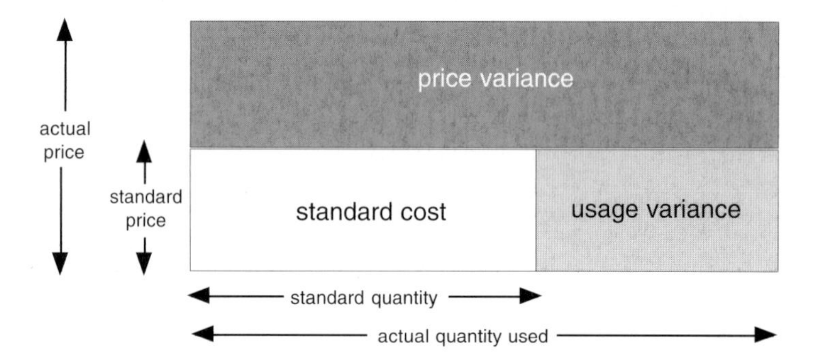

total materials variance =

(standard quantity x standard price) – (actual quantity x actual price)

This variance can then be analysed further by calculating the *sub-variances:*

materials price sub-variance =

(standard price – actual price) x actual quantity

materials usage sub-variance =

(standard quantity – actual quantity) x standard price

notes from the diagram

- The change in the price of materials, based on the quantity actually used, forms the materials price variance – shaded in the diagram. This variance is the responsibility of the *buying department.*
- The change in the actual quantity used, based on the standard price, forms the materials usage variance – shaded in the diagram. This variance is the responsibility of the *production department.*
- As noted, for clarity of presentation, the diagram shows adverse price and usage variances; these variances can, of course, be favourable, ie less than the standard cost.

CASE STUDY

CALCULATING MATERIALS VARIANCES

situation

Wyvern Walling is a manufacturer of garden wall blocks. The management accountant has prepared the following costs for a batch of 1,200 wall blocks:

- the standard price of concrete is 25p per kilo
- the standard usage is 1,200 kilos

The results achieved for the latest batch are:

- the actual price of concrete used was 30p per kilo
- the actual usage was 900 kilos

In short, the concrete has cost more, but less has been used for each wall block. What are the variances and sub-variances for materials costs?

solution

Here both the price and usage have differed from the standard to give the following *total materials variance*:

(standard quantity x standard price) – (actual quantity x actual price)

(1,200 kgs x 25p per kg) – (900 kgs x 30p per kg) =

£300 – £270 = £30 FAVOURABLE

While the total materials variance is favourable by £30, as both price *and* usage differ from standard, the sub-variances must be calculated:

Materials price sub-variance

(standard price – actual price) x actual quantity

(25p – 30p) x 900 kgs = £45 ADVERSE

Materials usage sub-variance

(standard quantity – actual quantity) x standard price		
(1,200 kgs – 900 kgs) x 25p	= £75	FAVOURABLE
TOTAL MATERIALS VARIANCE	£30	FAVOURABLE

For a batch of 1,200 wall blocks, the materials variance is £30 FAV. This agrees with the standard cost report shown in fig 17.6. As a consequence, the rise in price (the adverse sub-variance) must be investigated, together with the reason for the reduced usage of materials (the favourable sub-variance).

THE CALCULATION OF LABOUR VARIANCES

The variances and sub-variances for labour costs (see fig 17.4) are:

variance

- total labour variance, *which is caused by*

sub-variances

- labour rate variance – the rate of wages paid
- labour efficiency variance – the level of efficiency of the workforce

The money amounts of these are calculated from the areas indicated in the diagram set out below. Note that for clarity of presentation, both actual labour rate and the actual hours worked are greater than standard, ie they are adverse variances:

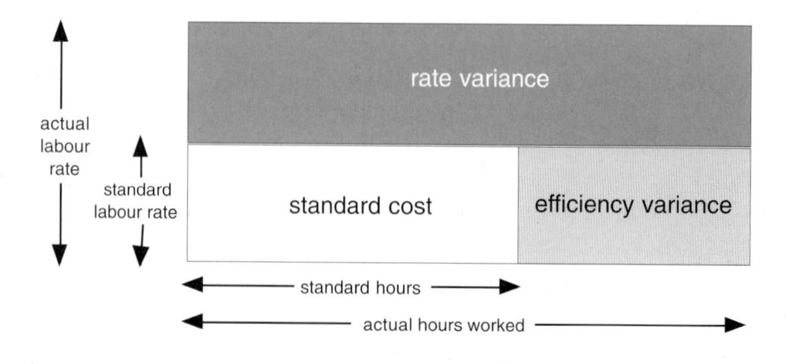

The variances are calculated as follows:

total labour variance =

(standard hours x standard rate) – (actual hours x actual rate)

This variance can then be analysed further by calculating the *sub-variances:*

labour rate sub-variance =

(standard rate – actual rate) x actual hours

labour efficiency sub-variance =

(standard hours – actual hours) x standard rate

notes from the diagram:

- The change in the labour rate, based on the actual hours worked, forms the labour rate variance – shaded [dark grey box] in the diagram. This variance is the responsibility of the *personnel department.*
- The change in the actual hours worked, based on the standard hours, forms the labour efficiency variance – shaded [light grey box] in the diagram. This variance is the responsibility of the *production department.*

CASE STUDY

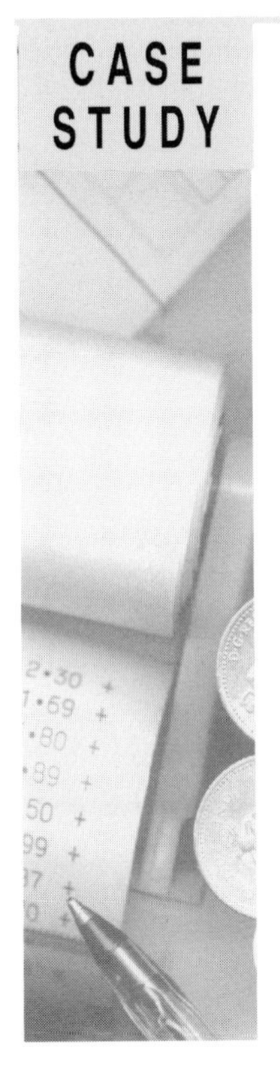

CALCULATING LABOUR VARIANCES

situation

The management accountant of Wyvern Walling has prepared the following labour costs for a batch of 1,200 wall blocks:

- the standard cost of direct labour is £6.00 per hour
- the standard efficiency is 50 hours per batch

The results achieved for the latest batch are:

- the actual cost of direct labour was £5.00 per hour
- the actual production took 65 hours

In short, the wage rates are lower, but the employees have not worked as efficiently. What are the variances and sub-variances for labour costs?

solution

Here both the rate and efficiency have differed from the standard to give the following *total labour variance*:

(standard hours x standard rate) – (actual hours x actual rate)

(50 hours x £6.00 per hour)	–	(65 hours x £5.00 per hour)	=
£300	–	£325	= £25 ADVERSE

Note: The calculation gives a negative figure of £25; this means that the actual cost is more than the standard cost, ie it is adverse, and profits will reduce. By contrast, a favourable cost variance is a positive figure, ie the actual cost is less than the standard cost, and profits will increase.

While the total labour variance is adverse by £25, as both rate and efficiency differ from standard, the sub-variances must be calculated:

Labour rate sub-variance

(standard rate	*– actual rate)*	*x actual hours*	
(£6.00 – £5.00)	x 65 hours		= £65 FAVOURABLE

Labour efficiency sub-variance

(standard hours	*– actual hours)*	*x standard rate*	
(50 hours	– 65 hours)	x £6.00	= £90 ADVERSE
TOTAL LABOUR VARIANCE			= £25 ADVERSE

For a production run of 1,200 wall blocks, the labour variance is £25 ADV. This agrees with the standard cost report shown in fig 17.6. The management of Wyvern Walling will wish, no doubt, to investigate the reasons for both variances.

OTHER VARIANCES

overhead variances

Overhead variances take into account the fixed and variable nature of costs. The sub-variances for overheads are based on changes in expenditure, volume of output, and efficiency. The calculation of these is normally undertaken by the management accountant, who is especially trained to calculate and present them.

Fixed overhead variances consist of two elements:

- the budgeted cost *less* the actual cost of the overhead
- the actual output *less* the budgeted output, *multiplied by* the overhead rate per unit

Variable overhead variances are calculated in a similar way to the labour variances (page 324):

- the variable overhead expenditure variance is the equivalent of the labour rate variance
- the variable overhead efficiency variance is the equivalent of the labour efficiency variance

An *adverse* overhead variance shows that more has been spent on overheads than has been charged to production; thus profit will be reduced. A *favourable* overhead variance is the opposite, and will increase profits.

sales variances

The main sales variance is to compare budgeted sales with actual sales. This can then be broken down into a number of sub-variances of which the two main ones focus on changes in the selling price and in the number of units sold. Sales variances – like those for overheads – are best calculated by the specialist management accountant.

OPERATING STATEMENTS

Variance analysis can be summarised in the form of an operating statement for senior management. Such a statement reconciles budgeted profit with the actual profit in the following way:

	BUDGET	*ACTUAL*	*VARIANCE*	
	£	£	£	
Sales	95,000	96,500	1,500	FAV
Less Variable costs:				
Materials	33,500	33,250	250	FAV
Labour	21,200	22,300	1,100	ADV
Overhead	7,500	7,550	50	ADV
Total variable costs	62,200	63,100	900	ADV
Contribution	32,800	33,400	600	FAV
Less Fixed overheads	12,200	15,300	3,100	ADV
Profit	20,600	18,100	2,500	ADV

Such a statement is useful because it gives senior management an overall view of the way that the business has operated during the budget period.

Management will decide which income and expenditure headings warrant further investigation – for example, labour and fixed overheads in the above statement. Where appropriate, the sub-variances can be either discussed at senior management level or passed down to the budget holder with a request for an explanation of the variances. The important point is that the operating statement highlights the variances, and links budgeted profit with actual profit.

CONCLUSION

Standard costs are set in order to give individual departmental managers, who are responsible for aspects of the business' output, suitable targets to aim for. When actual costs are compared with standard costs, an analysis can be carried out to see why the variances and sub-variances have occurred, and to see what can be done about them for the future. Note, in particular, the way in which variances and sub-variances are calculated down to a responsibility level of an individual employee, or a small section within the business – *responsibility accounting.*

This chapter has shown the principles of budgetary control and of monitoring costs through variance analysis. It has explained the reasons why variances occur and has demonstrated, by means of Case Studies, how to calculate variances and sub-variances. There are other cost variances that can be calculated – for example, for overheads, and where actual production differs from standard: these are best calculated by a specialist management accountant.

CHAPTER SUMMARY

- Once budgets have been planned and put into action, they must be monitored so that the actual figures are compared with the budgeted figures.
- Where a standard costing system is used, a comparison is made between standard costs and actual costs.
- Variances – the difference between budgeted/standard costs and actual costs – are acted upon if they are significant.
- With standard costing, variances and sub-variances can be calculated for materials, labour, overheads and sales.
- An operating statement can be used to compare budgeted and actual activities – variances can be investigated to find out why they have occurred and corrective action taken where required.

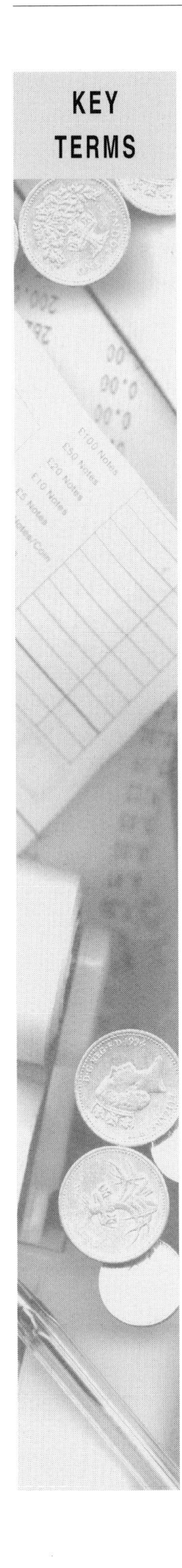

variance	budgeted/standard cost minus actual cost
favourable variance	an outcome that is better (lower) than budget/standard cost, or where sales/revenues are higher than budget
adverse variance	an outcome that is worse (higher) than budget/standard cost, or where sales/revenues are lower than budget
controllable costs	costs which can be influenced by the budget holder
non-controllable costs	costs which cannot be influenced by the budget holder
total materials variance	(standard quantity x standard price) – (actual quantity x actual price)
materials price sub-variance	(standard price – actual price) x actual quantity
materials usage sub-variance	(standard quantity – actual quantity) x standard price
total labour variance	(standard hours x standard rate) – (actual hours x actual rate)
labour rate sub-variance	(standard rate – actual rate) x actual hours
labour efficiency sub-variance	(standard hours – actual hours) x standard rate
fixed overhead variances	budgeted cost of overhead – actual cost of overhead (actual output – budgeted output) x overhead rate per unit
variable overhead variances	variable overhead expenditure variance variable overhead efficiency variance
sales variance	budgeted sales – actual sales

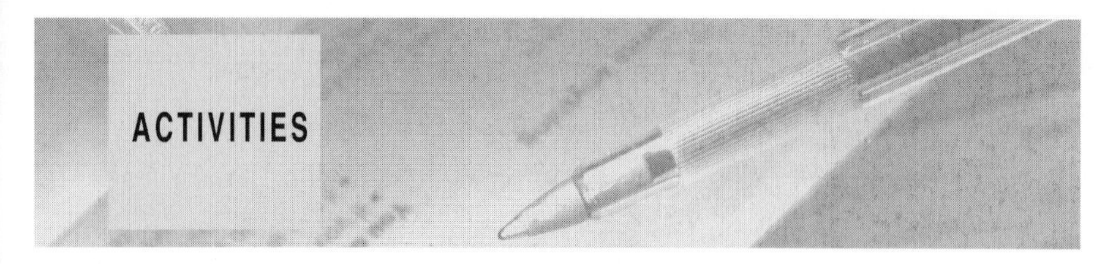

17.1 Using an organisation with which you are familiar:

- outline the budgetary control system that is used
- explain how significant variances are identified
- suggest improvements to the budget monitoring process

17.2 Identify a product or service with which you are familiar:

- determine the standard cost
- compare the standard cost with the actual cost for a particular time period
- identify any significant variances
- discuss the control limits used by the business or organisation in its budgetary control system

17.3 From the following information prepare a standard cost report:

product: 500 cardboard boxes, size 750 mm x 400 mm x 300 mm

standard costs:	£
materials	28
labour	36
fixed overheads	18
variable overheads	15
actual costs:	
materials	38
labour	29
fixed overheads	20
variable overheads	12

- What factors do you think may have caused the variances?
- What further analysis of the cost information would you advise?

17.4 The following standard cost report for the manufacture of 600 ornamental clay garden pots, showing sub-variances for materials and labour, has been passed to you for further action:

	standard cost		*actual cost*		*sub-variances*			
		£		£		£	£	
materials	900 kilos		800 kilos		price	40		ADV
	at 75p per kilo	675	at 80p per kilo	640	usage	75		FAV
							35	FAV
labour	150 hours		140 hours		rate	70		ADV
	at £5.00 per hour	750	at £5.50 per hour	770	efficiency	50		FAV
							20	ADV
overheads								
fixed		250		260			10	ADV
variable		80		60			20	FAV
TOTAL COST		1,755		1,730			25	FAV

You are to:

- show how the sub-variances for materials and labour have been calculated
- explain how you will use the variances and sub-variances as part of the process of monitoring costs

17.5 From the following data you are to calculate:

(a) materials price variance

(b) materials usage variance

(c) total materials variance

(Indicate whether each variance is *adverse* or *favourable*.)

	Standard Price	*Standard Usage*	*Actual Price*	*Actual Usage*
Material A	£5 per kg	100 kgs	£4 per kg	120 kgs
Material B	£20 per unit	120 units	£22 per unit	100 units
Material C	£10 per litre	600 litres	£9 per litre	500 litres
Material D	£2 per metre	300 metres	£3 per metre	250 metres

17.6 From the following data you are to calculate:

(a) labour rate variance

(b) labour efficiency variance

(c) total labour variance

(Indicate whether each variance is adverse or favourable.)

	Standard Hours	*Standard Wage Rate*	*Actual Hours*	*Actual Wage Rate*
Product 1	8	£5.00	7	£5.50
Product 2	3	£4.50	4	£5.00
Product 3	24	£6.00	30	£5.75
Product 4	12	£8.00	15	£8.50

17.7 From the following information for the month of January, you are to prepare an operating statement which will be of use to the senior management of the business:

	Budget	*Actual*
	£	£
Sales	155,000	133,500
Materials (variable)	33,400	34,100
Labour (variable)	26,200	30,500
Overheads:		
fixed	18,500	21,350
variable	19,200	19,450

Write a briefing note to the senior managers giving your thoughts on the operating statement and suggesting the action they might wish to take.

Section 7

business planning

In this section we look at the ways in which financial data is compiled and presented and how a business plan is constructed

presentation of data

sources of finance

break-even

business plan

balance sheet

cash flow forecast

profit and loss

18 ANALYSING BUSINESS INFORMATION

this chapter covers ...

- *the use of business information*
- *the use of averages in dealing with data*
- *the techniques used for forecasting future trends*

INTRODUCTION

Business information is a critical tool for managers. Figures such as sales, profits, customer buying patterns, wages costs, are all needed to provide an accurate picture of how a business is performing. It is important therefore that this information is gathered, analysed and presented accurately and systematically, using statistical techniques.

Statistics is a scientific method of collecting, organising, summarising, presenting and analysing information.

In this chapter we will examine the basic statistical techniques which may be used for organising, summarising and analysing financial data in a reliable and scientific way.

In the next chapter we look at the way this data is presented for the benefit of business owners and other interested parties. Those of you familiar with graphs showing sales trends and pie or bar charts setting out the break-down of profits are seeing the end-product of the use of statistics. Statistical techniques are used in finance:

- for the analysis of *past events* and the *present* situation.
- for the forecasting of *future trends*

THE NATURE OF DATA

Data is normally categorised as follows:

- *quantitative data* is data which can be measured in some way, eg sales for the year, hours worked on the production line, distances travelled by sales representatives
- *qualitative data*, on the other hand, reflects opinions rather than facts and is a valuable product of market research

In this chapter we will be dealing with *quantitative data.*

USING AVERAGES

A statistical technique which is useful to the management of a business in assessing the *present* situation and making decisions about the *future* is the use of *averages.*

It is important that the management of a business knows the answers to questions such as:

- how much credit are we given by our suppliers?
- what sales are we likely to achieve in December?
- how long do we keep stock in the warehouse before it is sold?
- how long a credit period do we give to our debtors?

Only by keeping firm control over areas such as these does the business increase efficiency and profitability. Control is only possible when the precise answer to these questions is known. It would be an easy option to reply " about . . ." or "approximately . . . " and give a 'rule of thumb' answer. The scientific and statistical approach is to calculate an average.

There are three types of average:

- the arithmetic mean
- the median
- the mode

which average?

Suppose the finance manager of a kitchen installation business wanted to know for budgeting purposes the average job completion time in days, from initial enquiry through to final installation. He has just received the figures for the jobs completed last month. The figures are (in days):

20, 25, 35, 35, 35, 36, 37, 55, 60, 65, 65

What is the average job completion time? We will look in turn at the mean, median and mode averages.

the mean

The arithmetic mean is probably the most commonly used and statistically reliable form of average.

The arithmetic mean is the sum of all the figures divided by the number of figures

The sum of 20, 25, 35, 35, 35, 36, 37, 55, 60, 65, 65 = 468

The arithmetic mean = $\frac{468}{11}$ = 42.5 days

This tells the manager that, on average, a job takes approximately 43 days to complete. This will help him in the planning and budgeting process. Note

- the result is not a whole number of days – rounding up to 43 is necessary
- the result takes into account all values – if there had been an exceptional job taking 165 days instead of 65, the result will have been a mean average of 568 ÷ 11 = 51.6 days

the median

The median is the value of the middle figure in a series of figures.

Note that if there is no middle figure, as with an even number of values, the median is the arithmetic mean of the two figures nearest to the middle.

Here the median is 20, 25, 35, 35, 35, **36**, 37, 55, 60, 65, 65 = 36 days.

This will not be as useful to the manager as the mean in this context; its use lies mainly in the way it is not distorted by extreme values (eg 165 days).

the mode

The mode is the value that occurs most often in a series.

In this case the most common period is 35 days (3 jobs), followed closely by 65 days (2 jobs). Note that these two time periods are very widely dispersed. This would suggest that this type of average is not as helpful in the planning process.

The mode is more useful in areas such as market research in answering questions such as

"How much do people on average spend on a meal?"

"What is the most commonly occurring size of shirt?"

THE DISPERSION OF DATA

We have seen on the previous page that a rogue result (eg 165 days for completion of a kitchen installation) can distort the accuracy of statistical analysis. The spread of the data – the *dispersion* – can be dealt with in a number of ways.

the range

Look again at the number of days used in the example on the previous page:

20, 25, 35, 35, 35, 36, 37, 55, 60, 65, 65

They run from 20 to 65. This spread of data, from lowest to highest, is known as the *range*. Here it is 65 minus 20 = 45.

As we have seen from calculating the averages:

- the range can be affected by extreme values
- the range does not tell you how the data is grouped – for example, the following values also have a range of 45, and present a very different picture, with most of the values at the lower end of the range:
  20, 25, 25, 25, 25, 26, 27, 30, 31, 35, 65

quartiles

A common technique in statistics which helps to get rid of distortions caused by extreme values is the division of the data into four equal sections divided by three *quartiles*. In the example below there are eleven numbers in the range. If you use the data between the first and third quartiles (the interquartile range), extreme values will be disregarded. Note that the second quartile is the median.

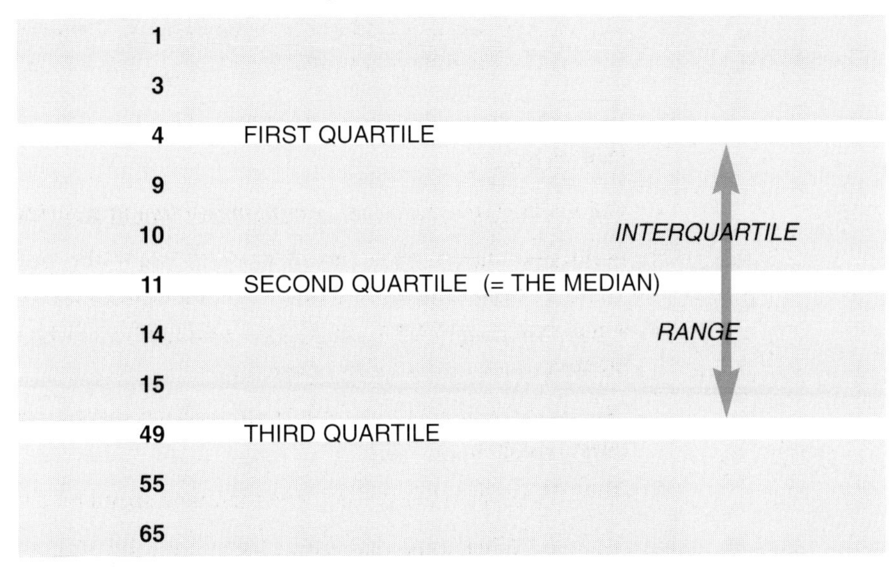

standard deviation

The *standard deviation* is a statistical method of expressing how widely dispersed the data is either side of the mean (arithmetic average) – in basic terms 'how near is the data to the average?' This is useful in many business contexts, for example in quality control judging whether the quality of a product diverges too far from the standard (the mean).

To take a practical example: if the value of orders received by a business was totalled up, the mean could be calculated (money total of orders divided by the number of orders). The readings – which are likely to be evenly distributed around the mean – could be plotted as shown in the chart below. This is known as 'normal distribution.' The frequency (the number of times each value occurs) is plotted on the vertical axis and the order values on the horizontal axis. You will see that most of the order values are near the mean amount, and as they diverge more from the mean they occur less frequently.

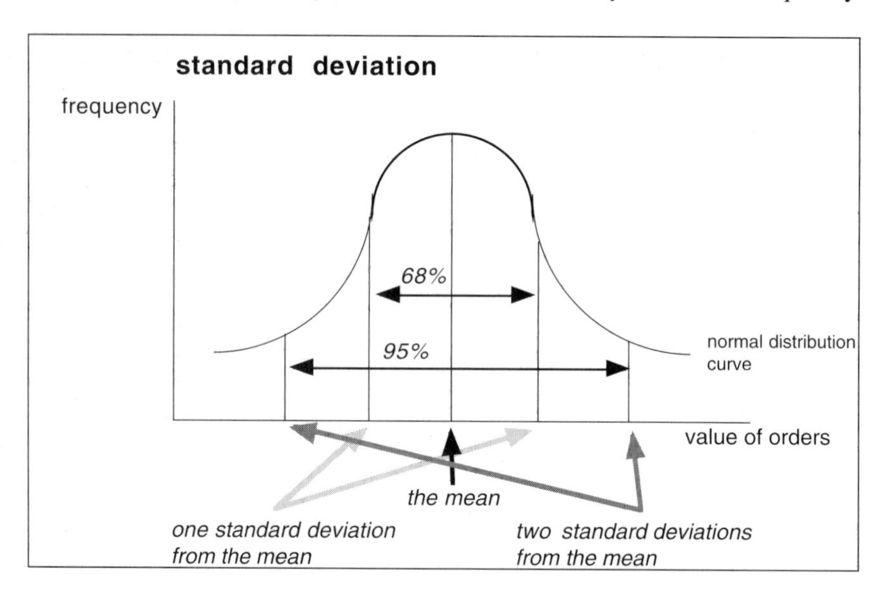

The standard deviation, once calculated, would show that

- approximately 68% (about two-thirds) of the order values would be within one standard deviation of the mean (written 1σ)
- approximately 95% of the order values would be within two standard deviations of the mean (written 2σ)

The *mean* and the *standard deviation* are key values in statistical analysis as they enable values within a range to be predicted and monitored with accuracy.

CORRELATION

Statistics are useful in pointing out how one variable depends on another. For example, in general terms:

- sales of a product increase in line with spending on advertising
- sales of a product increase as the price is lowered

In the first case there is *positive correlation* between sales and advertising expenditure, ie they both go up together.

In the second case there is *negative correlation* because sales go up as prices go down.

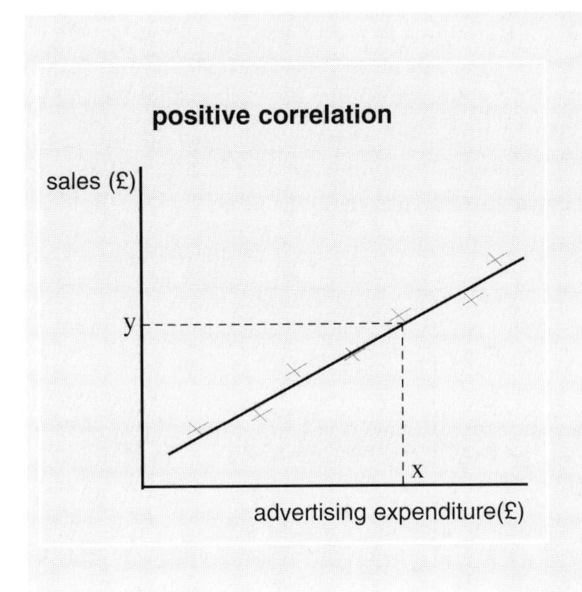

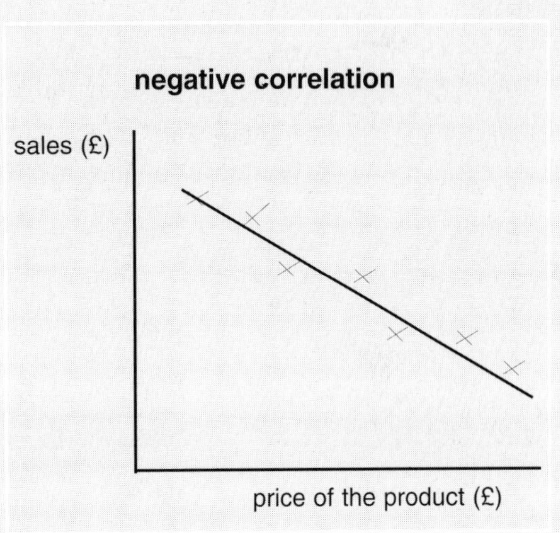

regression lines

Here the trends are shown in graphical format. In each case the 'line of best fit,' known as the *regression line* is calculated mathematically, and can be used for forecasting purposes.

In the case of the diagram on the left showing *positive correlation*, a certain level of sales can be expected from changing levels of advertising expenditure. Advertising spending of £x, for example, would suggest, from past experience, sales of £y.

STATISTICAL TECHNIQUES USED IN FORECASTING

Forecasts in financial management are based on information about the way in which trends have established themselves in the past and are showing themselves in the present. It is then assumed that these trends will continue into the future. If one takes a profits trend, for example, established in the past, it is possible to predict a trend for the future by using a number of techniques, including the *moving average.*

The use of moving averages is the technique of repeatedly calculating a series of different arithmetic mean values for a dependent variable along a time series to produce a trend graph.

A moving average will move forward in time (the independent variable) step by step along the trend line, calculating a new average from the given data at each step, removing in the averaging process data which is literally "out of line" with the trend. Some data will be above the line, some below it; in the averaging process these fluctuations will offset each other to produce a smooth line. The following example,. assuming the date is now 1998, shows the profit figures of a company, Arco plc, over 15 years.

Year	annual profit	5 Year Moving Average
	£M	£M
1984	10	
1985	4	
1986	8	64 ÷ 5 =12.8
1987	18	17.6
1988	24	20.8
1989	34	21.6
1990	20	23.2
1991	12	26.4
1992	26	26.8
1993	40	26.4
1994	36	30.4
1995	18	34.0
1996	32	34.0
1997	44	
1998	40	

This chart has been produced as follows:

- the profit figures were plotted on a line graph (see below)
- a five yearly fluctuating cycle was noted
- the profit figures for the first five years were added and divided by five to find the first of the moving averages: (i.e. 10 + 4 + 8 + 18 + 24 = 64; 64 ÷ 5 = 12.8)
- the next arithmetic mean is calculated over the five years 1985 to 1989, i.e.the average moves forward a year: (4 + 8 + 18 + 24 + 34 = 88; 88 ÷ 5 = 17.6)
- the process is repeated for the following years until the data is exhausted
- the moving average line is plotted on the same axes as the annual profit (see below)

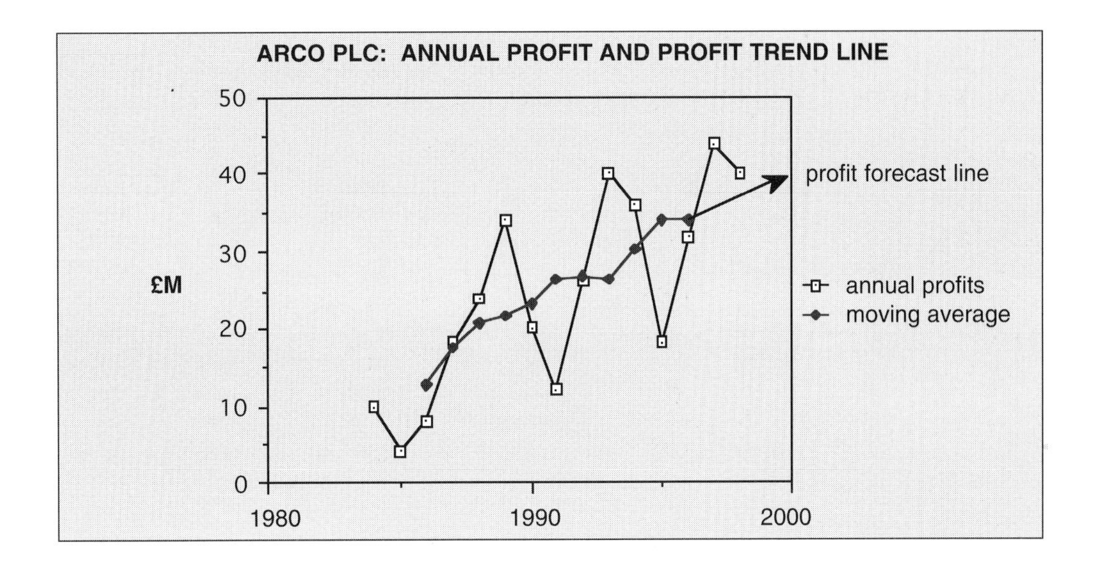

It is clear from this line graph that the moving average smooths out the fluctuations, providing an upward moving profit trend line.

The actual forecast line into the future (the line with the arrow) is a 'ruler' extension of that trend, by eye, rather than a calculation, as with regression (see page 339).

CHAPTER SUMMARY

- Statistics may be used for organising, presenting and analysing a wide variety of accounting data.
- Statistics can be used for the analysis of past events and present trends, and for making forecasts of future trends.
- Data can be quantitative (measurable) or qualitative (recording opinions).
- Averages (mean, median and mode) can be used to provide information for managers.
- The dispersion of data is measured by the range and by standard deviation.
- Correlation of data shows how one variable can be dependent on another.
- Regression lines may be calculated mathematically and used for forecasting purposes.
- A common forecasting technique is the moving average.

KEY TERMS

arithmetic mean — the sum of all the figures divided by the number of figures

median — the median is the value of the middle figure in a series of figures

mode — the mode is the value that occurs most often in a series of figures

range — the spread of data from the lowest to the highest figure

standard deviation — a scientific method of expressing how widely dispersed the data is

positive correlation — where an increase in one variable causes an increase in another or a decrease in one causes a decrease in another

negative correlation — where an increase in one variable causes a decrease in another or a decrease in one causes an increase in another

moving average — the technique of repeatedly calculating a series of different arithmetic mean values for a dependent variable along a time series to produce a trend graph

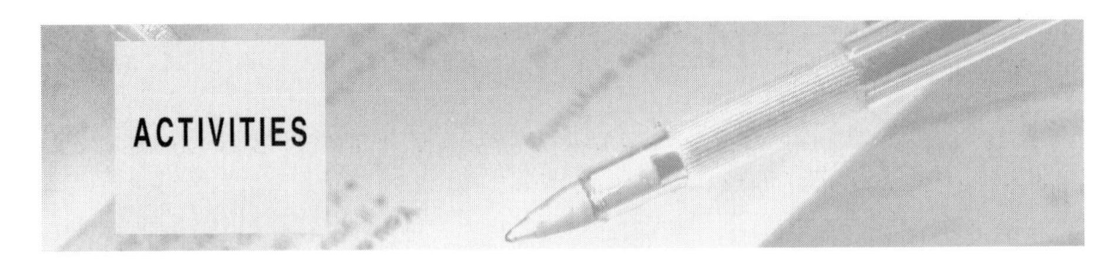

18.1 Calculate the average (mean, median and mode) hourly rate of shopfloor workers pay from the following figures:

£5.50, £5.75, £5.80, £5.85, £5.90, £8.00, £10.00, £10.00, £35.00.

Which average(s) are you likely to use to support your case in pay bargaining if you are

(a) in management

(b) in a union?

18.2 Identify factors which might have

(a) a positive correlation with a company' sales

(b) a negative correlation with a company' sales

18.3 The following figures represent the daily staff absentee numbers over the last 15 working days, following the introduction of new working practices.

2, 5, 10, 7, 4, 9, 12, 10, 6, 12,14,11,7,13,18

Work out a moving average on these figures, using as a base for the average the number of figures which you think appropriate.

Plot the original figures and the moving average figures on a line graph.

What general trend do you predict on the basis of these figures?

19 PRESENTING BUSINESS INFORMATION

this chapter covers ...

- *the statistical methods used to present financial data*
- *the techniques of network analysis in business planning*
- *the use of Gannt charts in the business planning process*

INTRODUCTION

We saw in the last chapter how business data is collected, analysed and used for forecasting of *future* trends. In this chapter we turn to the ways in which statistical data is presented in the form of graphs and charts in order that *past* financial trends can be clearly understood by business managers and owners. It is generally accepted that a visual image can convey a statistical message more effectively than any list of figures. The charts that will be illustrated include:

- the line graph
- the bar chart (simple,compound and component)
- the pie chart

The use of index numbers to illustrate trends is also explained.

The chapter concludes with an examination of the way business planning can be clarified by the use of charts and diagrams: the techniques we will look at are critical path analysis and the Gannt chart. This part of the chapter looks ahead to Chapter 20 'The Business Plan' in which we look at the format of a formal business plan prepared for a potential provider of finance.

STATISTICAL ANALYSIS OF PAST EVENTS

As we have seen in Chapter 6, when a large public company announces its annual results, it will publish the details of the figures in a number of forms:

- the published annual report and accounts sent to shareholders (sometimes in summarised form)
- press releases for the financial newspapers and journals
- employee reports distributed to the workforce and management of the company, and sometimes also to the shareholders

In all these written reports the accounting data is usually presented in tabular and also in pictoral form, because it is generally recognised that the average individual can understand a picture – a graph or a chart – better than a paragraph of descriptive prose.

There are two main types of statistical analysis used when presenting accounting data:

- *time series analysis*, which presents numeric data recorded at set intervals of time, eg line graphs, bar charts, and indices
- *proportional analysis*, which break down a single figure into its constituent elements, eg pie charts

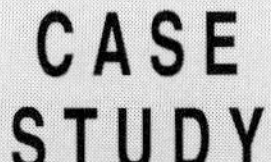

CASE STUDY

VECTOR CARS PLC

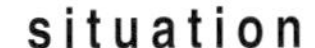

situation

For the purpose of illustrating time series analysis we will take as an example the sales figures for Vector Cars plc, a major UK car manufacturer:

- for the last three years (the time series) – quoted here as Years 1, 2 and 3
- broken down into UK sales and overseas sales
- in comparison with the total sales projections for the three years

The starting point for any statistical presentation is a table of the constituent figures:

Vector Cars plc: Projected and Actual Sales

	Year 1 £M	Year 2 £M	Year 3 £M
UK Sales	3 102	3 593	4 239
Overseas Sales	3 815	3 692	2 470
Total Sales	6 917	7 285	6 709
Projected Sales	*6 800*	*6 950*	*7 100*

the line graph

This data has been collected and summarised by the accounting process, but not yet analysed. In order to detect trends from looking at this table, it is necessary first to read each row of figures, relate them to the other figures, and then to interpret them. The process is slow and laborious because there is no pictorial assistance. Contrast this table with the line graph presentation of the Vector Cars plc sales figures illustrated below.

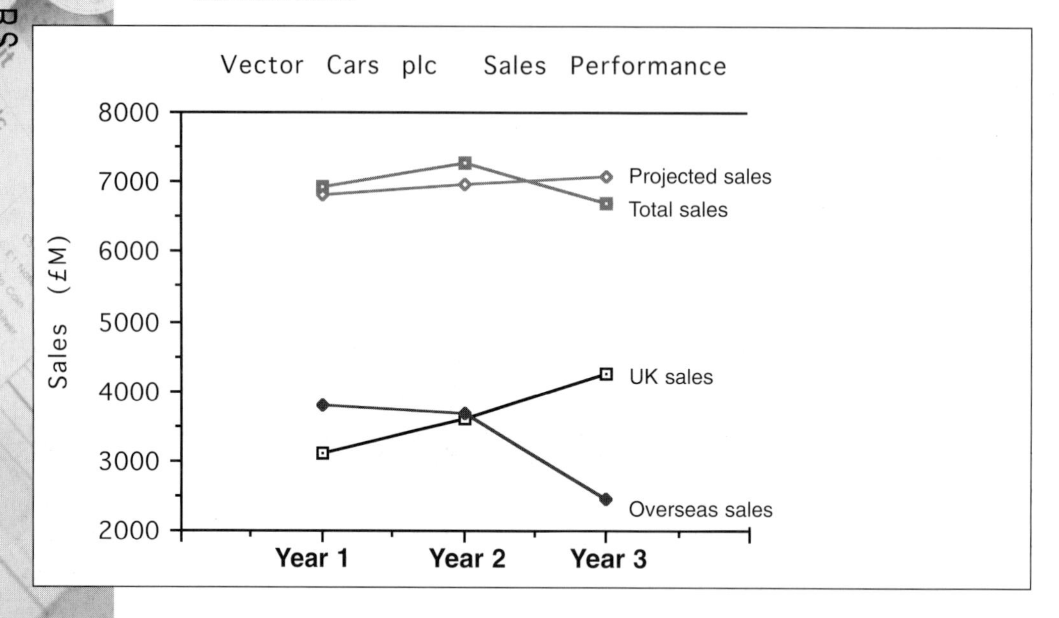

the simple bar chart

A bar chart is a series of bars drawn between two defined axes. The height of the bars represents the amount of the dependent variable.

The following bar chart shows the total sales for Vector Cars plc over the three years:

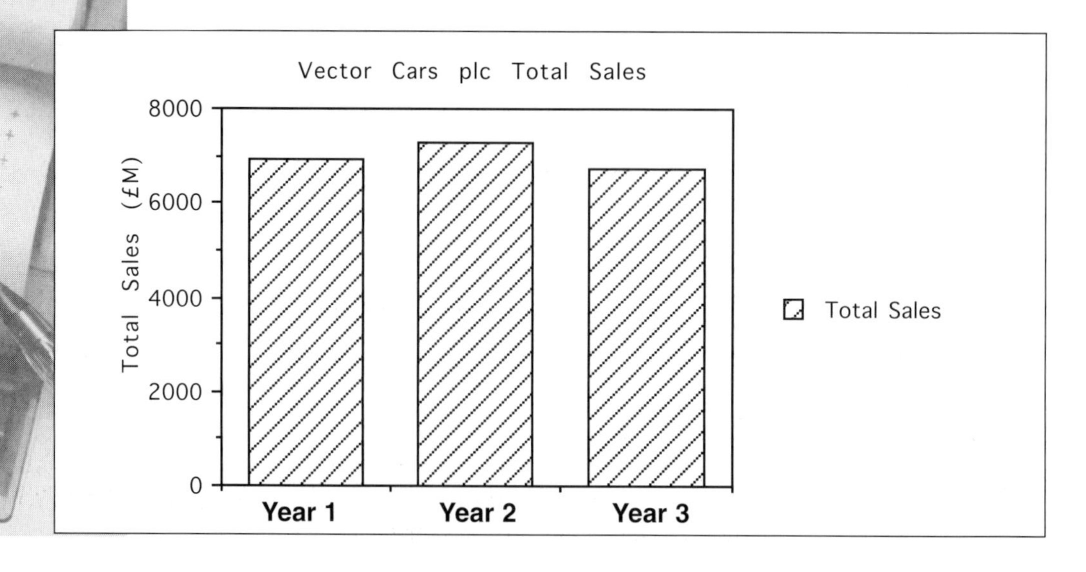

The simple bar chart on the previous page is limited because it can only compare individual items from one set of data over the time series. Its visual impact is strong, and it is consequently very popular. Note that it is the height of the bar that must be accurately charted. The width is of no statistical significance (but must be standard).

the compound bar chart

A compound bar chart is a bar chart which sets out more than one variable for each of the points in the time series

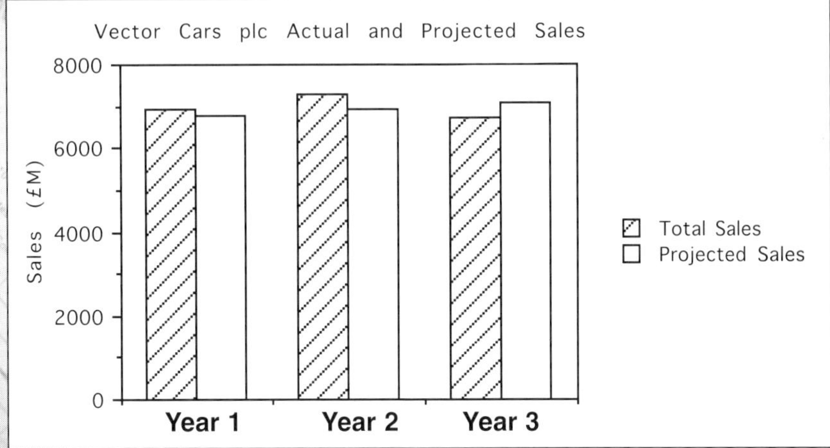

This compound bar chart sets out the total sales and projected total sales for Vector Cars plc. Note that the two separate bars should be clearly distinguished by a contrasting infill.

component bar chart

A component bar chart is a bar chart which subdivides each bar into its component elements.

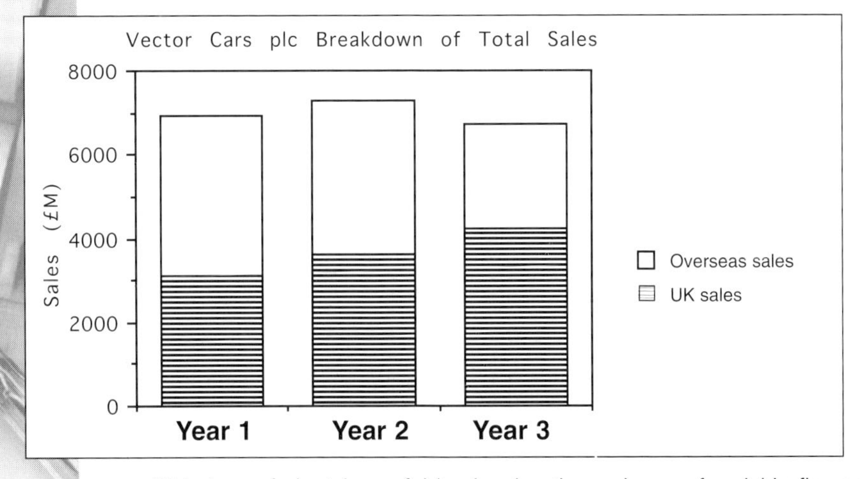

This type of chart is useful in showing the make-up of variable figures over a time series. In the example shown above, the total sales figure for Vector Cars plc is subdivided into UK and overseas sales.

TIME SERIES ANALYSIS: INDEX NUMBERS

A further method of presenting a numeric trend over a time series, such as sales or profit over a period of years is converting the numbers in question into an index number sequence.

An index is a sequence of values where the first or base value is equated to 100 and the subsequent values are proportionally related to 100.

The object of using an index system is to simplify comparison of complex values by replacing the complicated figures with simple ones, all related to a base of 100. Commonly quoted indices are the Retail Price Index (RPI) which measures the cost of living and the Financial Times Share Indices which measure the value of shares quoted by Stock Exchange market dealers.

The procedure for creating an index series is as follows:

1 Take a series of values, for example the total sales for Vector Cars plc over the three years:

Year 1 £6,917M

Year 2 £7,285M

Year 3 £6,709M

2 Equate the first figure (the base year) with 100, ie assume £6,917M = 100

3 Convert each of the subsequent years' figures to index numbers by applying the formula:

$$\frac{\text{subsequent year's figure}}{\text{base year figure}} \times 100 = \text{index number of subsequent year}$$

The calculation for the index for the sales of Vector Cars plc is therefore:

Year 1 6,917 (base year figure) = 100

Year 2 $\frac{7,285}{6,917} \times 100 = 105$

Year 3 $\frac{6,709}{6,917} \times 100 = 97$

As Vector Cars plc adopts Year 1 as its base year and equates total sales with 100, it is then easy to see that there has been a rise to 105 (+5%) in Year 2 and a fall to 97 in Year 3. In due course subsequent years' sales could similarly be given an index number and comparison be made with previous years. Another advantage of using indices is that like can be compared meaningfully with unlike, eg sales with inflation, sales with unemployment.

PROPORTIONAL ANALYSIS: THE PIE CHART

Whereas time series analysis shows a trend derived from a series of figures over a period of time, proportional analysis examines a single figure divided into component elements at a single moment in time. It is commonly presented in the form of a pie chart.

A pie chart is a circle divided into sectors to represent proportionally the parts of a whole.

A pie chart might be used to show the breakdown by area of the sales of Vector Cars plc. The starting point is the financial data:

Sales of cars by area by Vector Cars plc in Year 3

Area	*£M*
UK	4,239
Europe	1,040
North America	912
Japan	518
Total Sales	6,709

The total sales of £6,709M will become the whole circle of the pie divided into segments, each of which will proportionally represent a geographical sales figure.

The pie chart is set out below. Note the labelling and shading.

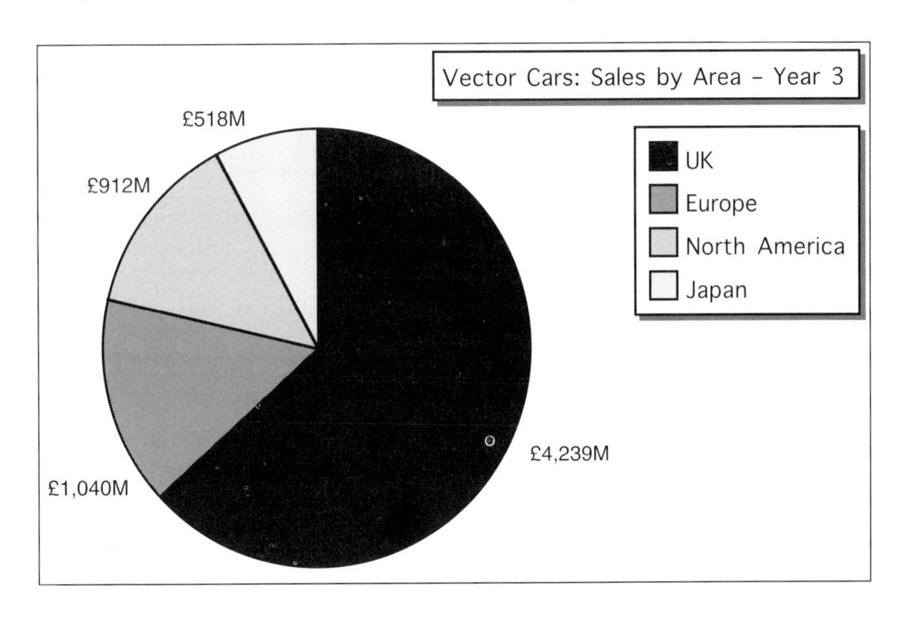

PLANNING CHARTS

We will now look at some techniques used when a business is undertaking a project which involves planning to make capital investments in the form of fixed assets, eg premises, plant and machinery and current assets eg stock and materials. These techniques are based on two types of chart:

- critical path analysis
- bar charts known as Gannt charts

The results obtained from the planning process – for example how long it will take to complete a project – will contribute to the *business plan* which we will examine in detail in the next chapter.

critical path analysis

Critical path analysis is a technique for working out the minimum time a project is likely to take. It is a form of what is termed 'network analysis'. Critical path analysis operates by examining all the individual actions which contribute to the project, eg ordering, constructing, testing, and determining the minimum time the project will take. The process can be very complex, and may be introduced by looking at a simple operation such as making a cup of instant coffee, eg "take the kettle, fill it up, plug it in, take a cup" … and so on. This form of analysis is presented in visual form by a network of arrows. Each arrow represents an individual activity, and is normally labelled with the activity and the time it takes (in, say, weeks) to carry out the activity, for example:

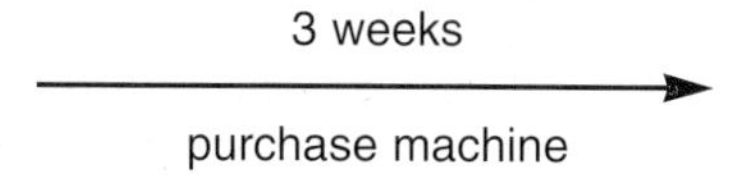

Arrows start and finish in circles known as *events* or *nodes*. Activities shown by arrows pointing into a circle (event) must be completed before any activity shown on an arrow coming out of an event can be started. For example:

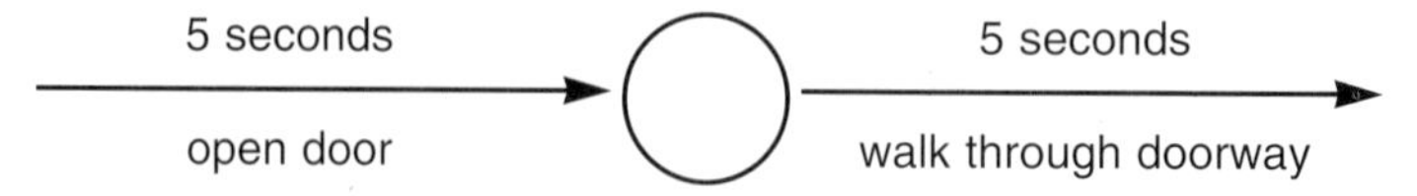

It is common for a number of activities to take place *simultaneously*. If you are making a cup of instant coffee, the kettle will be boiling while you are getting a spoon and putting the instant coffee in the cup. In this case there will be arrows denoting these parallel activities, and these arrows will converge on the event which marks the pouring of the water into the cup. It is important to note that all activities on the converging arrows must be completed before any activity on any arrow leaving the circle can be started.

the critical path

You will know that if you are making a cup of coffee that you will have to wait for the kettle to boil before you can make a decent cupful. You therefore have to wait the longest time of the two alternative arrows (presumably boiling the water!) before completing the event - the steaming cupful of coffee. In critical path analysis the activities which take the longest time to complete are known as *critical activities*, and are shown with a thicker arrow.

In an analysis of a complex project, the *quickest* time the project will take to complete will be the *sum of the time taken for the critical activities in sequence.* In visual terms there will be a thick black line running through the network of activities: this will be the critical path, shown in the illustration below.

labelling the network

In critical path analysis, there are certain labelling conventions:

- The circle (event) is often annotated with numbers to show the stage in the project which has been reached. The number is the event number.
- The arrows (activities) are also given abbreviated labels:
  - the time taken for the activity is shown as a simple number which could stand for minutes, days, weeks as appropriate
  - the activity itself may be given a letter which is explained in a separate list (this would give clarity to the network when the activity descriptions are long and involved)

A critical path analysis is illustrated below. Note how the sum of the numbers on the critical path (the thicker arrows) indicates the activities which take the longest time - a total of 13 as opposed to the other route, which totals 8.

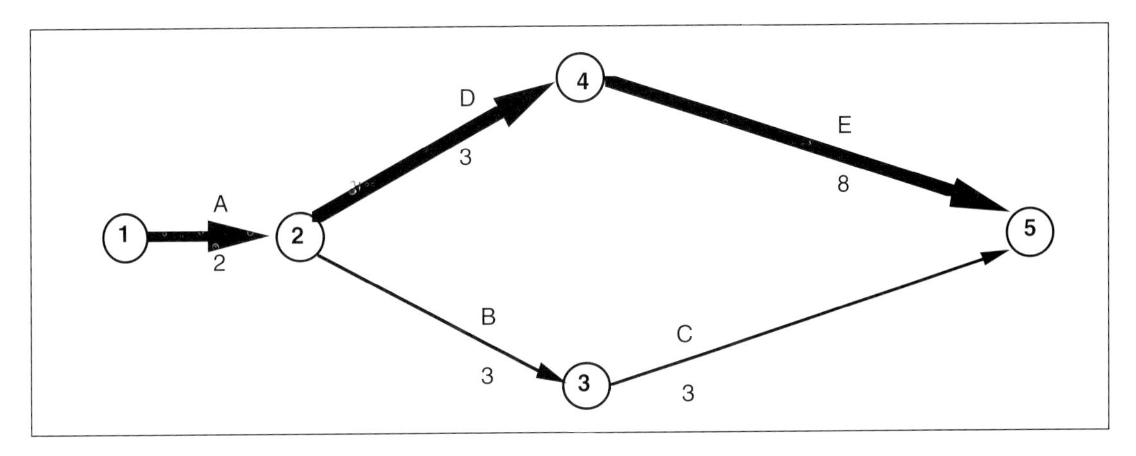

The case study on the next page shows how critical path analysis can be used by a business investing in new premises.

HERMES BUREAU: INVESTMENT IN NEW PREMISES

situation

You run a computer bureau - Hermes Bureau - which provides accounting, payroll and other computer services to a wide range of commercial customers. You are planning to invest in new premises shortly, and have purchased the lease of an office in the town, and will be able to move in six months' time.

You are taking the opportunity when moving to update your computer hardware and software systems. There are a number of important tasks to carry out before you move, and after consultation with your colleagues you have made the list set out below. Your software needs updating and customising for your bureau by programmers, and this will be the task which will take the most time. You see that all the tasks will have to be completed before you can become operational, and the obvious fact that the ordering of software and hardware can only take place after full assessment. You allow yourself a clear two week planning period before starting the process. You are very busy at the moment. When should you start planning?

Task A	time available for detailed planning	2 weeks
Task B	assessment of computer hardware	2 weeks
Task C	ordering new computers	2 weeks
Task D	assessment of new software	4 weeks
Task E	ordering software	10 weeks
Task F	obtaining quotes from removal firm	3 weeks
Task G	ordering the removal van	3 weeks

solution

The planning process can be carried out using critical path analysis, which will set out the different activities in the form of a network and will determine the maximum time, and thus the project time. The procedure is as follows:

step one

List the activities and the times which they will take, and give them a code letter. This has already been done (see above)

step two

Draw a sketch setting out the different activities in the forms of arrows, starting on the left, making sure that

- the arrows are annotated with the activity coding and the time taken (in weeks)
- all activities follow Task A - the planning process
- C follows B, E follows D, G follows F

step three

Set out the 'events' which mark the completion of activities in the form of circles, and give them consecutive numbers

step four

Add up the time taken by each alternative route taken by the arrows. This produces the result:

- planning and ordering software 16 weeks (2 + 4 + 10)
- planning and ordering new computers 6 weeks (2 + 2 + 2)
- planning and arranging removal van 8 weeks (2 + 3 + 3)

step five

Draw up a final neat copy of the network, marking in the critical path - the 16 week software upgrading - in heavy ink. The final version appears below.

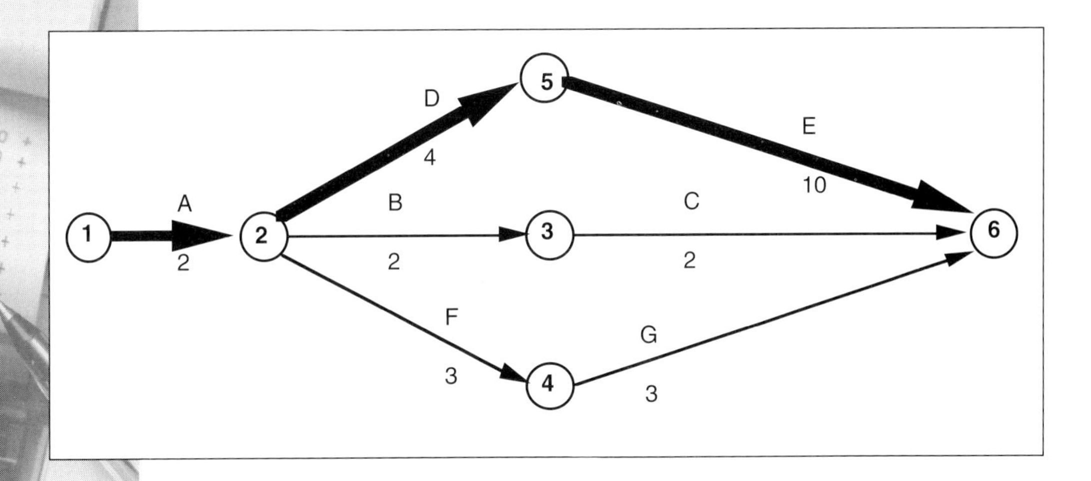

USING A GANNT CHART

It would also be possible to set out the planning process on a bar chart known as a *Gannt chart* (illustrated below). This shows:

- the activities on a weekly schedule (the weeks are numbered across the top)
- the critical activities as black bars
- the activities which are not on the critical path as shaded bars
- float times for non-critical activities – ie times during which a delay can occur which will not hold up the project – as white bars

A Gannt chart is useful because each week it can be consulted to see what is due to start, to finish or to continue. Note that the chart shows the activity letters allocated to the critical activities.

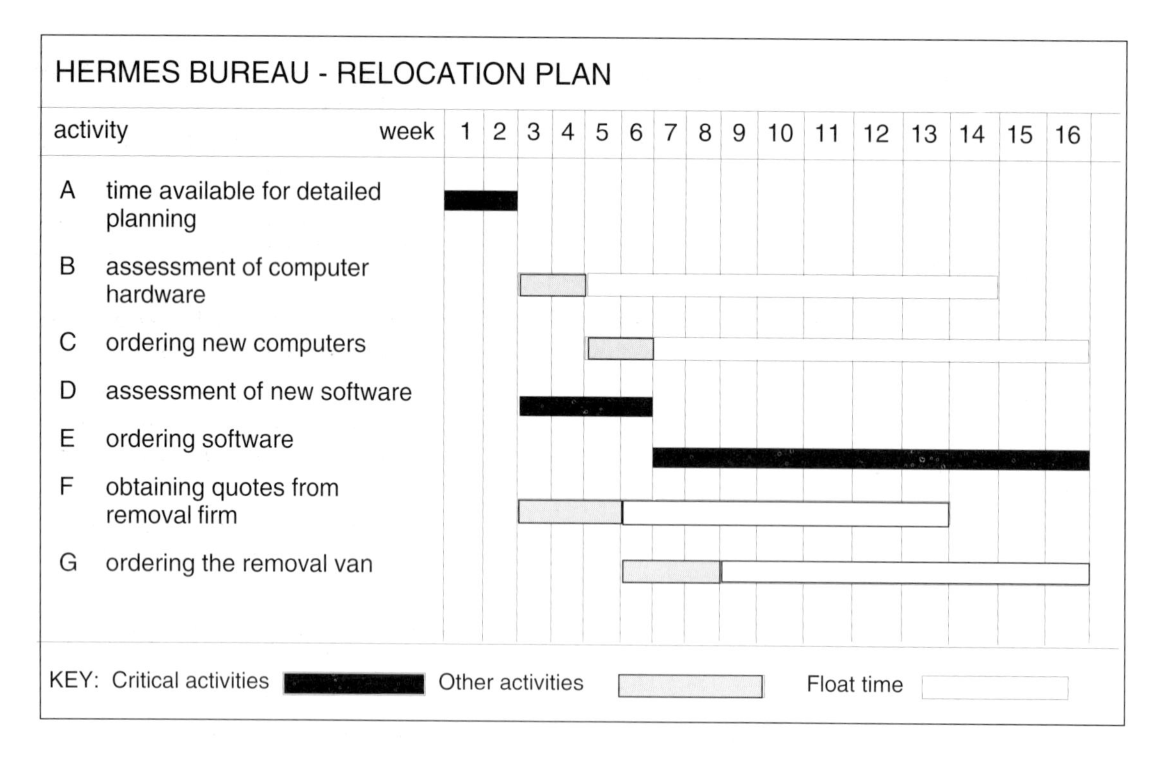

Gannt chart showing the relocation plans from the Case Study 'Hermes Bureau'

CHAPTER SUMMARY

- Methods of statistical presentation include time series analysis and proportional analysis.
- Time series analysis is best presented in the form of line graphs, bar charts and indices.
- Proportional analysis is best presented in the form of pie charts.
- Critical path analysis is used in the business planning process to work out the minimum time a project will take.
- The planning process can also be displayed in the form of a Gannt bar chart.

KEY TERMS

time series analysis — the presentation of numeric data at set intervals of time

proportional analysis — the breaking down of a single figure into its constituent elements

compound bar chart — a bar chart that sets out more than one variable for each of the points in the time series

component bar chart — a bar chart which subdivides each bar into its component elements

index — a sequence of numbers where the first or base number is equated to 100 and the subsequent numbers are proportionally related to 100

pie chart — a circle divided into sectors to represent proportionally the parts of a whole

critical path analysis — Critical path analysis is a technique for working out the minimum time a project is likely to take. It is a form of what is termed 'network analysis'.

Gannt chart — A Gannt chart is a horizontal bar chart which shows the planning process in terms of critical activities, non-critical activities and float times.

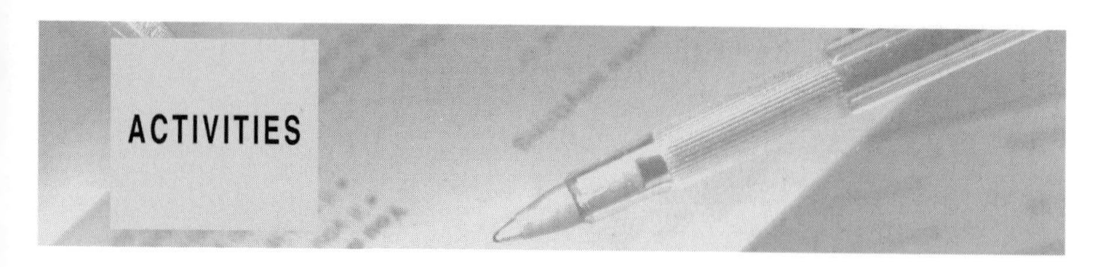

19.1 Obtain a set of financial statistics which are illustrated by graphs and charts. These could be documents produced by an organisation with which you are familar, or they could be found in a published set of Report and Accounts.

Identify and list the different types of graph and chart, and state for what purpose they are used. Distinguish in your analysis between the illustration of past trends and the forecasting of future trends. How successful do you think the graphs and charts are in getting their message across?

19.2 You work in the finance department of Hyzaku Limited, the UK subsidiary of a Japanese car manufacturer which has made substantial inroads into the UK market with its revolutionary "Trojan" multi-purpose vehicle, manufactured in the UK. You are given three sets of statistics and are asked to present them to the board of directors and to comment on the results.

Market Share: UK Market for MPVs (multi-purpose vehicles)

	1995	1996	1997
	£M	£M	£M
MPVs manufactured in the EU, imported into the UK	295	280	275
Hyzaku MPVs (manufactured in the UK)	150	195	250
US MPVs imported into the UK	140	130	115

(a) present this data in the form of a line graph

(b) comment on the trends shown

Actual and Projected Sales of Hyzaku MPVs (multi-purpose vehicles) in the UK Market

	1995	1996	1997
	£M	£M	£M
Actual Sales	150	195	250
Projected Sales	140	180	220

(c) present this data in the form of a compound bar chart

(d) comment on the trend shown

Breakdown of UK Sales by Area

	1995	1996	1997
	£M	£M	£M
South East	100	125	175
Midlands	25	45	25
Other Areas	25	25	50
Total Sales	150	195	250

(e) present this data in the form of a component bar chart

(f) comment on the regional trends; what should be done about the Midlands?

(g) one of your directors doesn't like your bar chart; present the data in another form that will show the trends clearly

(h) take the figures for the UK sales of Hyzaku vehicles in 1997 and draw up a pie chart showing the breakdown of sales by area

19.3 Cool Drinks plc manufactures and sells soft drinks in Europe. The directors are concerned about the profit trends of some of the overseas operating companies. The relevant figures are as follows:

Country	*Year 1*	*Year 2*	*Year 3*	*Year 4*
	£M	*£M*	*£M*	*£M*
Austria	8.6	7.8	9.5	9.7
Belgium	5.6	4.1	3.6	3.8
France	9.1	10.5	11.8	12.5
Germany	10.3	11.4	12.6	14.2
Spain	4.5	5.5	4.7	3.8
UK	12.5	11.6	12.9	13.5

You are to

(a) present the data in suitable graphical form

(b) convert each country's results to index numbers and explain why this process helps the analysis of the results

20 THE BUSINESS PLAN

this chapter covers ...

- *the structure and contents of a business plan*
- *the formulation of business objectives*
- *how to write the marketing section of the business plan*
- *how to write the production section of the business plan*
- *how to present the requirements for human, physical and financial resources in the business plan*
- *the importance of the financial data to the plan – the cash flow forecast, profit and loss account and balance sheet*
- *the need to set up a system to monitor progress – to compare actual results with the figures projected in the business plan*

INTRODUCTION

So far in this book we have looked at the business planning process as it affects the finance function of the business. The process of budgeting and costing all form part of day-to-day financial planning and can be described as operational planning. It will be mirrored in other functions of the business by a similar process – there will be sales plans, production plans, marketing plans, and so on. In this chapter we turn to a specific document, the *business plan*, which is written to present the business to outsiders and combines aspects of all the operational plans. As the business plan is produced to help raise finance, it follows that much of the content will be financial in nature.

definitions

A business plan could be defined as:

> *A plan presented to a bank or other provider of finance, describing what the business intends to do, explaining what its costs will be, what it expects to earn, how it will repay money it has borrowed, and how soon it will make a profit.*

In other words it is a confident statement to a lender or investor of what a business is, where it plans to go, and how much money it needs to get there.

The business plan normally comprises some form of presentation folder – an A4 ringbinder for example. It should be presented in a professional manner appropriate to the user.

THE PURPOSES OF THE PLAN

The writing of a business plan is a very useful exercise . . .

for providers of finance

A business plan will help to persuade a lender such as a bank or venture capital company to lend money. Providers of finance need financial information about the business – a cash flow forecast and final accounts – set out in a clear and detailed way.

for the management of the business

A business plan will help the management of a business to see clearly where the business is going. All too often a person running a business does not have time to see further than the next week; a business plan will make the business owner sit down and think through business objectives and financial requirements.

monitoring the business

Once a business is up and running, the regular writing (or re-writing) of a business plan will enable the management of a business to monitor its progress; it will also enable a provider of finance to see that repayment of loans and overdrafts will take place on schedule.

BUSINESS OBJECTIVES

If you are starting a business, the type of business will depend on your objectives. The profit motive remains the most important goal of any business organisation, although there are, of course, other motives, such as environmental and social improvement.

business objectives – the mission statement

If you are starting or expanding a business you should have very specific objectives – targets which you hope to achieve. These objectives can be short-term and long-term. You are likely to adopt a "Mission Statement".

short-term objectives

For example, the owner of Express Pasta, an Italian fast-food store, might have the following short-term objectives:

In the next twelve months I intend Express Pasta:

- to offer the best standard of customer care in Stourminster High Street
- to turn over £100,000 of business
- to achieve a profit after all expenses and deductions of £15,000

long-term objectives

Long-term objectives might be:

Within three years, I intend Express Pasta:

- to open a further two branches in St Martins and in Wimbury
- to increase annual turnover to £300,000

mission statement

These objectives might be summed up in a mission statement:

Express Pasta will provide the best quality Pasta, offer the best service, and be the most profitable fast food outlet in Stourminster High Street.

the case study – Sonic Deco Limited

In this chapter we will set out the format and an example of a five-part plan, which is a fairly typical structure. The business is Sonic Deco Limited, a loudspeaker manufacturer. The five sections, which we will deal with in turn, are as follows:

- setting of objectives
- marketing plan
- production plan
- resource requirements
- financial support data

We will concentrate here on the practicalities of selecting the appropriate information and presenting it in a persuasive way. As we mentioned above, a business plan is about *selling a business idea.* The effective use of communication skills is vital to the plan's success.

CASE STUDY

SONIC DECO LIMITED – THE BUSINESS PLAN

situation

In this Case Study we set out the five part business plan compiled by John Eliot and Edward Gardiner, the owners of Sonic Deco. They are forming a limited company to manufacture hi-fi loudspeakers. The product, the "Presence" loudspeaker, has already been successfully launched on the market by John Eliot working as a sole trader; he is now being joined by Edward Gardiner. A large increase in production is planned, and the two directors need to approach the bank for finance of £110,000.

You should now read the notes set out below and study the sections of the business plan which follow. The notes cover all parts of the business plan, the sample pages cover the financial sections of the plan.

introductory page

A business plan, like any document, needs careful thought about the order in which material is arranged. The first page is critical. It should include:

- the name and address of the business
- a summary setting out the business idea positively and clearly, quoting appropriate detail
- a list of contents – so that the reader can find the information he or she wants without having to thumb through pages of material

business objectives and mission statement

The nature of the business and its legal status (here a limited company) should be set out, together with the objectives of the business. The short-term (12 months) objectives should state:

- the type of product – whether it be a manufactured item or a service
- the expected sales volume (number of items sold)
- the sales value (the amount of income to be received from sales)
- the projected market share
- the profit target, eg net profit figure

It is common practice to summarise these objectives in a clearly-expressed message known as a "Mission Statement" (see previous page).

personnel

An important determining factor of the success of a business is the people that it employs. It is customary to list in a separate section the management of the business, showing their qualifications and experience. If necessary their CVs can be attached as an Appendix. The extent of the other staff of the business should also be listed, although in less detail.

marketing plan

A successful business should invest time and money in marketing. The business plan should convince the reader that the product or service will fulfil a specific need. The plan should set out details of:

- the product and its price (sales brochures could be included in the Appendix)
- the present market and the expected market share
- the competition, and why the proposed product is better
- promotion plans – showing timings
- distribution and sales
- the marketing budget (brief details)
- break-even calculations

It should be stressed that the marketing plan which appears in the business plan is an abbreviated version of the internal marketing plan of the business.

production plan

The production will set out details of the physical resources needed for the production of the manufactured item. It will contain:

- a summary of the production method
- the premises used, showing full details of cost, valuation, whether freehold or leasehold
- the machinery and vehicles required, together with details of cost, valuation and expected life
- raw materials needed, stating cost, supplier details and expected stock levels
- labour and training requirements
- quality control procedures

You should note that if the plan is presenting a service, the appropriate details will be listed, although there will obviously be no raw materials requirement.

resource requirements

This section summarises in financial terms:

- the resources that will be needed
- the amount of money being contributed by the owner(s)
- the amount of finance required
- the assets available for security

This section summarises for a potential lender the essential questions of

- how much finance is being requested in proportion to the capital sum being invested by the owner(s)?
- what assets are available for security?

financial data

This section will contain for a new business:

- a twelve month cashflow forecast
- the balance sheet at the beginning of the twelve months
- projected profit and loss statement for the first twelve months
- projected balance sheet at the end of twelve months

If the business is already trading, the financial data should also include past financial statements, normally over a three year period.

monitor and review performance

When looking at the figures in the financial statements in this Case Study, remember that the cashflow forecast will include VAT, and the profit statement will not.

You should also note that the financial projections contained in the plan will enable the business to *monitor and review performance* during the course of the year.

Specifically the business will be able to look at:

- *cashflow* – the business can compare the projected cash flow forecast figures with the actual figures on a monthly basis; if the figures are going widely adrift, the cashflow forecast can be redrafted
- *monthly profit and loss account* (a standard report if the business has its accounts on a computer) – against the projected figures in the plan (normally divided by twelve)

It will be useful for the business each month to produce cumulative (year-to-date) figures for the profit and loss account. This will show any adverse or positive trend much more accurately.

BUSINESS PLAN

name Sonic Deco Limited

address Unit 1b Severnside Industrial Estate
Link Road
Stourminster ST2 4RT

summary

Sonic Deco Limited is a hi-fi loudspeaker manufacturing business founded by John Eliot and Edward Gardiner in 19-1. John Eliot has fifteen years' experience of loudspeaker design and has pioneered as a sole trader a new Deco'Presence' speaker which is now in production in rented premises, and has already sold 500 units in six months to hi-fi dealers in London and the West Midlands. There is proven market demand for an estimated 5,000 units a year.

The new company proposes to takeover and expand the sole trader business. It will purchase an industrial unit, machinery and delivery vehicle. Total cost of assets will be £219k. The owners are contributing £125k of capital, and the company seeks a further £110k from the bank: £50k by way of commercial mortgage on the premises, £20k by way of business loan for the machinery, and £40k by way of overdraft for working capital purposes.

contents

- 1 -

business and objectives

name Sonic Deco Limited

address Unit 1b Severnside Industrial Estate
Link Road
Stourminster ST2 4RT

Tel 0605 577455 Fax 0605 577498

legal status Limited company
Shareholders:
John Eliot 50%
Edward Gardiner 50%

business Hi-fi loudspeaker manufacturer

start date 1 January 19-1

mission statement

"Sonic Deco Limited will become a leading manufacturer of quality loudspeaker systems and a household name in the UK"

short-term objectives

Sonic Deco will within the first twelve months of trading:

- produce and sell 4,800 units (pairs) of loudspeakers
- achieve sales turnover of £480,000
- achieve a pre-tax profit of over £45,000
- supply over 50 major hi-fi retailers throughout the UK
- take 10% of UK market in similar units

long-term objectives

Sonic Deco will within the first three years of trading:

- increase the product lines to six loudspeaker models
- increase annual turnover to £1,000,000
- establish sales through agents in the EC, USA and Japan

resources requirements

resources required

item	*cost (£)*
freehold premises	125,000
production machinery	45,000
office equipment	12,500
vehicle	12,500
materials and working capital	40,000
TOTAL	235,000

financial requirements

item	*finance(£)*	
freehold premises	50,000	commercial mortgage*
production machinery	20,000	business loan**
stock/working capital	40,000	overdraft
TOTAL FINANCE REQUIRED	110,000	
CONTRIBUTION FROM OWN RESOURCES	125,000	
TOTAL	235,000	

* commercial mortgage with annual repayments of capital and interest requested

** business loan with first year interest only repayments requested

assets available for security

security	*value (£)*
freehold premises	£127,000 (valuation Dec. 19-0)
other fixed assets	£70,000 (at cost)

financial data – projected profit statement

PROJECTED TRADING AND PROFIT LOSS ACCOUNT OF SONIC DECO LIMITED FOR YEAR ENDING 31 DECEMBER 19-1

	£	£
Sales		480,000
Purchases	288,000	
Less closing stock	10,000	
Cost of Goods Sold		278,000
Gross Profit		202,000
Wages	43,750	
Directors salaries	48,000	
Rates	2,900	
Insurance	1,500	
Services	2,400	
Telephone	1,200	
Vehicle expenses	2,400	
Stationery	600	
Postages	1,800	
Advertising	12,000	
Packing	6,000	
Bank charges	600	
Interest	7,500	
Depreciation	14,625	
		145,275
Net profit		56,725

Note:

The figures for purchases and sales on the cash flow forecast differ from those quoted above because the figures here *exclude* VAT.

financial data – opening balance sheet

PROJECTED BALANCE SHEET OF SONIC DECO LIMITED AS AT 1 JANUARY 19-1

	Cost	Dep'n	Net
	£	£	£
Fixed Assets			
Premises	125,000	0	125,000
Machinery	45,000	0	45,000
Vehicle	12,500	0	12,500
Office equipment	12,500	0	12,500
	195,000	0	195,000
Current Assets			
Stock		24,000	
Less Current Liabilities			
Overdraft		24,000*	
Working Capital			0
			195,000
Less Long-term Liabilties			
Bank Loans			70,000
NET ASSETS			125,000

FINANCED BY

Authorised Share Capital	
125,000 ordinary shares of £1 each	125,000
Issued Share Capital	
125,000 ordinary shares of £1 each, fully paid	125,000

*Note that the overdraft of £24,000 results from the initial stock purchase of £24,000. The full overdraft requirement of £40,000 shown in the Resources Requirement Section (p.8) will not be utilised until the end of the first month of trading.

financial data – year-end balance sheet

BALANCE SHEET OF SONIC DECO LIMITED AS AT 31 DECEMBER 19-1

	Cost	Dep'n	Net
	£	£	£
Fixed Assets			
Premises	125,000	0	125,000
Machinery	45,000	9,000	36000
Vehicle	12,500	3,125	9,375
Office equipment	12,500	2,500	10,000
	195,000	14,625	180,375
Current Assets			
Stock		10,000	
Debtors		40,000	
Bank		53,450	
		103,450	
Less Current Liabilities			
Creditors		34,100	
Working Capital			69,350
			249,725
Less Long-term Liabilties			
Bank Loans			68,000
NET ASSETS			181,725

FINANCED BY	
Authorised Share Capital	
125,000 ordinary shares of £1 each	125,000
Issued Share Capital	
125,000 ordinary shares of £1 each, fully paid	125,000
Profit and loss	56,725
	181,725

financial data – cashflow forecast

Name of Business: Sonic Deco Limited								
Period: January - Dec 19-1								
	Jan	Feb	Mar	Apl	May	Jun	July	Aug
	£	£	£	£	£	£	£	£
RECEIPTS								
Cash sales								
Cash from debtors		47000	47000	47000	47000	47000	47000	47000
Capital	125000							
Loans	70000							
Interest								
TOTAL RECEIPTS	195000	47000	47000	47000	47000	47000	47000	47000
PAYMENTS								
Cash purchases	28200							
Credit purchases			28200	28200	28200	28200	28200	28200
Capital items	195000							
Wages	7645	7645	7645	7645	7645	7645	7645	7645
Rent/rates			290	290	290	290	290	290
Insurance	1500							
Services	200	200	200	200	200	200	200	200
Telephone				300			300	
VAT				7000			7000	
Vehicle expenses	200	200	200	200	200	200	200	200
Stationery	50	50	50	50	50	50	50	50
Postages	150	150	150	150	150	150	150	150
Bank charges			150			150		
Interest			500					
Loan repayments								
Advertising	1000	1000	1000	1000	1000	1000	1000	1000
Packaging	500	500	500	500	500	500	500	500
TOTAL PAYMENTS	234445	9745	38885	45535	38235	38385	45535	38235
NET CASHFLOW	-39445	37255	8115	1465	8765	8615	1465	8765
OPENING BANK	0	-39445	-2190	5925	7390	16155	24770	26235
CLOSING BANK	-39445	-2190	5925	7390	16155	24770	26235	35000

financial data – cashflow forecast

Sept	Oct	Nov	Dec	TOTAL		
£	£	£	£	£		
47000	47000	47000	47000	517000		
				125000		
				70000		
				0		
47000	47000	47000	47000	712000		
				28200		
28200	28200	28200	28200	282000		
				195000		
7645	7645	7645	7655	91750		
290	290	290	290	2900		
				1500		
200	200	200	200	2400		
	300			900		
	7000			21000		
200	200	200	200	2400		
50	50	50	50	600		
150	150	150	150	1800		
150			150	600		
			7000	7500		
			2000	2000		
1000	1000	1000	1000	12000		
500	500	500	500	6000		
				0		
				0		
38385	45535	38235	47395	658550		
8615	1465	8765	-395	53450		
35000	43615	45080	53845	0		
43615	45080	53845	53450	53450		

monitoring of financial results

CASHFLOW FORECAST

Monthly figures will be recorded and compared with forecast figures and inspected by the directors.

If results fluctuate significantly the situation will be investigated and the forecast redrafted.

PROFIT AND LOSS STATEMENT

Monthly figures will be extracted from the computer system and compared with the projected monthly equivalent from the forecast.

Year-to-date figures will also be calculated and compared with the forecast. The directors will investigate significant adverse and positive trends and take action accordingly.

All monitored figures will be supplied to a lender on request.

appendix A

accounting formats and worksheets

This appendix contains

- a specimen format of the internal use (ie not for publication) profit and loss account and balance sheet for a limited company
- a specimen format of a cash flow statement
- a worksheet for the main accounting ratios

***** NAME OF COMPANY *** LIMITED**
Profit and loss account
for the year ended * date *****

	£	£	
Sales	x	(a)	
Opening stock	x		
Purchases or production cost	x		
	x		
Less Closing stock	x		
Cost of sales		x	(b)
Gross profit (a) – (b)		x	(c)
Less overheads:			
eg Selling and distribution costs	x		
Administration costs	x		
Finance costs	x		
		x	(d)
Net profit for year before taxation (c) – (d)		x	(e)
Less corporation tax		x	(f)
Profit for year after taxation (e) – (f)		x	(g)
Less interim dividends paid			
ordinary shares	x		
preference shares	x		
final dividends proposed			
ordinary shares	x		
preference shares	x		
		x	(h)
Retained profit for year (g) – (h)		x	(i)
Add balance of retained profits at beginning of year		x	(j)
Balance of retained profits at end of year (i) + (j)		x	(k)

Notes:

- for a manufacturing business, production cost (ie the factory cost of manufacturing the products) is shown instead of purchases
- depreciation of fixed assets is included in the costs for production, selling and distribution, and administration, as appropriate
- directors' remuneration and debenture interest is included in the overheads

*** NAME OF COMPANY *** LIMITED

Balance sheet as at * date *****

Fixed assets	*Cost* (a)	*Dep'n to date* (b)	*Net* (a) – (b)	
	£	£	£	
Intangible				
Goodwill	x	x	x	
Tangible				
Freehold land and buildings	x	x	x	
Machinery	x	x	x	
Fixtures and fittings	x	x	x	
etc	x	x	x	
	x	x	x	(c)
Current assets				
Stock *(closing)*		x		
Debtors		x		
Bank		x		
Cash		x		
		x		(d)
Less Current liabilities				
Creditors	x			
Bank overdraft	x			
Proposed dividends	x			
Corporation tax	x			
		x		(e)
Working capital (d) – (e)			x	(f)
(c) + (f)			x	(g)
Less Long-term liabilities				
Debentures			x	(h)
NET ASSETS (g) – (h)			x	(i)
FINANCED BY				
Authorised share capital				
x (number) preference shares of £x (nominal value) each			x	
x (number) ordinary shares of £x (nominal value) each			x	
			x	
Issued share capital				
x (number) preference shares of £x (nominal value) each, fully/partly paid			x	
x (number) ordinary shares of £x (nominal value) each, fully/partly paid			x	
			x	
Capital reserves				
Share premium account		x		
Revaluation reserve		x	x	
Revenue reserves				
Profit and loss account		x		
General reserve		x	x	
SHAREHOLDERS' FUNDS			x	(i)

Note: balance sheet balances at points (i)

***** NAME OF COMPANY *** LIMITED**
Cash flow statement for the year ended * date *****

		£	£
Operating activities:			
Operating profit (note: before tax and interest)		x	
Depreciation for year		x	
Increase or decrease in stocks	(x) or	x	
Increase or decrease in debtors	(x) or	x	
Increase or decrease in creditors	x or	(x)	
Net cash inflow from operating activities			x
Returns on investments and servicing of finance:			
Interest and dividends received		x	
Interest and dividends paid (dividends on ordinary shares shown below)		(x)	
			x or (x)
Taxation:			
Corporation tax paid (note: amount *paid* during year)			(x)
Capital expenditure and financial investment			
Payments to acquire fixed assets and investments		(x)	
Receipts from sales of fixed assets and investments		x	
			x or (x)
Acquisitions and disposals			
eg purchase of subsidiary undertakings		(x)	
eg sale of a business		x	x or (x)
Equity dividends paid: (note: amount *paid* during year)			(x)
Cash inflow or outflow before use of liquid resources and financing			x (or (x)
Management of liquid resources:			
eg purchase of treasury bills		(x)	
eg sale of treasury bills		x	
			x or (x)
Financing:			
Issue of share capital		x	
Repayment of share capital		(x)	
Increase in loans		x	
Repayment of loans		(x)	
			x or (x)
Increase or decrease in cash			x or (x)

Note: money amounts shown in brackets indicate a deduction or, where the figure is a sub-total, a negative figure

Accounting ratios worksheet

This worksheet will assist in calculating the main accounting ratios from a set of financial statements. Use it as follows:

- *enter the figures from the profit and loss account and balance sheet against items 1 – 11*
- *calculate the ratios and percentages using the numbered figures, as indicated on the next page*

Note that this will assist in the calculation of the main accounting ratios; but it will not provide the all-important interpretation.

FIGURES FROM FINANCIAL STATEMENTS

		financial year-end	
		previous year	current year
		£	£
	Profit and loss account		
1	Sales (or turnover)		
2	Cost of sales (or cost of goods sold)		
3	Operating profit (or net profit + interest payable)		
4	Net profit (or profit on ordinary activities) before taxation		
	Balance sheet		
5	Current assets sub-total		
6	Stock		
7	Debtors		
8	Current liabilities sub-total (or creditors: amounts falling due within one year)		
9	Trade creditors		
10	Long-term liabilities (or creditors: amounts falling due after more than one year)		
11	Capital and reserves total		

ACCOUNTING RATIOS

	figures from the table on the previous page		previous year	current year
Profitability				
Gross profit/sales percentage	$\frac{1 - 2}{1}$	x $\frac{100}{1}$	%	%
Operating profit percentage	$\frac{3}{1}$	x $\frac{100}{1}$	%	%
Net profit/sales percentage	$\frac{4}{1}$	x $\frac{100}{1}$	%	%
Return on capital employed	$\frac{3}{10 + 11}$	x $\frac{100}{1}$	%	%
Return on equity (pre-tax) * less preference dividend (if any)	$\frac{4^*}{11}$	x $\frac{100}{1}$	%	%
Solvency/liquidity				
Working capital ratio	$\frac{5}{8}$		:1	:1
Liquid ratio	$\frac{5 - 6}{8}$		:1	:1
Capital gearing percentage	$\frac{10}{11}$	x $\frac{100}{1}$	%	%
Asset utilisation				
Stock turnover (days) * ideally, this should be the average of opening stock and closing stock	$\frac{6^*}{2}$	x 365	days	days
Debtors' collection period (days)	$\frac{7}{1}$	x 365	days	days
Creditors' payment period (days) * ideally, this should be the purchases figure	$\frac{9}{2^*}$	x 365	days	days
Working capital cycle: stock turnover + debtors collection period – creditors payment period = working capital cycle			days	days

appendix B

answers to activities

This appendix contains:

- full answers to numerical activities
- key points for non-numerical activities

CHAPTER 1: THE ROLE OF BUSINESS IN THE ECONOMY

1.1 Points to consider include:

- The reason why the organisation is classified as private or public sector.
- The reason why the organisation is categorised as primary, manufacturing, or service.
- Is the primary objective that of profit? If so, what do you see as the secondary objectives? How do these link with the objectives set by the organisation? If not profit, then what is the primary objective – eg to provide a service to the local community?
- Does the organisation strive to incorporate the three 'E's (page 5) or does it pay lip-service to them? What is the evidence?
  - Have costs been reduced?
  - Has throughput (products/services) improved?
  - How closely have targets been achieved?

1.2 Personal contacts will be particularly useful for the sole trader and partnership aspects of this Activity. The accounts of a private limited company can be obtained from Companies House. There is much more information readily available on public limited companies – the report and accounts can be obtained from the Company Secretary, or from Companies House; alternatively some financial newspapers offer a report and accounts service for well-known plcs.

The discussion should centre around the following:

- The reason for the current form of business unit (and whether the business has changed from one form to another as expansion or decline has taken place).
- Whether there is any link between type of product/service, size of business, and the form of business unit.
- Whether sources of finance are common to all the businesses, or whether some are not used/unavailable to certain businesses.

1.3

Compsoft Limited

Statement of added value for the year

	£	£
Income		
Receipts from repairs	100,000	
Sales of software and computer supplies	108,000	
		208,000
Less Costs		
Spare parts for repairs	25,000	
Software and computer supplies bought for resale	72,000	
Rent and rates of premises	11,000	
		108,000
Added value		100,000
Less distribution of added value:		
Wages and salaries	42,000	
Finance costs: interest paid on bank loan	3,000	
leasing of office equipment	12,000	
		57,000
Surplus of added value for year		43,000

The surplus of added value of £43,000 will be used for
- paying corporation tax
- repaying the bank loan
- providing dividends to the company's shareholders
- retained in the company to build for the future

$$\frac{\text{spare parts for repairs}}{\text{receipts from repairs}} = \frac{£25{,}000}{£100{,}000} \times \frac{100}{1} = \underline{25\%}$$

$$\frac{\text{software and computer supplies bought for resale}}{\text{sales of software and computer supplies}} = \frac{£72{,}000}{£108{,}000} = \underline{67\%}$$

- Repairs will take a major part of the wages and salaries bill; sales will take a small part.
- Thus the cost of the added value for repairs is spare parts, a high proportion of the wages and salaries, plus a share of the other costs of the business.
- The directors need to apportion costs to the two sections of the business so that they know which is providing the most added value.

1.4 *Local economy*

As the topic is the closure of various organisations, the points to consider include:
- reduction in local facilities (department store, college, bank) and, therefore, a need for local people to travel to a nearby larger town
- increase in local unemployment
- reduced wages and other costs going into the local economy, possibly leading to reductions in local services
- the closure of the factory will affect the national economy, with an increase in the balance of trade as more goods are imported

Business objectives

The discussion should focus on the effect that secondary objectives have on the primary objective of maximising profits, at least in the short-term. However, in the longer-term, secondary objectives could well increase profits, for example:
- to increase market share, prices may be cut; this will reduce profit in the short-term, but the increased business may lead to greater long-term profitability
- money spent on research and development may well create modified or new products
- being positive about green issues will add to costs in the short-term, but may well increase sales in the future as people examine environmental issues

Effect on local businesses

Include in the discussion points such as:
- closure of smaller retail businesses in the town centre (with effects of downward spiral on local economy)
- will the job opportunities of the new businesses lead to a net increase in employment?
- will the new businesses result in increased standards of service from the existing businesses as they seek to compete, and cut their profit margins?
- the new businesses that will need to be established to provide support services to the new

operations, eg the telephone banking will need staff (from local recruitment agencies), maintenance work, sandwich shops, etc

CHAPTER 2: THE ACCOUNTING FUNCTION

2.1 Points to consider include:

- The form of the financial statements – whether profit and loss account and balance sheet, or income and expenditure account, or final accounts.
- Whether the financial statements are produced for the use of insiders who run the organisation, or for outsiders, such as shareholders. Are the accounts available for public inspection?
- Whether the objective of the organisation is to make a profit, or to show the stewardship of money allocated to it.
- Look for the different accounting roles within the finance function. Who is responsible for producing financial statements, for budgeting, for financing capital expenditure?
- In the audit report, look for the words 'true and fair view', but also read the rest of the report.

2.2

- The financial accountant is mainly concerned with control of the accounting records, financial statements, tax matters. What tasks are undertaken?
- The management accountant is mainly concerned with financial decision-making, planning and control of the business. What tasks are undertaken?
- Besides technical accounting skills, consider others such as communications, information technology, management of people.

2.3 Don't dismiss these topics! Consider:

- The benefits brought to the organisation by the accountant/accounting function:
  - provision of accounting controls to prevent fraud
  - completed financial accounts
  - accounting returns (eg for VAT and payroll) submitted on time
  - management accounts prepared to help with decision-making
  - monitoring of performance through accounting reports
  - liaison with providers of finance
- How do these benefits compare with those of other functions, eg personnel, administration, marketing?
- Is it too simplistic to say "if we don't employ accountants we can have more front-line staff (eg nurses)"?
- How is a balance struck between producing goods and services, and accounting for them? Look for ways in which accounting helps the production process by analysing costs and revenues, in particular:
  - looking for cost reductions
  - focusing on improving financial performance

CHAPTER 3: BASICS OF FINANCIAL STATEMENTS

3.1

Profit and loss account
Gloria Golding, trading as "Gloria's Garden"
for the year ended 31 March 1997

	£	£
Sales		109,950
Opening stock (1 April 1996)	1,750	
Purchases	67,500	
	69,250	
Less Closing stock (31 March 1997)	10,400	
Cost of sales		58,850
Gross profit		51,100
Less overheads:		
Wages	16,500	
Rent paid	8,450	
Telephone	1,430	
Interest paid	780	
Administration	9,720	
Depreciation of shop fittings	3,000	
		39,880
Net profit		11,220

Balance sheet as at 31 December 1996

	£ Cost	£ Dep'n to date	£ Net
Fixed assets			
Shop fittings	15,000	9,000	6,000
Current assets			
Stock		10,400	
Debtors		1,450	
Bank		1,210	
Cash		150	
		13,210	
Less Current liabilities			
Creditors		6,250	
Working capital			6,960
NET ASSETS			12,960
FINANCED BY			
Capital			
Opening capital			16,100
Add net profit			11,220
			27,320
Less drawings			14,360
Closing capital			12,960

Points to discuss include:

- the busines is profitable
- high level of closing stock
- high cost of wages and administration
- high level of creditors (are they pressing for payment?), with very little money in the bank to meet them
- owner's drawings in excess of net profit

3.2 *For Wyvern Stationery, the interested parties will include:*

- the owner, Peter Simpson
- the bank manager – the business has both an overdraft facility and a bank loan
- the Inland Revenue – to assess Peter Simpson for tax

As the turnover is increasing, HM Customs and Excise – the VAT authority – will wish to ensure that the business registers for VAT at the correct time.

Net profit percentages:

last year

$$\frac{£5,410}{£27,500} \times \frac{100}{1} = 19.7\%$$

this year

$$\frac{£6,604}{£48,200} \times \frac{100}{1} = 13.7\%$$

From the profit and loss account:

- The net profit percentage has fallen by six percentage points – a dramatic fall; Peter Simpson needs to investigate the reasons for this
- Sales have increased by 75% but net profit has increased by only 22%; Peter Simpson needs to look at increases in cost of sales and overheads:
  - cost of sales has gone up by 92% (greater than the increase in sales); it seems likely that selling prices have been reduced in order to generate a greater volume of sales
  - wages have increased almost four times: is there enough business to justify the use of part-time employees? (Remember that Peter Simpson's drawings are not shown here; instead they are listed in the balance sheet)
  - interest paid has more than doubled, a reflection of increased borrowing from the bank

From the balance sheet:

- Stock and debtors have more than doubled
- Money in the bank of £1,820 has now become an overdraft of £2,955
- Creditors have almost doubled
- Working capital has fallen from £3,405 to £1,600
- Fixed assets have been purchased
- A repayment of £200 has been made on the bank loan
- Peter Simpson's drawings have exceeded net profit for both years
- Over the two years shown here, his capital in the business has shrunk from £6,000 (on 1 January last year) to £4,550 (on 31 December this year)
- Sales have increased by 75%; however, the balance sheet shows a business facing financial

problems – particularly with the decline in working capital and the increase in the bank overdraft

The bank manager will note:

- The bank overdraft of £2,955 – which is close to the overdraft facility limit of £3,000, ie there isn't much financial leeway for the business
- Bank loan £1,800 + overdraft £2,955 = £4,755, which is greater than Peter Simpson's capital of £4,550 at 31 December this year; a worrying sign
- The level of Peter Simpson's drawings in relation to profit over the last two years
- The decline in the net profit percentage over the last two years
- The decline in working capital
- The lack of any suitable security in the balance sheet for the bank to hold (ie no premises – they are rented)

In return for continued bank loan and overdraft facilities, the bank will be looking for Peter Simpson to address the problems of declining profitability and liquidity with urgency; an early repayment of part of the bank facilities will be sought in order to bring the bank's liabilities well below that of Peter Simpson's capital.

3.3 (a) See text

(b) Under the consistency concept, the owner should continue to use the reducing balance method (it won't make any difference to the bank manager anyway).

(c) Under the prudence concept, the bad debt should be written off, with debtors being shown on the balance sheet as £27,500. This is a closer figure of the amount that the business expects to receive and is, therefore, a better reflection of the financial strength of the business.

(d) If the rate of inflation over the twelve months is less than 2.5%, then the business has improved; if higher than 2.5%, then the business has declined.

(e) Under the business entity concept, as the car is not owned by the NHS Trust, it will not be shown on the Trust's balance sheet. However, petrol and other running costs paid to the district nurse will be recorded as an expense of the NHS Trust.

(f) The going concern concept presumes that the business will continue to trade in the foreseeable future. The alternative is 'gone concern', when assets may have very different values.

CHAPTER 4: FINANCIAL STATEMENTS: LIMITED COMPANIES

4.1

Jobseekers Limited
Profit and loss account (appropriation section)
for the year ended 31 December 1996

	£	£
Net profit for year before taxation		68,200
Less corporation tax		14,850
Profit for year after taxation		53,350
Less interim ordinary dividends paid	10,000	
final ordinary dividend proposed	40,000	
		50,000
Retained profit for year		3,350
Retained profit at 1 January 1996		7,350
Retained profit at 31 December 1996		10,700

Jobseekers Limited
Balance sheet as at 31 December 1996

Fixed assets	*Cost* £	*Dep'n to date* £	*Net* £
Intangible			
Goodwill	20,000	6,000	14,000
Tangible			
Premises	175,000	10,500	164,500
Office equipment	25,000	5,000	20,000
	220,000	21,500	198,500
Current assets			
Stock		750	
Debtors		42,500	
		43,250	
Less Current liabilities			
Creditors	7,250		
Bank overdraft	13,950		
Proposed dividends	40,000		
Corporation tax	14,850		
		76,050	
Working capital			(32,800)
			165,700
Less Long-term liabilities			
Bank loan			55,000
NET ASSETS			110,700

FINANCED BY	
Issued share capital	
100,000 ordinary shares of £1 each	100,000
Revenue reserve	
Profit and loss account	10,700
SHAREHOLDERS' FUNDS	110,700

Points to discuss include:

- company is very profitable
- high level of dividends for year – better to retain profits to build the company for the future?
- main asset strength of the company is in the premises – is balance sheet value accurate?
- high level of debtors – are any overdue, and what is being done to reduce debtors?
- who are the creditors and are any pressing for payment?
- a bank overdraft of £13,950, with payments due soon for dividends and corporation tax – is the bank prepared to increase the overdraft limit?
- would it have been more prudent to retain more of the profits in the business?
- a negative figure for working capital
- bank loan of £55,000, together with overdraft of £13,950, means that the company is heavily in debt to the bank – have the premises been used as security?

4.2 (a) Depreciation is a non-cash accounting adjustment to record an estimate of the fall in value of fixed assets. As a further issue, it is possible to make transfers out of the bank account into a separate account set up to meet the cost of replacing fixed assets. The balance on such a separate account will be shown on the balance sheet of the organisation; any interest earned will be shown as income.

(b) Reserves are not cash; instead they are profits which have been retained to build the business for the future. They are represented by assets but can rarely be linked to specific amounts.

(c) There are two acceptable accounting treatments for writing down (amortizing) purchased goodwill; it should be

- either written-off immediately to reserves through the appropriation section of the profit and loss account
- or written off to profit and loss account over the estimated economic life of the goodwill

Non-purchased goodwill cannot be recorded in the accounts, so the figure cannot be increased.

(d) Share capital is an investment in a company. Thus, to the investor, it is an asset while, to the company, it is money that might be repaid at some time in the future (depending on the terms of the share issue).

(e) The ordinary shareholders might be persuaded by this, as the share price should increase as the company expands. In this way, they will receive a capital gain rather than income. However, some investors may have bought the shares in order to obtain a regular income and will not wish to see a change in dividend policy. There may also be tax implications between income and capital gains.

The preference shareholders are most likely to have invested for income. The terms under which the preference shares were originally issued are most likely to require that a preference dividend is paid when sufficient profit is made. If a dividend is not paid in one year (because a loss has been made), most preference shares are *cumulative* and require any missed dividends to be paid once profits are available. It is most unlikely that the preference shareholders will agree to the proposal, especially as their shares will not significantly change in value as the company expands.

(f) For taxation purposes, depreciation is added back to net profit and then standard *writing down allowances* are deducted. Thus the tax paid will be the same whatever depreciation method is used. Also, the accounting concept of consistency requires the accounting treatment to be similar from year-to-year.

(g) Two issues here:

- Share premium account is a *capital reserve* created when shares are issued to the public at a higher amount than nominal value. Capital reserves cannot be used to fund the payment of dividends.
- A reserve is not represented by cash – (see (b), above).

CHAPTER 5: CASH FLOW STATEMENTS

5.1 Cash flow statement of John Smithfor the year ended 31 December 1997

	£	£
Operating activities:		
Operating profit (before interest)	11,250	
Depreciation	1,000	
Increase in stock	(3,500)	
Increase in debtors	(800)	
Increase in creditors	250	
Net cash inflow from operating activities		8,200
Returns on investments and servicing of finance:		
Interest paid		(250)
Taxation:		
Corporation tax paid		not applicable
Capital expenditure and financial investment:		
Payments to acquire fixed assets		(2,000)
Equity dividends paid: (drawings)		(9,000)
Cash outflow before use of liquid resources and financing		(3,050)
Financing:		–
Decrease in cash		*(3,050)
Bank balance at start of year		850
Bank balance at end of year		(2,200)
* Decrease in cash		(3,050)

Comments to include:

- quite a high level of operating profit, larger than drawings
- large increase in stocks – why is this? are they saleable?
- debtors have doubled – any bad debts?
- new fixed assets have been bought for £2,000

The business has financed a large increase in stock and new fixed assets through its bank account – resulting in a decrease in cash of £3,050 over the year.

5.2

Retail News Limited
Cash flow statement for the year ended 31 December

	1995 £000	*1995* £000	*1996* £000	*1996* £000
Operating activities:				
Operating profit (before tax and interest)	* 31		§ 50	
Depreciation	* 24		§ 20	
Increase in stock	(14)		(6)	
Increase in debtors	(40)		(40)	
Increase in creditors	16		6	
Net cash inflow from operating activities		17		30
Returns on investments and servicing of finance:				
Interest paid		(3)		(15)
Taxation:				
Corporation tax paid		(4)		(5)
Capital expenditure and financial investment:				
Payments to acquire fixed assets		(24)		(26)
Equity dividends paid:		(16)		(20)
Cash outflow before use of liquid resources and financing		(30)		(36)
Financing:				
Issue of share capital		10		–
Decrease in cash		** (20)		** (36)
Bank balance at start of year		10		(10)
Bank balance at end of year		(10)		(46)
** Decrease in cash		(20)		(36)

* Operating profit (before tax and interest) for 1995:

	£
increase in retained profits	3,000
proposed dividend, 1995	20,000
corporation tax, 1995	5,000
interest, 1995	3,000
operating profit before tax and interest	31,000

Depreciation for 1995: £98,000 – £74,000 = £24,000

§ Operating profit (before tax and interest) for 1996:

	£
increase in retained profits	11,000
proposed dividend, 1996	16,000
corporation tax, 1996	8,000
interest, 1996	15,000
operating profit before tax and dividends	50,000

Depreciation for 1996: £118,000 – £98,000 = £20,000

Comments to include:

- a good cash flow from operating profit in both years – well above the amounts paid for corporation tax and dividends
- stock, debtors and creditors have increased each year – in particular the debtors have increased dramatically
- interest paid in 1996 is high because of the increasing bank overdraft (and will, most probably, be even higher in 1997)
- new fixed assets have been bought each year – £24,000 in 1995 and £26,000 in 1996. Apart from a share issue of £10,000 in 1995, these have been financed through the bank account

The business appears to be expanding quite rapidly, with large increases in fixed assets and the working capital items. As most of this expansion has been financed through the bank (apart from the share issue of £10,000 in 1995), there is much pressure on the bank account. It would be better to obtain long-term finance – either a loan or a new issue of shares – rather than using the bank overdraft.

5.3 (a) See text

(b)
- Profit is the surplus of income over expenditure.
- Cash is the surplus of receipts over payments.
- A profitable business could be spending money on expansion now in order to generate increased profits for the future, which will generate cash once the expansion is completed.
- A business with cash in the bank might now be benefiting from past expansion schemes. Does it need to invest in new products/services before receipts begin to fall? Also a declining business might be selling off assets to generate cash.

(c)
- *Profit and loss account:* depreciation for the year on the new computer system will be recorded as an expense (unless it is company policy not to depreciate fixed assets in the year of purchase).
- *Balance sheet:* the new computer system will be shown as a fixed asset at cost, less depreciation (if any) to date, and net book value is the figure to be added into the assets.
- *Cash flow statement:* the cost of £100,000 will be shown under the heading of 'capital expenditure and financial investment'.

(d)
- Only produced once a year.
- Historical – it is not a guide to the future.
- User needs to look at trends.
- Does not measure performance (the profit and loss account does this).
- Need to compare with cash flow statements of similar companies.

CHAPTER 6: PUBLISHED ACCOUNTS OF LIMITED COMPANIES

6.1 This Activity is principally concerned with:

- *initial reading* in order to get an overview of the company's accounts and an understanding of the industry
- *horizontal analysis* in order to compare certain figures from the financial statements with the figures from the previous accounting period

The Activity can be developed to look at various aspects of:

- the company's structure and its own industry
- the stage of its development
- both internal and external influences on the company

6.2 (a) A bonus issue of shares does not bring in any new money to the business. In this example, after the issue, there will be twice as many shares, so the share price will, in theory, halve. (In practice, for Stock Market reasons, the price will often not quite halve, so the shareholders may see a small gain in value.)

(b) Revaluation of property is a non-trading transaction, so the reported profit will be unaffected. Instead, the revaluation will be recorded in a capital reserve account called 'revaluation reserve'. The technique of revaluing assets – commonly property – is to formally record on the balance sheet the increase in value which belongs to the shareholders.

(c) Depreciation of fixed assets is an application of the concepts of prudence and consistency. It would go against the consistency concept to change the accounting treatment from year-to-year. There will be no effect on the amount of tax paid because, for tax purposes, depreciation is added back to net profit and then standard *writing down allowances* are deducted.

(d) Retained profits are not represented by cash – see also Activity 4.2(b). The capital expenditure programme can only be financed through the bank (or other financial facilities).

(e)
- A rights issue is an appropriate way to finance a major capital expenditure project
- Cash is raised by offering additional shares to existing shareholders at a favourable price (usually a little below the current market price)
- Extra shares are offered in proportion to the shareholders' existing holding
- The shareholder either takes up the rights by subscribing the cash, or sells the rights on the Stock Exchange
- The benefit to the company is that a rights issue is cheaper than an issue to the general public; also, existing shareholders have an interest in the future of the company and are likely to subscribe

CHAPTER 7: INTERPRETATION OF FINANCIAL STATEMENTS

7.1

	A plc	*B plc*
• gross profit percentage	11.85%	54.26%
• net profit percentage	2.87%	21.08%
• operating profit percentage	3.95%	26.01%
• return on capital employed	18.18%	13.70%

- primary ratio:
  net profit percentage x asset turnover = return on capital employed

A plc	2.873%	x	6.33 times	=	18.18%
B plc	21.08%	x	0.65 times	=	13.70%

7.2

	C plc	*D plc*
• working capital ratio	1.51:1	1.04:1
• liquid ratio	0.82:1	0.65:1
• debtors' collection period	37 days	3 days
• creditors' payment period	57 days	46 days
• stock turnover	41 days	18 days
• gearing ratio	0.54:1	0.16:1

C plc is the chemical manufacturer, while D plc runs department stores.

All of the ratios for C are close to the benchmarks for a manufacturing business: eg working capital and liquid ratios, although a little low, are near the 'accepted' figures of 2:1 and 1:1, respectively. Debtors, creditors and stock turnover show quite a high level of stock being held; debtors' turnover indicates that most sales are on credit; creditors' turnover is rather high. The gearing ratio is acceptable – medium-geared.

For D plc, the ratios indicate a business that sells most of its goods on cash terms: low working capital and liquid ratios, with minimal debtors' turnover. The stock turnover is speedy, whilst creditors are paid after one-and-a-half months. The gearing ratio is low, indicating that there is scope for future borrowing should it be required.

7.3

	ABC plc	*XYZ plc*
• dividend yield	10%	1.39%
• earnings per share	30p	36.67p
• earnings yield	20%	6.11%
• price/earnings ratio	5:1	16.37:1
• dividend cover	2 times	4.4 times

XYZ plc is the better company for capital growth: less than a quarter of its earnings is paid out as dividends – the rest is retained in the company to build for the future, which should be reflected in its share price in the years to come.

ABC plc has a much higher dividend yield than XYZ and is the better company for income. Nevertheless, ABC retains half of its earnings, which should help its share price in the future.

7.4

	Business A	*Business B*
(a) gross profit percentage	13.4%	44.0%
(b) net profit percentage	1.4%	4.2%
(c) stock turnover	10.9 times per year or 4.8 weeks	3.8 times per year or 13.5 weeks
(d) working capital ratio	1.3:1	2.4:1
(e) liquid ratio	0.05:1	1.3:1
(f) debtors' collection period	0.1 weeks*	8.6 weeks
(g) return on capital employed	11%	8.1%

* sales figure used for this calculation; this is unrealistic because most supermarket sales will be for cash rather than on credit

Business A is a grocery supermarket chain; business B the heavy engineering company

Reasons:

Business A low net profit percentage; high stock turnover; short debtors' collection period, low working capital and liquid ratios; few debtors

Business B higher net profit percentage; low stock turnover; long debtors' collection period; good working capital and liquid ratios; high figures for fixed assets and debtors

7.5 **Profitability**

- Gross profit percentage has declined by only one percentage point. Whilst this may have been due to pressures of competition within the industry, the relationship between production costs and sales appears to have been maintained.
- Operating profit has fallen considerably and the reason for this needs to be investigated urgently. It may be that one (or more) of the expense items has increased by proportionately more than any increase in sales; alternatively, a fall in sales has resulted in a lower figure of gross profit, but without a consequent reduction in expenses (perhaps because some of the costs are fixed, rather than variable).
- The very large decline in net profit percentage (much greater than the fall in operating profit percentage) indicates that the company's interest costs have risen: this is confirmed by the increase in capital gearing.
- As a consequence of the above, the return on capital employed has fallen by 50 per cent to a low level that may well not be acceptable to the owners.

Liquidity

- Last year, both the working capital and the liquid ratios were close to the benchmark 'norms'.
- This year, both have fallen to lower levels and the company could well face liquidity problems in the near future.
- The company has borrowed money over the year and now is high geared. This does not leave much scope for further borrowing, should it be needed.

Asset utilisation

- Both stock turnover and debtors' collection period are similar for both years. Both would seem to be acceptable figures for this type of business.
- Creditors' payment period has increased by almost 50 per cent to an unacceptably long 48 days. The company could find that suppliers are reluctant to continue delivering goods and services until they are paid.

Conclusion

A company that appears to be facing a profitability and a liquidity crisis. Action needs to be taken to correct the reasons for the fall in operating profit and net profit percentages. On the balance sheet, working capital and liquid ratios have fallen, whilst capital gearing has increased considerably. The problems indicated by the ratios can be resolved provided that steps are taken very soon.

7.6

Profitability	1994	1995
Gross profit/sales	33.3%	25.0%
Net profit/sales	25.0%	17.5%
Expenses/sales	8.3%	7.5%
Return on capital employed	136.0%*/103.4%§	120.0%*/85.4%§
* opening capital used	§ closing capital used	

Reduction in selling prices is shown by the fall in gross profit/sales percentage. The policy has been successful, as the sales increase has been sufficient to give higher gross and net profits. Expenses/sales percentage has fallen, showing that overheads are under control. The return on capital employed has been reduced, but is still very high.

Liquidity	1994	1995
Working capital ratio	3.33:1	2.16:1
Liquid ratio	2.17:1	1.44:1

Both ratios have fallen, but are still very satisfactory and indicate that the business does not have liquidity problems. The business is nil geared.

Asset utilisation	1994	1995
Stock turnover	32 days	44 days
Debtors' collection period	37 days	66 days
Creditors' payment period	27 days	37 days
Asset turnover ratio	4.14:1	4.88:1

Stock turnover has slowed; debtors' collection period has lengthened – Mr Rowles may have relaxed debtors' terms in order to achieve higher sales; creditors' payment period has lengthened – the creditors may become reluctant to supply the business unless they are paid more promptly. The asset turnover ratio has increased, indicating the policy of increased sales.

Conclusion

A profitable and expanding business. The decision to reduce selling prices has increased turnover and profits. The expansion has not caused liquidity problems, but there are warning signs of possible future problems in the asset utilisation figures. The business provides an excellent return on capital employed.

7.7 Take a logical approach to this Activity. In particular, before calculating the accounting ratios, use the analytical review technique (page 124) to understand the company and to highlight unusual trends and other items.

It is essential to be able to interpret accounting ratios and it may help to think in terms of:

R atio
T rend
C omment

For example, using net profit percentage:

- *Ratio*

  "Net profit percentage measures net profit in relationship to sales and indicates how effectively the company has controlled costs."
- *Trend*

  "For Zed Limited, in 1996 the net profit percentage was 10%; in 1997 it was 8.75%."
- *Comment*

  "The fall in net profit percentage is a worrying sign and indicates a failure to control costs – expenses have increased by a far greater proportion than sales."

Remember that one accounting ratio by itself gives just one viewpoint and, to highlight the cause of a company's difficulties, needs a number of ratios – all of which are likely to point in a similar direction, eg a company in decline, or a company doing well.

This Activity can be developed into a full 'financial exercise' which investigates all aspects of the selected plc's accounts.

CHAPTER 8: THE MANAGEMENT OF WORKING CAPITAL

8.1 (a)
- *current assets,* £17,865
- *current liabilities,* £20,460
- *working capital,* £17,865 – £20,460 = (£2,595), ie negative working capital
- *liquid capital,* (£17,865 – £13,700) – £20,460 = (£16,295), ie negative liquid capital

(b)
- *working capital ratio,* £17,865 ÷ £20,460 = 0.87:1
- *liquid ratio,* £4,165 ÷ £20,460 = 0.20:1

(c)
- *working capital,* (£1,765)
- *liquid capital,* (£14,095)
- *working capital ratio,* 0.90:1
- *liquid ratio,* 0.18:1

Note: stocks £12,330, debtors £1,925, cash £1,230, total £15,485
creditors £13,200, bank overdraft £4,050, total £17,250

The amount of working capital has improved slightly, being the profit of £830 on the stock sold. Liquid capital has improved by £2,200 being the cost of the stock and the profit. However, both working capital and liquid capital are negative. The ratios are low, although they are not untypical of the retail trade.

8.2

	(a)	(b)	(c)	(d)	(e)
Stock	158,000	132,000	138,000	138,000	138,000
Debtors	110,000	120,000	110,000	110,000	110,000
Bank	8,000	8,000	68,000	–	18,000
	276,000	260,000	316,000	248,000	266,000
Creditors	100,000	80,000	80,000	80,000	80,000
Bank overdraft	–	–	–	8,000	–
	176,000	180,000	236,000	160,000	186,000

Working capital ratio	2.76:1	3.25:1	3.95:1	2.82:1	3.32:1
Liquid ratio	1.18:1	1.6:1	2.22:1	1.25:1	1.60:1

All of the working capital and liquid ratios are above the accepted 'norms' of 1.5 – 2.0 and 1.0 respectively. Indeed, the ratios are almost too high, especially under (c); however, the share issue may well have been made with the intention of funding a forthcoming capital expenditure project.

Notice how the amount of working capital is affected by inflows or outflows from activities outside of stocks, debtors, creditors and bank. For example, the share issue, payment of a dividend, and sale proceeds of fixed assets affect the monetary total of working capital.

8.3

- Remember to relate the calculations to the type of business, eg an engineering company will have quite different ratios from a supermarket chain
- Look at the make-up of the working capital cycle:
  - are the number of days for stock, debtors and creditors what you would expect?
  - do the two businesses have similar figures? If not, what are the reasons for the differences?
- It is good practice to calculate the working capital cycle for two consecutive years; then comparisons can be made horizontally. What are the reasons for the changes? Note, however, that a reduction in stock days, while seeming to represent good working capital management, might adversely affect sales if items are regularly out of stock. Likewise, an increase in creditor days could well cause problems with suppliers declining to deliver more goods and services until they are paid promptly.

8.4

	1995	*1996*	*differences*
Stock turnover	63 days	80 days	17 days
Debtors' collection	24 days	36 days	12 days
	87 days	116 days	29 days
Less creditors' payment	36 days	51 days	15 days
Working capital cycle	51 days	65 days	14 days

- Stock turnover has slowed. Which stock lines are affected? Is any of the stock unsaleable?
- Debtors' collection period has increased. What are the stated terms of payment? Have debtors signed a credit agreement with the company? Are there any bad debts?
- Extra credit is being taken from creditors. This could lead to supply problems in the future. Can extra credit terms be negotiated with major suppliers?

8.5 (a) The discussion should centre around the following points:

- Increased sales – up 324 per cent
- Increased net profit – up by £26,000 or 4.3 per cent
- An analysis of the profit and loss account to show those costs which have increased proportionately more than sales. This can be used to explain why the percentage increase in sales is not affected in a similar increase in profits
- Note especially the increase in interest paid
- Aspects of the balance sheet, particularly liquidity, gearing and return on capital employed, and including the way in which the capital investment has been financed
- Accounting ratios include:

	1996	*1997*
– gross profit percentage	60%	41.25%
– operating profit percentage	34.89%	17.88%
– net profit percentage	33.56%	10.79%
– return on capital employed	30.52%	18.18%
– gearing	10.77%	125.79%
– working capital ratio	3.47:1	4.44:1
– liquid ratio	2.64:1	3.13:1
– stock turnover*	30 days	52 days
– debtors' collection period*	34 days	73 days
– creditors' payment period*	36 days	37 days

* using year-end figures; for debtors, assuming that all sales are on credit; for creditors, using cost of sales instead of purchases

(b)

- The new debtors figure under this proposal will be £720,000, so generating £446,000 of cash

- A bonus issue of shares has no effect on the cash position
- The new stock figure under this proposal will be £376,000, so generating £110,000 of cash
- 328,000 new shares will be issued at £1.50 each, so generating £492,000 of cash.

Other points include:

- effect on sales of reducing debtor days; also the possibility of using debt factoring
- the balance sheet management benefits of converting some of the revenue reserves into share capital
- the need to maintain sufficient stocks to meet customer demand
- the effect of the rights issue on gearing; also the need for existing shareholders to take up the rights issue if they do not wish to see their holdings diluted

8.6

	JUN	JUL	AUG	SEP	OCT
Current assets	£	£	£	£	£
Stock	7,000	27,000	7,000	7,000	7,000
Debtors	1,100	1,100	31,100	31,100	1,100
Bank	1,200	1,200	1,200	–	11,200
	9,300	29,300	39,300	38,100	19,300
Less current liabilities					
Creditors	3,300	23,300	23,300	3,300	3,300
Bank overdraft	–	–	–	18,800	–
WORKING CAPITAL	6,000	6,000	16,000	16,000	16,000
Working capital ratio	2.82:1	1.26:1	1.69:1	1.72:1	5.85:1
Liquid ratio	0.70:1	0.10:1	1.39:1	1.40:1	3.73:1

The business becomes very illiquid in July; bank overdraft facilities will need to be negotiated. Danger of bad debts (credit references to be taken) but, if transactions are completed satisfactorily, there are large profits.

CHAPTER 9: INTRODUCTION TO COST AND COSTING SYSTEMS

9.1 (a)

- The principle behind this Activity is the identification of relevant costs
- Whilst the type of organisation selected may well not fit with the exact layout for a manufacturing business, as shown in fig 9.1, the Activity should generate thought and discussion of costs involved
- As an example, an outline of the costs incurred by a school or college is as follows:

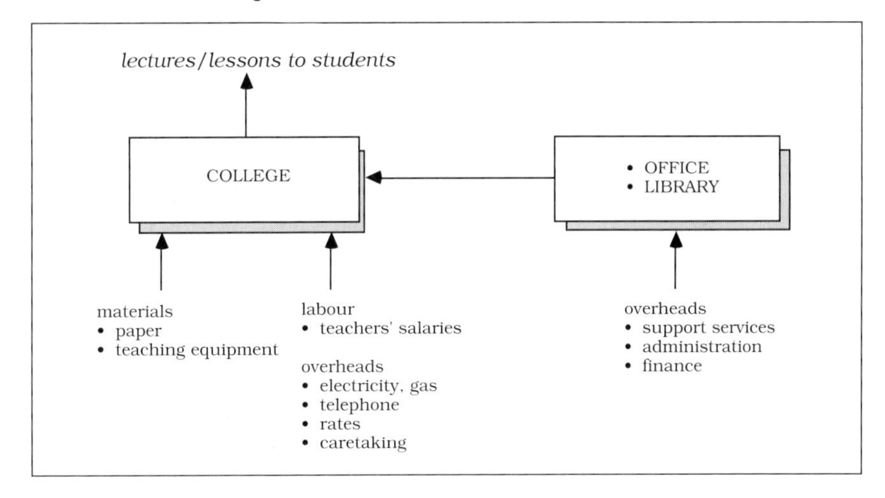

(b)

- For this part of the Activity, identify the main sections of the organisation and the costs which each incurs. Does the costing system in use identify these sections as cost centres? If not, what are the cost centres that should be used?
- Are cost units identified, and are they relevant to the organisation?

9.2 (a) See text, page 166.

(b)

- raw materials: variable
- factory rent: fixed
- telephone: semi-variable
- direct labour: variable
- indirect labour: fixed
- commission to sales staff: variable

Classifying costs by nature identifies them as being fixed, variable, or semi-variable. This helps with decision making – the business might be able to alter the balance between fixed and variable costs in order to increase profits. For example, a furniture manufacturing business will have to make decisions on whether to use direct labour (variable cost) or machinery (fixed cost) for many of the production processes. The decision will be based very much on the expected level of sales, ie for lower sales it is likely to make greater use of direct labour, while for higher sales a more machine-intensive method of production might be used.

9.3

• tubular steel	direct materials
• factory supervisor's salary	indirect labour
• wages of employee operating moulding machine	direct labour
• works canteen assistant's wages	indirect labour
• rates of factory	indirect expenses
• power to operate machines	indirect expenses*
• factory heating and lighting	indirect expenses
• plastic for making chair seats	direct materials
• hire of special machinery for one particular order	direct expenses
• cost of oil for the moulding machine	indirect materials
• depreciation of factory machinery	indirect expenses
• depreciation of office equipment	indirect expenses

* Note: The cost of power to operate machines has been classified above as an indirect expense. This is often the case because it is not worthwhile for the management accountant to analyse the cost of power for each unit of production. An industry that uses a lot of power will often have meters fitted to each machine so that costs may be identified and allocated to production as a direct expense. Other, lesser users of power, are unlikely to calculate the separate cost and will consider power to be an indirect expense.

9.4

(a) cleaning materials for the machines: indirect materials

(b) wages of factory supervisor: indirect labour

(c) clay from which pots are made: direct materials

(d) royalty paid to designer: direct expenses

(e) salary of office clerk: indirect expenses*

(f) electricity used to heat the kilns: indirect expense (or possible a direct expense – see note to question 9.3, above)

(g) rates of factory: indirect expense

(h) depreciation of office equipment: indirect expense

(i) wages of production line workers: direct labour

(j) salesperson's salary: indirect expenses*

(k) interest charged on bank overdraft: indirect expenses

* Note: Both the salary of the office clerk and the salesperson's salary have been classified as indirect expenses, rather than indirect labour. This is because neither of them work in the factory and so the cost cannot be attributed directly to production. By contrast, the

wages of the factory supervisor are classified as indirect labour – here the employee does work in the factory, and the cost is more closely linked to production.

- *factory overheads:* (a), (b), (f), (g)
- *selling and distribution overheads:* (j)
- *administration overheads:* (e), (h)
- *finance overheads:* (k)

9.5 (a)

Hughes Limited
Total cost statement for the year ended 31 December 1996

	£	£
Direct materials		118,830
Direct labour*		117,315
PRIME COST		236,145
Factory overheads:		
rent and rates	16,460	
factory power	3,825	
factory heat and light	1,185	
factory expenses and maintenance	4,095	
depreciation of factory plant and machinery	3,725	
		29,290
PRODUCTION COST		265,435
Selling and distribution costs:		
advertising		11,085
Administration costs:		
office salaries and wages	69,350	
office expenses	3,930	
		73,280
TOTAL COST		349,800

* *Note:* It has been assumed in the cost statement that all of the factory wages are direct labour. With additional information, it would be possible to split the cost between direct and indirect labour.

(b)

Hughes Limited
Profit statement for the year ended 31 December 1996

		£
	Sales	426,350
less	Total cost	349,800
	PROFIT	76,550

Note: It is assumed that all the goods manufactured have been sold.

9.6 (a)

Absorption cost per pair of trainers	£
direct materials (per pair)	15.00
direct labour (per pair)	12.00
PRIME COST (per pair)	27.00
overheads (fixed) £245,000 ÷ 25,000 pairs	9.80
ABSORPTION COST (per pair)	36.80

(b)

Marginal cost per pair of trainers	£
direct materials (per pair)	15.00
direct labour (per pair)	12.00
MARGINAL COST (per pair)	27.00

(c)

John Walker Limited
Profit statement: 25,000 pairs of trainers

	£	£
sales (25,000 x £40)		1,000,000
direct materials (25,000 x £15)	375,000	
direct labour (25,000 x £12)	300,000	
PRIME COST	675,000	
overheads (fixed)	245,000	
TOTAL COST		920,000
PROFIT		80,000

9.7 *Standard cost of producing 100 castings*

	£	£
materials		
550 kg of ordinary steel at £3.50 per kg,	1,925.00	
200 kg of high tensile steel at £10.00 per kg	2,000.00	
		3,925.00
labour		
60 hours of foundry-workers' wages at £10.50 per hour	630.00	
155 hours in machine shop at £12.75 per hour	1,976.25	
		2,606.25
		6,531.25
overheads (factory and office)		
210 hours at £25.00 per hour		5,250.00
STANDARD COST		11,781.25

9.8 (a) *calculation of weekly overheads for set ups and quality inspections*

			£	£
set ups:	product A	5 x £250	1,250	
	product B	50 x £250	12,500	
				13,750
quality inspection:	product A	5 x £150	750	
	product B	50 x £150	7,500	
				8,250
TOTAL				22,000

At present the weekly overheads are charged on the basis of labour hours:

	£
product A (500 hours)	11,000
product B (500 hours)	11,000
TOTAL	22,000

(b) *activity based costing:*

	£	£
product A		
5 set ups at £250	1,250	
5 quality inspections £150	750	
		2,000
product B		
50 set ups at £250	12,500	
50 quality inspections £150	7,500	
		20,000
TOTAL		22,000

(c)
- By using the activity based costing system, there is a more accurate reflection of the cost of demand on the support functions of set up and quality inspection.
- The cost of 50,000 units of product A is reduced by £9,000 (ie £11,000 – £2,000), while the cost of 50,000 units of product B is increased by £9,000 (ie from £11,000 to £20,000).
- This may well have implications for the viability of product B, and for the selling prices of both products.

CHAPTER 10: OVERHEAD ANALYSIS AND METHODS OF COSTING

10.1 (a) The discussion should include:

- the inputs and outputs of the organisation
- whether the outputs (goods/services) are identical or different
- the way in which the outputs are achieved
- how the outputs are costed

(b) The method of costing for each business should be justified; however, the following are the most likely methods:

- *oil refinery* – process costing, because of the continuous nature of the operation
- *accountant* – job costing, because each job will take a different length of time and is likely to involve a number of staff, each with different skill levels
- *bus company* – service costing, where the object is to find the cost per unit of service, eg passenger mile; job costing used for 'one-offs', eg quoting for the transport for a trip to the seaside for an old people's home
- *baker* – batch costing, where identical units are produced in batches, eg loaves; job costing could be used for 'one-off' items, eg a wedding cake
- *sports centre* – service costing, or job costing for 'one-off', eg hire of the main sports hall for an exhibition
- *hotel* – different methods of costing are likely to be used, eg service costing for the rooms, batch costing in the restaurant, and job costing for special events

10.2 (a) and (b)

Cost	Basis of apportionment	Total £	Machining £	Finishing £	Maintenance £
Rent and rates	Floor area	5,520	2,760	1,840	920
Buildings insurance	Floor area	1,320	660	440	220
Machinery insurance	Value of machinery	1,650	1,200	450	–
Lighting & heating	Floor area	3,720	1,860	1,240	620
Depn. of machinery	Value of machinery	11,000	8,000	3,000	–
Supervisory salaries	No. of employees	30,000	18,000	9,000	3,000
Maintenance Dept salary	Allocation	16,000	–	–	16,000
Factory cleaning	Floor area	4,800	2,400	1,600	800
		74,010	34,880	17,570	21,560
Re-apportionment of maintenance dept.	Value of machinery	–	15,680	5,880	(21,560)
		74,010	50,560	23,450	–

(c) 35 hours x 47 weeks = 1,645 direct labour hours per employee

Machining Dept: 6 employees = 9,870 hours = £5.12 per direct labour hour

Finishing Dept: 3 employees = 4,935 hours = £4.75 per direct labour hour

(d) Depending on the method and type of production, the company could use overhead absorption rates based on:

- units of output
- direct labour hour
- machine hour

These are discussed in the text (pages 193 to 195); in addition, the company could consider the use of activity based costing (pages 176 to 179). Alternative methods could be based on a percentage of certain costs, eg direct wages.

10.3 (a) $\frac{\text{total overheads}}{\text{total hours}} = \frac{\text{£59,900}}{\text{3,290}} =$ £18.21 per partner hour

(b) $\frac{\text{£59,900 + £60,000}}{\text{3,290}} =$ £36.44 per partner hour

(c) 2 hours x 47 weeks x £18.21 = £1,711.74 per partner (ie £3,423.48 in total)

10.4 (a) Units of output: 80 + 40 = 120 units per month = £8.33 per unit.

Direct labour hour: (3 hours x 80 seats) + (3.5 hours x 40 seats) = 380 direct labour hours per month = £2.63 per hour.

Machine hour: (1 hour x 80 seats) + (2.5 hours x 40 seats) = 180 machine hours per month = £5.56 per hour.

Alternative methods could be based on a percentage of certain costs, eg direct labour.

(b) *Units of output*

'Standard' £36.50 + £8.33 = £44.83

'De Luxe' £55.00 + £8.33 = £63.33

Direct labour hour

'Standard' £36.50 + £7.89 = £44.39

'De Luxe' £55.00 + £9.21 = £64.21

Machine hour

'Standard' £36.50 + £5.56 = £42.06

'De Luxe' £55.00 + £13.89 = £68.89

(c) See text. Units of output method charges same amount to different models; machine hour rate charges most to 'de luxe' model. On balance, direct labour hours may be the best method to use because the products are more labour-intensive than machine-intensive.

10.5 (a)

	500 copies	1,000 copies	2,000 copies
	£	£	£
Fixed costs:			
Setting up machine	60.00	60.00	60.00
Artwork	84.00	84.00	84.00
Typesetting	300.00	300.00	300.00
Direct materials:			
Paper	100.00	200.00	400.00
Other printing consumables	50.00	100.00	200.00
Direct labour	65.00	130.00	260.00
Overheads	52.00	104.00	208.00
COST PRICE	711.00	978.00	1,512.00
Profit (25% of cost price)	177.75	244.50	378.00
SELLING PRICE	888.75	1,222.50	1,890.00

(b) Cost per book to author	£1.78	£1.22	£0.95

(c) Point out high fixed costs which must be met however many copies are printed. Variable cost of production is only £0.53 per copy.

10.6

Process 1	£6,044	(including £744 production overheads)
Process 2	£2,466	(including £496 production overheads)
Process 3	£2,665	(including £620 production overheads)
	£11,175	

Cost per litre

Process 1	£0.242
Process 2	£0.099
Process 3	£0.107
Total cost per litre	£0.448

10.7

Cost element	Costs	Completed Units	Work-in-progress			Total Equivalent Units	Cost per Unit	WIP valuation
			Units	% complete	Equivalent Units			
	A	B	C	D	E C x D	F B + E	G A ÷ F	H E x G
	£						£	£
Direct materials	97,300	18,000	7,000	100	7,000	25,000	3.892	27,244
Direct labour	43,650	18,000	7,000	50	3,500	21,500	2.030	7,105
Production overheads	50,700	18,000	7,000	50	3,500	21,500	2.358	8,253
Total	191,650						8.280	42,602

18,000 completed units at £8.28 each	=	£149,040.00
work-in-progress valuation	=	£ 42,602.00
total costs for month	=	£191,642.00 *

* Note that the discrepancy of £8 (ie £191,650 – £191,642) is caused by working column G to only three decimal places.

10.8 *Total costs:*

	£
Depreciation of diesel trains* £30,000 x 6 trains	180,000
Leasing charges for track	500,000
Maintenance charges for trains	455,000
Fuel for trains	105,000
Wages of drivers and conductors	240,000
Administration	260,000
	1,740,000

* (£650,000 – £50,000) ÷ 20 years = £30,000 per train per year

Cost per passenger mile:

$$\frac{£1{,}740{,}000}{2.5\text{m journeys} \times 5 \text{ miles}} = £0.1392$$

CHAPTER 11: COST BEHAVIOUR AND BREAK-EVEN ANALYSIS

11.1

- This Activity focuses on the nature of costs.
- For the section of the organisation, classify costs into:
  - fixed
  - variable
  - semi-variable (there is no need to subdivide between the fixed and variable elements)
- Look at the effect on costs if output doubles:
  - fixed costs may well remain unchanged unless new assets, eg premises, have had to be acquired (note the stepped nature of fixed costs)
  - variable costs, in theory, will double, but there may well be savings at higher levels of output, eg bulk buying
  - semi-variable costs will increase, but the main part of the increase will be in the variable element
- The relationship between fixed and variable costs can be examined, even if it is not in the form of a break-even analysis; for example, the introduction of technology to automate a labour-intensive process can apply to virtually all organisations – the use of a new switchboard, or a faster photocopier with a stapling facility. Show how the costs of such proposals were used by management in the decision-making process.

11.2

- This Activity applies the costs and revenues (or savings) to the concept of break-even.
- All the costs (including semi-variable) must be identified and allocated to either fixed costs or variable costs.
- The margin of safety is an important concept which measures the 'cushion' which current production/sales gives beyond the break-even point.
- Critically examine the balance between fixed and variable costs and sales revenue. Are fixed costs a large proportion of total costs? If so, what are the implications if there should be a downturn or an upturn in sales? What if fixed costs are a small proportion of total costs? How sensitive is sales revenue to changes in economic conditions?

11.3 table method

units of production	fixed costs	variable costs	total cost	sales revenue	profit/(loss)*
	£	£	£	£	£
100	12,000	2,000	14,000	3,500	(10,500)
200	12,000	4,000	16,000	7,000	(9,000)
300	12,000	6,000	18,000	10,500	(7,500)
400	12,000	8,000	20,000	14,000	(6,000)
500	12,000	10,000	22,000	17,500	(4,500)
600	12,000	12,000	24,000	21,000	(3,000)
700	12,000	14,000	26,000	24,500	(1,500)
800	12,000	16,000	28,000	28,000	nil
900	12,000	18,000	30,000	31,500	1,500
1,000	12,000	20,000	32,000	35,000	3,000
1,100	12,000	22,000	34,000	38,500	4,500
1,200	12,000	24,000	36,000	42,000	6,000

* brackets indicate a loss

graph method

Note: for illustrative purposes, a break-even graph is shown for this question only.

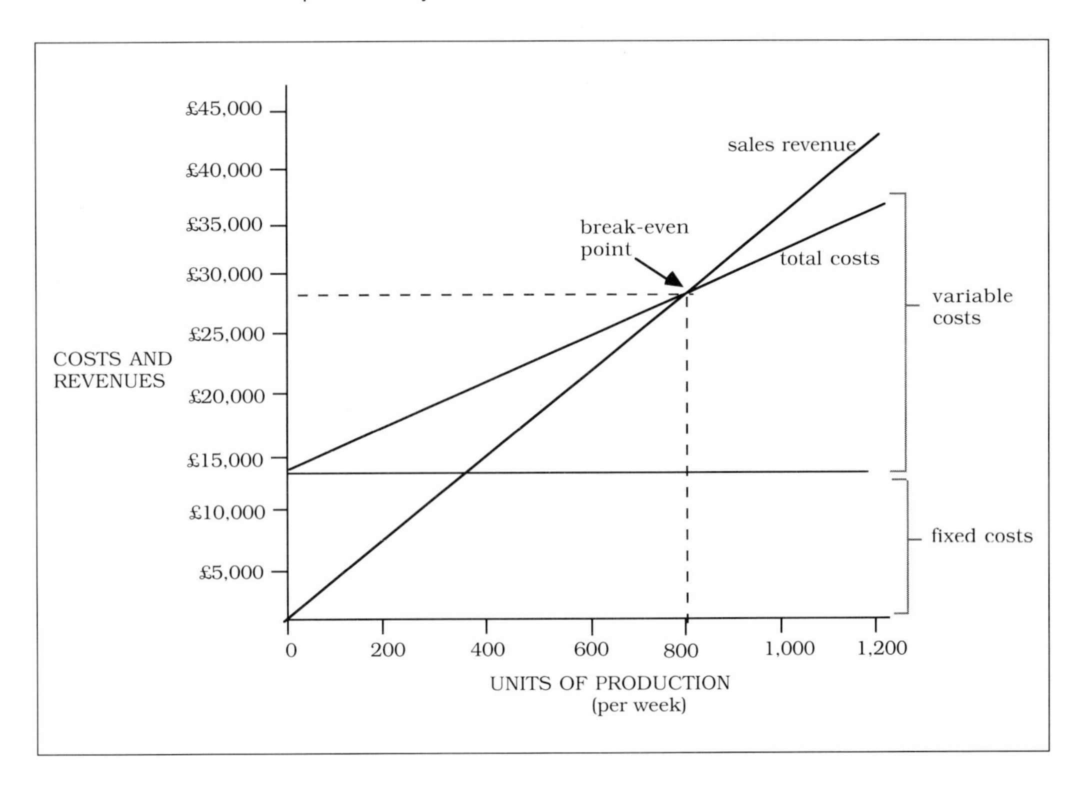

calculation method

Fixed costs of £12,000 ÷ contribution of £15 per bat = 800 bats to break-even.

profit/(loss)

- *200 bats*

	£
Sales (£35 per bat)	7,000
Less variable costs (£20 per bat)	4,000
Contribution	3,000
Less fixed costs	12,000
Loss for month	(9,000)

- *1,200 bats*

	£
Sales (£35 per bat)	42,000
Less variable costs (£20 per bat)	24,000
Contribution	18,000
Less fixed costs	12,000
Profit for month	6,000

margin of safety

$$\frac{\text{current output} - \text{break-even output}}{\text{current output}} \times \frac{100}{1} = \frac{1,000 - 8,000}{1,000}$$

= 20 per cent, or 200 units

11.4 table method

petrol (litres)	fixed costs	variable costs	total cost	sales revenue	profit/(loss)
	£	£	£	£	£
1,000	750	600	1,350	650	(700)
2,000	750	1,200	1,950	1,300	(650)
3,000	750	1,800	2,550	1,950	(600)
4,000	750	2,400	3,150	2,600	(550)
5,000	750	3,000	3,750	3,250	(500)
6,000	750	3,600	4,350	3,900	(450)
7,000	750	4,200	4,950	4,550	(400)
8,000	750	4,800	5,550	5,200	(350)
9,000	750	5,400	6,150	5,850	(300)
10,000	750	6,000	6,750	6,500	(250)
11,000	750	6,600	7,350	7,150	(200)
12,000	750	7,200	7,950	7,800	(150)
13,000	750	7,800	8,550	8,450	(100)
14,000	750	8,400	9,150	9,100	(50)
15,000	750	9,000	9,750	9,750	nil
16,000	750	9,600	10,350	10,400	50
17,000	750	10,200	10,950	11,050	100
18,000	750	10,800	11,550	11,700	150
19,000	750	11,400	12,150	12,350	200
20,000	750	12,000	12,750	13,000	250

graph method
Not shown

calculation method
Fixed costs of £750 ÷ contribution of £0.05 per litre = 15,000 litres to break-even.

profit/(loss)

- *12,000 litres*

	£
Sales (65p per litre)	7,800
Less variable costs (60p per litre)	7,200
Contribution	600
Less fixed costs	750
Loss for week	(150)

- *18,000 litres*

	£
Sales (65p per litre)	11,700
Less variable costs (60p per litre)	10,800
Contribution	900
Less fixed costs	750
Profit for week	150

margin of safety

$$\frac{18{,}000 \text{ litres} - 15{,}000 \text{ litres}}{18{,}000 \text{ litres}} \times \frac{100}{1} = 16.67 \text{ per cent, or } 3{,}000 \text{ litres}$$

11.5 (a) 9,000 units: £12,000 loss
12,000 units: break-even point
15,000 units: £12,000 profit
20,000 units: £32,000 profit

(b) The break-even point is at 12,000 units made and sold – see (a).

(c) Fixed amount of production overheads £30,000 (£2 per unit of overheads is variable).

	£
At 25,000 units of production:	
direct materials	75,000
direct labour	25,000
production overheads	80,000
administration, selling and distribution expenses	18,000
	198,000
sales revenue	250,000
profit	52,000

Limitations of calculation: see text.

11.6 (a) *Method 1*

Contribution: £60 - £35 = £25 per unit

Fixed costs: £60,000 + £40,000 (depreciation) + £48,000 (20% return on capital) = £148,000

Break-even point: 5,920 units

Method 2

Contribution: £60 - £45 = £15 per unit

Fixed costs: £29,000 + £16,000 (depreciation) + £24,000 (20% return on capital) = £69,000

Break-even point: 4,600 units

(b) On the face of it, Method 2 is more attractive – lower investment, earlier break-even, and required return on capital at a lower production level.

However, at maximum available production level, Method 1 produces more profit, eg 4,080 beyond break-even equals £102,000 after return on capital, as compared with Method 2 – 5,400 units beyond break-even is £81,000 after return on capital.

At higher production levels potentially higher profit is available from Method 1's higher contribution per unit.

Algebraically, or by using a break-even chart, break-even profit (ie identical profit for 1 and 2) arises on a production of 7,900 units*.

Beyond break-even profit, the higher contribution of Method 1 provides £10 more profit per unit. Below break-even profit, Method 2 with its lower contribution per unit (£10 less) shows the smaller loss or greater profit.

Summary

The method to be selected should therefore be related to the probable production/sales levels of units, ie beyond an average of 7,900 units use Method 1; below, use Method 2.

* calculated by formula: Method 1 F + VQ = Method 2 F + VQ, where:

F = fixed costs

V = variable cost per unit

Q = quantity of units sold

Thus:	£148,000 + £25Q	= £69,000 + £15Q
	£25Q – £15Q	= £148,000 – £69,000
	£10Q	= £79,000
	Q	= £79,000 + £10
	Q	= 7,900 units

CHAPTER 12: MARGINAL COSTING

12.1 (a)
- Check the limiting factors listed on page 239 against the organisation you are investigating.
- Which one do you see as being the main limiting factor?
- Can it be overcome by maximising contribution from some sections of the organisation to the detriment of others? How will this affect the organisation as a whole?

(b)
- Consider the relevance of the use of marginal costing to the organisation. For example, consider the application of:
  - decisions about products/departments that do not make a profit;
  - the use of spare capacity for special orders;
  - make or buy decisions;
  - the allocation of scarce resources.
- If marginal costing is used, what problems will be created? See page 242 for possible points.

12.2 There are a wide range of marginal costing applications in the service industries mentioned. For example:

- *hotel*
  - 'bargain break' weekends to make use of rooms occupied by business people during the week
  - last minute bookings, which are discounted from the normal tariff
- *transport*
  - season tickets
  - weekend fares
  - cheaper fares after the morning rush
  - discounts for categories of people in slack travel months
- *cinema or theatre*
  - standing or cheap tickets released only on the day of the performance
  - 'half-price' ticket booths on day of performance
  - special cheap ticket deals with transport companies
  - family tickets
- *holiday companies*
  - discounts for last minute bookings to fill empty places on planes and at hotels
  - discounts for early bookings, which help with planning the travel companies' operations
  - special deals with transport companies
  - off-peak prices

Consider also the benefits and restrictions/problems for both the customer and the supplier. Often only a limited number of products are available at special prices, or there are restrictions on the time that they are available. The major disadvantage for the supplier is that those customers who have paid the full price will be disgruntled when they learn the lower price paid by others.

12.3 • The first step is to present the financial results in order to show the contribution made by each department:

	shrubs and trees *£000s*	*plants* *£000s*	*hardware* *£000s*	*coffee shop* *£000s*	*total* *£000s*
Sales	150	200	100	60	510
Materials	50	60	45	30	185
Labour	35	40	15	20	110
VARIABLE COSTS	85	100	60	50	295
CONTRIBUTION	65	100	40	10	215
Overheads (fixed)					153
PROFIT					62

- This shows that each department makes a contribution towards the fixed overheads of the business. The contribution/sales ratios are:

shrubs and trees $\frac{£65,000}{£150,000}$ = 0.43 or 43%

plants $\frac{£100,000}{£200,000}$ = 0.50 or 50%

hardware $\frac{£40,000}{£100,000}$ = 0.40 or 40%

coffee shop $\frac{£10,000}{£60,000}$ = 0.17 or 17%

- Before taking the decision to close the coffee shop, points to consider include:
  - as the coffee shop makes a contribution of £10,000 towards fixed overheads, its closure means that overall profits will fall to £52,000 (assuming that fixed overheads do not reduce in the short-term)
  - closure of the coffee shop may well have implications for sales in the other departments, eg some customers will call in for coffee, and then buy other items from the garden centre
  - the floor space currently occupied by the coffee shop could be used for other retailing purposes; will this give a higher contribution than £10,000 per year?

12.4 *Absorption cost per seat (based on sixty seats sold)*

		£
direct materials	£12.50 x 60	750.00
direct labour	£10.00 x 60	600.00
direct expenses	£2.50 x 60	150.00
fixed overheads		3,500.00
TOTAL COST		5,000.00

The absorption cost per seat is £5,000 ÷ 60 = £83.33

Marginal cost per seat

	£
direct materials	12.50
direct labour	10.00
direct expenses	2.50
MARGINAL COST (per seat)	25.00

Profit or loss if no further tickets sold

	£
revenue 60 seats at £100 each	6,000.00
less total cost (see above)	5,000.00
PROFIT	1,000.00

profit statements

	60 seats sold	60 seats + 30 sold to travel firm	60 seats + 40 sold to newspaper
	£	£	£
sales revenue for flight:			
60 seats at £100 each	6,000	6,000	6,000
30 seats at £45 each	–	1,350	–
40 seats at £35 each	–	–	1,400
	6,000	7,350	7,400
less costs:			
direct materials (£12.50 per passenger)	750	1,125	1,250
direct labour (£10 per passenger)	600	900	1,000
direct expenses (£2.50 per passenger)	150	225	250
fixed overheads	3,500	3,500	3,500
PROFIT	1,000	1,600	1,400

The conclusion is that the offer from the firm selling cheap flights should be taken up, while the newspaper offer should not be considered on this occasion. The contribution (selling price minus marginal cost) is 30 seats x (£45 – £25) = £600; the newspaper provides a contribution of 40 seats x (£35 – £25) = £400. So, provided that the flights firm can sell more than 20 seats, the contribution will be greater than that from the newspaper.

12.5 *Absorption cost*

	£
direct materials (per pair)	20.00
direct labour (per pair)	18.00
PRIME COST (per pair)	38.00
overheads (fixed) £200,000 ÷ 12,500 pairs	16.00
ABSORPTION COST (per pair)	54.00

Marginal cost

	£
direct materials (per pair)	20.00
direct labour (per pair)	18.00
MARGINAL COST (per pair)	38.00

Profit or loss at existing production of 12,500 pairs of boots, see below

THE LAST COMPANY

profit statements	Existing production 12,500 pairs of boots £	Existing production + 2,500 pairs @ £45 each £	Existing production + 5,000 pairs @ £37 each £
sales revenue (per week):			
12,500 pairs at £60 per pair	750,000	750,000	750,000
2,500 pairs at £45 per pair	–	112,500	–
5,000 pairs at £37 per pair	–	–	185,000
	750,000	862,500	935,000
less production costs:			
direct materials (£20 per pair)	250,000	300,000	350,000
direct labour (£18 per pair)	225,000	270,000	315,000
overheads (fixed)	200,000	200,000	200,000
PROFIT	75,000	92,500	70,000

- The conclusion is that the first 'special order' from the mail order company should be undertaken, and the second declined.
- Under the first special order, the price is £7 above marginal cost (£45 – £38 = £7); thus profits increase by £17,500 (2,500 pairs x £7) to £92,500
- With the second special order, the price is £1 below marginal cost; thus profits decrease by £5,000 (5,000 pairs x £1) to £70,000

- The rule is that, once the overheads have been recovered, provided additional units can be sold at a price above marginal cost, then profits will increase

12.6

- The solution is to switch production to the product which gives the highest contribution from each unit of the limiting factor
- As the limiting factor is direct materials, the company should maximise the contribution from each kilo of materials:
  - product A: contribution per kilo is £30 ÷ 2 kg = £15 per kg
  - product B: contribution per kilo is £50 ÷ 4 kg = £12.50 per kg
- Therefore, the company should utilise fully its direct materials in manufacturing product A, ie 250 units will be made (500 kg ÷ 2 kg per unit)
- The forecast weekly profit statement will be as follows:

forecast weekly profit statement

	£
sales of product A (250 units x £150)	37,500
contribution (250 units x £30)	7,500
less overheads (fixed)	4,000
PROFIT	3,500

- Note however that, by taking this action, no units of product B will be produced – the marketing director will not be too keen on this as it may be difficult to re-establish the product in the market when production can be restarted following an increase in supplies of direct materials. In practice, it is likely that both models will be made, but with preference being given to product A.

12.7 *Buying from the Far East*

The marginal cost of producing each pair of the 'Paris' design pair of shoes is:

	£
direct materials	10.00
direct labour	5.00
variable overheads	3.00
marginal cost	18.00

Although the Far Eastern supplier's price of £20 per pair of shoes is below the absorption cost of £23, it is £2 (£20 – £18) above the marginal cost of in-house manufacture.

As there is no other use for the factory space and production machinery currently used to make the 'Paris' design, the financial decision should be to continue in-house manufacture.

Other considerations

- Will it be possible, in the future, to use the factory space and production machinery currently used for the 'Paris' design for other purposes? If so, what contribution is likely from these other purposes?
- If the company considers buying in from the Far East, it must be sure of the supplier's abilities regarding:
  - quality
  - reliability
  - price
  - confidentiality
  - legal requirements and other standards

12.8 *In-house manufacture*

Marginal cost of manufacture per pump motor:

	£
direct materials	40.00
direct labour	25.00
variable overheads	20.00
marginal cost	85.00

The marginal cost of making 3,500 pump motors per year:

	£
3,500 units at £85	= 297,500
plus contribution which will be lost from 'olde worlde' handpumps: 750 units at £250 – £150	= 75,000
	372,500
Buying in cost from outside supplier	
3,500 units at £95	332,500

Therefore, by buying in pump motors from an outside supplier, the company has the potential to increase profits by £40,000 (£372,500 – £332,500).

CHAPTER 13: PRICING DECISIONS

13.1 This Activity is concerned with the use of relevant costs in decision-making. Identify which of the following costs were used:

- sunk costs
- notional costs
- opportunity costs
- differential costs
- cost benefit analysis

Assess how relevant each of the costs was in the decision-making process. Did management have sufficient or too much information when making the decision? If alternative causes of action were considered, which costs and revenues were considered?

13.2

- The factors influencing the pricing of goods or services will include:
  - the need to make a profit
  - prices of competing products
  - under-used capacity

  Show why the prices of the goods or services of the organisation are influenced by these factors. If transfer pricing is used, how are these influenced by the above factors?
- The pricing strategy is likely to be based on:
  - cost-plus pricing
  - market led pricing
  - marginal cost/contribution pricing

  Consider how the price is calculated in relation to the pricing strategy. Are there variations of pricing strategy within the organisation? If transfer pricing is used, what basis is used for establishing the price – marginal cost, full cost, market price, negotiation?

13.3 *25 per cent mark-up on cost price*

	£
total costs	950,000
25 per cent mark-up (25% x £950,000)	237,500
selling price	1,187,500

The price per minor operation will be:

£1,187,500 ÷ 2,500 operations = £475 per operation

20 per cent return on capital employed

	£
total costs	950,000
20 per cent return on capital (20% x £1,000,000)	200,000
selling price	1,150,000

The price per minor operation will be:

£1,150,000 ÷ 2,500 operations = £460 per operation

13.4

- The objective of establishing a transfer price is to allow the producer of the output to be paid by the recipient for the cost and effort incurred by production.
- The basis for establishing a transfer price – marginal cost, full cost, market price, negotiation – can be discussed and linked to the objective.
- Whatever the transfer price, it has no effect on the overall profitability of the organisation.
- The transfer price provides a benchmark against which performance can be measured.
- Running the internal information technology course will involve a number of opportunity costs, principally:
  - staff time, both for teachers and for computer technician staff

- use of the computer room
- stationery requirements, such as floppy disks, listing paper, handouts
- administration

There may be grants or funding available to offset some of these costs.

- The price for the course could be based on any of the methods for establishing a transfer price. However, it is unlikely that the Department of Management will wish to pay the full cost or the market price. In practice a marginal cost or negotiated price will be agreed, based on the cost of the time of the teaching staff; alternatively, the Department of Management might offer the Department of Computing a management course requiring the same amount of staff time!

CHAPTER 14: CAPITAL INVESTMENT APPRAISAL

14.1

- This Activity requires an investigation of all aspects of a capital investment appraisal project. The size of the project can vary from the relatively small, such as a new photocopier, to something more major, such as the commissioning of a new or relocated department of the organisation.
- As well as the non-financial aspects of the project, ascertain the investment appraisal techniques used by the organisation. Does the organisation require projects to satisfy more than one technique, eg "projects must pay back within three years, *and* give a positive net present value at a cost of capital of 10 per cent"?
- For discounted cash flow techniques, how does the organisation establish the cost of capital to be used?
- The audit of the project (see page 263) is important for ensuring that costs are in line with the estimates. Once a project has been approved, how carefully is it then monitored within the organisation? What happens if there are variances between estimates and actual results?

14.2 (a) Project Exe pays back after two years

Project Wye pays back after three years

(b) Project Exe

	Cash Flow		*Discount Factor*		*Discounted Cash Flow*
	£				£
Year 0	(80,000)	x	1.000	=	(80,000)
Year 1	40,000	x	0.893	=	35,720
Year 2	40,000	x	0.797	=	31,880
Year 3	20,000	x	0.712	=	14,240
Year 4	10,000	x	0.636	=	6,360
Year 5	10,000	x	0.567	=	5,670
		Net Present Value (NPV)		=	13,870

Project Wye

	Cash Flow		*Discount Factor*		*Discounted Cash Flow*
	£				£
Year 0	(100,000)	x	1.000	=	(100,000)
Year 1	20,000	x	0.893	=	17,860
Year 2	30,000	x	0.797	=	23,910
Year 3	50,000	x	0.712	=	35,600
Year 4	50,000	x	0.636	=	31,800
Year 5	49,000	x	0.567	=	27,783
			Net Present Value (NPV)	=	36,953

(c) Project Exe

$$\frac{£120{,}000 - £80{,}000}{5 \text{ years}} \times \frac{100}{£40{,}000} = 20 \text{ per cent}$$

Project Wye

$$\frac{£199{,}000 - £100{,}000}{5 \text{ years}} \times \frac{100}{£50{,}000} = 39.6 \text{ per cent}$$

- No one project appraisal technique is entirely satisfactory by itself (see chapter for advantages and disadvantages)
- Project Wye has higher NPV (and higher initial investment) and accounting rate of return, but longer payback – the latter could be a major disadvantage if likely to be out-of-date very soon
- See also internal rate of return (Activity 14.4)

14.3

	Cash Flow		*Discount Factor*		*Discounted Cash Flow*
	£				£
Outright purchases					
Year 0	(10,000)	x	1.000	=	(10,000)
Year 5	1,000	x	0.621	=	621
			Net Present Value (NPV)	=	(9,379)
Hire purchase					
Year 0	(4,000)	x	1.000	=	(4,000)
Year 1	(4,000)	x	0.909	=	(3,636)
Year 2	(4,000)	x	0.826	=	(3,304)
Year 5	1,000	x	0.621	=	621
			Net Present Value (NPV)	=	(10,319)
Hire					
Year 1	(2,500)	x	0.909	=	(2,272.50)
Year 2	(2,500)	x	0.826	=	(2,065.00)
Year 3	(2,500)	x	0.751	=	(1,877.50)
Year 4	(2,500)	x	0.683	=	(1,707.50)
Year 5	(2,500)	x	0.621	=	(1,552.50)
			Net Present Value (NPV)	=	(9,475.00)

- Outright purchase is marginally more attractive than hiring (hire purchase ranks third); a lot depends on the firm's financial position
- Note that, as these are costs, the best project (in financial terms) has the lowest cost

14.4 trial and error

Separate calculations not shown

Project Exe: 20% NPV = £1,500

22% NPV = (£1,090)

∴ Internal Rate of Return (DCF yield) = 22% (to nearest two per cent)

Project Wye: 22% NPV = £6,430

24% NPV = (£321)

∴ Internal Rate of Return (DCF yield) = 24% (to nearest two per cent)

interpolation

Project Exe: NPV at 12% = £13,870

NPV at 24% = (£3,640)

$$12 + \left(\frac{£13{,}870}{£17{,}510} \times 12\right) = 12 + 9.5 = 21.5\% \text{ or } 22\%$$

(to nearest two per cent)

Project Wye: NPV at 12% = £36,953

NPV at 24% = (£321)

$$12 + \left(\frac{£36{,}953}{£37{,}274} \times 12\right) = 12 + 11.90 = 23.90\% \text{ or } 24\%$$

(to nearest two per cent)

graph

Not shown

comment

- Project Wye has the higher IRR and is, therefore, the preferred option
- There should be a good margin of IRR over the actual borrowing cost

CHAPTER 15: PRINCIPLES OF BUDGETING

15.1 This Activity requires a full investigation of the budgetary planning and control process of the selected organisation. In particular the Activity should focus on:

- Links between long- and short-term objectives. Are the long-term objectives translated into the short-term objectives of the budget period?
- As different organisations adapt the budgetary planning and control process to suit their individual needs, it is appropriate to see how they apply the principles of budgets. These will prove a useful discussion point within a student group.
- Responsibility accounting is where budget holders manage their own budgets. How far are budget holders involved in the planning and control process?
- Management by exception is where only those variances considered to be of significant size (relative to the business) are drawn to the attention of management for further investigation.
- Are budgets for the next period set using incremental budgets or zero-based budgeting? Would it be appropriate to consider use of the latter from time-to-time?

15.2 Points to consider include:

(a)
- How far are budgets delegated down the organisation?
- Are employees involved in the budgetary planning process?
- Are the budgets fully co-ordinated?

(b)
- Is the supervisor a budget holder? If not, how far down the organisation are budgets delegated?
- Why is it important for supervisors to make a contribution to the organisation's budgets?

(c)
- Was the manager involved in the budgetary planning process?
- On what basis were the current budgets set? Incremental or zero-based?
- Which aspect of the budgets is "set far too high"?

(d)
- Managers and supervisors are given responsibility as budget holders to manage the finances of their section of the business
- Budgets are delegated down the organisation
- Budgets can be used to
  - encourage the achievement of targets set
  - as a form of punishment if targets are mised

(e)
- Senior managers work on the principle of management by exception, ie only those variances of significant size relative to the business need to be drawn to their attention
- Nevertheless, some form of feedback to budget holders would be good practice

(f)
- The system here is that of incremental budgeting. This is used where the area budgeted for is stable, but the disadvantage is that it doesn't analyse costs
- From time-to-time it would be appropriate to consider zero-based budgeting. This would ensure that inefficiencies and overspending are avoided

(g)
- Budgets can be expressed in either units of output or in financial terms
- However, at some point, the organisation will need to know the costs and revenues associated with the output
- The master budget is expressed in monetary terms

15.3
- The most likely budgets will be
  - sales budget
  - production budget
  - selling and distribution budget
  - administration budget
  - capital expenditure budget
- Each of these is likely to involve the production of a number of subsidiary budgets. For example, the production budget is likely to require subsidiary budgets for
  - purchases of materials
  - direct labour
  - direct expenses
  - production overheads
- The various budgets will be combined to produce
  - cash budget
  - master budget, comprising forecast profit and loss account, and forecast balance sheet
- Limiting factors will include:
  - quantity of product that can be sold
  - availability of raw materials
  - availability of skilled labour
  - factory or office space
  - finance
- For Radionics Limited, the most likely limiting factor will be that of sales. The other limiting factors will soon feature if the business expands rapidly

15.4 (a) This Activity is concerned with production schedules. A suggested answer is that 7,500 units are produced each month, except for:

- April 5,625 (holiday week)
- July 7,583 (7,500 plus 83 overtime)
- August 4,125 (7,500 ÷ 2, plus 375 overtime)
- December 5,625 (holiday week)

This gives a closing stock of 14,458 units

The production budget is as follows:

UNITS	Jan	Feb	Mar	Apr	May	Jun	Jul	Aug	Sep	Oct	Nov	Dec
Opening stock	8,500	10,500	13,500	17,500	19,125	19,625	14,625	7,208	1,333	6,833	11,333	13,833
add Units produced	7,500	7,500	7,500	5,625	7,500	7,500	7,583	4,125	7,500	7,500	7,500	5,625
less Units sold	5,500	4,500	3,500	4,000	7,000	12,500	15,000	10,000	2,000	3,000	5,000	5,000
Closing stock	10,500	13,500	17,500	19,125	19,625	14,625	7,208	1,333	6,833	11,333	13,833	14,458

(b) For Shades Limited, the limiting factors will include:

- quantity of the product that can be sold
- availability of skilled labour

Other factors will be:

- availability of raw materials
- factory, warehouse, or office space
- finance

15.5 (a) *Fixed budgets* remain the same whatever the level of activity of the organisation.

(b) *Flexible budgets* change with the level of activity and take into account different cost behaviour patterns

- A fixed budget is used where circumstances are stable – where a set amount of money is allowed to be spent during a year
- A flexible budget is prepared where the activity of the business is likely to vary quite widely from the target figures in the budget; thus a series of flexible budgets is prepared at different levels of activity
- In a flexible budget
  - fixed overheads normally remain the same whatever the level of activity
  - variable overheads change in line with the activity
- Thus a flexible budget allows the budget to be 'flexed' to the level of activity, and appropriate variances calculated

(b) **Seats Limited**

	Fixed budget	Flexible budgets	
	90,000 units	81,000 units	112,500 units
	£	£	£
Sales revenue (£10 each)	900,000	810,000	1,125,000
Less:			
materials (£2.50 each)	(225,000)	(202,500)	(281,250)
labour (£2.75 each)	(247,500)	(222,750)	(309,375)
variable overheads			
(£0.50 each)	(45,000)	(40,500)	(56,250)
Contribution to fixed overheads	382,500	344,250	478,125
Less: fixed overheads	(242,000)	(242,000)	(242,000)
Budgeted profit	140,500	102,250	236,125

Contribution per chair is £10 – £5.75 = £4.25. At lower production levels there is lower contribution but still the same amount of fixed overheads; at higher production levels, the reverse is true.

15.6 **Greenlawn Limited**

	Fixed budget	Flexible budgets		
	1m litres	1.5m litres	2m litres	2.5m litres
	£	£	£	£
Sales revenue	5,000,000	6,750,000	8,000,000	8,750,000
Less: variable overheads	(2,000,000)	(3,000,000)	(4,000,000)	(5,000,000)
semi-variable overheads	(750,000)	(1,000,000)	(1,250,000)	(1,500,000)
fixed overheads	(1,500,000)	(1,500,000)	(1,500,000)	(1,500,000)
Budgeted profit	750,000	1,250,000	1,250,000	750,000

- Output of 1.5m is recommended
- Contribution per litre is £2.50 (at 1m litres), £2.00 (at 1.5m litres), £1.50 (at 2m litres), and £1.00 (at 2.5m litres).
- Reduction in contribution at higher levels of production is not offset by spreading the fixed costs over greater number of units

CHAPTER 16: CASH BUDGETS AND MASTER BUDGETS

16.1
- This is an on-going Activity to compare a cash budget with actual results.
- It can be used both for businesses with receipts and payments, and for organisations when the receipt is a lump sum and the main priority is control of payments.
- The Activity will be more appropriate if it relates to a section or department of the organisation rather than the organisation as a whole.
- It is suggested that, for each of the months, columns are used for budget, actual and variance. In this way a direct comparison can be made between the budgeted and actual results. However, the format of the cash budget should be adapted to suit the needs of the organisation; indeed, it is expected that the organisation will have a cash budgeting system in use already.
- The analysis of variances is an important part of this Activity.

16.2 There are a number of points to consider, including:

- Mike Anderson has knowledge of selling the products and has business contacts.
- Previously he has been employed, but he is now setting up in business by himself.
- He is investing £20,000 of his savings into the new business. Of this, £13,000 will be used to pay for fixed assets and initial stocks.
- The cash budget shows cash deficits in the early months so that, in the first six months, bank finance of up to £8,000 will be required.
- The reason for the cash deficits in the early months is because
  - sales are relatively low
  - there is an imbalance between credit allowed and credit received
- In particular, by allowing two months' credit to customers instead of one month, there is an additional £10,500 tied up in working capital by 30 June – this is more than sufficient to clear the overdraft
- The cash budget shows that, from June onwards, there is expected to be a net cash inflow of £900 per month. If this continues, it will clear the overdraft by the end of March 1999 (including an allowance for bank interest).
- The business is expected to earn a net profit of £5,100 in the first six months. Drawings of £1,000 per month are reasonable but are greater than profit; thus capital will be reduced.
- Gross and net profit percentages are 33.3% and 11.0%: both are acceptable.
- The working capital and liquid ratios are 1.84:1 and 1.49:1: both are acceptable.
- The forecast accounts cover only the first six months of business – results for a full year will be much better, provided the estimates are fulfilled and sales stabilise at £10,500 per month:

	£	£
Sales (12 months at £10,500 per month)		126,000
Less: Cost of sales		84,000
Gross profit		42,000
Less: Running expenses	19,200	
Depreciation	1,600	
		20,800
Net profit		21,200

- The business will need to be registered for Value Added Tax. Will this have any effect on sales and expenses?
- Mike Anderson must also remember that he will be liable for income tax on profits made; however, as payments are based on the preceding year's accounts, there is nothing for him to pay for some time.
- Overall, if the estimates prove to be correct, this should be a profitable business. However, much depends on Mike Anderson's ability to generate sales at the volume and profit margins suggested in the budget.

16.3 (a)

Wilkinson Limited

Cash budget for the six months ending 30 June 1998

	Jan	Feb	Mar	Apr	May	Jun
	£	£	£	£	£	£
Receipts						
Debtors	57,500	65,000	70,000	72,500	85,000	65,000
Total receipts for month	57,500	65,000	70,000	72,500	85,000	65,000
Payments						
Creditors	26,500	45,000	50,000	34,500	35,500	40,500
Wages and salaries	17,500	18,000	18,250	18,500	16,500	20,000
Other expenses	14,500	19,500	18,000	17,500	19,500	21,000
Total payments for month	58,500	82,500	86,250	70,500	71,500	81,500
Net cash flow	(1,000)	(17,500)	(16,250)	2,000	13,500	(16,500)
Add bank balance (overdraft) at beginning of month	2,250	1,250	(16,250)	(32,500)	(30,500)	(17,000)
Bank balance (overdraft) at end of month	1,250	(16,250)	(32,500)	(30,500)	(17,000)	(33,500)

(b)

Wilkinson Limited
Forecast profit and loss account for the six months ending 30 June 1998

	£	£
Sales		465,000
Opening stock	15,500	
Purchases	232,000	
	247,500	
Less Closing stock	17,350	
Cost of sales		230,150
Gross profit		234,850
Less overheads:		
Wages and salaries	108,750	
Depreciation of fixed assets	6,000	
Other expenses	110,000	
		224,750
Net profit		10,100

16.4 (a)

Jim Smith
Cash budget for the six months ending 30 June 19...

	Jan	Feb	Mar	Apr	May	Jun
	£	£	£	£	£	£
Receipts						
Capital introduced	10,000					
Debtors	–	1,250	3,000	4,000	4,000	4,500
Total receipts for month	10,000	1,250	3,000	4,000	4,000	4,500
Payments						
Van	6,000					
Creditors	–	4,500	4,500	3,500	3,500	3,500
Expenses	750	600	600	650	650	700
Total payments for month	6,750	5,100	5,100	4,150	4,150	4,200
Net cash flow	3,250	(3,850)	(2,100)	(150)	(150)	300
Add bank balance (overdraft) at beginning of month	–	3,250	(600)	(2,700)	(2,850)	(3,000)
Bank balance (overdraft) at end of month	3,250	(600)	(2,700)	(2,850)	(3,000)	(2,700)

Notes:

- no depreciation – a non-cash expense – is shown in the cash budget
- purchases are two-thirds of the sales values (selling price is cost price plus 50 per cent)
- customers pay two months after sale, ie debtors from January settle in March
- suppliers are paid one month after purchase, ie creditors from January are paid in February

(b)

Jim Smith
Forecast profit and loss account for the six months ending 30 June 19...

	£	£
Sales		22,750
Purchases	23,500	
Less Closing stock	3,250	
Cost of sales		20,250
Gross profit		2,500
Less overheads:		
Expenses	3,950	
Depreciation of van		
(6,000 x 20%) ÷ 2, ie six months	600	
		4,550
Net loss		(2,050)

(c)

Jim Smith
Forecast balance sheet as at 30 June 19...

	£	£
Fixed assets		
Van at cost		6,000
Less depreciation to date		600
		5,400
Current assets		
Stock	3,250	
Debtors	6,000	
	9,250	
Less Current liabilities		
Creditors	4,000	
Bank overdraft	2,700	
	6,700	
Working capital		2,550
NET ASSETS		7,950
FINANCED BY		
Capital		
Opening capital		10,000
Less net loss		2,050
Closing capital		7,950

16.5 (a)

Mayday Limited
Cash budget for the year ending 31 May 1999

	Jun	Jul	Aug	Sep	Oct	Nov	Dec	Jan	Feb	Mar	Apr	May
	£	£	£	£	£	£	£	£	£	£	£	£
Receipts												
Debtors	–	–	50,000	50,000	50,000	50,000	50,000	50,000	50,000	50,000	50,000	50,000
Total receipts for month	–	–	50,000	50,000	50,000	50,000	50,000	50,000	50,000	50,000	50,000	50,000
Payments												
Creditors	–	40,000	40,000	40,000	40,000	40,000	40,000	40,000	40,000	40,000	40,000	40,000
Wages and expenses	6,000	6,000	6,000	6,000	6,000	6,000	6,000	6,000	6,000	6,000	6,000	6,000
Total payments for month	6,000	46,000	46,000	46,000	46,000	46,000	46,000	46,000	46,000	46,000	46,000	46,000
Net cash flow	(6,000)	(46,000)	4,000	4,000	4,000	4,000	4,000	4,000	4,000	4,000	4,000	4,000
Add bank balance (overdraft) at beginning of month	20,000	14,000	(32,000)	(28,000)	(24,000)	(20,000)	(16,000)	(12,000)	(8,000)	(4,000)	–	4,000
Bank balance (overdraft) at end of month	14,000	(32,000)	(28,000)	(24,000)	(20,000)	(16,000)	(12,000)	(8,000)	(4,000)	–	4,000	8,000

(b)

Mayday Limited
Forecast profit and loss account for the year ending 31 May 1999

	£	£
Sales		600,000
Opening stock	50,000	
Purchases	480,000	
	530,000	
Less Closing stock	50,000	
Cost of sales		480,000
Gross profit		120,000
Less overheads:		
Wages and expenses	72,000	
Depreciation of fixed assets	13,000	
		85,000
Net profit		35,000

Forecast balance sheet as at 31 May 1999

	£	£
Fixed assets		
At cost		130,000
Less depreciation to date		13,000
		117,000
Current assets		
Stock	50,000	
Debtors	100,000	
Bank	8,000	
	158,000	
Less Current liabilities		
Creditors	40,000	
Working capital		118,000
NET ASSETS		235,000
FINANCED BY		
Capital		
Share capital		200,000
Add net profit		35,000
		235,000

CHAPTER 17: BUDGET MONITORING AND VARIANCE ANALYSIS

17.1

- This Activity requires an investigation into the budgetary control system used by the organisation. The control system might well be linked to a standard costing system.
- Two aspects of the organisation should be investigated:
  - the method of identifying variances
  - the corrective action that is taken (examples could be given of the use of control limits and management by exception)
- Examples of good practice in budget monitoring within the organisation should be highlighted.
- Consider how responsibility accounting might be used to improve budget monitoring.

17.2
- This Activity is applicable to all organisations – whether the output is in the form of products or services.
- The results are likely to be easier to interpret if the output selected is relatively simple and with clearly identifiable costs.
- The Activity is divided into two sections:
  – a quantitative part requiring the calculation of standard cost, actual cost and variances for a particular time period
  – a qualitative discussion of significant variances and how these will be handled within the organisation's budgetary control system

17.3

STANDARD COST REPORT

product 500 cardboard boxes 750 mm x 400 mm x 300 mm **date**

supervisor **period**

	current period			*comments*
	standard cost	**actual cost**	**variance**	
	£	£	£	
materials	28	38	10 ADV	
labour	36	29	7 FAV	
overheads:				
fixed	18	20	2 ADV	
variable	15	12	3 FAV	
TOTAL COST	97	99	2 ADV	

Factors which may have caused the variances:
- materials
  – the cost may be higher or lower than standard
  – the use of materials may be higher or lower than standard
- labour
  – wage rates may be higher or lower than standard
  – the workforce may be more efficient or less efficient than standard
- overheads
  – fixed overheads may be more or less than standard
  – variable overheads may be more or less than standard

Further analysis:
- variances and sub-variances should be calculated
- for materials, the sub-variances are price and usage
- for labour, the sub-variances are rate and efficiency
- sub-variances can also be calculated for overheads
- the managers responsible for each section of the business will be asked to explain the reasons for any significant variances and sub-variances of their section
- corrective action will be taken where appropriate

17.4 *The sub-variances:*

(see text, pages 322 and 325, for the methods of calculating the sub-variances)

Materials price sub-variance
(75p – 80p) x 800 kg = £40 ADVERSE

Materials usage sub-variance
(900 kg – 800 kg) x 75p per kg = £75 FAVOURABLE
TOTAL MATERIALS VARIANCE = £35 FAVOURABLE

Labour rate sub-variance
(£5.00 – £5.50) x 140 hours = £70 ADVERSE

Labour efficiency sub-variance
(150 hours – 140 hours) x £5.00 per hour = £50 FAVOURABLE
TOTAL LABOUR VARIANCE = £20 ADVERSE

Using the variances and sub-variances:

- the managers responsible for each section of the business will be asked to explain the reason for any significant variances and sub-variances of their section
- the buying department should explain the 5p per kilo adverse variance in the cost of materials
- the production department should explain the favourable variance in materials usage – perhaps better quality materials have been used with less wastage
- the personnel/human resources department will need to explain the 50p per hour higher labour rate – perhaps there has been a pay rise; alternatively, overtime rates may have had to be paid, which the production department will be asked to explain
- the production department should be asked to explain the favourable variance in labour efficiency – perhaps more use has been made of machines
- it may be that sub-variances are linked, eg more expensive materials have less wastage; skilled employees (on higher pay rates) work more efficiently
- the managers responsible for the fixed and variable overheads will need to explain the variances in these items
- corrective action may need to be taken in some areas despite the overall favourable variance in total cost

17.5

	Material A	*Material B*	*Material C*	*Material D*
	£ p	£ p	£ p	£ p
materials price variance	120.00 FAV	200.00 ADV	500.00 FAV	250.00 ADV
materials usage variance	100.00 ADV	400.00 FAV	1,000.00 FAV	100.00 FAV
total materials variance	20.00 FAV	200.00 FAV	1,500.00 FAV	150.00 ADV

17.6

	Product 1	*Product 2*	*Product 3*	*Product 4*
	£ p	£ p	£ p	£ p
labour rate variance	3.50 ADV	2.00 ADV	7.50 FAV	7.50 ADV
labour efficiency variance	5.00 FAV	4.50 ADV	36.00 ADV	24.00 ADV
total labour variance	1.50 FAV	6.50 ADV	28.50 ADV	31.50 ADV

17.7

Operating statement

	BUDGET	ACTUAL	VARIANCE	
	£	£	£	
Sales	155,000	133,500	21,500	ADV
Less Variable costs:				
Materials	33,400	34,100	700	ADV
Labour	26,200	30,500	4,300	ADV
Overhead	19,200	19,450	250	ADV
Total	78,800	84,050	5,250	ADV
Contribution	76,200	49,450	26,750	ADV
Less Fixed overheads	18,500	21,350	2,850	ADV
Profit	57,700	28,100	29,600	ADV

Briefing note to managers:

- All of the actual figures are adverse to the budget. The cumulative effect is that actual profit is 49% of that budgeted.
- Variances that need particular investigation are sales, labour and fixed overheads.
- For sales, sub-variances should be calculated by the management accountant which show:
  - changes in the selling price
  - changes in the number of units sold
- For labour, sub-variances should be calculated which show
  - changes in wage rates
  - changes in the efficiency of the workforce
- For fixed overheads, sub-variances should be calculated by the management accountant which show:
  - changes in costs
  - changes in output, multiplied by the overhead rate per unit
- Although the adverse variances for materials and variable overhead will probably be classed as not significant (both being within 2.5 per cent of budget), a watch should be kept for more significant variances on future operating statements. For materials, it would be appropriate to calculate the sub-variances of price and usage to see if the variance is more attributable to one than the other
- All-in-all, urgent action needs to be taken to ensure that, in the future, actual figures are more in line with those of the budget

CHAPTER 18: ANALYSING BUSINESS INFORMATION

18.1

- mean £10.20
- median £5.90
- mode £10.00

(a) Management is likely to use the lowest figure as a bargaining point: this is the median (£5.90)

(b) The union is likely to use the higher figures (mean and mode), again for bargaining.

18.2 (a) Positive correlation with a change in sales:

- increase in advertising expenditure
- increase in spending on distribution
- increase in spending on R & D (new products and improvements to existing products)

(b) Negative correlation with a change in sales:

- reduction in price
- falling number of competitors
- fall in value of the home currency will boost export sales

18.3 Moving average data starting from day 4: 6, 6.5, 7.5, 8, 8.75, 9.25, 10, 10.5, 10.75, 11, 11.25, 12.25

The trend shows a rise in absenteeism, possibly as a result of the new working practices.

CHAPTER 19: PRESENTING BUSINESS INFORMATION

19.1 Your analysis of charts should ideally:

- distinguish between the different types of chart
- identify which type of chart is best for which type of task

  For example, analysis of time series data is best shown by line graphs and bar charts whereas proportional analysis is best shown by a pie chart or component bar chart.

  Further source material can be found in newspapers (economic and financial reports) and in publications such as Social Trends (HMSO).

19.2 (a)

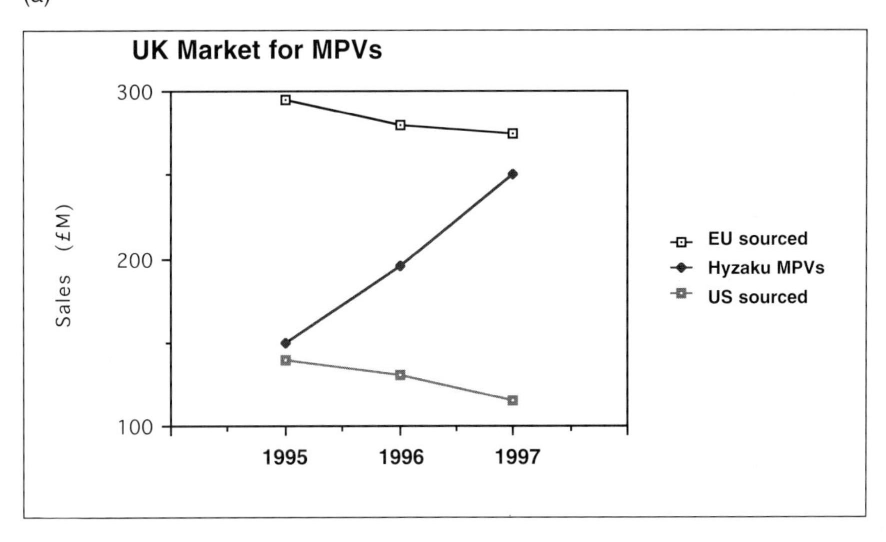

(b) The trend here is for a very healthy rise in sales of Hyzaku MPVs at the expense of EU and US sourced vehicles.

(c)&(d) The trend is encouraging: sales are above budget over 3 years.

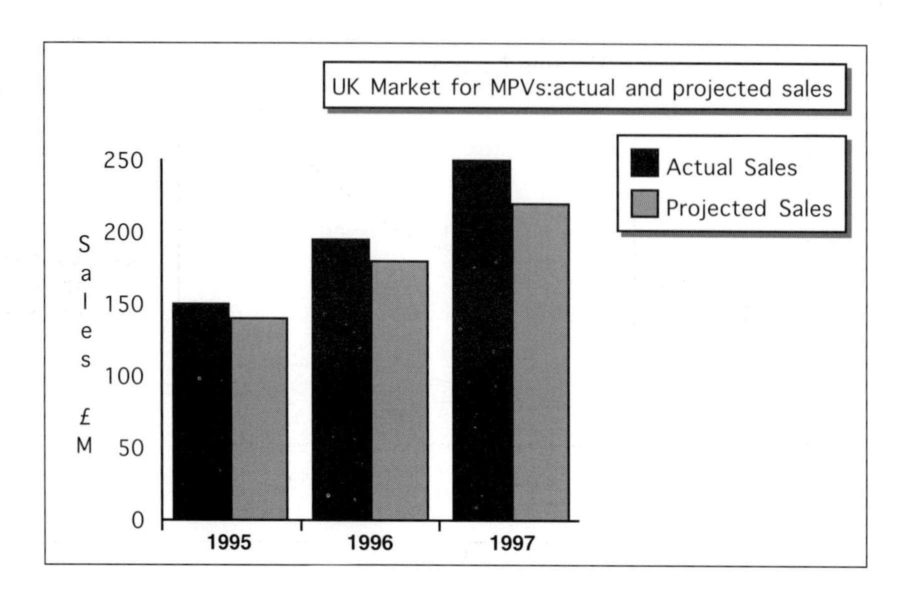

(e)

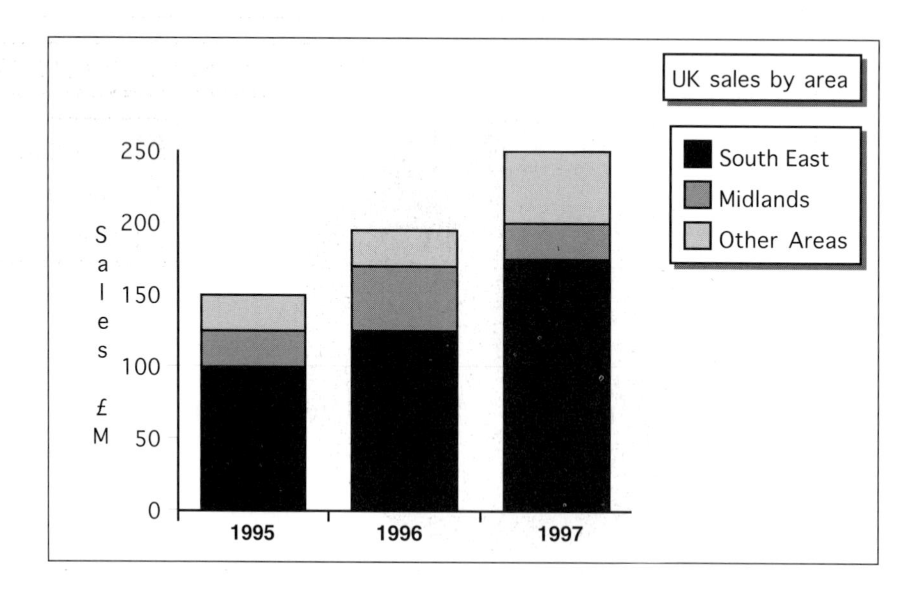

(f) The big growth area is the South East, probably reflecting the fashionable nature of the MPVs. The Midlands needs investigating: it may just be a marketing weakness, or there could be other contributory trends, eg economic problems.

(g) A line graph is an alternative method of presentation.

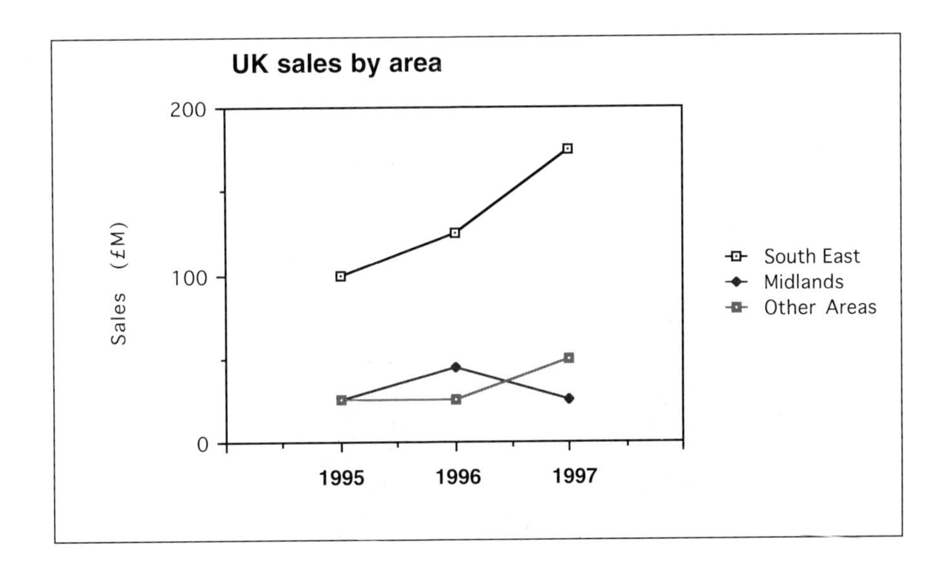

(h)

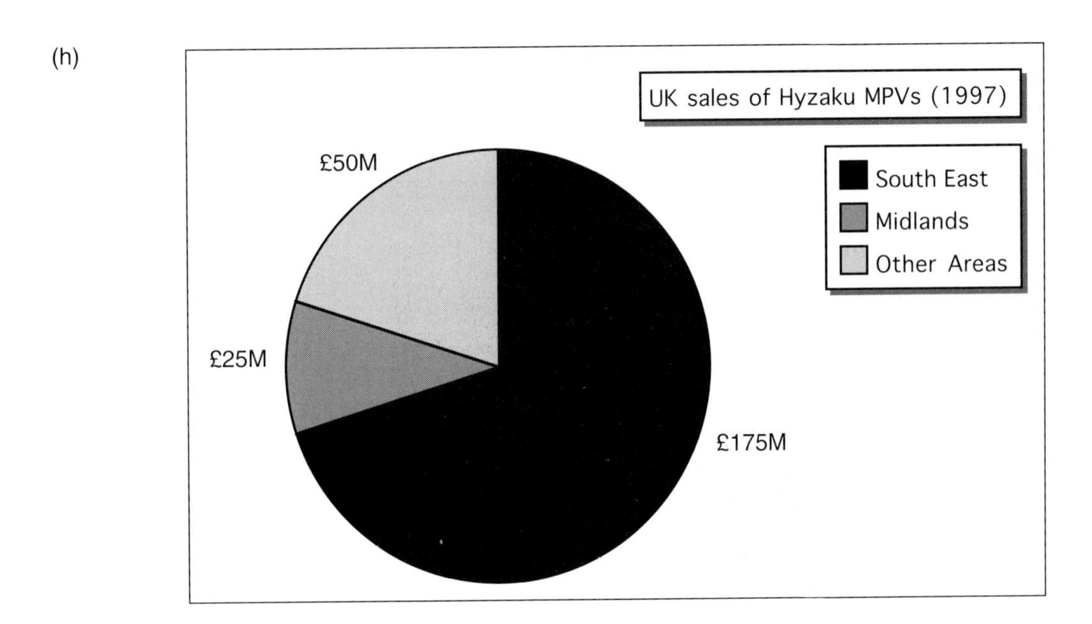

19.3 (a) A line graph would be most appropriate. There are too many countries for a bar chart and a series of pie charts would not show the trend so clearly.

(b)

	Year 1	Year 2	Year 3	Year 4
Austria	100	91	110	113
Belgium	100	73	64	68
France	100	115	130	137
Germany	100	111	122	138
Spain	100	122	104	84
UK	100	93	103	108

The indexation of these numbers provides a *precise* means of comparison. Although a graph will show trends, the indexation will show the comparitive growth and decline in sales in the various countries. Clearly Germany leads the field and Belgium gives cause for concern.

INDEX